Six countries. What could *possibly* go wrong... In Asia?

SHAVE MY SPIDER!

Tony James Slater

ISBN: 978-1720054856

Copyright © Tony James Slater 2016

All rights reserved. No part of this publication may be reproduced, stored in a retrieval system or transmitted, in any form or by any other means without the prior written permission of the author, nor be otherwise circulated in any form of binding or cover other than that in which it is published and without a similar condition being imposed on the purchaser.

Although this is a work of non-fiction, some names have been changed by the author.

An e-book edition of this title is also available.

Paperback edition published by **Various Things At Different Times**
Cover Design by **Various Things At Different Times**
Formatted for paperback by **Tony James Slater**

Please visit the author's website for a selection of photographs that accompany this book:

www.TonyJamesSlater.com

Books by the same author:

Travel Memoirs:
That Bear Ate My Pants!
Don't Need The Whole Dog!
Kamikaze Kangaroos!
Can I Kiss Her Yet?
Don't You Know Who I Am?

Science Fiction:
Earth Warden

Contents

Prologue..11
To Buy Or Not To Buy..13
Trouble And Strife...21
Sucks in the City...28
Bus-ness As Usual...35
Howard's Way..41
Paradise Lost...47
Hotel KinaballloooOOOO!..53
Slip n' Slide..59
Sandakan...64
People Of The Forest..70
Discovering Ends..76
Messing About In Boats...83
River Monster...89
Breaking News..96
Expedition...102
Carry On Climbing..109
Pinnacle of Success..116
To Cave, Or Not To Cave?..123
The End Of The Beginning...130
Good Morning Vietnam!...138
Going With The Flow..145
High-Jinks..151
Breakage...156
Things That Go Bump In The Night..................................162
Paradise City..169
Market Forces..177
Tunnelling Out...184

Crazytown	191
Stitched Up	198
Hué To Close	206
Getting Hanoi'd	213
Culture Shock	221
Ha Long Awaited Trip	228
Where Complaining Gets You	238
Mongolia By Night	245
Into The Wild	251
In Tents Workout	257
Follow The Yellow Dirt Road	263
Nature Calling	270
One Small Steppe For Man	277
The Hot Springs	283
A Steppe Too Far?	290
The Kindness of Strangers	296
Back To The Future	303
City Of The Lost	310
The End Of An Era	316
Red Tape	323
Best Served Cold	330
Double Dutch	338
Farewell To Mongolia	344
A Change Of Track	352
Beijing Dreamin'	358
Dying To Explore	364
Monumental Mission	370
Tempeled Out	379
Commercial Success	385
Mortal Instruments	392
Training Day	398
Lost In Transit	405
Hostel Negotiation	413
Monkin' About	419
Circumnavigatxi'an	426
Buried In The Ground	434
Getting High	439
What Goes Up	449
Water Features	459
Pandamonium	465

Slumber Party	474
The Difference A Day Makes	479
Coming To Kunming	488
There And Back Again	494
Cloud Nine	500
Escape	506
Poison Cafe	515
Drugged	521
Alternative Therapy	527
Circles Of Life	533
Vertical Limits	540
Vientiane	546
Temple Of Manhood	547
Hammock Time	555
Vespa Mandarinia	560
Rough Crossing	567
Road Rage	574
Delicate Matters	580
City Of Stone	586
Best 'Til Last	593
Beach Baby!	600
Repatriation	608
Sitting Dogs	615

For Chris

We really miss you, mate.
Hope you enjoy the view.

– Prologue –
Somewhere in China

Halfway up the concrete ramp, I broke into a jog. I swung around the bannister at the top and surged onto the station platform, adrenaline pumping. The train beside me stretched off into infinity, but it wasn't moving; doors were standing open here and there, so I still had a chance. I took a break from scanning the carriage numbers to check behind me, and immediately wished I hadn't. A pair of what looked like SWAT troopers were giving chase, charging down the platform towards me, machine guns jangling against their body armour. I passed a window with a '13' in it; my carriage was only three cars ahead. With little choice, I accelerated, running like a drunkard with the weight of my rucksack swaying me from side to side.

Just... Don't... Fall... Even the voice inside my head was out of breath.

I was close now; I'd passed the mid-point of the previous carriage, and there had been no whistles or obvious signs of departure. I was going to make it!

An angry cry sounded behind me as I came abreast of the

door and hauled myself up through it. By some miracle the train wasn't crowded, and I pushed my way down the aisle with minimum commotion. My wife wasn't hard to spot – her rainbow-coloured hair, her pale face, and the terror writ large across it – all these were visible from the other end of the carriage. I bustled up to her, dripping sweat, panting from my exertions, and grabbed the back of the chair opposite her to keep myself upright.

"I'm here love!" I gasped.

"Thank God for that!" she sobbed.

"But I've got a bit of bad news..."

Her eyes went wide – and then focused on the heavily armed officers storming down the aisle towards me.

"Tony, what...?"

And that was when they grabbed me.

I'd made a few mistakes in China.

Going there in the first place could be considered one of them...

To Buy, or Not To Buy...

I never planned on going to China.

Back when I first conceived of this trip, it was meant to be easy; an extended foray into the tourist hot spots of South-East Asia. I was developing a reputation as some kind of travel writer, but with one major stumbling block; I hadn't actually *been* anywhere. My first attempt at a round-the-world trip had ended in France, where I was swindled out of hundreds of pounds, got molested by an old-age pensioner and narrowly avoided being incinerated in a prune-drying furnace by a gypsy-murdering farmer.

It wasn't exactly a rip-roaring success.

My second trip took me as far as Ecuador, where I spent most of my time bleeding from monkey bites, or bleeding from machete wounds, or just bleeding for no good reason.

It might not sound like it, but that trip was a lot of fun.

Eventually I washed up in Australia, by way of a lengthy stay in Thailand – I only left there because I couldn't afford to eat. And if you can't afford to eat in Thailand, you're in real trouble anywhere else. But I was lucky. I was born that way, I think, and it never manifested itself more profoundly than when I met Roo. Tall, slender and gorgeous, her permanently sunny disposition matched my own. She even shared my outlook on life; that it shouldn't be taken too seriously, and that we should enjoy every single moment as though it were our last.

On quite a few occasions, it nearly had been.

Roo's playfulness and enthusiasm make her seem much younger than she is – for example, she was recently ID'd whilst trying to buy superglue. Her love of fancy dress may also have been a factor; despite being 31 years old, it's quite likely she was wearing wings at the time.

Roo was my sister Gill's best friend, yet I shamelessly stole her, made her my wife, and we've been together ever since.

And for most of that time, neither of us could afford to eat.

But things were starting to change for us.

Against all odds, my first book, about my three-month-long near-death experience in Ecuador, was selling well. The second one, about Thailand, wasn't doing quite as well. But that's okay, because it was rubbish. Somehow I'd saved up enough money to buy the campervan of our dreams...

So long as it was still on sale second hand for $8,000.

I'd already decided not to get it, though. For starters, it was in Cairns – a little over 5,000 kilometres away on the opposite side of Australia. If I'd really wanted the thing, I probably should have bought it the previous week, when my wife and I were *in* Cairns on holiday. I'd been stopped by the thought that, perhaps there was something better I could do with that money. I mean, we weren't exactly the right kind of people to own nice cars.

I'd recently gotten around to washing our current car, by way of a surprise for Roo. I'd used a scouring sponge to get the accumulated bird crap off the bonnet, without realising that it would actually take most of the paint off, too.

Mission accomplished – she'd been surprised all right!

The car's resale value would have dropped dramatically, except it didn't have a resale value, because she'd crashed it into the back of a taxi only a few weeks after buying the thing.

So there was that.

And there were other things to consider. My next book was one; I was writing about Australia, and whilst it stirred up a certain nostalgia for traveling around the country in a beat up old van, extended road trips are not the ideal circumstances for writing. Sitting on a beach, on the other hand…

Or even a series of beaches.

It occurred to me that $8,000 would take us halfway around the world.

Then we wouldn't even need a car! An extended trip away had so much more potential, and was so exciting that pretty soon we couldn't think of anything else.

I came up with a list of destinations that would be fun to travel to and cheap, the idea being to take that $8,000 as our budget, and to stretch it into as long a trip as possible.

My list included Thailand (obviously), Indonesia and Malaysia – the kind of places where you can live on the beach for a few dollars a day, eat unlimited fried rice and drink cocktails out of coconuts. Honestly, I think I was selling myself on a six-month long tropical holiday.

Within minutes, my wife Roo (that's her nickname from Camp America) had countered with a list of her own, full of exotic, unusual places.

Tibet was on there.

And Burma.

And Outer Mongolia, which I hadn't actually realised was a real country until she pointed to it on the map.

Her list looked a lot more challenging than mine.

But there was a silver lining to undertaking so much effort. I'd been suffering something of an identity crisis since realising that most nineteen year olds on a gap year had visited more countries than me. How could I pass myself off as a travel writer when I hadn't left home in over a year? I was starting to depend on my books as a source of income, and already thinking of building a career as an author. Sooner or later I was going to have to start taking it seriously.

This looked like the perfect opportunity.

Visit cool places.

Write books about them.
Make a living from it.
Now *that* was the stuff of dreams...

Our plans evolved a little once we started looking into the options.

Tibet, for example, had been closed to foreigners by the Chinese government; the last two years had seen tensions rise, and almost a hundred Tibetan people had set themselves on fire to protest their treatment by the Chinese. UN monitors and aid workers had been kicked out of the region, along with foreign journalists; this made me think we probably shouldn't go there.

Burma was also going through a period of upheaval. Or, as *Human Rights Watch* put it, 'The Burmese military continues to engage in extrajudicial killings, attacks on civilians, forced labor, torture, pillage, and use of antipersonnel land mines.'

So, you know. There's off the beaten track, which sounds arduous, but then there's being beaten shitless whilst still on the track. That sounds like no fun at all.

Plus, it was *really* hard to get visas.

All of which left us with a grab-bag of countries and a similarly eclectic mix of reasons for visiting them. Roo had fixated on the island of Borneo because (as she put it), "Hello? Orangutans!"

I really wanted to go to Thailand, but it was vetoed on the grounds that once I entered the country I might never leave it.

Vietnam was my next choice, for the sole reason that forever afterwards I could put on a husky voice and tell people, "I was in 'nam..."

With our first destinations picked out, the rest of the trip fell into place.

At only six hours away from Perth, Borneo (which is split in ownership between Indonesia and Malaysia) offered the cheapest flights.

From there we would take a short hop over the South

China Sea to Vietnam, where we'd be joined by Roo's younger sister, Vicky.

Vicky was super-keen to meet up with us and do a spot of traveling – presumably because she'd never read my previous books – but the harsh realities of having a real job meant she was restricted to four weeks off work.

The two countries she wanted to see most of all were Vietnam and Mongolia, which was a bit tricky as they are separated by nearly two and a half thousand miles of China.

As a result of this, our route became a little more complex.

Or arse-about-tit, as it's known in the trade.

In the end we managed to find a flight that bypassed China, taking us from Vietnam in the south to Mongolia in the north – with a convenient eighteen-hour layover in Seoul Airport.

After Mongolia, Vicky would fly home and Roo and I would continue down through China, eventually hitting Laos and then Cambodia.

Laos was on the itinerary purely because it shared a border with China, and Cambodia was on there because it contains Angkor Wat – the largest complex of ancient temples anywhere in the world, and a staple on most people's bucket lists.

It was definitely on mine.

With the route roughly mapped out, we had work to do. The pre-trip stage consists of three phases: Planning, Shopping and Packing.

We decided to prioritise shopping because, of all three phases, it is by far the most fun.

First things first: Roo needed a new camera.

Strictly speaking she needed *a* camera, but she had quickly established that this trip had to be documented *properly*.

"I'm thinking about getting one of those big cameras," she said, in that whimsical tone that means she already has the make, model and serial number inscribed on her shopping list.

I figured I owed it to her. Roo had been the

photographer-in-chief on all our trips to date, for the simple reason that I break every camera I touch. It was a position she relished, filling hard drives with photos of our adventures. Until our brief holiday in Fiji, when she had mistakenly handed me the camera to put away in our room.

It had a lot of sentimental value, that camera.

I think she still has the pieces of it somewhere.

It was the week before her birthday, and we happened to be in Perth city, browsing deals on the latest DSLR models. For non-camera geeks, 'DSLR' stands for Delicate Sodding Lens, Ridiculously-huge – they're the brick-sized things you only used to see in Japanese tour groups. Because they were the only ones who could afford them. They have since become beloved of backpackers worldwide, which makes no sense at all to me. In a world where you can get cameras that fit on a tie, it seems unnecessarily ambitious to devote half your luggage allowance to something that can be destroyed by dust, water, shock, vibration...

Especially when it costs $600.

"It's my birthday," Roo gushed, as the sales assistant swiped my credit card.

"Wow!" said the girl, "I wish I got birthday presents like that! I need a better boyfriend."

It did make me feel kind of proud.

The lens was another $600.

Roo was beside herself with excitement as we walked out of the shopping centre.

"Can I have it early?" she pleaded, "I need to practise with it before we go to Asia!"

"Of course, love. So long as we can wrap it up on your birthday."

"Can I carry the bag?"

"Of course, love. Here you go."

That was the last time I was allowed to touch that camera.

When it was my turn to buy something, I went online and ordered a Steripen. This cool invention is a battery-powered ultraviolet water steriliser. It sounds too good to be true, but according to the marketing material, one minute of stirring with the Steripen would make even puddle water safely drinkable – well, unless it was full of poo. You still had to fish any lumps out yourself.

I also needed a watch.

I've never owned a decent watch because most of them are analogue, and I can't tell the time on an analogue clock (or 'proper clock' as most of my family call it).

Don't get me started! I have some sort of weird mental block about it, and have to count the numbers from the nearest quarter. Roo teases me endlessly about it. She wouldn't be allowed to tease me if I were fat, or had a club foot, but because clock-blindness has yet to be diagnosed as a disorder, it's apparently still fair game. Anyway, there were sure to be occasions on this trip when we'd need to know the time, so I was granted the rare luxury of spending an hour on eBay, browsing all the possibilities. What I *really* wanted was a watch with a retractable garrote built into it, because that would be *awesome*. Sadly, they seemed to be in short supply, so I settled on one which had a digital compass instead. It wasn't nearly as useful.

There were other purchases, of course.

In fact there were *a lot* of other purchases.

There were conventional things, like head torches and hiking shoes, a mosquito net and insect repellent, and occasionally some weirder things; for example, I'd never heard of 'leech socks' before. I didn't even know leeches had feet. But Roo had done her research. She assured me that, in the steaming jungles of Borneo, these socks would be essential. Except they were ridiculously expensive, so we bought football socks instead.

Apparently Roo's research was satisfied with this.

As five out of the six countries we planned on visiting were currently in the middle of malaria epidemics, Roo thought it would be a good idea to take some precautions. Internet research taught me there are three main kinds of anti-malaria tablets; there were the good ones, which had relatively few side-effects, and there were the *really* good ones, which you only needed to take once a week. And then there were the ones we could afford, which had neither of these benefits. We emerged from the pharmacy with a six-month supply – so many packets of pills that they practically needed a backpack of their own.

When the dust settled on our shopping spree, we didn't dare count the cost.

I decided not to take the money we'd spent off our travel budget, or this six-month odyssey would rapidly become a wet weekend in Malaysia. Instead I called upon the gods of Visa and Mastercard to make it all disappear.

So long as my books kept selling we'd have some form of income, no matter where we were – hopefully this would make up any shortfall, allowing us to complete the trip even if we blew the original $8,000.

Of course, we'd be utterly broke by the time we got back, but that was part of the adventure. Right? I'd read somewhere that travel writers are supposed to be broke, owing largely to the twin facts that travel is damn expensive, and hardly any bugger reads travel books. Being permanently penniless and surviving by blagging free stuff off tour companies is a way of life in this industry; for the true professionals it's like a badge of honour.

Well, maybe.

I could be wrong.

Trouble And Strife

The planning phase now required our full attention. In the past, I'd gone off on trips with no more thought than most people give to a night on the town.

It has since been explained to me that this is not a good thing, and that a lack of preparation is the cause of most of the problems I encounter – animal attacks and being shot at notwithstanding.

This time would be different. The love of my life was accompanying me on this expedition, and I was determined to make sure everything went to plan.

The first step in this process, of course, is actually having a plan.

So we nipped out to the local library, before expanding our search to libraries in other areas. In one day we had amassed a treasure trove of information; at least one guidebook for each of our destinations, with some relief-reading for when those got too dry. This consisted of a guide to DSLR photography, for Roo, and a book on Thailand for me. Just in case.

I was so proud of us! Having all this knowledge at our fingertips made me feel all grown-up and responsible. I spread all the books out on the bed and took a photo, to show the world just how prepared we were going to be this time around. Then I piled the books up again and stacked them at the side of the bed, in easy reach.

And that is where they stayed, completely untouched, until Roo made a panicked phone call from Borneo, sending her sisters to return them to the library.

It wasn't the most successful of planning strategies.

Packing we left until the last possible moment, as always, because there isn't enough stress in our lives. It doesn't feel like a major trip unless I spend the day before it flinging stuff around the room in a blind panic.

It started serenely enough. I did what I'd been doing since my very first trip abroad: put everything I want to take out on the bed, and got rid of half of it. I'd read this advice as a teenager, in a book I could no longer remember owning, but I regularly espoused this piece of wisdom as though it were the cornerstone of my faith as a backpacker.

However.

I was no longer just a backpacker.

I was now one half of a married, backpacking couple, and for those of you that don't know, life tends to change a bit when you get married. Rules you'd always held dear suddenly go up in smoke, or get re-written to accommodate new realities. Like this, for example: women need more shit.

Why?

I dunno. They just *do*.

It's one of the universe's eternal mysteries.

Take underwear, for example. It's been years since I've worn any. That's why my balls hang out of my trousers so much. But Roo, despite not having testicles to risk accidentally displaying, was determined to take underwear; everyday stuff, which was comfy to travel in, and nicer stuff to wear when we were 'going out'. Oh, and the extra-special stuff, which she only wore in the bedroom. I couldn't really complain about that now, could I?

There were other issues. Hair straighteners, for example, lingered in the 'to take' pile far longer than I expected. To me they were a no-brainer, but Roo was only forced to discard them at the last moment when it came down to them, or three bottles of brightly-coloured hair dye.

It was around this time that, for sanity's sake, I decided to concentrate on what I was packing instead.

Electronics are typically my domain. Top of the essentials list was a miniature netbook-style laptop, that Roo's sister Wendy loaned us. I say loaned – I think she knew, deep down, that she was never getting that thing back. Hell, after six months of me sweating over it, I don't think she'd want to be in the same room as it. The laptop was vital, because I needed to get some serious writing done on this trip. It didn't have a charger, so I bought a replacement one from eBay and prayed night and day that the thing would arrive in time. It did – just. We verified that the laptop was working, filled it full of music and movies, and managed to charge it once completely before the new power pack exploded rather spectacularly.

I had a few stern words with the eBay seller, and he promised he could get a replacement to me in less than two weeks.

I wasn't entirely sure I trusted him – or his stock – but it didn't matter, as we were leaving for Borneo tomorrow morning.

Luckily, Roo's Dad is a Dutch version of MacGyver, and he managed to make us a temporary adaptor out of several old ones he had lying around. "Be gentle with it," he suggested, holding out a wire wrapped in gaffer tape. This was slightly worrying, as the laptop would be our lifeline – needed to book tickets and excursions, hotels and onward travel, to research our destinations and to communicate with home.

Ah well. At least if it died, I'd have a good excuse for not writing.

Alongside the computer I packed a matching pair of his n' hers hard drives, to keep my manuscripts and Roo's photographs securely backed up.

And this is where it began to get ridiculous.

Roo's beautiful new camera, with its beautiful new lens, also came with a beautiful new charger. Our back-up bomb-proof camera also had a charger, as did the phone we were taking. And my Kindle. And Roo's nifty little 7-inch Samsung Galaxy tablet, which she was using as a Kindle. The video camera, which I'd bought solely for the purpose of making video blogs, could do its business whilst plugged into a USB port – which was no problem, because we had the laptop with us. Oh, and Roo had her epilator, which also came with its own charger. In case you're wondering, an epilator is some kind of feminine torture device with spinning blades on one end, that makes a screech like a badly-tuned dentist's drill. It looks a bit like a handheld combine harvester. I have no idea what it does, but once a week Roo locks herself in the bathroom with the thing and swears at it for an hour straight, before emerging in such a foul mood that I have to break out the emergency chocolate.

Anyway – that was coming with us, too.

Rather than struggle to pack country-specific plug adaptors for all of these devices, I excelled myself by taking one multi-adaptor and a cheap, four-way power strip. On the one hand, I reckoned this was a triumph of logistics; on the other, it was kind of depressing to think that we couldn't go backpacking without a socket-quadrupler.

Amazingly, defying all known laws of physics, we managed to cram it all in.

Including a four-foot tall inflatable Velociraptor.

"It'll be so funny," Roo explained, "we'll get him out and take photos of him in all these different countries, doing all sorts of crazy things!"

I had my doubts. Specifically because Vince the Velociraptor added about 2kg of scrunched-up plastic to my burden. But then, how does that old saying go?

Oh, that's right – there is no old saying about traveling with an inflatable Velociraptor. I guess we were the first.

With packing completed and only a few hours until our flight to Borneo, I posted on Facebook that we were going away for six months. Amidst a flurry of replies from well-wishers, I got an email from Tim and Charlotte, a couple who were amongst the first of my readers to contact me. They were also travelling around Asia, and wanted to know if there was a chance we could meet up. At first I thought this was a great idea – not least because they were currently in Thailand – but then it occurred to me to wonder just who they thought they'd be meeting. They might be expecting some battle-scarred travel veteran, a larger-than-life adventurer who'd survived crocodile bites, jaguar attacks, sailing disasters and more.

Whereas, in reality, I'm pretty average. Medium height, medium build. Brown eyes, brown hair. No impressive scars. The only remarkable thing about me is the size of my nose; it's frikkin' *huge*, like a comedy prosthetic I forgot to remove.

There was a good chance I'd be a disappointment.

Tim and Charlotte were the real deal. They even had a proper travel blog, which they actually bothered to post to. I showed it to Roo.

"Check it out! They've been traveling together for a year already. They've visited most of the places we want to go to, plus Russia, Japan, Finland… They jacked in their jobs, sold everything, and have been bouncing around the world ever since. They sound like proper travellers. I bet *they* could write a book about what they've done."

"But my love, you're… *different*. You don't write books about travel because you're good at it. You write them because you're absolutely terrible at it! I've never known anyone get into as much trouble as you. As soon as you set foot out the door, everything goes wrong – it's like you're the eye of a disaster-hurricane! Traveling with you can be a real pain in the bum, but that's what makes it so entertaining to read about."

I let this information sink in for a few seconds before I responded.

"So, I get to write about travel because I'm so crap at it?"

"That's basically it, yeah."

It was good to know how she felt. Because now I had two goals on this grand adventure we were planning. Not only would I visit enough exotic destinations to feel validated in my chosen career, I would also prove to Roo that I could be *good* at travelling. I can't cook, sing, dance, act, tell the time or reliably tell my left from right. But God damn it I was going to be good at *something*. Even if it killed me.

And six months around Asia wouldn't kill me.

Would it?

BORNEO

Sucks In The City

Our flight left Perth at stupid o' clock in the morning, because that's when all the cheapest flights leave.
It didn't matter; neither of us could have slept, even if we'd wanted to. We were revved up, bursting with anticipation. Not only did we have six months of adventure stretching out ahead of us, our first destination was one of the most exciting; Borneo, a largely undeveloped island blanketed by dense jungle. I could almost smell it; undergrowth steaming in the morning sun, the calls of exotic birds close at hand. It was all I could do to stop Roo from travelling in her football socks – I had to point out that there were unlikely to be leeches in the airport. And if there were, it was only our cash they were after.

As it happened, there was no-one at the airport.
I'd booked a pick-up from our hotel, but a quick call to the manager revealed the car we'd booked was already on the way back to hotel with us inside it.
I had a feeling this wasn't entirely accurate.
But whatever. We jumped in a regular taxi, which the manager promised wouldn't rip us off too badly.
It took almost an hour to make the 8km trip, sitting in the kind of infinite traffic jam I'd thought Borneo would be

exempt from. But it *was* rush hour, our two connecting flights having taken most of the day, and we *were* heading into Borneo's capital city. That city was called Kota Kinabalu, and was known to locals as 'KK'. Neither of us could pronounce the full name, so I'd taken to calling it 'Kenny BalloooOOOOOO' – generally keeping the sound going until Roo hit me.

She'd taken to calling it KK.

The taxi deposited us close to the 'Summer Lodge', a converted 1960s apartment block which had once been painted bright yellow – presumably around the time it was built.

The manager explained that he couldn't find our booking, but had plenty of rooms available; for $12 per night we could have a double room, with a bathroom, but no window. Windows apparently cost extra.

Roo and I were both knackered, having not slept in two days, so I nodded to the man and shambled upstairs after him.

The room with no window was unspeakably dingy. By the sparse light of the single struggling bulb I could make out the rough dimensions of the room – about two metres square – and its rough condition. I've never been interred in a concentration camp, but that's what ran through my head. The stained mattress looked like generations of backpackers had been tortured to death on it. I felt I'd seen the room before; quite possibly in the movie *Saw*.

"I... ah... I think we'll try the room with windows after all..." I was trying to be polite; being English means I'm terrified of offending anyone. "It's nice though," I added.

I glanced at Roo and saw her expression mirroring my thoughts. 'RUN THE FUCK AWAY!' it said.

"Ah okay. I show you window."

The room with a window was also unspeakably dingy. It wasn't much of an upgrade; I half expected to see Terry Waite in there, chained to a radiator. It *did* have a window though, which cast a stale beam of daylight across the minuscule room's contents. A bed, with a mouldy headboard, and... well, that was it. For $15 a night I wasn't expecting the

Ritz, but this redefined my concept of 'basic'. And 'habitable'.

I looked at Roo. This time her face framed resignation; 'I'm too tired to run,' it said, 'let's just lay down here and die.'

"We'll take it," I told the manager.

He handed me a slab of wood nearly as big as the window, with our room key attached, muttered something indecipherable which probably had to do with how picky westerners were, and backed out of the room.

And we were alone.

We ditched our rucksacks in the corner and eyed the bed wearily. The duvet had once been white, but mildew had taken its toll some time in the past. It was decorated with outlines of love hearts, which of course made everything all right.

"Do you want me to put a towel down?" I asked Roo.

"Too late," she said, and collapsed face-first onto the bed.

"How is it?"

"It smells like feet."

"Are you sure that's not just you?"

"It smells like the feet of a dead yak."

"Okay, so that's probably not you then."

I joined her on the bed. It really did stink, but I was too tired to care. I drifted off to sleep fully clothed, dreaming of strange people screaming endlessly...

I woke to scraps of sunlight forcing their way in through the slats in a bamboo window blind. Seeing no string or mechanism, I gingerly lifted one edge. The whole blind promptly ripped out of the wall and fell to the floor, showering me with plaster dust. It was an instant improvement. Daylight blazed in, proving we'd slept all through the night and for most of the day.

"Is it time to get up?" came a groggy moan from the bed.

"I dunno. Maybe."

"I don't want to get up."

"No, me neither."

But this was Day One of our adventure – we had to seize it! So we dragged ourselves up and set off to find breakfast in Kenny BallooooOOO.

Kenny BaaallllooooooooOOOOOOOO!

punch
"Ow!"
"Stop it."

KK city, though tiny, was a far cry from the pristine jungles we'd been looking forward to.

In fact, it was much like any other city in south-east Asia; stained concrete apartment blocks bristling with battered air-con units, traffic in permanent honking gridlock, and a sidewalk so broken and irregular it was more akin to an assault course. The music of the streets was a cacophony of horns blaring, and the smells rolled in like waves – one minute tasty noodles frying, the next a dead badger's arse. These Pockets of Random Stink, as we came to call them, arose for no discernable reason, striking without warning when you least expected them.

The only defence was to blunder forward, gagging, and hope you didn't trip on a metal bar sticking out of the pavement and fall ten feet through a crevasse into the storm drain.

We did a fairly decent circuit of the city, and spotted a supermarket in what looked like a derelict high school gymnasium. Inside, one whole wall was dedicated to meat – at least, I think it was meat. A long chiller held open trays in which internal organs marinated in their own juices. A cloud of flies flew circuits, chasing each other from tray to tray.

"I feel a bout of vegetarianism coming on," Roo warned.

"Well, it's either that or a bout of Botulism," I told her.

Feeling vaguely nauseous, we bought biscuits and ice creams, and sat on the curb between two parked cars to eat them.

It was alarming how far our standards had fallen in the last 24 hours.

I put my arm around Roo. "You know, two days ago we were lying in a comfy bed in our air-conditioned room, sleeping off a delicious restaurant meal. And today we're sitting in the gutter eating junk, about to return to a cell from Guantanamo Bay. Do you ever get the feeling that we're doing something wrong?"

"Oh, don't worry," she said, "I'm sure we'll stay in worse places."

This wasn't really what I wanted to hear.

But the ice creams were delicious.

After a short nap, we went in search of a viewpoint that was supposedly the number one attraction in Kota Kinabalu.

We followed a busy road up a hill which rose just behind the city. Buses, cars and scooters whipped past us at top speed, the locals obviously used to the twisting route. The complete absence of footpaths for long sections was a bit nerve-wracking, as we were forced to walk on the edge of the road, tucking ourselves as far over as possible in the hope that no-one took the bends too tightly.

"I don't think you're meant to walk up here," Roo commented.

"No. Probably not," I agreed.

We marched on in single file, holding our breath every time a tour bus swung around the corner and bore down on us.

"The book said it was a twenty-minute *walk*," Roo complained.

"Doesn't mean the author walked it," I pointed out.

A long and hair-raising hike finally brought us to a circular viewing platform that looked like the remains of a flying saucer crashed into the hillside.

Downtown KK spread out below us, the lights beginning to come on as evening approached. Roo took plenty of photos to justify lugging her precious camera all the way up here, and we marvelled at the regular turn-around of tour buses; they sped up, fifty-odd Asian tourists disembarked and posed excitedly for photos in various groups, and then they all scurried back on board and disappeared just as quick. We were there for about an hour, as Roo wanted to catch the sunset over the harbour, and in that time we saw at least twenty tour groups come and go.

The sunset, when it arrived, was spectacular. The sun sank between two sea-front hotels, affording Roo some dramatic images. Another hotel was already under construction in the gap, so before long this view would be gone; lingering there though, I couldn't help but wish that we were headed back to one of those luxurious establishments.

Budget travel certainly has its limitations.

"Time to go?" I asked.

"Yeah, might as well. Thanks for waiting for me! I *love* my new camera. I got some great pics."

I turned towards the road, and realised something. "Hey, love, there's a slight problem with taking sunset photos in a place like this."

"What's that?"

"Well, you know how long it took us to get here? And how scary it was?"

"Yeah?"

"Well, we've got to walk back now. And it's gone dark."

"Oh. Crap."

That evening we dragged ourselves out again, determined to experience KK in all its guises. We headed to the night market, as it was listed by *Lonely Planet* as the number two attraction in Kota Kinabalu. What they neglected to mention, however, is that it's a *fish* market. We could smell it before we saw it; dozens of stalls where you could pick your seafood, before having it cooked right in front of you on a camping stove and sitting down to eat it on a collection of patio furniture. The place bustled with locals, although much like the rest of the city it seemed bereft of Westerners. Roo's arrival, therefore, caused quite a commotion.

Tall, slim and gorgeous, she gets attention anywhere we go – but her hair, dyed six colours of the rainbow (every one except green, which I think looks like seaweed) – made her an instant celebrity. Calls and waving came from all sides as the stallholders (and quite a few of their customers) competed for Roo's business.

"It's nice..." Roo admitted, shyly, "but I don't want to eat fish."

Which pretty much ruled out the night market.

Luckily, the supermarket was still open.

"There's an offal smell in here," I said, standing in the meat aisle.

"It's your off-colour jokes that stink," she retorted.

"So what do you want to eat?"

"Um… we did pass that Burger King not long ago…"

So that was what we ate, for the first proper meal of our adventure.

I'm not ashamed; it tasted like home.

Though I did pause, halfway through my Whopper, to wonder whether or not they got their meat from the supermarket down the road.

I thought about mentioning it, but Roo was still eating, so I decided not to.

Bus-ness As Usual

We spent several days in Kota Kinabalu.
 How many days is several? I honestly don't know. It wasn't because some rustic charm arose from the smog-laden shadows and enticed us to stay there; it was because neither of us could persuade the other to get out of bed. A strange, all-pervading lethargy had washed over us, leaving us bemoaning even the simplest of tasks, like going to the bathroom. By day we drowsed, throwing off the bedspread so the stale air could reach our sweaty bodies. We shambled out as far as a string of restaurants just over a block away, marvelling at how stiff and leaden our limbs felt. By night we lay awake, cursing the all-night Karaoke bar that occupied the building directly opposite us. It was an oddity, that place; a couple of times we roused ourselves, determined to take advantage of such tangible night life. But every time we got down there it was deserted. The music pounded on regardless, as a resident duo took turns trying to draw in customers by murdering top ten hits of the last decade. For professionals they were pretty awful, getting most of the lyrics wrong and glossing over the ones they didn't understand by wailing volubly in time to the music. But it was the lisping that really killed me. Especially when they cranked up the volume for Lady Gaga's *'Bad Womance'*.

We decided not to stay for a drink.

Back upstairs, our squalid room pulsed to the 500-decibel strains of Katy Perry's *'I Kithed A girl'*. It was in this way that I discovered the vibrating walls – including the exterior one, housing our foot-square inoperable window – were made of thin plywood. Now, you kind of expect this with internal walls. Sure, it means you can hear every burp, scratch and fart for ten rooms in every direction, but that's pretty much par for the course. But external walls? This was an eight-storey building, and we were on the sixth floor. I'd assumed it was built of concrete, or something similarly sturdy, but closer inspection (of the cracks in our walls, through several of which I could actually *see* the karaoke bar) revealed the truth. The frame of the building was concrete; great beams and columns formed in a grid pattern. But the walls in-between were filled in – not with bricks, or more concrete, or high-spec glass – but with plywood. If a shabbier high-rise exists anywhere in the world... well, I don't want to stay there.

Hell, I didn't want to stay *here*.

Unsurprisingly, neither did Roo. She'd downloaded *Lonely Planet: Borneo* to her tablet, and was paging through it seeking escape. "There's this beach resort to the north of here, that sounds pretty cool," she suggested. "Tampat Do Aman – it's run by this bloke called Howard, and his phone number is right here."

"Eh? His phone number can't be in *Lonely Planet*."

"Yeah, look. Where it says Call Howard."

She was right. *That guy must be something special,* I thought. "Shall we go then?"

"We've got to do something. I feel like I've been drugged! We've only got a month in Borneo, and I don't want to spend it half-comatose in this dump."

With the decision made to hit the beach, we had only to get there.

It was a short, hot walk to the bus station – a rather grand title for a rough stretch of car park on the northern edge of the city. A row of decrepit wooden ticket booths marched along the nearest edge, though all were closed and shuttered. I couldn't tell if they'd been open for business half an hour ago, or if they'd been derelict for the last decade. There was plenty of help on offer though – a veritable swarm of elderly men dressed in shirts and trousers engulfed us on arrival, all shouting place names at us and tugging on our arms.

"KUDAT!" I yelled, hoping for some relief, and the effect was immediate – the swarm dissolved, apart from two men in front of us who beckoned us urgently. We followed them across the cracked tarmac to a line of shiny white minivans, and that's when I knew we were about to get the hard sell.

"Twenty dollar each!" the old man demanded, waving at the minivan.

Five western tourists were already sitting cramped in their seats, wearing the expressions of people who'd been there for quite a while.

Indicating the four empty seats, the man added brightly, "pay forty each, we go now!"

Anxious faces peered through the windows, all watching to see what would happen. If we coughed up enough dough, we could potentially be on our way immediately – but there was no way I was paying for two empty seats as well as our own. Hell, I wasn't paying for any seats on this tourist-trap.

"No," I told him, "we take local bus."

"Ha! No local bus," he countered. "Sit, sit! We wait for two."

"No." I pointed at a pair of knackered buses parked beyond the ticket booths. "We take big bus."

There was a brief argument, which we won by walking away, shedding our backpacks in the shade of a ticket booth, and sitting defiantly on them.

It was just after midday; we had plenty of time. And we were in no rush.

After repeatedly imploring that he would "only wait for two more," the driver finally gave up on us and stomped back to his minivan. I could almost feel the disappointment radiating from his passengers.

Another old bloke in even more dishevelled formalwear strolled over with a sly smile, and told us, "Kudat bus come soon! The driver, he is my brother!"

That seemed to settle it. We'd stuck to our guns, refused to be ripped off, and an authentic Bornean travel experience would be our reward.

We'd been sitting there, baking on the side of the road for what felt like hours. I glanced at my watch – it had *been* hours. The bus driver's brother was no longer in sight. Or maybe he was? We were surrounded by diminutive old men dressed like homeless office workers, and I'd long since lost track of the guy in question.

It was time to face facts: this bus wasn't coming.

We had two choices; pay the exorbitant fee for seats in the minivan, or head back for another night at the Summer Lodge...

Ugh! Just thinking about that made the decision a whole lot easier. Reluctantly, I hauled myself upright and headed towards the row of vehicles.

"Okay," I told the driver, "we go to Kudat."

"Oh!" he brightened. "How many seat? You want all?"

"No, not all. Just two." I held up two fingers for emphasis. I'm not saying which fingers they were, but I poured several hours of frustration into the gesture.

The driver, oblivious, grinned back at me. He waved me towards an empty minivan that was now standing exactly where the previous one had been. "So! We wait for seven."

Roo was less than ecstatic when I broke this news.

On the upside, the driver was working hard to recruit more passengers.

He called out to every passer-by – I mean, every single one, from overburdened old ladies to trendy young urbanites – plucking at their sleeves, if they came close enough. "Kudat, KUDAT!" was his battle cry.

Unsurprisingly, it wasn't getting him very far.

Kudat was over a hundred and twenty miles away, at the extreme northern tip of Borneo. There was absolutely nothing there – just one hotel and a golf course, left over from British colonial days. I got the feeling that, if you were going to Kudat, you generally knew about it in advance.

"Kudat, KUDAT!" he yelled, echoing himself to no

discernable effect.

How had he not figured this out already?

I wanted to shake the guy, and say, "No-one is going to suddenly need a ticket to Kudat! It's a three-hour drive into the middle of nowhere. It doesn't matter how much effort you put in – it's just not an impulse-buy!

Four hours later, at 6pm precisely, we left for Kudat.

To be honest, I was already a bit sick of the place.

The journey itself could best be described as 'rough'.

The surface of the road was so damaged it looked like it had been raining hand grenades. Every time a wheel hit a pot hole, the person sitting opposite it bounced out of their seat and cracked their head on the roof. As there were nine of us in the car, it gave a remarkably good impression of a game of Whack-a-Mole.

At one point we passed a crew of guys with diggers and steamrollers, with signs claiming they were resurfacing. I was hard pushed to figure out which direction they were working in, as the road on both sides of them was equally crap.

We'd have got a smoother ride if we'd driven down the scar of deforestation that paralleled the road for most of its length.

The minivan dropped us by the corner of Kudat's aging hotel, but this was not our final destination. One of the few chores we had managed to achieve in KK was buying a Malaysian SIM card for our phone, so I was able to call Howard using the number in *Lonely Planet*. I could hardly believe it when he answered, and promised to come and pick us up.

It was late, and dark, and after a while Roo began to get nervous.

"How will we know who Howard is?" she asked.

Just then, with a spray of gravel, a pickup truck screeched to a stop in front of us.

And out climbed Howard.

There was no mistaking him; three parts Indiana Jones, one part English geezer, he was dressed the way a *real* explorer dresses; in battered khaki shorts, faded t-shirt and trainers, rather than head-to-toe Gore-Tex.

He looked every inch the kind of bloke who could come to a place like this, carve out a small niche in the jungle, and build a whole complex of cabins by hand.

He'd also learnt the Malaysian language, married a local girl, become a pillar of the community and built a museum to the tribal people of the area.

Not bad for a bloke from Stratford-on-Avon.

"Tony, is it?" he offered his hand.

It was like shaking hands with the Terminator.

"Jump in!"

I eyed the truck. This, too, was the real deal; not the blatantly unnecessary 4x4 of the suburban soccer-mom. This truck looked like it had won a tough rugby match, gone straight out on the town without showering, then got steaming drunk and slept in a ditch.

"Can I... ride on the back?" I asked.

Howard thought about it for a few seconds. "Yeah mate, why not? Just hold on tight, it gets a bit bumpy. And watch out for low-hanging branches. And we might get chased by some dogs, but ignore them. And don't worry about the army checkpoint, I'll do the talking."

I was already stood in the truck's tray, holding on to the roll-bars, when that last bit sunk in.

Army checkpoint? Where the hell were we going...?

Howard's Way

Tampat Do Aman was a slice of paradise.

The beach, a flawless expanse of sand, extended right up to the tip of Borneo; I know, because there was a sign on it which said 'Tip Of Borneo'.

I've heard beaches described as unspoiled before, but this was the definition of it.

There were no hotels along the sea-front, and no high-rises. No resorts, or souvenir shops, or bars, or market stalls; nothing.

Just pure white sand, bordered by jungle; crystal-clear waters and the sound of the surf hitting the beach.

Oh, and Howard's restaurant.

He'd built the place himself, of course, with a little help from local craftspeople. His staff came entirely from the nearby villages, and were paid a sensible wage to cook the kind of food which made me weak at knees just anticipating it.

Malaysian Beef *Rendang*, fresh fruit salad – fresh as in, picked that morning fresh – and homemade Oreo cheesecake.

Ahhh!

They even ran cooking classes, the latest string to Howard's highly-strung bow.

We watched intently as Lorinna, Howard's tiny Malay

wife, poured the ingredients of her traditional *Mee Goreng* (fried noodles) recipe into a giant wok.

The pan sizzled, exuding a scent so delicious I had to clutch the worktop to keep me upright.

Needless to say, we ate well there. At least when Howard was around.

"It's a problem with the local work ethic," he confided in me. "These people don't do nine-to-five, and they haven't developed the same sense of urgency we have in the Western world. For the most part that's a good thing, but it means that as soon as I leave, all the staff stop work and start chatting."

It was a measurable phenomenon; *mee goreng*, ordered in Howard's presence, took ten minutes to arrive. Ordered in his absence, it either arrived two hours later, or ten minutes after Howard did.

But it was hard to complain in paradise.

One night, strolling the mile from the beach to the resort, we were treated to the sight of a civet, slinking along the power lines that followed the road. Far above our heads, the cat ignored us completely, demonstrating its amazing agility by using the cluster of cables as easily as we were using the road. Or easier – it didn't have to worry about the dogs, half a dozen of which came charging out of every house and hovel we passed, barking so loudly it set their neighbours' dogs off. Pretty soon we were walking cocooned in the sound. It made me wonder just how thrilled the locals were about guests walking back to Howard's jungle lodge, if this happened every time.

Personally, I'd have shot us.

The lodge itself was another wonder.

Perfectly replicating the traditional long-houses of the native Rungus people, it was a palm-thatched stick hut the size of a tennis court. Chunky logs held it a metre off the ground, rough-split planks formed the flooring – and the beds – and every other part of it was made from thousands of interwoven skinny branches.

More than anything, it looked like a retirement home for Tarzan.

The whole lodge swayed slightly with every footstep,

and we soon learned which boards were safer to put our feet on, and which ones complained loudly about it. There was a long, central corridor with plank doors lining both sides. These led to the rooms, which were only separated from each other by panels of woven reeds. Privacy would have been moot, except that we were the only people there. Lying in bed, gazing through the gauze of the mosquito net, it was impossible not to follow the sticks, noting where they were cut together, where tied, where woven under or over or accidentally missing…

It was good to have something to occupy me in bed. There'd be no sex in this place; too vigorous a thrust might bring the whole thing down on top of us. Hell, I was stifling my sneezes out of the same fear.

But it was beautiful.

Simple.

Peaceful.

Or so you'd think.

Late on that first night, lulled by the ever-present drone of cicadas, I was just about to doze off when I felt Roo go tense.

"Stop breathing so loudly! I can hear something."

"Wha…?"

"Shhh! It's right *underneath* us," she hissed.

My ears strained downwards. There were undeniable scuffling sounds, all the more audible because the floor had gaps I could put my hand through.

"It can't get us, can it?" Roo's whisper sounded nervous.

"Don't think so, love. It sounds big though…"

Just then, an ear-splitting cry rent the still night air.

ACK-ACK-AOOOOOOOOOOOWWW! ACK-ACK-AWWOOOOOOOO!

I had a minor heart-attack, but Roo recovered quickly.

"Oh no," she said.

"It's a fucking rooster!" I wailed.

Then, in the distance, we heard a flurry of answering cries. Our rooster also heard them, and sent out another deafening warble.

"How the hell do roosters survive in the jungle?" I moaned. "Surely the first time they do that, every predator in the place will be queuing up to eat them?"

"They're probably pet roosters. Kept by farmers."

"So? There has to be something here that kills roosters!"

"Try and ignore it," Roo advised me. "If you start obsessing now…"

Another piercing chicken-shriek issued from below us.

"Ignore *that*? He's sitting right under my head! The little bugger's taunting me!"

Roo sighed. "Just go to sleep."

There was no sleep that night.

The rooster had commenced his serenade shortly after midnight; he continued with gusto, crowing every thirty seconds or so until 6am.

I had earplugs; I pushed them in so far they came out dripping brain, but all it accomplished was adding the sound of the sea to the cries of the creature.

I friggin' hate roosters.

"Yeah, I've been meaning to get rid of that rooster," said Howard, when we broached the subject.

"No worries," I told him, "if he tries the same thing tonight I'll do it for you. And then we can make him into burgers."

Howard just laughed and went about his business, obviously immune to me threatening his chicken.

Our plans for that day involved a spot of light sunbathing, followed by more of the same. The long trip from KK, coupled with the lack of sleep, had left us exhausted again; doing very little seemed like the antidote.

The only fly in the ointment – apart from the flies, and the lack of any kind of ointment – was the sunburn. It had been too dark inside the longhouse to tell, but once undressed for the beach it became painfully obvious. Somehow we'd managed to arrive at the beach more burned than most people left it.

Once, in New Zealand, I spent an entire day snowboarding in gorgeous weather, and never thought to apply sunscreen. Two days later, I'd been able to peel the burnt skin off my right ear in one piece, creating a perfect ear-cast (which I kept until it disintegrated, because it was *awesome*). But even that didn't compare to this.

A crazy-paved pattern of angry red welts twisted and turned across our bodies like the scars from a flogging. I had a ring of fire all around one shoulder – and yet the shoulder itself was unblemished! It was like we'd had sun block applied by Picasso and then been left naked in the desert for three days. It was weird. It was painful. It was…

"Those bloody Malaria pills! The side-effects include increased sensitivity to sunlight!"

Roo's eyes widened. "But we've hardly been out in the sun! Only yesterday, walking to the bus station."

"Well, that must have been enough." Something else dawned on me at that moment. "Oh… bloody hell! You know what? The other side effects of Dioxy-cyclone, or whatever it is?"

"Yeah?"

"Lethargy."

"Ohhh…"

"Yup."

It all made sense. I'd read about extreme reactions to the pills back when we'd ordered them, but I never suffer from side-effects – even when testing experimental medicines in paid medical trials, I'd mostly survived unscathed. But there was no denying it – debilitating tiredness and agonizing sunburn. Those pills have ruined our first week away, and we couldn't keep taking them.

"I'd rather have malaria," Roo joked. Then she laughed. "Back in the Summer Lodge, I was starting to worry that we'd been drugged. And we were – only we were doing it to ourselves!"

With our skin raw and blistering, the sun felt as sharp as a scalpel.

We spent the rest of that day hiding from it, and wishing that the beach was a little *less* undiscovered. A string of cocktail bars would have been ideal about now, and maybe a bloke renting out beach umbrellas. And an internet café, as WiFi was one thing Tampat Do Aman couldn't supply. And a stall selling sunglasses – Roo's snapped in half the first time she tried to put them on.

"You can wear mine," I offered.

"Huh. No thanks," she pouted.

I knew she was jealous. Mine had Batman on them.

"We picked a bad time for a beach holiday," Roo mused, as we sat in the restaurant, sweating into full-length hiking pants and long-sleeved shirts.

It would be a while before the Doxycycline was out of our system, and in the meantime any part of us that saw the sun sizzled like it was being molested with a red-hot poker.

"It's funny. What I wanted most of all when we left KK was exactly this: endless beach, swimming, kayaking, sunbathing, exploring... and now what I'm craving is air-con, a soft mattress, somewhere comfy to hide from the sun during the day and a bit of internet to plan the rest of the trip."

"You think we're getting too old for this shit?" I asked her.

Roo shook her head, charitably ignoring my use of the royal 'we' – and the fact that she's nearly a decade younger than me. "No, I still love backpacking," she said, "but I used to think people were crazy to come to a place like Borneo and blow loads of cash on five-star resorts with swimming pools and room service. I used to think, what's the point of traveling halfway around the world to sit in a posh hotel watching satellite TV? And yet, now..."

She looked at me.

I didn't dare nod. Not because I was ashamed of agreeing with her, but because I was afraid of splattering her with drool.

Five-star luxury! If only we had a five-star budget.

Then something occurred to me. "Hey love, I know a place where we could afford that kind of thing..."

Roo rolled her eyes in response. "Tony, for the last time – we are *not* going to Thailand!"

Paradise Lost

We spent several more days at Tampat Do Aman.

We saw Howard as he bounced back and forth, ferrying new arrivals from Kudat town to the long house, from the long house to the restaurant, and back. He was never in one place for longer than a few minutes, though he didn't seem bothered by the relentless stream of busywork.

"Just got to fix a hole in the school fence," he explained, heading to his dusty truck once more. He'd built the school himself, of course, and provided ongoing maintenance as well as classes on environmental awareness and local wildlife.

"I'll be back in time for that night walk, if you guys are still up for it?"

He'd offered us this by way of an excursion – a trek through the wildlife reserve he was currently creating, at night because that was when the animals came out.

"Yeah, sure!"

That evening, Howard collected us from the longhouse and led us across the road to his private reserve. Equipped with a machete and a powerful head torch, he made his way uphill, setting a blistering pace. The humidity was so high we almost needed snorkels to breathe, yet Howard forged his way upwards like a sweaty version of the Energiser Bunny. Every so often he stopped to show us something – plants and insects for the most part, as the larger creatures tended not to stray too close to human habitations.

"Watch out for this one," he warned, pointing his machete at a plant with broad, waxy green leaves. "The sap is pretty bad, if it gets on your skin, and whatever you do don't rub your eyes or you could go blind."

"Oh! Fair enough. What's it called?"

"Dunno. The locals call it poison-tree."

"Well. That sounds about right."

"Oh, and watch out for those." Howard gestured at my head. I turned, confused – and the beam of his head torch picked out a dark brown spider bigger than my hand, sitting with its legs splayed out around the tree next to me. I've seen a lot of spiders in my life, but this one looked big enough to swallow my head.

"Do... do they bite?" I asked.

"Oh hell yeah. Very nasty, those tarantulas."

"Right."

"I'd come away from there," said Howard, as though I'd wandered close to the thing intentionally. "They can be bad-tempered."

The walk passed without serious incident, and was every bit as exciting as I'd imagined. It had been too dark to see much, and we'd blundered through the undergrowth so clumsily that everything within a mile radius heard us coming, but that didn't alter the experience. To be out in the jungle at night, surrounded by the sounds you only hear on David Attenborough documentaries, with only Howard's knowledge (and his machete) between us and disaster – it was a thrill I won't soon forget.

We went for a swim in the sea to cool off, marvelling at the phosphorescence. Millions of tiny pinpricks of light sparked to life with every move we made, trailing our arms and legs like fairy dust. I'd experienced this before, in Thailand; bioluminescent plankton glowing suddenly to confuse predators – but never as dramatically as here. The water was alive with the stuff, and swimming underwater was a magical, ethereal experience.

The next day we found a jellyfish the size of a dustbin lid washed up on the beach. Even Howard was impressed when we showed him the photos. "Sometimes we get the really big ones here," he enthused.

Howard was impossible to faze.

I mentioned my time in Ecuador, volunteering in a wildlife refuge. He said I was welcome to come and volunteer in the refuge he was currently building.

I told him I'd done a bit of diving, and he said he had, too.

So I told him I was a PADI Divemaster, with over a hundred dives under my weight belt.

And he said that was great! And then told me he'd been a search and rescue diver in the Caribbean, with more than three-thousand-five-hundred dives.

He'd also been in the army. I didn't need to ask – I could just tell he'd been SAS, or something equally ass-kicking.

I decided not to mention my own stint in the army. As a weekend warrior. And that, since I'd taken leave to go on holiday in Thailand and never returned, I was *technically* still AWOL…

"He's amazing," I gushed. "I want to be just like him when I grow up!"

Roo eyed me as if to say, you've left that a bit late.

She'd seen all the hallmarks of a new fixation. I was still having an identity crisis – approaching thirty-five, yet insecure about my place in the grand scheme of things. I was starting to question my choices, and to wonder how things might have turned out differently if I'd taken other paths. Idolising Howard was a symptom; the man was so focussed, so confident, so dedicated to what he was doing. As a result of this, he was an overachiever – talented, experienced, and charismatic to boot.

It was when I started talking about him in bed that she decided to draw the line.

"The thing is," she explained, "Howard has a lot of stuff going on around here. It's very impressive, for sure, but it *is* all around here. As in, he's tied to this place. He's made his decision, and devoted his life to this tiny corner of Borneo. He's become part of the place, and one of its people – but what about everything outside of here? There's a whole world to explore, yet this place revolves around him. If he wants to keep it in one piece, he can't leave. So long as he's happy that way, then it's perfect for him. But I wouldn't be. And you wouldn't be."

I sighed. She made a good point.

"And if I have to spend one more night listening to that rooster..." she added.

And that was a *very* good point.

Much as I loved Tampat Do Aman, and what it stood for – what Howard stood for – it was time to take our leave. The next morning we caught a lift with the legend himself back into Kudat town, and to the deserted main square, where we were introduced to the Kota Kinabalu minibus driver.

"We go soon," he told us, holding up one hand with his fingers splayed. "Only wait for five..."

It took a couple of hours, but eventually the driver decided to make the most of what he'd got. Four more people had arrived, including a father and son, and a very frail-looking old woman who proceeded to load the entire back of the vehicle with watermelons. The seat next to me was left empty, as I'd opted to sit in the middle next to Roo; I'd been hoping my terrifyingly blotchy complexion, which looked not unlike the evidence of some tropical disease, would be enough to keep the natives away.

And it seemed to be working.

But then we pulled up on the outskirts of town, near what looked to be the equivalent of a convenience store. The driver made a quick phone call, and the door to the shop yawned open – and out of it squeezed the largest woman I have ever clapped eyes on. She was gargantuan. Swathed in what appeared to be a floral-print double bedspread, she waddled towards the car, clutching a handbag under one arm and a sack of fruit under the other.

The driver did a double-take when he saw her. He had to get out and push on her to get her all in. Her flesh undulated, filling up all the available space, rubbing up against mine in a way that made me wish I hadn't worn shorts. She was...

Moist.

And so, now adequately laden, we set off for Kota Kinabalu.

I kept catching the driver's eyes in the mirror, as he glanced back at the huge woman in something approaching fear. I think he was genuinely concerned that she would eat him en-route. Finally he could take no more, and started babbling nervously to the car's occupants. Confusion reigned for a few minutes, while he struggled to articulate his point. Then the father and son in the back started squirming, and the boy slid over his dad to swap seats.

"Everything okay?" I asked.

The driver had great English for someone who lived so remotely. He groped briefly for the words, and then explained. "Is fine! But car... falling... to one side. Too heavy that side!"

Then he fired off an apology to the huge lady in Malaysian, which she took in good spirits. She was so fat the driver couldn't steer his minivan, but she didn't seem to mind one bit. She was a jolly giant, and colourful too, with her duvet-sized sarong.

She reached into her bag and produced a cellophane pouch filled with brown liquid, which she opened. The stench was immediate and potent – rotting fish assailed my nostrils, causing Roo to gag.

Pulling a cocktail stick from the bag, she proceeded to spear a chunk of something unmentionable in the brown liquid, lifted it clear of the pouch, and then slurped it down noisily. Other chunks bobbed ominously in the goop. I couldn't take my eyes off the stuff. I'd been in the van on the way here. I knew it was about to get bumpy. And by bumpy, I mean surface-of-the-moon bumpy. I mean this minibus was going to get air-time, no matter how heavily laden it was. And when that happened, whatever the hell it was she was eating... well, we'd all be wearing it.

As for the implications of travel sickness...

Roo lowered the window, ignoring the driver's complaint about it affecting his air-con. We just needed plain

old air back here, and quick.
   It was going to be a long trip.

Hotel KinaballoooOOO!

Getting back to KK was a huge relief. We both let out breaths we'd been subconsciously holding – mostly because there hadn't been room to breathe in that minivan – and appraised our surroundings.

We'd chosen Hotel Kinabalu hoping it would be an upgrade from the Summer Lodge. At twice the price, it couldn't be worse; nothing could, short of prison. Although, the location didn't look too promising. Bordered on one side by the main road, the back of the building overlooked the kind of alleyway you see on *Crimewatch.* Narrow and claustrophobic, it led to a small square which acted like a catchment pond for the tidal wave of litter sweeping down the streets. Boxy air conditioners bristled from every wall like a paused game of Tetris. It would have been impossible to commit suicide from this building; no matter which window you jumped from, you'd simply bounce back and forth between air-con units like a human pinball, all the way to the ground.

Thankfully, the lobby looked more inviting. It's a weird trend I was already noticing, which was to be echoed throughout all the Asian cities we visited; no-one seemed to give a damn what the outside of their building looked like. From the most expensive hotels and presumably slick, inner-city offices, to apartments and shopping centres; the entrance hall was quite often dripping in luxurious finishes, right up to the doorway. But step outside, and the building looked derelict. Smog-stained concrete, decades-old paint, filthy, broken signs and, of course, my personal favourite – sidewalks that looked like they'd barely survived a nuclear holocaust.

Safely ensconced in our room on the twelfth floor of Hotel Kinabalu, we could finally relax. The bed looked clean and comfy. We had our own bathroom, a TV on the wall and the WiFi worked a treat. It might not have been a beach, but for my weary, sunburned body, *this* was paradise.

Tampat Do Aman had been too remote. At first I worried that we'd grown soft in our old age – or at least, in our middle age. I've never had much faith in my ability to survive past 40, a calculation which now placed me firmly in the last decade of my life. Had marriage changed us? Had we lost the spirit of adventure that had seen us through so many peculiar predicaments? Was this the start of a long, slow decline, which would see me sitting in front of daytime TV wearing sweat-pants and slippers in a few years' time?

As usual, Roo had a more real-world appraisal of our problems.

"We went a beach holiday," she explained, "and we fucked it up."

I liked her version much better. And it *did* sound like us.

"We need to recover," she continued, "and we need to rest. We need to shower, and then we need to take a nap."

This plan was sounding better by the minute.

"And then," she added, "we need a chainsaw."

She was right, of course.

The centre of town was nearly ten minutes' walk away from our new location, but the lure of food was strong. Chainsaw was a dish we'd discovered on our first few days in KK. Struggling to get ourselves out of bed, our path-of-least-resistance mentality had led us to a Chinese café just over the road from the Summer Lodge. Recognising nothing from the photo-menu covering one wall, we'd each pointed to something that looked vaguely appetising. Roo's had turned out okay, but forgettable, whereas I had stumbled onto something labelled (in felt-tip pen) 'Chan-Suw'. Thin slices of barbequed meat on a bed of plain rice, it was simple, non-threatening and utterly delicious. After that, we ate there every time we passed, regardless of whether or not we were hungry, and we both ordered the same thing every time. It was always served with a bowl of steaming hot, clear liquid with chives floating in it. We were never quite sure what to do with this, and on different occasions I variously drank it, poured it over my rice, or washed my fingers in it. No-one in the restaurant seemed to care either way, though I suspect the staff had a running bet on what I'd try next. I made surreptitious attempts to see what the locals did with theirs, casting sidelong glances until Roo thought I was having some kind of fit.

Apparently I don't do surreptitious very well.

Anyway, Chan-Suw quickly became Chainsaw, and it was the first contender for our favourite meal in Asia.

We also ate of lot of *Mee Goreng*, that delicious Indonesian staple of fried noodles. It was our fail-safe, one thing we could order anywhere and know it would be good. I could even order it in the local lingo: *Mee* (fried) *Goreng* (noodles) *Ayam* (chicken). Fried food was impossible to avoid here, unless you went for soup; I'm pretty sure I saw fried soup advertised on at least one occasion. Expanding waistlines looked set to be our next crisis, and we steered clear of another Chinese restaurant, despite it being only a few doors down from our hotel, because the name of the place seemed worryingly prophetic; *Soon Phat*, it was called.

The next day we visited Suria Sabah, an immense, upmarket shopping mall with a conical glass façade that loomed over downtown KK. It was an anomaly; a dazzling shopping mecca of the kind I'd expect to find in Singapore or Hong Kong. Boutiques for the likes of *Gucci* and *Prada* rubbed shoulders with nail-art salons and bubble-tea bars, and between it all were acres of gleaming, cream-coloured marble floor tiles.

And no people.

Perhaps because it offered *Gucci* and *Prada* – and yet was embedded within a city lined with *Proton* cars and street vendors selling single cigarettes from a packet – Suria Sabah was completely empty every time we set foot in it.

There's only one other place you can go to from Kota Kinabalu. Well, technically two, but one of them is the Kingdom of Brunei; a tiny, oil rich country ranked as fifth-wealthiest nation in the world. It sort of went without saying that we weren't going there.

So, Sandakan, the second city of the northern state of Sabah, was our destination.

We planned to stop en-route, to hike in the national park surrounding Mount Kinabalu, Malaysia's highest mountain. Roo and I had both been looking forward to climbing the mountain – at least, until we started researching it. Taking a guide was compulsory, as was a variety of passes and permissions, and spending the night in a hotel halfway up. All up, the total cost would be $400 *each* – for a two day, one night trek.

And even at those prices, the climb was booked up for weeks or months in advance.

I tried to make myself feel better by remembering that climbing Mount Kinabalu – or attempting it – was the single most touristy activity in all Borneo. It would be a solid queue all the way up and back down again; I was unlikely to discover anything new up there.

The minibus to Sandakan was 'only waiting for four', but it was crammed to the roof with boxes and baggage, practically burying the other passengers. After we squeezed in, the driver had no choice but to pile our enormous rucksacks onto the two empty seats. At which point, he demanded we pay him for four tickets.

"Screw this," I said, climbing out and dragging my backpack out after me. Another night in the Hotel Kinabalu seemed on the cards, but the driver chased us across the car park and eventually offered to let our bags ride for free. It was a sudden revelation; haggling *was* possible here – I'd just been too timid with my attempts. Walking away hadn't been a bluff, but it had worked like one. I felt a warm glow of triumph spreading through me as I hopped in next to my backpack and the driver fired up the engine. Then I remembered I'd only succeeded in negotiating the price down to what it should have been in the first place – standard tourist rates for two seats instead of four. *Setting the bar for success fairly low,* I thought, as we joined the traffic queuing out of KK.

Most of the other passengers were bound for Sandakan, which both *Lonely Planet* and our driver agreed were a six-hour drive away. I thought that was a bit optimistic, as it took us nearly two hours just to get out of KK. Very optimistic, as it turned out; it took five hours to reach Mount Kinabalu National Park, our destination of choice – and the halfway point for the minibus.

"Traffic bad," the driver explained, shrugging away any responsibility.

"Isn't it always bad?"

"Yes, always bad, yes."

Yet it never occurred to anyone to mention that, traffic being a constant, the average journey time had escalated somewhat – from six hours to around ten-and-a-half.

The driver pulled up about a mile short of the Kinabalu National Park entrance, and kicked us out on the side of the road.

We were expecting it though; the picturesque-sounding Mountain Lodge, where we had booked in for the night, was set back in the forest along a winding dirt track.

We could have tried hailing a taxi, but couldn't bring ourselves to be that lazy. The crippling lethargy had disappeared not long after stopping the malaria pills, and we were both feeling strong and energetic for the first time since leaving Perth. I didn't care that it was starting to rain, and neither did Roo. We shouldered our backpacks, delighted that we could do so without our knees buckling.

"How far is it?" Roo asked.

"Only a mile," I scoffed, "shouldn't take us more than twenty minutes."

"That's good," Roo said, "because we've got to hike in

there, ditch our bags, then hike back out again and along this main road for another mile to the park entrance if we want to eat anything tonight. It's the only restaurant in the area. And after that, we've got to hike back in again. There's a good chance we'll be sick of this road by the time we're finished."

"Ha! Well, the website says it's an easy walk."

She laughed suddenly, and slapped her forehead. "I just had a thought. You know what would have made it even easier?"

"What?"

"If we'd brought a sandwich."

Slip n' Slide

The easy one-mile hike to the Kinabalu Mountain Lodge took us an hour and a half.

I blame their website; I think whoever wrote it had confused the word 'easy' with the word 'death-trap'.

Leaving the sealed road behind, we followed a rough track uphill. The rain, which had started as soon as we got out of the minivan, was light enough to ignore; between that and the humidity, the air seemed overburdened with moisture. We reached the top of the hill and stopped for a breather. On our left, the flank of Mount Kinabalu rose, heavily forested. To our right the land dropped away abruptly, just like it did in front of us – the track plunged back down the hillside disappearing into a mass of tropical vegetation.

Mist rose to greet us we set off downwards. At first this only added to the sense of adventure; we were halfway up the side of a mountain, surrounded by exotic foliage and enveloped in the haze. It was like descending into the Land of the Lost; anything could emerge from that impenetrable fog.

I was picturing a T-rex.

Roo looked at me, then rolled her eyes.

She can always tell when I'm picturing a T-rex.

The road undulated, going from steep downhill slope to steep uphill again almost immediately. And it continued in this fashion for the entire mile, so that by the time we arrived, we felt like we'd walked five. But the difficult bit wasn't the distance – it was the surface. Most of the road was, blessedly, dirt. But in order to help cars climb the hills, the steepest part of every section had been overlaid with great slabs of concrete. Rainwater, which was being absorbed harmlessly by the dirt track, was pooling on the solid surface; by the time we crested the second rise and stood looking down, the centre of the slope had become a river.

Few surfaces are as slippery as wet concrete. That's why they don't make roads out of it – and why people etch brick-relief patterns into their patio slabs.

For grip.

What these people had done was to rake rough grooves in the concrete, about a foot apart. Which would be all well and good, if we had giant clown-feet. Or giant clown shoes at least, with customised grippy rubber soles. Or if we were cars.

But we weren't.

We were pedestrians, laden down and shambling like arthritic tortoises, and those grooves were absolutely sod all good to us. What we faced at the top of that hill was roughly twenty metres of rain-slicked concrete pitched at around forty-five degrees downwards.

Basically a giant water-slide.

We must have looked like a pair of drunks, clinging to each other, our spare arms flailing frantically for balance as we edged down the slope an inch at a time.

"Shit, shit!" Roo cried, "I'm slipping!"

She clutched my arm tighter, until one of my feet slid out from under me. "Shit!" I yelled, "Me too!"

When we reached the bottom we stood together, shaking. Frustration gave way to hilarity as we realised how ridiculous we must have looked on the descent.

"Good job no-one can see us in this," Roo waved an arm

at the swirling fog.

"Yeah," I agreed. Good job no-one is out here to see us.

Because as well as up and down, the track curved blindly around the side of the mountain. I'd seen how the locals drove, and the thought of a pickup speeding round the bend ahead and barrelling down the slope towards us in this weather...

"Let's get moving," I suggested.

The next hill began immediately, so we started up it – and halfway up, we met concrete again.

It was like trying to ice skate uphill, but with a twenty-kilo rucksack on my back.

"Crap! I think they've done this on every slope..."

Several waterslides later, I was starting to lose my sense of humour.

"What gets me is, the Mountain Lodge people *know* about this. It's not like it's normally dry here – it's a *frigging rainforest!* Half the buggers who hike into this place must give them grief about nearly breaking legs, but they don't bother mentioning it on the website. Better to deny all knowledge and take flak from every new arrival, than to risk losing business by putting a warning in their description. It takes the piss!"

It was going dark by the time we arrived, as well as raining. When we saw the lights of the Mountain Lodge looming out of the shadows, we were immensely relieved; there'd been no signage at all en route, no clue that our destination was ever going to emerge. We'd passed private houses and long driveways disappearing off at odd angles into the fog, and slightly more concerning, a series of big bushes that were entirely cocooned in spider webs.

Around that point I started to worry that we'd made a horrible mistake. I was so grateful to get there that I didn't unleash the rant I'd been forming furiously in my head. An hour-odd of pent-up frustration melted away when I recognised the gorgeous, timber-clad chalet poised on the hillside above us.

A last push up a set of stairs, past a raised deck hung with sodden laundry, led us to a wide, covered balcony overlooking the valley below.

And at last, we could relax.

Our room was on the top floor, tucked away under the eaves. The bed was a mattress on the floor, which the owners had cleverly turned into a virtue by calling this 'The Japanese Room'. I have to admit, it did sound more appealing than the 'Not Tall Enough To Stand Up In' room.

We'd been there less than five minutes when the heavens opened fully, rain lashing down hard enough to shake the lodge. We could hardly believe our luck. If we'd been caught halfway by that downpour we'd have been washed off the road like a couple of crisp packets.

Consequently, we decided to wait out the storm before setting off on our return journey.

After all, we had to eat...

The final trip that night was accomplished in full darkness, with head torches. It was still raining, though not as heavily, and we were forced to scoot down some of the steeper sections on all fours.

Back at the lodge, the drumming of the rain on the roof soothed us, and lulled us into sleep.

Or it would have.

Unfortunately, the sturdy wooden structure conducted sound like a bell. Every noise, from hikers knocking mud off their boots on the back steps to someone chopping veg in the kitchen, resonated throughout the whole building.

The paper-thin walls offered no resistance at all; I could hear the bloke in the next room all night, and he wasn't even snoring.

At 5am, a large tour group occupying most of the rooms got up to prepare for their mountain climb. That was the end of sleep for us; the whole lodge trembled as they stomped around in hiking boots, shouting and jeering at each other in Malay. It was also the end of breakfast. After they left, we dredged ourselves up from the floor, where every vibration had been concentrated, and went down to the lounge area. The kitchen staff had prepared our fried eggs – at 5:30am, along with the tour group's. They sat there on the counter, cold and fly-blown, and the staff merely shrugged when I tried to complain about it. Our toast had also been ready since 5:30, despite breakfast not officially starting until 7. As far as I could tell there wasn't anything left to cook fresh – either that, or the girls in the kitchen didn't care enough to offer. The last straw came when we went to fill our water bottles. "Our filter is slow," one of the girls explained, unapologetically. By which she meant, she'd allowed the tour group to take all the available drinking water, and it would be hours before there was any for us.

Luckily I had the Steripen, and it didn't take long to make a litre of water from the bathroom tap drinkable. Otherwise it would have been a long, thirsty hike back to the park entrance, with full backpacks to boot. As it was, the heat was bearable, and I spent most of the trip writing an angry Trip Advisor review in my head.

Breakfast in the national park put us both in a much better frame of mind, so we stored our bags in the park office and spent a good few hours getting lost on miles of cryptically-signposted jungle trails. More than anything, Roo wanted to see a Rafflesia – Borneo's most infamous plant, also known as the corpse-flower.

It blooms only once per year, unfurling a single, red-and-yellow spotted flower over a metre wide. It also produces a pungent stench like rotting flesh, attracting flies and other insects to carry its pollen. It's the world's largest, heaviest flower (at up to 11kg!) – and one of the rarest.

So I didn't hold out much hope of stumbling across one.

There was a huge concrete replica though, which we climbed inside for photos, and then – as we forced our way down a heavily overgrown path that seemed long unused – Roo froze. "Smell that?" she breathed.

"Smell what?"

"That *stink!* It can't be... can it?"

"Be what?"

"A rafflesia!"

"Oh, no. No, that's just my ass. Sorry!"

"God damn it! That's the last time you have beans for breakfast."

Sandakan

Six and a half hours later, the bus to Sandakan dropped us off in a place that looked suspiciously not like Sandakan. Everyone else got off, including the driver, so we didn't have much choice, really.

There's a growing trend amongst Asian cities of relocating their long-distance bus terminals to an area well outside the city. The benefits are obvious: keep huge coaches out of chaotic city centres, avoid adding to the already problematic congestion, and reduce air pollution for the urbanites. It also shaved two hours off a bus's effective journey time – one spent getting out of the city, and one getting back into it.

But the downside was that we had to find another form of transportation to get us to and from the bus stations. That almost always meant a taxi, which typically cost more than the bus journey itself.

And that is what we had to do now, more than doubling the cost of our journey. I tried to haggle with the driver, but he just smirked and shook his head – without a lift to a recognisable part of the city we were buggered, and he knew it as well as I did.

Research had taught me two things about Sandakan; one,

that it was the site of a notorious Japanese POW camp in World War 2, from where the mostly Australian prisoners set out on forced Death Marches. Of around 2,500 POWs, only six survived the ordeal.

And two; Sandakan's busy sea-port is the jumping off point for Sipadan Island, one of the world's most famous diving destinations.

I'd expected to find the city bustling with holidaymakers, but the streets were oddly quiet and empty.

As we made our way to the Sea View Budget Hotel, Roo had an idea.

"We should tell them you're a travel writer," she suggested.

"Ah… I dunno. What if they ask where I've been published? I hate that."

"But my love, you *are* a travel writer! Your books are published, by you, and they're about your travels. That totally counts. Your royalties are paying for this trip."

"Yeah… I guess so…"

"No, really! We've got to start telling more people. We could get discounts, free upgrades, all sorts of stuff. We should be telling everyone!"

Our host for our stay in Sandakan was a very friendly middle-aged lady, who owned the Sea View and ran it herself. She seemed delighted to see us, as most of her other bookings had been cancelled.

"All because of the attacks," she explained, "and now, no-one will come to Sandakan! Everyone is too scared, but the attacks happened very far from here."

Roo and I exchanged glances. She shrugged. We hadn't seen any news in weeks, and we weren't about to squander our precious internet time looking into it.

So long as no-one actually attacked our room while we were in it, I was happy enough.

"We don't worry about things like that," I told her.

Roo surrendered her passport as the room deposit, and the woman touched its blue cover with reverence. "Australian!" she said, "That's very good!"

"And my husband is a travel writer," Roo explained.

Shave My Spider!

The woman looked at me, her eyes going wide. "Really?"

Inwardly, I cringed. "Oh, I ah, well, I wrote a couple of books, you know, about my travels..."

"Oh, that's *fantastic!*" she declared. "You're just what I need!"

"Eh?"

"In Australia you have big ANZAC celebrations every year, yes?"

"Erm... we have ANZAC biscuits...?" I glanced at Roo.

"Australia and New Zealand Army Corps," she explained, "we have a church service at dawn on ANZAC Day."

"So!" the lady exclaimed, "You know, Sandakan is the most important place for ANZAC celebrations. Thousands of Australians would love to come here, to view our memorial, but until now I don't have a link to the Australian travel industry!"

She gazed at me. "*You* can be that link. You can help me! We'll organise special trips for Australian tourists, and bring them directly here, to the memorial. We can do everything for them, arrange the whole ANZAC Tour package. You must tell me how we can get started."

"Ah..." I looked at Roo. "Can we... check in, first?"

"Oh! Sorry! Yes, of course. You check in and have a nice rest. It must have been a long bus ride, yes?"

"Yes."

"Okay. So you go relax, have showers maybe. Then I'll come to your room and we can make some plans. Very exciting!"

And she handed me a key.

I led Roo into the room, dumped my bag on the bed, and turned to her in disbelief. "What did you do?"

We spent the rest of our stay in Sandakan trying to avoid the woman. She didn't make it easy – every time we came or went from the hotel, we had to pass reception first. And every time we passed reception she'd bestow an urgent reminder; "We must talk about that plan! When are you coming back?"

"Ur... we're going out for a meal, so, sometime later?"

"Great! I'll be waiting!"

I felt kind of sorry for her. Because she had this grand idea, and she was utterly convinced that I was the one to help her realise it. Only, I wasn't going to help her at all, because her idea was rubbish. And even if it wasn't, what the hell kind of contacts did I have in the Australian travel industry? And even if I did, what could I tell them? "I met this lady who thinks Australians are queuing up to look at her war memorial, and she wants to do some kind of deal…?"

I also felt sorry for her because she was very nice, and quite possibly bat-shit crazy.

We ate dinner in her restaurant, where she served us an infusion of lemongrass, which she claimed to have invented. I was pretty sure lemongrass tea had been done before, but I said nothing – until she served us pancakes, made especially thin in a style she had also invented. Roo raised an eyebrow at me. We'd both eaten crêpes plenty of times, and I was confident the French had something to do with their creation. She buttonholed me again as we left the restaurant, so I promised to discuss our ideas later. I wasn't even sure what she wanted me to do, but whatever it was, she *really* wanted me to do it.

That night we pleaded exhaustion, hiding in our room, and decided to check out a day early due to a 'miscalculation in our schedule'.

"But you must leave me your contact details, so we can talk about our plans," she said. "You have a mobile phone in Malaysia?"

"Ah, no," I lied.

"You have Skype?"

"Um… it, ah, doesn't work on my computer…"

"You have email though?"

I could hardly deny that. So I gave her a fake email address, and we fled.

As we hiked down the main street following directions to the local bus station, I made a deal with Roo.

We were never, *ever* going to tell anyone I was a travel writer, ever again.

Shave My Spider!

The streets of Sandakan were as empty on our way out as they'd been on the way in. Much later, whilst trying to write a blog about our time there, I discovered why. Shortly before we arrived in the country, a group of 235 armed insurgents from the Philippines had invaded Borneo, capturing and holding the small coastal town of *Lahad Datu*. Led by the Sultan of Sulu, they claimed ancestral ownership of the state of Sabah – which included both Sandakan and KK city. After a month of skirmishes and bombing raids by the air force, the stand-off had been resolved less than a week ago, when Malaysian Army forces stormed the town. Seventy-two people had been killed in the battle, including six civilians, and the ongoing situation of unrest had caused no-travel advisories to be issued worldwide.

At the time of our trip, the advice from the UK Foreign Office went like this:

'The FCO advise against all but essential travel to an area east of Kudat, to the Indonesian border in the southern part of Sabah. This region has been declared a 'Special Security Area' by the Malaysian government. It includes the towns of Sandakan and Lahad Datu and their respective airports, and the islands immediately off the coast, including Sipadan. Foreign nationals have been kidnapped in East Malaysia, particularly in the islands off eastern Sabah. Those currently in the region should consider leaving as soon as practicable and follow the advice of local police authorities.'

That explained the army check-point near Kudat – Howard's beach being a prime insertion point for armed forces seeking to attack Kota Kinabalu. But of course, all the actual violence had taken place over a hundred kilometers from where we were in Sandakan.

I generally don't pay much attention to this sort of thing. I mean, the odds of actually getting shot or kidnapped are pretty astronomical – unless of course everyone else follows the travel advisory, and suddenly you're the only white person left in town. But I truly believe that this kind of dramatic, blanket overreaction does far more harm than good. It wrecks the local tourist industry and feeds into people's fears of travel and foreign cultures.

On the upside, hotel rooms suddenly got a lot cheaper.

The same thing happens whenever there's a plane crash – suddenly everyone becomes scared of flying. I think that's the safest time to fly. All that paranoia makes even the laziest maintenance dudes step up their game. Meanwhile, passenger lists dwindle and prices plummet…

For extra discount, I usually buy tickets from the airline that had the crash.

But then, I also buy beef anytime there's a 'mad cow' scare. Oh yeah – living on the edge, that's me.

It was only after our trip was over that I realised why Sandakan was so devoid of tourists; there is nothing between it, and the scene of the troubles, but jungle. In fact, the only thing substantially closer to Lahad Datu is the Kinabatangan River – which, as luck would have it, is where we were headed next.

People of the Forest

On our way out of Sandakan, on our second week in the country, we finally managed to catch a local bus.

We even managed to get a seat – right at the front, facing a giant speaker the size of a coffin and its surrounding system of multicoloured strobe lights. It was a rolling disco, and definitely the most entertaining half hour I've spent on a bus. It took me three days to get my hearing back, but still – such is the price you pay for an authentic travel experience. The fare wasn't bad either; the whole trip cost us less than a dollar each.

Incidentally, a sign on the back end of the vehicle informed us that the Malaysian word for bus is 'bas'. No wonder we hadn't found any! We'd been asking for the wrong vowel all along. If they were trying to hide the fact that they'd hijacked the English word, they needed to work a bit harder at disguising it.

We staggered off the local bus at the junction for Sepilok Orangutan Sanctuary, and called the hostel I'd booked for a pick-up. Their minibus driver collected us minutes later and whisked us off into the jungle, past a tranquil lake, up a steep hill, and dropped us off at *Paganakan Dii Tropical Retreat*.

And we were in heaven.

All around us, the rainforest pulsed with life. Paganakan Dii was essentially a tree house, a series of large, raised, log cabin-type structures built right into the heart of the forest. Clicks and cries and calls and buzzing came from all around us, forming a background cadence that ebbed and swelled like waves on the shore.

The huge dorms were like barns on stilts, nestling within the canopy. Beneath them were individual toilet cubicles and shower rooms, and more hammocks than you could shake a lazy buttock at.

Organising our trip to the orangutan sanctuary was as easy as strolling down to the bar area and checking the time of the shuttle bus. Without hesitation, I booked us in for a couple more nights. There was just something in the air at that place; the peace and the vibrancy didn't clash at all – they blended.

After all the places we'd stayed so far, this was... *serenity*.

I could write here, I knew. It would be easy.

I could almost feel the magic gathering.

*   *   *

We caught the morning shuttle into Sepilok, positively bursting with excitement. Both Roo and I are animal lovers first and foremost; long before I found myself in Ecuador, helping to sew the head back onto a partially decapitated crocodile, Roo was volunteering in not one but two wildlife parks in Western Australia. At *Cohunu*, not far from her family home, she was the koala handler (which I appreciate sounds one step removed from koala molester) – whilst at *Marapana* Wildlife Park, she spent her work experience being bitten by wombats. She was only seventeen at the time and couldn't drive, so her mum Frieda had to take her – an hour there, drop her off, and an hour home – and go back to pick her up again afterwards.

Now *that's* dedication!

So it's no exaggeration to say that seeing orangutans this close – even tame ones – was pretty much our entire motivation for coming to Borneo.

But you can never be sure, with these kind of places, just

what kind of a show you're in for. We paid our entrance fees and started off down the log walkway into the sanctuary, automatically speaking in hushed tones. Foliage closed in on both sides, leaving a narrow gap between the vine-laden trees.

"I wonder if we'll actually see any—" I said.

And there he was – a slightly scruffy, bright orange monkey, sitting on the bannister, looking at me.

Come here, he beckoned, then got up and sauntered along the wooden railing.

We followed slowly, spellbound, trying to keep our distance and move quietly. The young orangutan cared not one bit for our stealth. When we started to lag behind, he sat down and waited for us. *Come on,* he beckoned again, leading us onwards once more. It was like something from Alice in Wonderland. Roo and I hardly dared look at each other for fear of spooking him, but this guy wasn't even remotely afraid. I think he wanted a hug, but I couldn't bring myself to get close enough, to break that cardinal rule of wild animal care – *DO NOT TOUCH.*

Very few non-domestic animals react well to having their personal space violated. Some humans are kind of touchy about it, too. This orang, though, seemed almost a little sad, as he led us most of the way to the feeding area. Then, with a final wave, he leapt off into the jungle. I don't think I'd taken a breath since we started following him.

"That was just…" Roo let the sentence hang. Neither of us could put a word there that would adequately describe the experience.

The viewing area was an extension of the wooden walkway, only much wider and with raised benches on one side. Opposite the benches, a clearing in the jungle had been turned into a multi-level monkey play area, festooned with log platforms and bristling with ropes and cables. Several keepers were already waiting, looking very fetching in their bright yellow welly-boots. The viewing area was filling up as more and more people arrived from the entrance. It was a hot day, stifling rather than cooling in the forest clearing, and sweat was already trickling into places it shouldn't.

One at a time, the orangutans swung in from the surrounding trees. A gasp would go up from the crowd and all eyes would swivel to track the source, fixing on the latest arrival in a blur of camera flashes. "No! No flash!" called one of the keepers, but most of the group completely ignored him. I doubted this was a unique experience for him. The older orangs' fur tended more towards brown, especially while they were hanging around in the shadows. In direct sunlight, a halo of burnt-orange fringed their shaggy silhouettes. Their expressions seemed so placid, so human – at least until one opened its mouth in a yawn, exposing massive teeth that seemed altogether too terrifying for a vegetarian.

A young orangutan arrived from behind the crowd, opting to walk right through the middle of the viewing area. The keeper bawled at people to keep out of the way, and this they respected. A large female orang swung in, hand over hand along a rope. Clinging tightly to her waist was a tiny bundle of orange fluff, its face dominated by large, unblinking eyes. Both mother and baby were unruffled by the attention they were getting, and seemed in no real hurry to do anything. They hung back from the gathering, the mum chewing idly on a few leaves that hung in front of her.

One of the keepers climbed a ladder onto a raised deck in the centre of the clearing, carrying a wicker basket the size of my backpack. Before he had a chance to distribute any food, he was accosted by one of his charges – a cheeky little orangutan rushed up to him and wrapped its long, skinny arms around him.

How badly did I want his job at that moment?

After he was done hugging, the orangutan grabbed a battered tin tray from a pile of them and held it up expectantly. The keeper fished in his basket for a bunch of bananas and dropped them into the tray, which pleased his little friend immensely. That done, he upended the basket on the platform, creating a giant fruit salad. Apples, papaya and watermelon rolled every which-way, along with bananas of course, and several fruits I didn't recognise. But most of the orangs present seemed content just to chill out – there was no mass-move to mob the platform as I'd have expected. These guys weren't bullies, and didn't even move a muscle when a gang of black squirrels darted in to steal bits and pieces of their breakfast. It was like an all-you-can-eat buffet, and the orangs took it in turns, swinging in languidly to cast an eye over the offerings.

Then the keeper returned with a bucket, and poured out several trays of milk, and these *were* a big hit. I say milk; presumably it was some sort of vitamin-rich, scientifically designed formula, rather than semi-skimmed from the local supermarket. But the orangs lapped it up – literally, some of them sporting the charming foamy moustache familiar to eight-year-olds everywhere.

With the food all dispensed, the orangs become more active. One little guy ran down a rope like a slackline, waving his hands above his head as though to prove he didn't need them for balance. These apes seemed even more agile than monkeys. Not faster, but so much stronger that they could hold the most peculiar poses. A favourite seemed to be hanging by both legs, but keeping their bodies upright. This resulted in a v-shape, with one foot next to each shoulder, leaving their arms free to drape around in an effort to look casual.

They really were incredible to behold, and I urge anyone who has the opportunity to go and visit a sanctuary like Sepilok. It really is hard to describe, but utterly mesmerising to watch!

Needless to say, Roo and I stayed until the bitter end.

With the show well and truly over, we wandered into the visitors centre and got chatting to one of the volunteers there. She turned out to be the co-ordinator, and chief amongst her current woes was how the recent attack near Sandakan had affected international travel to the area.

"It's not just tourists," she explained, "but the latest group of volunteers. They should be arriving next week, but now the company that sends them isn't sure it wants to."

I'd fantasised about volunteering in Sepilok, and never more so than after watching the young orangutans hug their keepers in gratitude.

"So, you might be needing replacements?" I asked.

It was a bit of a stretch. The rules for volunteering here included a minimum of two months' commitment, and it cost thousands of dollars. And places were booked up almost a year in advance. And yet...

"I'll take your number, and give you a call?" she suggested.

I spent the rest of that day and most of the next praying the King of the Philippines would try to conquer Sabah.

Of course I didn't *want* anyone to commit a terrorist act. I'm just saying that a *small* invasion wouldn't have gone amiss. Or even the threat of one. I mean, if the place *had* to become a war zone, someone may as well benefit. Right?

A few days later we had a missed call on our phone.

It was the only call we received during our entire time in Asia, which is probably why we missed it. I still lie awake at night, wondering if that had been our call to action – and if volunteering at Sepilok, had we managed it, would have changed our lives.

Or maybe it was just a telemarketer.

Bloody withheld numbers.

Discovering Ends

With Sepilok now completely empty, we followed the road for about a mile to the other main attraction in the area: the Rainforest Discovery Centre. Although blatantly put here to capitalize on the flow of trapped tourists waiting for the afternoon feed at Sepilok, the RDC was doing a lot of good work educating the local people about environmental issues. Having sat in minibuses staring out at mile after mile of deforestation due to palm-oil plantations, I knew this was a vital service; the $5 entrance fee was a contribution I was more than willing to make.

I baulked at $3 for a bottle of water, but the rest of the food prices were fairly reasonable, so Roo and I enjoyed a delicious meal of chicken and rice in their open-air restaurant. Then we headed for the RDC's star attraction – a vast series of steel walkways suspended twenty-five metres in the air, amidst the rainforest canopy. This was the spot where wildlife was most active, even in the daytime, and Roo had high hopes of capturing some of it on camera. Personally, I was afraid the camera was going to melt from overuse; she must have taken a least a thousand photos already, and we were only halfway through the day.

Editing them was going to be a bit of a chore.

By the entrance to the Sky Walk, we passed an information board bearing an artist's impression of it. It was a colossal structure; nine huge towers, most of which included helter-skelter style staircases going right to the ground. Between the towers ran hundred-metre spans of uninterrupted treetop viewing. It looked like it would take at least an hour to get around the circuit; fifteen times that, if Roo was allowed to stop and take photographs everywhere she wanted to. We decided to go halfway around, then take some stairs to the ground and walk a section through the undergrowth.

The entrance tower – marked with a helpful 'You Are Here' arrow on the map – was a giant. Twenty-five metres really doesn't sound that high, until you climb it and look down. From here we were on a par with all but the tallest trees; insects and birds flitted through the leaves, keeping us company with a constant chatter of birdsong, underscored by the bass drone of buzzing wings.

The first stretch of walkway was a sturdy, two-metre wide steel bridge. The views were amazing, although the noon sun kept most of the larger animals from showing themselves. We swivelled towards every crack and crash from the forest, hoping to see something moving, but could never quite locate the source. As the next tower approached we were moving faster, already considering climbing down for a trip across the ground.

Only, we couldn't.

This tower had no stairs, and beyond it the forest stretched off into the distance, undisturbed – no towers, no railings, nothing.

Apparently, that first stretch of walkway was also the last.

I could just make out a slab of reinforced concrete on the ground, about twenty-five metres further along. It was barely visible, having been reclaimed by the jungle.

"So... this is it?" Roo asked.

"I dunno. The picture was massive. Did we take a wrong turn?"

"No! There weren't any turns. They must have run out of money before they finished building it!" She pointed at the distant slab. "Looks like that was meant to become Tower

Three."

"But... why the hell would they have a diagram of the whole thing at the start? Talk about raising our expectations."

"They probably had the 'artist's impression' done first – and then couldn't afford to finish the actual walkway."

"Wow. Epic fail. That must have been a bloody expensive painting!"

"Or else their budgeting was faulty."

"Yeah! I bet someone got fired for that. 'Estimated cost, ten million ringgit? And we have how many towers now? Okay, own up – who forgot to add a zero?'"

Unable to reach the ground for our low-level foray, we returned along the walkway to the beginning. We climbed down and I got Roo to take a photo of the overly-ambitious picture.

"They must get a lot of complaints from disappointed tourists," she said.

"No kidding! They seriously need to re-word this title – Artist's Impression Of Final Structure – Less Than ¼ Of Which Currently Exists."

Shaking our heads at the peculiarities of the management's strategy, we forked out for another astronomically-priced bottle of water and headed back down the road towards Sepilok.

I was somewhat disillusioned with the RDC, until I remembered that most of their profits went towards education. The money was better spent teaching Malaysians not to completely destroy their rainforest than it was on giant steel walkways, I had to admit. But personally, I'd have invested a hundred bucks in asking that artist for a second impression – one that bore slightly more resemblance to reality. Or invested $3 in a pair of scissors, and cut the damn thing in half. And then in half again. And then displayed what was left. That might keep the public's expectations in check.

The second feeding at Sepilok followed the pattern of the first. It didn't matter; I could have watched this all day, everyday, for a long, long time before I got bored. The orangs were so gentle, so calm, as they reached for their dinner.

Dangling lazily from the slacklines they munched thoughtfully, looking out at us as though we were the curiosities and they the spectators. Every so often a foot would come up, giving a slight squeeze that popped a banana right out of its skin and straight into a waiting mouth. It looked effortless, relaxed; *unafraid*.

Again, we stayed long after the crowds departed, and this time there was a reward for our patience. With the orangs safely gone, a large troupe of monkeys descended to polish off the scraps. They were Macaques, with greyish fur and long tails, fairly large and obviously well-fed. As the most common species of monkey, and the least afraid of humans, they're considered a pest in most parts of south-east Asia – and a delicacy in the others. These guys weren't remotely bothered about us being there. They came within inches of us – one even gave me a cheeky slap on the back as he scampered past. I love monkeys, I always have, and it was a fitting end to a genuinely cool experience.

*   *   *

We spent the next couple of days at Paganakan Dii, resting and recharging our batteries (both figuratively and literally) before our trip to the Kinabatangan River. I wrote several chapters of my Australia book and a blog post, which as anyone who's ever read my blog can attest, is an exceedingly rare event. Roo spent most of her time swapping photography tips with Kat Dixon, a pretty, blonde English girl who had an even bigger lens than Roo did.

"It's on loan," Roo explained, "because it costs two-and-a-half thousand dollars to buy."

I threw up a little in my mouth, because the tone in her voice said she was mentally adding it to her Christmas list.

"It's *amazing*," she continued, and then went on to describe features and functions that made as much sense to me as midi-chlorians in Star Wars.

She was just explaining how it could balance on its white parts and stop if you said the f-word, when I looked down and noticed that a preying mantis the size of a Cuban cigar was paying rapt attention. It was a fantastic looking creature, with bulging, alien eyes and furled wing-cases that made it resemble a dried, curled-up leaf. It sat on my leg long enough for Roo to take some photos, then ventured onto my hand for a few more. An hour or so later we experienced the opposite end of the scale; a tiny, almost translucent green mantis not quite as big as my thumbnail.

Below the hill on which Paganakan Dii sat, a series of sturdy wooden walkways stretched out into a small green lake, joining up with platforms and pagodas on an island at its centre. Quite why we couldn't figure out; it was a pretty enough lake, but not spectacular.

Kat came with us on an exploratory stroll.

"I could swim across that in five minutes," I said, mostly to myself.

And then I saw the rings, dangling in a row just above the surface of the water. They hung from a thick wire which stretched clear across the lake. *Of course!* In season, this lake must be used for water-sports by the richer tourists staying in the posh resort next-door. They probably hired out jet skis and snorkels, and let swimmers use this aquatic assault course – in *season*.

Roo sighed when I announced my intention to cross the lake by the rings, but followed me out onto the walkways to see if it was possible. It wasn't – *not quite*.

"The buggers have taken the last ring away!" I moaned.

"Never mind then," she said, sounding relieved.

"Let's try the other side!"

On the other side of the lake was a steep, muddy bank. The nearest ring was tantalisingly out of reach again, but I wasn't going to be defeated that easily. I stripped off to my pants (grateful that, for once, I was wearing some – sleeping in a dormitory had its benefits after all). Kat did her best not to look embarrassed, while Roo did her best to convince her that she'd get used to it.

"I'm going in," I told Roo.

"I had a feeling you might be," she said, picking up my t-shirt.

The water was cold, and not the most inviting, but once I was away from the bank it lost some of its ickiness-factor. The first ring dangled above me, and I struggled to haul myself up on it. It was flat metal, like a bike wheel minus the spokes, and the edges bit into my fingers. I splashed back into the lake and tried the next ring over, treading water as the bottom fell away rapidly. They were the devil's playthings, these rings; just within reach, yet high enough to make me work for it. Painful to grip hard enough to pull myself out of the water, and too sharp and narrow to do much with once up there. The wire was thin, slicing into my palms like a cheese-cutter; there was no way I'd be able to climb from one ring to the next, much less complete a crossing that way. Defeated, I splashed back into the water, and swam over to the wooden platforms to see if it would be any easier at that end.

Nope.

"I can't do it," I called to Roo, "they're just too hard! I can't see how anyone could manage this."

"Maybe you're not supposed to, then?" Kat called back.

I thought about this for a second, as I kicked hard to stay afloat. The rings were too far apart. Made of skin-shredding metal. Above a murky green lake, in the middle of a forest...

It all came together.

"It's for monkeys!" I shouted. It made perfect sense. The walkways and platforms weren't for accessing the lake – they allowed spectators to observe wild monkeys, who probably came in troupes from the forest at certain times, expecting to be fed...

Which meant the lake was probably not designed for swimming in, either.

I caught movement out the corner of my eye, and turned to see a trail of bubbles circling round behind me.

"SHIT!"

The wooden deck was a fair bit higher than the rings, but I shot out of that lake so fast I nearly broke the railings.

"Did you have a nice swim, love?" Roo asked, when I caught up with her.

"Not really, no."

"Aww! Why not?"

I showed her the trails of blood snaking my legs, from where I'd pulled off a surprising variety of leeches.

"Did you get them all?" she asked.

I turned slowly, arms up, to let her examine me. "I think so."

"Did you check *in there?*" Kat levelled a finger at my underpants. "Because you wouldn't feel it, when it attached, and there's parts you really don't want to be bleeding from…"

I looked from one girl to the other, in rising panic.

I hadn't felt one attach, but I could bloody well feel one now.

Nowhere to hide round here.

"I'll just nip back up to the bathroom," I said, "I'll leave you girls to your photography."

"Little cock-suckers," Roo said, shaking her head.

Which, as it turned out, was a fairly accurate description.

Messing About In Boats

Malaysia had proven more expensive than I'd anticipated. It's easy to spot the flaw in my reasoning; actually, I think a five-year-old could. It went like this: I'd been to Bali. Bali was ridiculously cheap. Bali is part of Indonesia, which is right next to Malaysia. Therefore, Malaysia must also be cheap.

I mean, that's how it works, right?

While mathematicians and scientists may recoil in horror from this application of logic, I feel this would be a prudent place to remind you all that I am *terrible* at traveling. I love doing it, and consequently I do quite a bit of it – but that experience should in no way be construed as expertise. If you are ever in the position to receive any travel advice from me, please feel free to do exactly the opposite of what I recommend. I won't be hurt; hell, it might even save your life.

So, that said, let's get back to Malaysia – where I'd decided to break free from the constraints of our budget, and book us onto a three-day, two-night, river safari.

Because... well, bollocks to it!

Poor Roo had been getting disillusioned, as every activity we got excited about turned out to be drastically out of our price-range. In the end, there was only so much I could say no to before I felt like an evil miser, putting money before happiness. Climbing Mt Kinabalu and SCUBA diving near

Sandakan had been the most obvious casualties in this war of frugality, but there had been several others; it was high time we had a victory.

Three hundred dollars each bought us an all-inclusive stay at an eco-lodge on the banks of the Kinabatinanangana... ananagan... again... a nanna? ...an anagram? Well, it was a bloody big river with a name that took me ten minutes to pronounce.

Kinabatangan, Roo kept reminding me.

Which still didn't help; there were just too many repetitive syllables for me to know when to stop.

Whatever the case, it'd be a crap hand at Scrabble.

The minibus picked us up at the Sepilok junction, and made a couple more stops en route to the river. First we collected a young Polish couple, who seemed content to keep to themselves – and then we picked up a middle-aged American lady, who was not.

"Hey, you guys!" she yelled as she climbed aboard. Her voice was loud enough to echo around the bus, startling the Polish couple who were sitting at the back.

"Are we all going to the same place?" she asked. "The river safari? With the animals? The Nature Lodge?"

The barrage of rhetorical questions seemed a little unnecessary, seeing as how *Kinabatangan Nature Lodge* was emblazoned on the side of the bus. And it had come right into her resort, specifically to collect her; local buses almost never show that kind of dedication.

"Aren't we all excited!" she continued. There was not a trace of sarcasm in her voice. "I'm Annabel!"

She was right about that. She was, in fact, Annabel. However, as far as I can remember, that was the last time she was right about anything.

"I'm from the US, but I don't live *in* the US. I live on a tiny island called Maui, which is part of Hawaii. But it's not the big part of Hawaii! It's the little part. But not the littlest part." She looked around expectantly, awaiting a response to her introduction.

My English politeness kicked in, and I opened my mouth to speak – but Roo elbowed me in the ribs just in time.

"*Don't*," she hissed, "or she'll talk to us *all the way!*"
So I didn't.

And Annabel, who didn't seem even remotely phased by the complete lack of reaction, sat down next to the bus driver and talked to him all the way, instead.

It didn't seem to bother her that he spoke no English. Or if he did, he was doing a damn good impression of someone who didn't. Annabel ignored all that in favour of an hour-long monologue about herself, her interests, and the island she called home. From time to time, Roo glanced at me with an expression that said, *"See?"*

A slightly wider version of the common motor-canoe took us across the river to our accommodation. Low season was our friend once again. Row upon row of air-conditioned log cabins stretched off into the jungle, suggesting the Lodge's capacity when full would be uncomfortably large. For now, it was practically empty, so Roo and I had been given a four-bunk cabin to ourselves. Our small bus load were the day's only arrivals; a similarly-sized group, already in residence, would leave the following morning.

We stashed our bags in the cabin and reconvened in the open-air restaurant for a welcome talk/safety briefing/afternoon tea. As our guide Ramzan laid down some ground rules, I glanced over the balcony and saw a huge monitor lizard, well over a metre long, slowly wending its way across the garden. It seemed like a pretty good omen for the trip to come.

Next, Ramzan outlined our itinerary. It went like this:
3:30pm – Afternoon tea
4:00pm – River cruise (3 hours)
7:15pm – Dinner
9:30pm – Night walk (2 hours)
11:30pm – SLEEP! Ahhh...
5:45am – Wake up
6:00am – Dawn cruise (1 hour)
7:15am – Breakfast
9:00am – Jungle hike (3 hours)
1:00pm – Lunch
NAP TIME!

Then repeat, as above...

It was relentless, and it was knackering. And, out of all the things we did in Borneo, it was the best by far.

The emphasis on the cruises was the wildlife spotting, rather than the comfort. Our boat was a plain tin tub with plank seats and a single outboard motor – about the cheapest boat it's possible to buy. I was fine with that; it was a warm, sun-drenched afternoon, and rhythmically bouncing our way upriver in comfort would have been a good way to wind up sleeping through the whole trip. We waited for Annabel, who showed up ten minutes late, without apology. "I was asleep!" she laughed, as though it was the funniest thing in the world.

Ramzan was to be our guide for the entire stay, which was great. It meant we could develop a bit of a rapport with him, and as we motored off upstream we discovered another benefit; Ramzan had eyes like a —

"Hawk!" he pointed. All eyes turned towards the lone silhouette, barely visible amidst the foliage on a branch overhanging the water.

Roo's precious camera swung into life, its ridiculously long zoom lens shooting out to maximum extension. "Oh yeah!" she said, showing the camera's screen around the boat. A fine, greenish-coloured hawk with an orange face stared out from it. A prize-winning photograph, less than five minutes in.

From then on, my eyes combed the jungle on all sides. Everyone was doing the same, staring out of the boat in all directions – but we needn't have bothered. Ramzan was at home, in his natural environment. This was his job. And he was absolutely fantastic at it.

He pointed out giant monitor lizards as they lazed on the bank and lumbered through the undergrowth. He showed us a delicate white heron, perched on a floating log. When hornbills overflew us, he was already looking up, directing our gaze right at them. There were three major species of these bizarre-looking creatures in this area, in descending order of rarity. All had the trademark toucan-like beaks, with weird nubbins growing out the top, like someone had super-glued a Cheesy Wotsit to them. We saw all three of them on that first cruise.

About an hour in, Ramzan pointed urgently over the side. "Crocodile!" he told us.

Annabel borrowed his binoculars (by saying "Hey, gimmie those glasses,") and trained them on the croc, who was gliding along silently on the surface.

"Wow," she said, after a few seconds studying the creature, "it almost looks like a little reptile…"

I couldn't help myself. "That's because it IS a little reptile," I told her.

"Oh yeah!" came her reply – not only blithely unaware of my sarcasm, but clearly not appreciating she'd said anything dumb in the first place.

Although the jungle extended right to the edge of (and often into) the water, there were places where it peeled back, and we motored past swathes of rough pampas-like grasses. It was in one of these areas that we saw our first orangutan in the wild.

He was chilling out very photogenically, at the top of an exceptionally skinny tree. It was my turn on the binoculars, and I watched him stretch his long arms, reaching out half-heartedly for a handful of leaves.

"He's so small!" Annabel exclaimed, squinting through her camera lens.

It was a face-palm moment. Roo stared at her, incredulous – I could tell she was thinking exactly the same thing as me. *How is a person that stupid still breathing?*

"He's not small," I said, slowly, "he's just very far away."

"Oh yeah?" she replied.

Sometimes people ask me if I make these characters up, and I'm both shocked and ashamed of the answer: no. Not a word of it. Sad to say, these individuals really are out there – and are at least partially derived from the same genetic material as the rest of us.

Be afraid.

We were less than halfway through the cruise. We'd passed the jetties of several large nature camps, most of them looking significantly more upmarket than ours. We'd also been buzzed by a handful of boats, some labouring upstream, some shooting down. All were engaged in the same activity as we were, which was a frightening thought; if this was low season, and all the other resorts were as empty as ours... what on earth must it be like in the middle of summer? I shuddered just thinking about it, and felt blessed yet again by our incredibly lucky timing.

One downside was the river itself; swollen by the monsoon rains, it was the colour of a chocolate milkshake. It was in spate, flowing swift and strong, which meant the boat couldn't make as much distance upstream as might have been possible at other times. Specifically, this spelled the end of Roo's dream of sighting Borneo's elusive pygmy elephants. "They go far now," Ramzan apologised. But he didn't stop looking, just in case.

At the apex of our journey, Ramzan slewed the boat around for the return trip. Only one other boat seemed to have made it this far; with just an elderly Asian couple aboard, they probably had us beaten on the weight front. They also had Roo drooling in envy, as the lens mounted on their camera was telescopic almost to the point of being an actual telescope. It rested on its own tripod, and looked like it could overbalance their boat at any moment.

"Outlensed, eh?" I slid a conciliatory arm around Roo's shoulders. "One thing you get to learn, being a guy, is this: there will always be someone else with more impressive equipment. Remember – it's what you do with it that counts."

"I hear what you're saying," she replied, "but as a woman I learnt, if there's a bigger one available, then it's usually time to upgrade."

"Oh. Well. So long as we're still talking cameras, I have to say that looks like an expensive upgrade."

"It would be. But I'm thinking, that old man looks pretty frail. If we got close enough, I might be able to grab it..."

River Monster

Next morning, the dawn cruise began in mist so thick we could barely see each other. Yet still, we spotted an orangutan – a huge one this time, with the large cheek-flaps of an adult male, and close enough for Roo to take some amazing shots. "Biggest I ever see," said Ramzan. The awe in his voice suggested there were still moments when he genuinely loved his job.

The sky lightened and the mist, floating on the surface of the water, began to melt away. The jungle was coming alive; bird-calls, monkey-howls, and noises none of us could name filled the air around us.

Halfway in, we were staring at a hawk-like bird Ramzan had spotted. Roo was checking it out in his bird identification book.

"Hey, can I see that?" Annabel asked her.

Which would have been fine – except instead of leaving it there, she did her trademark trick of asking again – and again – without pausing for breath. "Hey, can I see that one from yesterday? You know, the one we looked at in the evening? That little bird? Is it in there? Can I see it? The one from yesterday? Remember? Can I see that one? From yesterday? I want to look at that one. The little bird, from yesterday? Can I see it? Can I—"

At which point Roo just shoved the book at her and said, "Take the damn thing."

Quite unaware that she'd done anything out of the ordinary, Annabel started flipping through the pages. "Oh, there are *lots* of little pictures in here! Lots of little birdies!"

She flipped a few more pages. "Wow, so many pictures! This is amazing! This whole thing is pictures! And they're all birds!"

She closed the book to study the cover in wonder.

It was called 'The Borneo Book Of Birds'.

Given how much success we'd had on the cruises, I was pretty excited as we gathered in front of the restaurant to begin our afternoon jungle walk. We waited almost twenty minutes for Annabel to arrive, but we put the time to good use, slathering ourselves in insect repellent, donning our (allegedly) leech-proof football socks and trying on the rubber welly-boots Ramzan offered us. When Annabel did show up, she was wearing pedal-pushers, flip-flops and a vest. "Is this okay?" she asked, indicating her outfit. She was displaying more flesh than I'd have though advisable for a visit to the supermarket.

Ramzan shook his head, torn between his duty to keep her safe and comfortable, and his desire to actually *go somewhere* today. "Is okay," he said eventually.

"Hey, nice socks," she said to me.

"Yeah, we bought them because proper leech socks are so expensive."

"Oh yeah, leech socks! I have a pair of those! I'll go get 'em."

There was a collective sigh, which she took as permission.

"Back in a jiffy!" she said, chuckling as though she'd said something witty. And then she strolled off, not even trying to hurry.

I really, *really* wanted to leave without her, and I don't think I was the only one.

The jungle walk was not about spotting wildlife. Which was probably for the best, as anything we could have seen would have been scared off by Annabel's non-stop chatter. Not having much luck with the rest of us, she attached herself to Ramzan, and spent the entire trek telling him about Maui, and how it differed from Borneo.

"Hey, we have that plant in Maui!" she'd say.

"Ah... no. This one only in Borneo."

"No, I'm pretty sure I have that one in my garden. I have this really great garden, not many people around me bother with theirs, but I like to have all kinds of plants in it. My mom used to do a lot of gardening too, and she loved flowers, so I think I inherited her green sleeves, you know, and I love to garden. I'm actually really good at it, I know all the names of the flowers, and oh, hey! I have that flower right there, too!"

"Ah... no. This one also only in Borneo."

"I'm tellin' ya, it looks just the same. We have the same trees too, in Maui, but not in my garden. But there's this place, near where I live..."

And on. And ON.

Until she got stuck knee-deep in the mud.

We'd all done it; the mud-trap was impossible to avoid. But we'd struggled through, us guys pulling our partners out – and leaving Annabel to Ramzan.

Who clearly didn't want to help her. So he left her there.

She pulled one foot out, leaving her boot behind in the mud, and moaned when she noticed. But then, seemingly incapable of learning from this mistake, she proceeded to do exactly the same with the other foot – leaving her shoeless, still mired, flailing around in confusion. It was too much; the whole group collapsed into laughter at the sight. Then Annabel found a stick, and tried to push it into the mud ahead of her, as though that could possibly help.

"Oh look," Roo said to me, "she's learning to use tools!"

Our destination was an oxbow lake, formed when the mighty Kinabatangan river had curved back on itself and then filled the loop in with flood water. We arrived at a wooden jetty protruding into the lake, and immediately set about divesting ourselves of leeches. I'd seen dozens of them during the walk, but of course it's the ones you don't see that get you. Usually hanging from leaves between knee and shoulder-height, they brushed off onto our clothing as we passed, then set about finding their way inside. Roo and I checked each other over, and pulled off nearly twenty of the little suckers. A more thorough inspection would have to be done when we got back to the lodge, but again it made me appreciate just how pointless the special 'leech socks' were. The last one I pulled off was a bit of a surprise – it had attached itself to the back of Roo's neck!

Then Ramzan produced a cookie. "Watch," he said, and tossed it into the water.

Immediately the surface roiled, as hundreds of tiny fish fell upon the cookie, reducing it to crumbs in seconds.

We gave a collective gasp.

"Now put hand in," Ramzan suggested.

I couldn't tell if he was joking or not, but I thought I'd call his bluff. "Alright," I said, approaching the edge of the jetty, "I'll do it."

I figured he'd stop me if I was about to lose my fingers.

Ramzan nodded and urged me on, so I knelt down and tentatively offered my hand towards the water. At the first tiny nip, I jerked it straight back out again.

"Is okay," Ramzan said, and thrust his hand into the water. A seething ball of fish surrounded it instantly, but he seemed unperturbed. "See?" he said, withdrawing the hand unscathed. "Is good... for skin!"

After that, everyone wanted a go. I was fascinated, giggling like a schoolgirl at the ticklish sensation as thousands of tiny fish nibbled the dead skin cells off my fingers. I fed them for a while, but every so often something bigger came in for a bite, which was a bit of a shock.

"Is the lake safe to swim in?" I asked Ramzan.

"No," he replied.

"What else lives in there?"

"Many other thing."

"Even crocodiles?"

"Sometime."

We were interrupted by the arrival of another group – this one consisting entirely of Scandinavian teenagers. Laughing, screaming, pushing each other, they burst out onto the jetty in a tidal wave of blonde hair and smooth, tanned limbs. I had no idea which resort they were from, but their preparation was even worse than Annabel's. Where we'd braved the mud and leeches in gumboots, every one of these kids was wearing flip-flops. The girls wore short-shorts and bikini tops, while the guys were decked out in sleeveless t-shirts and board shorts. How they'd made it this far was beyond me, but their guide didn't seem to care – he slouched on a bench and concentrated on rolling cigarettes, ignoring them completely. They never got to try the fish-feeding. Within minutes they'd all stripped off further, leaving piles of shirts and shorts strewn all over the deck. A group of lads took a running jump at the water, bombing in to shrieks from the girls they splashed. The rest of them followed suit, and their boisterous games continued in the water. I was jealous for a couple of heartbeats; they were young, sexy and single, probably on an organised gap-year adventure, and by the end of this holiday every one of them would have joked, partied, and shagged themselves into a coma. It was one thing I'd never quite managed to do, but I'd never stopped wanting to. Now… well, I was getting too old.

Too old…?

What a terrifying prospect.

"Ah… do we tell them about the crocodiles?" I looked at Ramzan.

"Huh." He snorted in disgust, and flapped a hand at their guide. "That his job."

The other guide was slumped down on the bench, taking a nap. It was pretty obvious that he gave not one shit.

So we left them to it.

The cruises continued to deliver. Every time the boat went out we saw something fascinating, from rare birds to lizards to whole troops of macaque monkeys, who swarmed around us as though we were invisible on their way down for a drink.

The best sighting of all came on our last morning when, just as the sun was rising, we spotted a female orangutan with her baby, sitting with their arms around each other and their backs to us, in a tree less than thirty metres from the boat.

Their posture was so familiar, so human, and Roo and I clasped hands as we gazed on in respectful silence.

Annabel was somewhat less delicate. "Oh my goodness!" she exclaimed. With her eyes glued to the screen of her camera, her whining voice ratcheted up several notches in volume; "Oh, you beautiful creature! Please turn around! Pretty please! Say hello to us! Say goodbye to us! Hello there! Oh please turn around! Please? Turn around! Say hello! Say goodbye! Give us your blessing! Please say hello! Say goodbye! Say hello! Please turn around! Please say hello! Please turn around! Say goodbye to us..."

She went on like this for five minutes straight.

I had to do something then which I've never done in my life (other than, occasionally, to my long-suffering sister). I put my hand on Annabel's shoulder and said rather firmly, "Shut up."

All I can say is, it's a bloody good job we were in a motorboat. Because if that thing had oars, I'd have beaten her to death with one.

When it came time to leave, both Roo and I were gutted. We'd had an amazing experience, and were already talking about a return visit; "As soon as I get a bigger lens," Roo decided. We agreed that this had been the perfect time of year for a visit; one of our boat trips had been conducted entirely in the rain, but somehow that made it seem more authentic and exotic. The night walks hadn't revealed much wildlife, but there was something so thrilling about being out in the jungle after dark that I didn't mind at all. The food, all hot and cold buffets taken in the open-air restaurant, had been superb. Only one thing had marred the experience, and I already knew I'd get a good chapter out of her.

"People will never believe she's real," Roo said, shaking her head. "You might as well write about meeting Bigfoot in the jungle, or finding the Missing Link."

We exchanged glances, both realising what she'd said.

"Oh my God! We *did* find the Missing Link!"

"Now I've got to write about her," I said, when we

stopped laughing, "it's my duty to science!"

As we sat enjoying our last breakfast in the rainforest, Annabel stood up to go.

"Well everybody," she announced, "I'm Oh-Eff-Eff!" She glanced around smugly, quite pleased with her joke – but she couldn't resist letting us in on it. "Off!" she explained, beaming at her own cleverness. And then, thank God, she *was* off – leaving us all to bask in the warm glow of her wit.

Breaking News

Having explored most of what the Sabah region had to offer, it was time for Roo and I to move on.

Malaysian Borneo is cut in half by the afore-mentioned Sultanate of Brunei, meaning the only way to reach the southern state of *Sarawak* is by plane.

Flying south meant we first had to make the unenviable trip north, back to KK and the airport – but we couldn't resist spending a couple more nights at Paganakan Dii, to break up our journey from the river. With a huge open deck covered in beanbags above the restaurant, it was the perfect place to chill out while Roo's shutter-finger recovered from RSI. We both felt the need to let our recent experiences marinate; I had a depressing amount of journaling to catch up on, and Roo began the painstaking task of sifting through the 5,000 photographs she'd taken in the few days since we were last here.

And no – that is not an exaggeration!

But we couldn't hide out for long. Adventure was calling, this time in the form of *Gunung Mulu* National Park. When shopping for plane tickets we'd discovered that most flights stopped at *Miri*, on the border between Sabah and Sarawak. If we were doing that, we figured we might as well take a quick side trip into the adjacent national park. After all, it *was* a UNESCO World Heritage Site – famous for having some of the largest caves in the world, including one which was home to over three *million* bats – and a correspondingly large (ie, 100m deep) pile of bat shit.

I know what you're thinking! How can *anyone* resist that?

We asked the Paganakan Dii staff to book our tickets back to KK, and the next morning we were dropped off right in the path of the coach.

So it was a bit of a shock when the thing drove straight on past us, the driver waving cheerfully in response to my frantic signalling.

Luckily, after a fraught hour of waiting and worrying, another one arrived.

That one didn't pick us up either.

It blasted past us as though we were invisible, and disappeared around the next corner at top speed.

I was still turning the air blue a few minutes later, when I noticed a strange thing; the back end of the coach re-emerged, reversing slowly and erratically back around the bend. It was a good job there was no other traffic – the massive 50-seater veered across both lanes as the driver struggled with his manoeuvre. Eventually he gave up, the door opened, and a skinny young lad in a track suit came jogging up the road towards us.

"Hello!" he grinned, seeming not at all phased by the rather unorthodox manner of his arrival. "This you?" he proffered a piece of paper with a list of names on it.

"Yes!"

"Oh! Ok. Come please!"

Back in the capital, we followed the path of least resistance and checked into the Hotel Kinabalu. The staff there seemed to remember us – hardly surprising, as we'd left them a present when we checked out. All the MSG in those fried noodles had done a number on Roo, and on our first night in the hotel she'd shit out an iron bar. I'd struggled to flush it for three days, but it wasn't going anywhere – whoever was lucky enough to clean our room must have had to fish the thing out with barbeque tongs.

Shave My Spider!

Amidst a few awkward giggles we received the key to the same room, and found it spotless. The helpful reception staff even directed us to a local lady who did our laundry, returning two huge carrier bags of filthy, jungle-stained clothes washed, dried and perfectly folded – even Roo's knickers, which had been transformed origami-style into individual triangular packages.

Taking advantage of the much better internet connection, we took turns using Skype to update our families – only to discover that my sister, Gillian, was about to undergo something of an adventure herself.

She pointed us towards a cartoon she'd posted on Facebook, of a bun and an oven, and my jaw just hit the floor.

My little baby sister was *pregnant!*

"HOW?" I asked.

"Um…"

"Okay, you don't need to answer that. Sorry, I'm just having trouble processing… WHERE?"

"Um…"

"Okay, sorry, you don't need to answer that either."

"I can tell you *when,* if you want."

"No, that's fine, that's none of my business…"

"I mean when the baby's due, dickhead."

"Oh! Right! There's going to be a baby. Of course there is."

"That is generally the way it works."

"So, when will you… get one?"

"Standard delivery is about nine months."

"No express post…"

"No. And I've been up the duff for three months already. Which means, in early September, you should be getting a little niece or a nephew!"

"Wow… and what will you do then?"

"I imagine I'll have a little lie down."

I was blown away.

Happy for her, obviously, but a little shell-shocked at the same time. Our parents were over the moon, as was Gill's husband, Chris – but Gill was understandably a bit freaked out. I mean, sure, they'd planned on starting a family, and the timing was right… but still. Getting pregnant meant two very real, very serious, very fundamental changes to her world.

One – her travelling days were over. She was irrevocably bound to settle down, abandoning the ways of the vagabond to create a life of responsibility and stability.

And two – at some point in the not-too-distant future, she was going to have to push a person out of her vagina.

Neither prospect particularly excited her.

Being her supportive big brother – and being safely tucked away in Asia, where I could hide from all the disturbing talk of baby stuff and womanly bits – I took it upon myself to wind her up as much as was humanly possible.

Okay, that sounds heartless. At first I spent hours chatting to her, sitting up late into the night talking philosophically, discussing the future and trying to find answers for all her panicked questions.

But there comes a point when you can't help but give into the temptation for a bit of a piss-take. Unless that's just me?

The moment came in the supermarket.

On a hitherto-undiscovered second floor, above the trays of unidentifiable raw meat and internal organs, we found a more civilized section of clothing and housewares. Roo bought a cheap umbrella to keep in her camera bag, while I wandered through the toy section – and that was where I found it.

Gill's perfect present.

It was a baby. A battery-powered plastic doll that crawled – 'with wiggly,' apparently. Glassy, lifeless eyes stared out of a disturbingly square-shaped head.

It was the kind of toy you might expect to find crawling across your ceiling with a kitchen knife in its teeth, intent on claiming your soul. In possibly the best display of 'Engrish' I'd seen so far, the packaging designers had come up with this alluring catch-phrase: 'The baby gives the not-general happiness!'

Awww!

How sweet. Every child should have one.

If nothing else, the nightmares would ensure their

virginity remained intact well into their thirties.

I think Gill would have loved it. Or at least seen the funny side. Unfortunately, I made the mistake of telling Mum about it on a Skype call, and I was instantly forbidden from sending it. I guess Gill's emotional state *was* a tad delicate at the moment. That doll may well have pushed her over the edge.

It certainly scared the crap out of me.

So we left it on the bed as a present for the cleaning staff.

Next morning we caught a taxi to the airport, and boarded a half-empty MAS-Wings plane bound for Mulu National Park. We loved the plane – a cute miniature version of a jumbo jet, only with propellers. The check-in counters were also rather quaint, with chattering dot-matrix printers that must have been older than Roo. But most of all, we loved the MAS-Wings slogan, which they had thoughtfully emblazoned on surfaces throughout the airport. 'Spreading Love Across Borders', the signs read. Which sounded messy.

"I'd check your seat before you sit down," I warned Roo, "in case anyone's spread love on it."

The flight was in two stages, each of less than an hour. The transfer process was ridiculous – we followed the other passengers off the plane and through the corridors of Miri airport, where we noticed a burly Malaysian bloke tapping people on the shoulder as they passed him. "Mulu? Mulu?" he was asking.

"Ah, we're going to Mulu…" I mentioned, as we approached.

"Ah! Good!" And he beckoned us over to the side of the corridor. There, on the narrow metal window ledge, lay a selection of boarding passes.

"Which you?" he asked.

I found the tickets for myself and Roo, and pointed them out.

Squinting at the print, he held them up. "An-toe-knee?"

"Yes, and this is Krista."

"Ha!" he waved the tickets in triumph, before handing them over. "Go this way," he said, "get stamp from immigration. Then back, quick!"

"Okaay...?"

Slightly bemused, we joined the immigration queue and were stamped out of Sabah and into Sarawak. Then we turned around and wandered back down the corridor. The big bloke was waiting for us. He'd managed to match up all his tickets to incoming passengers, in possibly the least-secure method of airport check-in I've ever encountered. They must have been keen on the personal touch. And as he chased us onto the tiny plane to Mulu National Park, we figured out why – there was only one other person on it.

And that was the pilot.

Mulu airport was a field.

There was a single, one-room building, which did duty as arrivals, departures, and everything in-between. The baggage handlers arrived with our luggage on a handcart, but they couldn't just wheel it over to us. No! They were a proper airport. So they took the cart to a set of rollers less than two metres long, stood on the opposite side, and slid our bags to us over the rollers one at a time.

There was a taxi waiting outside, so we manhandled our backpacks into the boot and climbed in. I was delighted to find out the fare would be just 5 *ringgit* – less than $2. The taxi set off down the airport driveway, turned left onto the main road, and stopped.

Right outside our accommodation.

The total journey time was less than ninety seconds.

It actually took longer for the driver to lift our bags out of the car, as they were about the same size as he was.

"Quickest ride of my life," Roo said.

I opened my mouth to correct her, and then thought better of it.

No point in incriminating myself, was there?

Expedition

At that time, the only accommodation bookable online was that run by Mulu National Park itself. They had several options available, so we'd decided to spend our first night in the dormitory, upgrading later if necessary. From the outside it was a large, rustic cabin – or, to be less charitable, a shed – with a little covered porch area. We kicked off our shoes and hauled our bags inside, to find the inside as simple as the out.

One long room, with twenty-four single beds in two rows and a door in the far end leading to a single shared bathroom. The whole place, walls, floor and ceiling, was lined with plywood, and apart from the beds there was no other furniture; just three dangling light bulbs and a pair of overhead fans.

"What the hell?" Roo said, dismay in her voice. "*How* many beds?"

"Quite a few, yeah."

"Imagine if this place was full? How much would it suck to be in here?"

"It'd be hot enough, that's for sure. Even if those crappy old fans work."

Roo picked the bed in the far corner, meaning she'd only have me next to her even if someone else arrived. I don't make much of a privacy screen, being fairly skinny, but for now it didn't matter; every other bed in the whole place was empty.

"Sweet! Unless there's another plane flying in later on, we've got the place to ourselves," I told her. "Looks like we booked into the most crowded dorm in the country and ended up staying in the world's biggest private bedroom! It's big enough to practice cartwheels."

Which I did, just to prove my point.

Access to the National Park was via a rope bridge over the wide, brown *Melinau* River. At least a dozen battered canoes were tethered to a jetty below us, and the forest canopy grew all around, enclosing the bridge in a tunnel of foliage. Sunlight broke through, dappling the rough planks beneath our feet, and we were immersed in a world of droning cicadas, buzzing insects and trilling, flitting birds. It was like walking into the Garden of Eden.

The Park HQ was surrounded by wooden walkways and beautifully manicured outcrops of rainforest, complete with benches to sit on and admire them. There was also a café, and the office, where activities and guides – who were compulsory – could be booked.

So that was our first plan of action.

In charge of the Park Office was a grizzled old Aussie battler. He looked like he'd come straight out of a 1930's jungle expedition, and could survive on the blood of snakes caught bare-handed.

"I really want to do some caving!" I explained.

"Oh," he said.

"I'd like to go on that 'Clearwater Cave Connection Trip' you do. Is that possible?"

"No. That one's very advanced. Very dangerous. You can only do it if you've done the Intermediate cave already."

"Oh." That was a disappointment, but I was not being dissuaded that easily. "Okay, can I do the intermediate cave then?"

"No. You can't do the Intermediate cave until you've done the Beginners Cave."

I was crestfallen. "Alright," I said, admitting defeat, "can

I please do the Beginners cave?"

"No. All of our guides are fully booked."

That was a bit of a blow. The bloke could see that I was gutted. "I'm really sorry," he added, "there's a big Chinese group here. They always book up everything. But we have space on the Pinnacles Trip tomorrow." He slid a brochure across the counter.

"Oh?" I brightened. "What's that like?"

"It's a two night expedition, first down the river to Camp Five, and then up at dawn to climb the Pinnacles. It's the only thing we have left, I'm afraid."

"Well, that actually sounds pretty cool. How come that isn't booked up?"

The bloke shrugged. "The Chinese, they never go on that one."

"Really? Why not?"

"It's too difficult."

I caught a gleam in his eye. He knew exactly what kind of person he was talking to. I glanced at Roo, and saw my excitement mirrored in her face.

"SOLD!"

We ate in the café before heading back over the bridge to our hostel. It was immediately obvious that something had changed; the place radiated noise and activity, even from outside. Hiking boots were piled high in the covered entryway. I opened the door and led Roo into the midst of chaos. Every single bed was occupied, and every single occupant was yelling across the room at a friend on the opposite side, all struggling to make themselves heard over each other. Vast suitcases were stacked next to the beds, make-up was being applied, snacks were sailing through the air, and at least a hundred grand's worth of high-end photography equipment was strewn callously across every surface in the dorm.

Roo and I looked at each other in despair.

"A big Chinese group," she said, wearily.

"So it would seem."

It goes without saying that sleep was impossible that night. I lay there for hours, cursing my luck that the loudest snorer of the entire bunch had picked the bed right next to me. Then I got up to visit the bathroom, only to discover that he hadn't; he was right over the other side of the dorm, twelve beds away in the furthest possible corner! Yet he still sounded like he was two feet from my lughole.

About 5am, we gave up and left, packing quietly and tip-toeing from the room. No matter how bad the temptation was to bang and clatter and stomp, I just couldn't bring myself to be rude.

I know, I know! It's a failing.

The first part of the Pinnacles Trip started from the jetty beneath the rope bridge. It was a kick-ass motor-canoe ride; five groggy westerners speeding through the dawn, with the jungle closing in on both sides. We stopped briefly at a 'handicraft village' – a blatant attempt to cash in on the tourist dollar, with 'tribes-people' relocated to a convenient spot where every tour group stops for an enforced shopping excursion. The satellite-dish-on-stick-hut phenomenon was very much in evidence here, and in the surrounding fields the skeletal columns of several new, concrete-framed villages were being erected. Business must have been good.

Still, you can't really go to one of these places without buying *something*. Which is what they rely on. It's like, bad karma is just floating around, waiting to attach itself to the miserly white man. I blew $2 on a carved wooden hornbill to send to Mum, as she's far less sceptical of these quasi-scams and would love it even though it was rubbish.

Our next stop was a pair of show-caves; Clearwater and the Cave of Winds, both of which form part of the longest interconnected cave system in the world. Both were spectacular; vast caverns bristling with stalactites, sensitively lit to accentuate the natural beauty of the rock. Boardwalks led us around most of them, and connected one to the other via a narrow walkway along the base of a cliff. I love caves; love the intense quiet, the shivering chill and the mystery of the impenetrable, inky darkness. I love the majesty of the living stone sculptures, and the way the tiniest of grottos can suddenly open out into jaw-dropping chambers – all carved by nothing more than the action of water over countless millennia.

But secretly I was a bit pissed off, because these were the caves from which I would have been emerging in triumph, had I been allowed to book the advanced trip. Damn Chinese.

We climbed back into the canoe for the next stage of our journey. Camp Five was a good two hours upriver, and it was a stunning route. Sheer cliffs and thick jungle fought for dominance, broken occasionally by shanty villages where children played and women washed clothes in the river. We even disturbed a few local men taking their baths in the river, complete with soap and shampoo.

The water grew more shallow as we worked our way deeper into the rainforest. At one point we shuddered as the boat grounded, and our pilot leapt out to drag the thing over the rapids. I jumped out to help, issuing a manly shriek at the unexpected coldness of the water, and a burly American lad joined me seconds later. Between us we hauled the canoe through the patch of white water, grinning madly at each other with excitement. At the next set of rapids we all had to get out, and by the time we reached our destination we'd pulled that canoe over five shallow stretches and were all soaked from the waist down.

This was already shaping up to be an adventure!

We waded ashore at a muddy riverbank, the canoe pilot pointing out the path to Camp Five before he let the water carry him gracefully back downstream. There were five of us, all suddenly released from the presence of a guide, like naughty school kids who'd gotten away from their teacher. So we babbled to each other as we started on the two-hour hike towards Camp Five.

Travis, the American dude, was a keen outdoorsman from Alaska. He looked every bit as tough and muscular as his Singaporean girlfriend Lydia was tiny.

"She sets the pace though," he explained, as she struck off into the jungle. "I just try to keep up." And that was what we all did, breathlessly, for the next two hours. That chick was like the Energiser Bunny on steroids, somehow walking at a speed that put most joggers to shame. Travis ploughed along behind her, followed closely by Cynta, a tall Dutch girl who seemed to have no problem maintaining the furious pace.

Roo was lagging behind the others, so I slowed to match her. "Are you okay?"

"Yes, I'm just letting the rest of them go on ahead for a second."

"Oh. Alright. Anything I can do…?"

"Not really. It's the wrong time of the month for me to be wading in rivers! My lady product got wet when we were pushing the boat, and now I'm all *soggy* up there."

"Ah. I had to ask."

"But you could stand guard for me while I change it?"

"Of course love. That's a perfectly normal thing to do on the middle of a hiking track through the forest. I'll just stand here while you get your fanny out."

"Don't make me laugh," she cursed.

I looked back the way we'd come, but it was unlikely there would be any more hikers through for a while. We might even have been the last boat for the day.

"Here," Roo said, passing something over my shoulder. I took it, and only then noticed it was a balled-up panty liner. Roo was right about one thing; it certainly was soggy.

"What am I supposed to do with this?"

"Just hold it," she hissed.

She rummaged in her backpack for a fresh pad, then dropped her pants again while she fitted it. "Okay," she said when she was done, "safe!"

"Cool. Um, what do I do with this one?" I held up the wadded ball.

"I dunno? It's a 'leave no trace' sort of place, isn't it?"

"Well I'm not putting it in the bag with the food! You could put it in your pocket?"

"Eww, no!"

"Well then. I'd better just chuck it. It'll biodegrade pretty quick out here."

"Oh… okay then. Just, throw it nice and far away, please! I don't want anyone noticing it."

"No worries." I wound my arm up, determined to pitch

the thing a substantial distance. I danced a funny little jig, like I'd seen baseball players do on TV, took a few fast steps, and let fly an almighty throw. In a wide open space, that thing would have gone for *miles*.

Not so in the jungle. It flew about a metre from the path, then hit dead centre on a large tangle of branches. It hung there like a flag, just out of arm's reach, slowly unfurling to present its true colours.

"SHIT!" said Roo.

"Oops! Bugger! It's butter-side up, too. What are the odds of that?"

"SHIT!" Roo said again. "What do we do?"

I considered our options. "I'm thinking... we leg it. And if anyone asks, we deny all knowledge."

"You think anyone else will... notice?"

The pad gleamed white amidst the dark green foliage. It couldn't have been more obvious if there was a flashing neon arrow pointing to it.

"Nah. No-one will notice."

"Right," she said. "*RUN!*"

So we did.

"And you are *not* putting this in your book," she growled, as we took off.

"Fair enough," I said.

So I didn't.

Carry On Climbing

By my estimation we were only minutes from the end of the trek when the heavens opened, soaking us completely. We squished into Camp Five like drowned rats, to find the rest of our group sitting in the covered dining area, sipping coffee and looking out at the rain. All of them were suspiciously dry.

"We arrived just before it started," Travis said, apologetically.

Roo followed me into the open-air dormitory, which was a three-sided wooden structure with rows of foam sleeping pads on a raised platform.

"At least we get to use the mosquito net," I consoled her, as she stripped off her sopping wet clothes.

The mozzie net had been one of our frantic last-minute purchases back in Perth. We'd thought it would be an essential piece of kit in tropical, malaria-prone Borneo, but so far it hadn't come out of my bag once. That's the thing about hotel rooms in tropical, malaria-prone countries; most of them have one.

Waterproof bags had also been a last-minute purchase, and they had just undergone their first real test.

They failed.

"Thank God we left all our electronic stuff at Park HQ," I

observed, as Roo wrung the water out of our 'dry' clothes. Our sandwiches also looked a mite moist.

"We can hang them up to dry, if you've brought that piece of string," Roo suggested.

"The sandwiches?"

"No, fool, the clothes! I don't care how soggy the sandwiches are, I'm eating them right now."

Camp Five was a handful of open structures collected in a bend of the river. It was an idyllic setting, and a photographer's dream.

Which is why, ten minutes later, a large group of Polish photographers rocked up. Roo looked horrified; these guys must have been right behind us on the trail. She nearly been caught with her trousers down – literally – and by a group of nerds festooned with cameras.

"I wonder if they took any pictures of…" I stared.

"Deny. Everything." Roo bit back. She was turning an interesting shade of red herself.

That evening, our little group sat together at one of the wooden picnic tables in the open-air dining shack. We listened to the jungle noises around us, and to the sound of the Polish photographers snoring; for some reason they'd all gone to bed at 6pm, about an hour after arriving.

Then Roo pulled something out of her pocket.

"Look!" she announced, "I brought Uno cards!"

I sighed.

I can't play cards.

I hate cards, largely because I struggle to retain any rule more complex than 'kick the ball *that way*'.

Roo on the other hand has an addiction to Uno which I will never understand – all the more confusing in that she never plays it. In the six-plus years we've known each other, she has never been more than an arm's length away from a deck of Uno cards. Even when packing extra-extra light for an insanely difficult climb tomorrow, she'd squeezed them in because, "we might need something to pass the time." All the while studiously ignoring the fact that I would rather pass the time by beating my own head against the nearest tree. We live together, we travel together, and we spend almost all our time together; we meet comparatively few other people.

And we *never* play Uno.

"Hey, that's a great idea," said Travis. "I used to play that all the time, up in the mountains!"

"Sure, I'll give it a go," said Lydia.

"Come on Tony," Roo pleaded, "it's so much fun, and it's really easy to learn!"

And then, before I had time to beat my head against something in protest, she was dealing out cards – skittering them across the rough wooden table like a pro, while she launched into a run-down of the rules.

I zoned out straight away. As far as I could tell Uno was designed to be confusing, with far too many house rules along the lines of; 'if the person to your right stands on their head whilst plucking their left nostril, play reverses three times and then goes back to normal, except that now you're the thumb-master.'

I picked up my cards and stared dumbly at them. Everyone else around the table began shielding their cards and sizing each other up surreptitiously. I sighed again. The game began, punctuated by Travis coming out with things like, "Oh, when we play back home, if you pick up Green Skip-A-Turn and you say 'Red Rover, Red Rover' the person opposite you has to play Green next time and you get to discard three times."

We played Uno all night. I lost every single game.

And I still have no idea how to play Uno.

The Polish were still snoring as we fought our way into the mosquito net. Sleep was looking less likely by the minute, but then the rain started, giving us something else to worry about. We'd been told that a wet morning meant no climb, as the route up the pinnacles was treacherous enough in dry conditions. What with the downpour at the end of the day, and now a light drizzle drumming on the tin roof, it was looking like we'd have all day tomorrow to sleep; if it was still raining when we woke, there would be no point getting out of bed in the first place.

Dawn found us huddled, shivering, around the breakfast table. The chill air seemed laden with moisture, but the rain had held off; the guide was happy for us to start the climb, though he gave a stern warning: if we weren't past the halfway point by eleven am, we'd have to turn around and come straight back. Along with rain, the biggest danger on this hike was nightfall. We had to beat it back to Camp Five, so if we weren't fast enough on the first section, we'd never get to see the second.

Laden with more than ten litres of water between us, Roo and I chose to walk near the back of the group. Our guide set a hectic pace through the jungle and we followed, excited to be on a new adventure but already too breathless to discuss it.

We came to a place where a series of black boulders jutted out of the forest floor, and it was all uphill from there.

But what a climb! The mountainside was much steeper than I'd expected. Our route twisted back and forth across it, scrambling up gullies and dry riverbeds that were more akin to waterfall-beds. Trees still covered the mountain, and we climbed with all four limbs, hauling ourselves up by branches and great gnarled roots which webbed the rock. In minutes I was panting like a dog, sweating like a pig, and crawling like a spider with half its legs missing. Roo, bless her, was struggling to keep up, and the gap between us and the front of the group grew as I fell back to help her. The frantic tempo seemed to be continuing unabated; although the incline had gone from zero to sixty degrees, our guide was powering uphill as though he'd been doing this for years.

Wait a minute – he *had* been doing this for years!

Immediately behind him was Travis, who we'd learned last night was a professional mountain guide, leading fishing and climbing expeditions all over the Rockies. Lydia was right up there with him; less than half his size, she was practically sprinting up the mountain. Cynta was forging on behind them with grim determination, her long legs pumping tirelessly.

"I... thought... we were... fit..." Roo gasped.

"Me too!" I hauled on another branch and glanced back

as Roo pulled herself up to join me. The steepness was even more apparent from this angle, as I could see the two Polish photographers who'd decided to tag along with us struggling way down below. On a plain, a twenty metre gap between walkers wouldn't seem much at all, but the twenty metre vertical gap meant the guys coming behind us looked like toys to me.

"At least we're not last," I said, putting my hands onto the rock in front of me and scrambling up it.

"I don't know," Roo panted, "how much longer... I can keep this up..."

Our first break came just half an hour into the climb.

And we needed it.

We caught up with the guide in a bowl scooped out of the rock. It was the only place we'd seen so far with enough flat space for our little group to stand together. Heads down, breathing heavily, we waited for the stragglers, extremely glad of their delay. Sweat was dripping off Travis and Lydia, and they did at least have the grace to look winded. The guide, on the other hand, cast a reproving look around the group.

"Must go faster," he said.

Well, shit.

On we climbed.

The humidity was off the scale, the air thick and unbearably close. We were out of breath again straight away, but our punishing pace left no chance for recovery. The guide had waited only as long as it took for the pair of Polish guys to catch up; I think they were starting to wish they'd gone with the rest of their group, on a quiet stroll by the river. As they stood panting, heads down, in that tiny clearing, the guide led the rest of us onwards again.

Onwards – and upwards.

The steepness of the mountain was the greatest part of the challenge. I was glad of my gloves – tough leather, yet partially fingerless, I'd bought them for a brief sailing adventure several years ago. They'd cost me a small fortune, and I'd carried them with me ever since, from country to country, around the world and back again at least twice.

And I hadn't worn them once.

We were properly climbing now, hauling ourselves up on the exposed roots of trees which grew directly above us. I kept expecting it to get easier, to find a level section where we could start walking upright.
I never did.
"This must... just be... the start..." I reassured Roo.
"Don't... make me... talk..." she panted back.
We pushed on.
Protruding rocks tripped us, and we scrambled back up and over them. The way forward was the only cleared route through otherwise impenetrable undergrowth, which closed off the view from all sides. The foliage steamed in the rising heat; animals calls resounded, mostly monkeys and exotic-sounding birds, but neither of us had the wind to speculate on them.
As killers of casual conversation go, this beat the snot out of X-Box.
Sweat was pouring off me by the time we reached the next stopping point. I'd seen flashes of the others up ahead, signalling that we weren't trailing by a substantial amount, but it was still a relief to collapse, exhausted, against an outcropping of boulders. Behind me, when I could spare the energy to look, was an incredible view. The jungle peeled back, offering us a window through which we could gaze out over the river below. Satisfyingly, it did seem a long way away; a slender ribbon, sparkling in the mid-morning sunlight.
"Leave extra water here," the guide said, indicating a hollow in the lee of a large boulder. The race-leaders had already deposited their spare two-litre bottles, and I quickly shrugged out of my backpack to do the same. Pulling it back on, after drinking more than half of the water still left in it, was a relief; suddenly, it felt almost weightless.
"I think I can handle this," I said to no-one in particular.
Roo was busy taking aerial photos of the landscape below, her sense of wonder somehow overcoming her need to recover.
"Okay," said our guide, after a couple of minutes. The

stragglers could be seen just below us, working their way doggedly closer. He knew they'd be able to hear him, and that was enough; no point wasting the time it would take them to actually *get* here.

"Done good!" He held up the point of his machete, and pointed at a rusty tin plaque nailed to the cliff in front of us.

'WARNING! If you have not reached this point by 11am, you must TURN BACK NOW!' it said.

We'd done it, I realised – we'd passed the point of no return! And it was only... I pulled back the sleeve of my sopping-wet shirt. 9:30am? We'd already been hiking for over three hours! No wonder we were knackered. I'd been concentrating so hard on keeping up, not falling, on pulling myself higher from root to branch to boulder, that I'd hardly noticed the passage of time.

"Okay. Now we go," he continued, before breaking into a rare grin. "Easy bit is finish!" he informed us.

Pinnacle of Success

Luckily, our guide was joking.

The climb didn't get harder at all – just *more technical*.

It was something I was more than ready for. The mindless exertion, forging on uphill at a speed most flat-road fun-runners would be appalled by, had pushed me to the limit. Roo had seriously impressed me just by staying with us; not that I'd have left her of course, but maintaining our place in the middle of the pack had forced her to dig deep. She was trembling with the exertion, and shooting alarmed glances at me in response to the guide's comments – but there was no need.

The next stage involved pulling ourselves up on ropes, climbing through clefts in the rock and up short sheer sections with the aid of pre-set lines. Another couple of hours passed in this fashion, and the pace naturally slowed to accommodate these more difficult elements. Then we hit the first ladder, and were surprised to find it was just that – a bog-standard, aluminium ladder of the kind you might buy at any budget hardware store. It was leaning upright against a boulder, indicating the route – but don't worry! For added security, it was tied on.

Yes, you read that right.

Tied. On.

With a few scraps of ragged rope.

I wasn't sure quite what I'd been expecting, and I guess I shouldn't have been surprised. This was a fairly remote part of the world, and I couldn't see an army of tradesmen hauling their tools up here – but still. *Tied* on?

Ah well. Up we went.

As we progressed, I was relieved to find not all the ladder sections were this temporary. Most were composed of thick steel bars, firmly embedded in the rock. They were rusty as hell, suggesting that their replacement would become an issue before long – maybe that's what had happened to the first section? Regardless, these metal bars meant business, and we were grateful for that.

Several of them were lengths of angle-iron, about two inches wide; these were used like a tightrope to span crevasses, where a split opened up in the rock beneath us. I edged across, sliding my feet along the narrow strip of metal, one hand out to steady myself on the cliff face. The gaping holes in the rock went down hundreds of feet, the guide told us, carved by heavy rains following fault lines in the mountain's crystalline structure.

"How does this compare to Mount Kinabalu?" I asked Cynta, as we waited for our turn on a long, blackened ladder. She'd mentioned earlier that she had made the legendarily difficult climb; her knees still hadn't forgiven her the punishment, and were currently strapped up with special tape.

"Mt Kinabalu took a lot longer," Cynta admitted, "but it was all walking. Pretty easy, really. This is way tougher!"

I took a grim satisfaction from that.

The ladders were the easy part for me. I love heights, I always have, and balancing on thin rungs with no safety harness and nothing behind me but empty air was quite refreshing. Some of the others struggled a bit more with the concept, but Roo overcame her niggling doubts and followed me all the way up.

By midday we were threading our way through rows of sharp, pointy rocks towards the summit.

The Pinnacles themselves were these same pointy rocks.

Viewed from a distance – which was only possible from this peak, looking over at the next one – they resembled hundreds of wavy-edged knife blades, protruding vertically in a forest of lethal stone spikes.

Probably not the best place to land a parachute, I mused.

Because our lunch spot was set amongst the same kind of rocks, finding a place to perch while we ate was quite a challenge. The blades tapered to their sharp edges, meaning at their base there was barely room to place a foot between them. Scattered all around the mountain peak, we found odd spots where an individual could squat long enough to scoff a sandwich, and that was that. A couple of giant black squirrels scampered effortlessly around the formations, and we indulged them with a few crusts of our well-earned meal. The rest were demolished in short order. We had to bid farewell to the view of our neighbouring pinnacles and get our asses in gear for the descent – because, inevitably this was what our guide referred to as 'the hard part'.

He was right, of course.

Hardened mountain-hikers are well aware of this truth; going uphill is easy.

Because you're fighting gravity the whole way, your muscles propelling you upwards, you have only the exertion to worry about. Going down, however, turns things on their head – especially if you fall, which we all did frequently. Now, gravity is pulling you inexorably onwards, and it's the job of your aching, fatigued muscles to resist it. Going slowly is agonising; thighs scream for relief after only a few minutes, and hips, knees and ankles soon start to ache with the repeated shock of impact. All your joints are being overburdened, as you step down (or jump down) repeatedly.

Going fast, however, is suicide. At least on a route like this.

The ladders were easy again, and waiting my turn gave me a chance to fully appreciate the spectacle. The top third of the mountain was bare rock, affording panoramic views for anyone who had the breath left to admire them. Often we were climbing between boulders or outcrops, and the view would narrow to the rope or rungs just ahead, but unfailingly it would open out again, rewarding the effort with another fleeting glimpse over the infinite, undisturbed rainforest.

When we hit the tree-line again the going became faster, but that in itself presented challenges; not tripping over my own feet was the biggest, as I'm not known for my grace or agility.

In fact I'm known for tripping over my own feet, which was not the best thing to remember at this point.

Especially as this usually happens to me whilst walking around supermarkets or paved town centres.

On we surged.

I was striving to find a kind of flow – like a series of movements where one action led smoothly into the next. We were using the same root-and-branch handholds to ease our passage, and I felt like I should be able to swing more, to reach some kind of efficient, effortless form of constant motion.

"There are no ambulances out here," Roo reminded me, as I picked myself up after one of these experiments.

"But monkeys manage it," I pointed out, "if we can only learn to move like them…"

Roo was not impressed with my hypothesis.

"Monkeys are tiny. It's not effortless, it's just that they weigh sod all!"

"Orangutans aren't tiny," I countered.

"Have you seen the *arms* on an orangutan? They could rip up that tree and beat you round the head with it. Might knock some sense into you."

"Yeah, I see your point…"

She sighed theatrically. "I can't believe after all this time you *still* have orangutan envy!"

My experimenting with arboreal animal emulation had caused us to become separated from the rest of the group. We'd been slowing down anyway, wary of our aching joints and the amount of work they still had mapped out for them.

We were less than a month into our six-month journey, and knees were bound to come in useful again; travelling the world is considerably less fun when you can't walk.

The rest of the group had pulled on ahead, and we were

happy to meander for a bit, chatting when we could, offering each other advice on better hand-and-foot-holds, and reminiscing about our recent adventures. Suddenly Roo threw an arm across to bar my path.

"Listen!"

I froze, and waited for Roo, with her vastly superior hearing, to tell me what she'd discovered.

"There!"

She pulled me down into a crouch, and pointed through the trees. Although underfoot was mostly rock, with patches of earth filling in the gaps and hollows, all around us the jungle had risen up again. We were once more in the thick of it – and we were not alone. Through a thinning in the trees I could see what Roo was pointing at – a family of large, golden monkeys were dangling lazily less than a tennis court away, munching on leaves.

"Are they...?" she whispered.

"Golden langurs!" I breathed.*

"Yes! I thought so. Wow!"

So we sat and watched the monkeys enjoy their afternoon snack.

Every so often one of them would look straight at us, as though to dispel our foolish human notions of stealth. They knew we were there, but they didn't seem to mind; it was a moment of delicious intimacy, and we couldn't believe our luck. If we hadn't let the rest of the group crash on ahead of us, we'd never have noticed the langurs – and more than likely, they'd have kept themselves much further away from the track.

A rumble from the sky broke our reverie.

"That doesn't sound good..." Roo said.

Rain was the enemy we'd been fearing all day. The rocky route up this mountain would become slick within seconds of a heavy downpour, and we were already cut and bleeding in numerous places from minor falls and spills. We'd reached the steepest section of the trail, where taking two steps forward required lowering oneself at least half a body-height. Most of our footing was on sharp, uneven, slippery, rocks; it was a scramble far more than it was a hike. Doing this in the rain would be impossible.

The sky gave another ominous rumble, and it was all the encouragement we needed. Roo blew farewell kisses at the golden-haired monkeys and we resumed our scramble with urgency.

The first fat drops of rain fell as we made it down the last slope. The path – which from this point actually *was* a path – sloped away through the rainforest, leading off towards the river and Camp Five. We'd made it!

We hugged each other, laughing at the rain that began to fall in earnest. It could pelt down as hard as it wanted to, now – it wasn't like it could possibly make us any wetter! Sweat ran down my cheeks and forehead, and dripped from my chin and nose. Roo's shirt was stuck to her, completely transparent in places. It had been an epic climb, a monumental effort, and we could hardly believe we'd managed to keep going. All that remained was a casual saunter through the downpour, and we arrived back at camp to find the others sitting in the dining area, still catching their breath. Going down had allowed all of us to push our limits a bit, and we weren't the only ones who'd suffered a few knocks as a result of them.

"Man we *stink*," said Travis, holding his arms up for emphasis.

Lydia pinched her delicate nose in agreement.

"We could go for a swim to wash our clothes," I suggested.

"What, in *this?*" he gestured out at the rain.

At which point we collapsed against each other, laughing.

And so it was that I spent the rest of that afternoon in the river, paddling against the current in a pool by the nearside bank.

Around me, three beautiful women wearing only their underwear also swam and frolicked; we'd all stripped off and washed our clothes in the fast-flowing water, and then proceeded to immerse ourselves for the same purpose.

As ends of adventures go, it wasn't half bad.

*AUTHOR'S NOTE: For those of you who'll email me about it – I later discovered that Golden Langurs are endemic to Northern India and Bhutan, and that what we saw was something else. In fact, the monkeys we were looking at turned out to be *Sarawak Surilis* – a critically endangered species, with an estimated 200-500 left in the wild, and one of the rarest primates on the planet!

To Cave, or Not To Cave?

The walk out of Camp Five the following day was uneventful, except to point out that tiny Lydia again set a furious pace, leaving Roo and me practically jogging to keep up. She was like a dynamo, that girl; some kind of perpetual-motion experiment given human form. I was extremely jealous, both of her apparent fitness and her motivation. I was considering not getting out of bed at all tomorrow, but I got the feeling that she already had plans; circumnavigating Borneo in a canoe, perhaps.

We met the boat at the same jetty we'd been dropped off at, two days previously. Back then we'd been fresh-faced and eager; now we were triumphant, if a bit battered.
And absolutely bloody knackered.
You can't just close the lid on an experience like this though, and even before we reached the park entrance we were chatting about what we could do for an encore. Having already conquered the toughest challenge Mulu had to offer, we were forced to settle for somewhat tamer options. We hiked around another show-cave, and I got pangs of envy when I spotted a sign that said 'Advanced Caving Trips Only Beyond This Point'. The cave was beautiful though, with a roughly circular section where the roof had collapsed,

allowing natural light to flood in. This rubble-strewn patch was bursting with plant-life, a miniature jungle-oasis surrounded by the cool, dank, darkness of the cave.

Then we settled in to watch the bat exodus, which was due exactly at dusk (that's a joke; we waited two hours for 'dusk', and still weren't sure it was happening).

In ones and twos bats streamed from the cave mouth, opposite which tiered benches had been constructed for our viewing pleasure. Each new arrival was greeted by a chorus of oohs and aahs from the seated crowd. When the bats began to issue forth in long streamers, hundreds strong, the flashbulbs flared around us. Like wisps of smoke barely visible against the darkening sky, the bats made terrible targets for photography.

All at once we realised, all these people would be leaving at exactly the same time, shuffling down the narrow, mile-long boardwalk back to the park entrance at the speed of the slowest pensioner. The thought of an all-tourist traffic-jam spurred us to make a break for it, and the only people we passed on the walk back were a group of Asian teenagers torturing an exceptionally hairy caterpillar on the railing.

Roo and I shared a conspiratorial smile as we rounded the next bend. "They'll regret that," she said.

Our guide at the pinnacles had pointed this particular beastie out to us on our hike, with a warning; "No touch this one," he'd told us, "very poisonous! Two men from my village die last year from this one."

The next day we said goodbye first to Travis and Lydia, and then to Cynta, as their travel plans caught up with them and whisked them off to horizons new. We still had a day left in the park, as we'd budgeted plenty of time for caving trips. It was shaping up to be a lazy day instead, and Roo was looking forward to a relaxing stroll around the boardwalks with her big camera.

And then I met Milos.

Milos was a small, wiry Aussie bloke with a small, wiry beard.

The first time I saw him, he was sticking needles into a

large German, so I tried not to get involved. I listened though, as Roo and I moved our belongings into a slightly more peaceful dorm room. It was hard not to hear; Milos was so enthusiastic it bordered on mania, explaining the concept of acupuncture and how he'd become so impressed with it that he'd left his successful career as a doctor of Western medicine to concentrate exclusively on the ancient Eastern art. His philosophy on acupuncture intrigued me – as did the idea of someone so dedicated to it that he travelled with a spare set of needles...

I still didn't speak to him though. In case he started sticking needles into me.

The second time I met Milos, he came barrelling into the dorm, strode right up to me, and asked me if I wanted to go caving.

Poor fellow, I thought. I sighed for his naïveté. "We can't. I tried. The guides are booked solid."

"No, no!" he replied. "I just came from HQ. They had a cancellation for today and tomorrow. I did the beginner cave today, and the HQ dude said I could skip to the most advanced one tomorrow – but only if I can find two more people to do it!"

I looked over at Roo. She was flat out on the bed, too sore from the Pinnacles trek even to prop herself up for reading.

"Uh, Roo, love, you fancy going caving tomorrow? It's probably not *that* advanced...?"

She gave a muffled "Mmff," which I took to be a no.

"I'll go, though," I said to Milos. "Hell, I'm desperate to go!"

"Right," he replied, "let's go find some people."

The thrill of caving had lit a fire under Milos, and it burned hot enough to melt through any sense of embarrassment or propriety. As I jogged along next to him, he completed a full loop of the HQ, restaurant and accommodation areas, accosting everyone he saw regardless of age, gender or nationality.

"Hey man! You wanna go caving?"

"Hey old lady! You wanna go caving?"

"Ah, Konnichiwa... Wanna go caving?"

We nearly convinced a pair of strapping young Danish lads. They'd wrangled a place on the beginner trip while I'd been at Camp 5, but they were too nervous to try the Clearwater Connection – they'd already asked about it, and had been told it was only for the most experienced of cavers.

Dinnertime came and went. We'd been trying all evening, and had asked every man, woman and child in the park at least twice – but no banana.

As morning arrived without success, Milos and I packed our stuff just in case, and went down to HQ to beg. It was no good. Although I exaggerated dramatically about having caving experience on three continents, the bloke in charge refused to send us out without a third person. It was a profitability thing, apparently, though at $70 per person, it begged the question of how much our guide would be earning. A damn sight more than either me or Milos did, that's for sure.

With the deadline for setting off approaching and no sign of potential companions, we retreated to the café to ponder our misfortune. We were sitting there with our coffees, downcast in defeat, when a shadow fell over us. It was one of the Danish lads. "Ah, my friend, he is not interested, but I can go caving with you?"

Milos looked at me. "Quick!" And we sprang from our seats, sprinting all the way to HQ.

Leaving the poor Danish bloke wondering what on Earth had just happened. And what he had let himself in for, no doubt...

We booked into the Clearwater Connection trip with minutes to spare. The Danish lad was sent to get changed immediately, and I took his order for a packed lunch to the restaurant. In less time than it takes to tell, we were hiking down the boardwalk towards the Cave of Winds.

The walk was familiar from the previous evening, as was the cave itself. But as we approached that little sign, with its forbidden gateway, I could feel my excitement rising. Crossing that barrier sent a thrill through me, and a surge of adrenaline flooded my body. I was rather surprised I had any left. I let Milos walk in front of me, behind the guide, as this trip was his baby; I didn't want my hyperactivity stealing his thunder.

The concrete walkway ended at that sign. From there on it was a scramble over uneven terrain; the cave floor in its natural, undisturbed state.

After a few minutes of picking our way through the boulders, our guide stopped to give us our pep-talk. It was a well-worn speech in clipped English, mostly about staying safe and listening to his instructions, but there was a twinkle in his eye which said this was more than just a day-job to him. He seemed like the kind of bloke who had fun at work – and I could hardly blame him. He had one hell of a nice office.

"How long does this cave take?" Milos asked. Everything about his body language said he was as jacked up as I was, and raring to go.

"Ah, that depend. Size of group, how fit, if many beginner…"

"But, normally?"

"Normally, take eight hour. If slow, take ten. If American… maybe more!"

"Ha! No way it'll take us that long."

I was starting to pick up on his train of thought. I could already tell how dangerously similar Milos and I were.

"How long does it take the guides to do it?" I asked.

An explosion of laughter was my reply, followed by an amused shake of his head. "Guide, all different. Some guide, four hour. Me? Three hour." He tapped his chest for emphasis, then started giggling again at some private joke. "Okay, three hour and half," he admitted finally.

"How long do you think it will take us?" Milos asked.

"PPfftttttt! Depend. If you fit."

Milos shrugged. "I'm pretty fit. Tony?"

I shrugged too, not being one for blowing my own trumpet. I *felt* pretty fit, but I'd been humbled on the Pinnacles trip – and not just by the guide. Lydia, Travis and Cynta had all beaten me quite handily, though I had consciously chosen to stay close to Roo rather than trying to compete with them.

But... Roo wasn't here right now.

I was alone.

I could do anything I wanted.

No limits.

My mind queried the boundless possibilities, and came back with only one suitable course of action.

GAME = ON.

"I reckon I'm fit enough," I admitted.

"Let's go," said Milos.

We ran through that cave. I mean that literally; in a sport known for careful deliberation over routes, delicate placement of hands, feet and ropes, Milos and I just *ran*. For the level of adrenaline coursing through our systems, mere caving wasn't enough. We invented a new sport: *speed caving*.

And we were good at it.

There was no path through that cave. There were no flat, level surfaces at all, and most of the time we were picking our own route up, over, across and between the kaleidoscopic rock formations. Not for the first time, I was grateful I'd picked training shoes over hiking boots when we were shopping for Asia. Boots would have been a far more sensible option; on this trip alone, I must have rolled my ankles at least a dozen times. But that's all good. I have very floppy ankles. Possibly because I roll them twice just walking around Asda.

The flexible, super-grippy soles allowed me to ignore some of the shorter climb-downs, as I simply jumped. I bounced off the odd rock face here and there, but who doesn't?

The guide stayed ahead, nimble as a rat; the Danish lad quickly fell behind, not quite prepared for our reckless haste, and I dropped back to encourage him.

He was being way more careful, climbing cautiously, obviously worried he might hurt himself. Which, in my opinion, is usually when that happens. I felt a bit bad. Milos had performed a hard sell to get him here, and none of this would have been possible without him, but it was pretty clear right from the start that he was just baggage.

We only paused for lunch, and spent ten minutes catching our breath and scoffing the cold cheese toasties I'd brought from the restaurant. They say hunger is the best seasoning, and it's true; I've never tasted anything finer in my entire life than that rubbery, congealed cheese between two slimy slices of toast.

We had to slow down for several technical sections. There were three 'squeezes', where a bit of contortion was required to squirm through tiny holes and short tunnels barely big enough for our bodies. There was a fair bit of free-climbing, some balancing on narrow ledges (with spectacular drops below us), and a few bits where we had to lower ourselves down on ropes. The clincher was climbing down a vertical crevasse, 15 metres deep yet barely as wide as our helmets. We had to enter it backwards, and lower ourselves down totally blind; there wasn't enough room to turn my head to look below me at what I was sliding into, and the drop at the bottom was a leap of faith.

I let Milos go first on that one, too.

As Wind Cave gave way to Clearwater Cave, we met the river which had helped to carve much of this system. The traditional way to exit the cave was by swimming, but after a refreshing dip in the icy-cold water, both Milos and I chose a tougher route, scrambling and climbing along the walls of the cave almost the entire way. Eventually, there was no choice but to swim, and we drifted with the flow out to the jetty where our boat had tied up on the way to the pinnacles.

Dripping and shivering from both the cold and the adrenaline rush, I hauled myself out of the river and onto the wooden deck. I looked at Milos, and saw a mirror-image of myself; bedraggled, swaying slightly, bleeding in a variety of places – and grinning so hard the top of his head was about to come off.

Now *this* was a triumph.

"Good," said the guide, twisting his wrist so we could read his watch.

Three hours and forty minutes.

"Next time, no stop for lunch," he suggested.

The End Of The Beginning

Mulu National Park had given us some fantastic experiences, but like all good things it had to end. We were now in the last few days of our Borneo leg, and it was time to return to civilization.

After much debate, we sprung for the world's shortest taxi ride back to Mulu Airport.

To be honest, the debate probably lasted longer than the journey.

But we booked the taxi thirty seconds early, in case he was running late.

The flight back to Miri was nearly as empty as the flight into Mulu. The same comedy hand-over process was repeated at Miri airport, with the big bloke stationed in the corridor, handing out tickets from the window ledge; this time he was wearing a Hawaiian shirt with bananas on it. He couldn't possibly have looked less official if he'd followed me into the toilets and offered to swap a ticket for my phone number.

Just for the record: that did not happen.

This time.

Arriving in Kuching, the capital of Malaysian Sarawak, wasn't nearly as exciting as we were hoping.

I'd booked us into the 'Grand Supreme Hotel' by way of a treat. We could wallow in comparative luxury for a few days, after weeks of sleeping in stick huts and dormitories – or so I thought. I mean, come on! It was called the *Grand Supreme Hotel* for crying out loud. That's like, one rung down from the Mega Ultimate Grand Supreme (which, interestingly enough, was just down the road). You can't give yourself a name like that and not live up to expectations. Right?

I'd promised Roo a bit of room service, and maybe the chance to watch some TV. However, their 'Cable TV' featured only three English channels – all of which were infomercials. We had to change rooms twice before we found one that got WiFi strong enough to open Facebook, and I very nearly gave up on room service, after spending twenty minutes sitting in the restaurant, struggling to explain the concept to the staff. A hefty bloke in a stained white t-shirt who I assumed was the cook kept storming out of the kitchen and glaring at me. I was the only person in the restaurant – and quite possibly the hotel. The old man on reception would shout at him, and a vehement slanging match would ensue across the lobby. The cook would then stomp off into the kitchen for another ten minutes, only to reappear and repeat the process at regular intervals.

By the time I got back to the room, Roo was trawling Malaysian news sites, looking to see if anyone had reported finding my body.

The food was crap, and cold; we'd only ordered noodles. I'd still ended up taking the tray to our room myself. I had a sneaking suspicion the cook didn't like me very much.

We went for a stroll outside, before deciding that the local area also wasn't the best; the hotel's stained, dated façade loomed ten stories above a patch of waste ground surrounded by derelict garages. A few scummy bars were scattered around the perimeter; the handful of shops and business looked run down or closed down. Piles of rubbish and old construction debris were scattered everywhere – it just needed a burnt out car to complete the ambience.

"I thought they said it was in a good location?" Roo asked. The tone of her voice suggested she didn't entirely agree.

"They said it was in the heart of the business district," I explained.

"Yeah? The sex-business district, maybe. This is, like, brothel central. I want to go back inside."

We checked out next morning, strapped our rucksacks on front and back, and hiked a couple of miles closer to town. There we found a hostel called 'Nomads', which Milos had recommended, and moved temporarily into the dormitory.

Which was worse.

There was one full-time, live-in staff member. He didn't shower much. He spent most of his time sitting out on the cramped balcony surrounded by the girls who were staying there, drinking with them, getting them stoned, playing his guitar for them – basically trying anything he could to get laid.

I'd chosen a bottom bunk, so that Roo would feel a bit safer sleeping above me. I lay down to test it, and it felt like I'd spread a picnic blanket over a loose collection of car parts.

I folded back the thin flap of foam that served as a mattress, and stared in disbelief. The bed was homemade, as was often the case in Malaysia, but on this one every single slat was a completely different-shaped piece of wood. Some were long and thin, some chunky and square, and most of them were broken in at least one place. It was like this bed had been purposefully designed for discomfort; there was simply no way it could possibly have worked. I had Roo take a photo by way of proof, because I couldn't imagine anyone would believe me. It would have cost about $5 to replace all the slats with matching strips of wood, and taken maybe half an hour. I've stayed in *a lot* of hostels, and slept everywhere from bus stations to park benches to hospital waiting rooms, but I've never spent a less comfortable night in my life. And that was after I stole the best slats I could find from the two neighbouring beds.

Faced with leaving Borneo on a bit of a downer, we decided to stash our big bags at the hostel and make a lightening-fast raid on another national park – this time *Bako,* which was less than two hours away.

On the bus there, Roo was reading about the rare proboscis monkeys that she hoped to photograph.

"Apparently, they're constantly aroused," she told me, "and due to their diet of largely indigestible leaves, also highly flatulent. So! Horny, hairy, and they fart all the time… now, who does that remind me of?"

There wasn't a lot to say to that.

I decided to take it as a compliment.

The second stage of the journey to Bako was by boat, and we waded ashore onto a wide, flat beach opposite the park entrance.

Two things were immediately abundant in the park; small, brownish-grey monkeys – and signs warning about the monkeys. Apparently they were not to be fed, and would steal anything not padlocked down. This was borne out even in the short time we were there; we watched as one lady chased her handbag down the beach, and saw another couple's picnic lifted from behind them as they sat canoodling. Later that night one of the guest bungalows was broken into by the thieving monkeys, through a window the occupant forgot to lock. Needless to say, they made quite a mess of the place before escaping with his camera and his passport.

They must have had customers waiting.

There was another interesting sign by the start of the hiking trails:

'The Sarawak Government shall not be responsible for any physical, mental or emotional injury sustained, or any loss of life within the National Park.'

I wasn't sure quite what they were trying to cover themselves against. Were there evil clowns in there? Cannibals? The Boogieman? Or did the park rangers like to hide in the bushes with their trousers down?

Physical danger was present in the bearded pigs – small, black, pot-bellied pigs that tended to hang around the accommodation areas. I'm ashamed to say, I've been terrified of pigs ever since my time in Ecuador, because they are such voracious and aggressive feeders. Roo finds this hysterical, and loves pigs – loves to taunt me with pigs, even. I generally like to get my revenge by eating as much bacon as I can find – which so far, in largely Muslim Borneo, was none.

The pigs followed us everywhere we went, and I inadvertently proved my point whilst sneakily feeding cookies to the 'Do Not Feed The Monkeys' monkeys. To avoid being too obvious about it, I stashed the cookies in my pocket. You wouldn't think a bearded pig was built for stealth, but these guys knew what they were doing. They stalked me while my attention was on the monkeys, snuck up behind me, and tried to eat the cookies *through* my pocket – along with the pocket itself, and everything else in that pocket.

Including my fingers, which were reaching for a cookie at that exact moment.

Shit, they were so focused on getting those cookies, I came perilously close to losing a testicle.

"You see how *dangerous* pigs are?" I demanded, trying to push them away with my knees.

Roo shook her head in wonder. "Only to you!"

That night we had a spacious four-bed dorm to ourselves, and got up at dawn to watch the monkeys playing on the beach. They sifted through a depressing amount of trash cast aside by thoughtless tourists, looking for fizzy drinks cans. Anytime they found one a fierce battle would be fought over it, with the victor tipping the can up to drink the dregs. It was shocking and appalling of course, but also a teeny bit hilarious, and Roo took plenty of close-up photos of the action. One of the cheeky chappies even wandered over to check out her camera, and managed to take a selfie!

Returning to Kuching, we spent a pleasant evening cruising up and down the Sarawak River on a traditional Malay gondola. We'd been treated to some stunning sunsets in Borneo, and our last night on the island was no exception. We strolled along the wide riverfront promenade, choosing what to eat from the stalls and huts that lined it. The sun sank past an elaborate modern temple complex on the far bank, which we'd run out of time to visit. The sky was pink, with wispy orange clouds like a baby orangutan's fuzz. It was a fitting end to our stay, which, whilst challenging on occasions, had been ultimately rewarding.

Kuching airport was smaller than I remembered, and completely deserted.

The immigration desk was unmanned; it took Roo twenty minutes to locate a staff member, while I waited with our backpacks. She convinced him to fire up the x-ray machine, and we scanned our bags ourselves.

Then we followed signs through empty, echoing halls to the departures gate – only to find there was nowhere to sit. I mean that literally – no benches, no chairs, nothing but the cold, tiled floor, and a row of coin-operated massage chairs.

We chose the latter.

Roo's chair, mercifully, was out of order, but not mine; every two minutes it emitted a piercing shriek of alarm, presumably to remind me (and everyone else in a five-mile radius) that I was sitting on it without paying.

"Can't you turn it off?" Roo moaned.

"I'm trying! But the power button has been nailed into the 'on' position!"

"Can't you unplug it?"

I looked behind the chair. "No! The bastards have screwed the plug into the wall as well! I get the feeling we aren't the first people to try turning these bloody things off."

In the end we sat on the floor, dozing against each other. Every few minutes we were startled awake by the same piercing bleep, as the chairs reminded someone down the other end of the airport that they'd forgotten to pay.

If this was a form of torture, it would have been outlawed by the Geneva Convention; only airports can get away with that shit.

At one point I staggered bleary-eyed into the bathroom, to be confronted with a rather graphic poster explaining how to use Western-style toilets. There must have been so many people trying to stand on them and squat to pee that a hard-hitting ad campaign had been mounted to stop it. One photo showed a shattered toilet bowl, and another showed what looked like the victim of a great white shark attack, but turned out to be the poor sod who'd been standing on the toilet when it shattered. In the world of embarrassing injuries, accidentally amputating your own arse whilst trying to take a shit had to be worth a medal.

And yet, it still hadn't worked; when I pushed open the door to my chosen stall, the first thing I saw was a pair of dirty bare footprints on the toilet seat.

Finally, we climbed aboard an ageing 737 bound for Hanoi, in the Socialist Republic of Vietnam.

"Any tips for when we get there?" I asked Roo, as she was paging through the guide book on her tablet.

"Only one," she replied, adopting her best impersonation of John Cleese in Faulty Towers; "Don't mention the war!"

VIETNAM

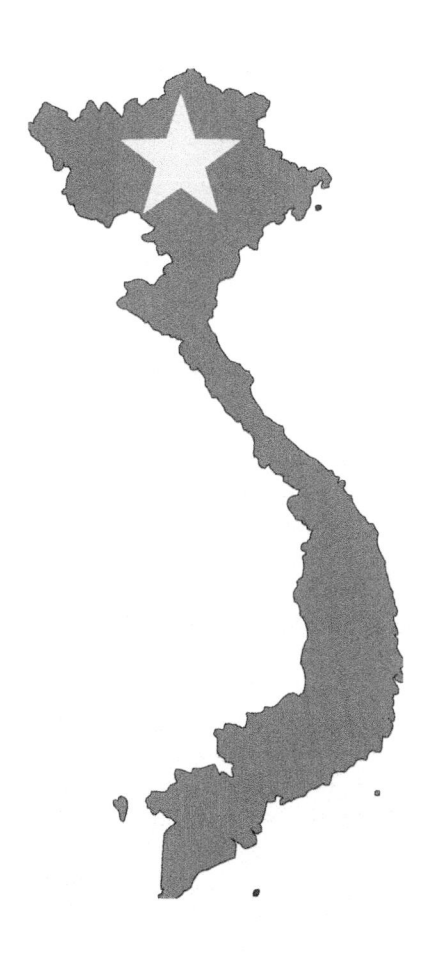

Good Morning Vietnam!

I'll confess to being a little nervous as we flew into Hanoi airport.

Not about Vietnam itself, you understand, but rather the slightly unorthodox way we'd obtained our visas. All the internet research in the world couldn't stop my Spider-sense from tingling; it was simply too weird. All I'd done is sent cash to a third party company, together with photocopies of mine and Roo's passports. And they'd emailed me back a poor-quality scan of a letter from the Vietnam Immigration Department, stating that visas had been issued for the following people. There was a list of names; Roo and I were tacked onto the bottom of it.

It smelled wrong. It smelled like trouble. It smelled like the most simplistic of scams, a rip-off so blatantly obvious that only the stupidest people would ever fall for it. No self-respecting Socialist government would allow such a lax system to regulate who was allowed into their country, surely?

Or let private companies profit from selling visas to foreigners?

A ten year old could have forged a more believable visa letter.

"You're sure this visa thing is going to work?" Roo

asked.

She sounded nervous, too.

"Yeah, sure," I told her. "Why wouldn't it?"

Following instructions I'd read online, I led the way through the airport to a wide counter, helpfully marked 'Visa On Arrival'.

"You see," I said to Roo, "this is the place I was telling you about."

"Where we get our real visas?" she asked, eyeing the mob that was already forming around the counter.

"Nope!" I replied, leading her around the crowd. We passed down a long corridor beside an office, where smartly-uniformed women rushed back and forth with files and stamps, and at the far end of it we found another waiting area with a much smaller counter. This was more or less what I was looking for: the desk for people who, like us, had paid their money to Visas'R'us.

There was no obvious sign, but a handful of people were standing around with their passports out, so I joined the queue. The person in front of me was handed his passport back, and then it was my turn. I showed the letter, handed over my precious brown book (and Roo's rather battered blue one) – and that was that! Or it would have been, had a tour guide not shoved his way to the front of the queue, barked something in Vietnamese, and thrust a stack of at least twenty open passports into the clerk's hands.

It wasn't hard to translate; "Just do these first," he'd said, and the ladies of the office were happy to oblige.

An hour later, with full-page stickers in our passports, we officially entered the Socialist Republic of Vietnam.

Hanoi has been the capital of Vietnam on and off for the better part of its thousand-year history. During that time it's been occupied more times than the toilet on a 747; the Chinese, the Japanese and the French have all left their marks. It's the fastest-growing city in the world – which is a bit frightening, given that it's already bursting at the seams with over seven and a half million people. In a land area roughly half the size of Perth, Hanoi manages to cram nearly quadruple the population. More promisingly though, it was ranked the fourth-best travel destination in the world by Trip Advisor – and the cheapest of all of them.

Our first port of call in any foreign land is always the same; the ATM, or cashpoint, or 'hole-in-the-wall' as we Brits tend to call them. They are an absolute godsend. When I first started traveling, the idea that my UK bank card would be accepted in some remote corner of southern Asia was laughable. I'd have been running around with my dong in my hand (because 'Dong' is the currency of Vietnam, you sickos!). For a trip like this, many months in many different countries, I'd have needed a shoebox full of cash; togrogs and bogrogs and wigwams... Okay, I may have made those last two up, but my point is there are some weird-assed currencies out there, and we would be collecting them as we went. Travellers Cheques used to be the trusted alternative to carting half your net wealth around the world in your underpants, but they came with all sorts of issues, especially when visiting far-flung and/or heinously corrupt locales. A four-star Parisian hotel can cash cheques while you eat cheese in their spa-bath, but the horse-nomads of the Mongolian Steppe probably charged an outrageous commission. And still made you ride a goat to the nearest city to collect the cash.

It was whilst we were partaking of this miracle of modern convenience that we met an English couple, Mary and Peter (presumably no relation to the followers of Jesus). They offered to split the cost of an official airport taxi with us, seeing as how we were all headed to the famous Old Quarter of Hanoi. I'd been a bit concerned with the taxi situation after reading some horror stories in online travel forums, so we gratefully accepted. Peter spent most of the journey adding to my fears with his own litany of woes – taxi drivers who had promised to use the meter, only the meter was rigged to charge ten times the going rate, drivers who held their luggage to ransom, or drove them around and around until they paid a bribe just to get out... All in all, it seemed like avoiding taxis completely was the way to go.

"But you can trust the green ones," he finished. "They say 'Mai Linh' on the side, and their company is honest. We only take Mai Linh taxis, now."

They dropped us right outside our hotel, on the edge of the Old Quarter.
Into a maelstrom.
Motorbikes swarmed around us, racing straight for us from all directions. I felt like bait thrown into a shark tank.
"SHIT!"
The scooters zipped by on all sides, missing us by inches without even acknowledging we were there.
"Get to the pavement!" Roo cried.
"What pavement?" I yelled.
The roar of engines drowned out her response. True enough, we were in the middle of the road. In fact we were now a miniature island in a sea of traffic. The front door of the hotel was clearly visible just a few yards down the street, but between us and it, in a space barely wide enough for a single car, three lanes of motorbikes were criss-crossing at breakneck speed.
I'd read about this issue, in the same place I'd read about collecting our visas. In Hanoi, the traffic waits for no man. The bold prosper, and the weak – the timid, touristy types – tend to die of old age, still standing on street corners without ever finding a gap big enough to cross.
There was nothing for it. Sooner or later, one of these 125cc death machines was going to plough right into us.
"Let's go!" I shouted to Roo.
"Are you fucking crazy?" she shouted back.
But this was it; it was do or die time.
I gripped Roo's hand, trusting her lightening-fast reflexes to yank me out of danger.
"One, two, three..." I cried... "SHUFFLE!"
And with all the boldness I could muster, I edged slightly forwards.

We survived, of course.
But doubtless there are people reading this, uncharitable souls who are starting to wonder if I'm not exaggerating this

experience *just a little bit*. To those people, I say: go to Hanoi! Try it yourself. Visit the Old Quarter in rush hour (pretty much anytime between 6am and 2am), pick a road, and try to cross it.

But take a change of underwear.

Safely ensconced in the narrow lobby of the Hanoi Asia Star Hotel, we recovered quickly. I had time to wonder about the odd shape of the building, which matched the endless parade of buildings I'd been studying from the taxi. Since leaving the airport, every structure we'd seen, whether commercial or residential, had seemed to be only one room wide. It was bizarre; often the buildings were ten or more stories tall, yet skinny to the point of absurdity. Great ranks of them lined every road, built right next to each other yet still separate, as though sharing a wall with your neighbours was unclean. It was like looking at row upon row of dominoes all stood on end, waiting for a giant finger-flick to set them falling.

Jimmy, the manager of the Asia Star, checked us in with an enthusiasm that bordered on creepy. He was a little guy, in keeping with Asians in general and the Vietnamese in particular, and very well presented in a smart suit. Jimmy had a nervous energy about him, a wide smile, and a mouth full of teeth that were as broken as his English.

"Stay two night?"
"Yes, thank-you."
"Where you go after?"
"Ah… we're going south. To Ho Chi Minh City."
"You want book train?"
"Ah, we're going to take the bus, I think."
"You want book bus?"
"No, thanks, that's okay."
"Okay. Where you go tomorrow?"
"Ah… not quite sure yet. We're just going to have a look around, you know?"
"Want book tour? Hanoi City tour?"
"Ah… no, thanks."
"Where you go tonight?"
"Um, well, I guess we'll go and find some dinner…"

"Want book restaurant? Very good restaurant!"

We managed to avoid booking a restaurant, and hauled our bags up six flights of stairs to our room. "It's all well and good having incredibly tall, incredibly skinny buildings, but they could at least think about installing lifts!" I moaned.

"I have a feeling Jimmy gets commission for anything he books for us," Roo mused, as we lay on the bed catching our breath.

"That's fine, so long as he doesn't hassle us every time we walk past him. There's no escape in that lobby, it's too damn narrow!"

"We should walk quickly, just in case," Roo suggested.

We explored the room, finding it surprisingly luxurious for $20 a night. It had no windows, but that was hardly surprising; the architects of the Old Quarter had studied at the 'put shit everywhere' school of urban design, and the Asia Star was hemmed in on three sides.

We briefly considered getting changed, but we were hungry, and eager to explore. And anything fresh we put on would smell like scooter exhaust fumes within minutes anyway.

Jimmy was waiting for us in the lobby. "Where you go now?" he asked, as we speed-walked past the check-in desk.

"Find some food," I said, without stopping.

"Want book taxi?"

Back outside, the heat and humidity hadn't diminished noticeably – and neither had the chaos. Roo gripped my hand. "I hope we can find somewhere to eat without getting run over."

"There's a street down that way where all the restaurants serve dog," I suggested, pointing to our left.

"They're not serving it to us," she said, setting off in the opposite direction.

We managed to find a restaurant without crossing the street, which was probably for the best; I didn't think we were ready for that yet.

After subsisting almost entirely on fried food in Malaysian Borneo, we were both keen to try something new.

Enter: pho.

Pho is a traditional Hanoian dish, the origins of which are hotly contested. It's a spiced, clear noodle soup made with either beef or chicken. We ordered one of each, and found it so delicious we very nearly ordered another one.

Roo was understandably impressed with the results of our experiment. "Wow, score one for us, trying the local cuisine!"

"I don't think we'll have much choice in Vietnam," I admitted, "there isn't a fast food outlet in the entire country."

"If it's all this tasty, I won't mind at all," she said.

"Good! So. Dog for dessert?"

Going With The Flow

Breakfast in the Hanoi Asia Star was served in the basement.

It consisted of miniature slices of stale bread, for which a toaster had been thoughtfully provided, and the lukewarm fruit juice of your choice. So long as it was orange.

Jimmy presided, standing at the end of the narrow room and focusing his undivided attention on our every mouthful.

We were the only people there, though I can't imagine why.

After three trips back to the toaster we were getting quite self-conscious, and decided we'd eaten enough for now. We stood up to leave, and Jimmy was on us like a starving piranha.

"Where you go now?"

"Ah, we, uh, might go back to our room, Jimmy…"

"Where you go after?"

"Ah, well, we thought we might take a walk around the lake."

"You want lake tour?"

"No, thank-you Jimmy, we just like to walk by ourselves."

"Oh, okay. Where you go after?"

"Ahhh… we haven't really thought about that…"

"You want tour of Hanoi?"

"Um, not right now, thanks."
And we fled.

"Jesus, he's persistent!" Roo said, as soon as we were safely back inside our room. Jimmy hadn't actually chased us up the stairs, but his eyes had; they told the story of his hunger from across the room.

"How the hell are we going to get past him?" Roo asked.

"I dunno... maybe we'll just stay in the room today?"

After recovering from the excitement of breakfast and spending a few hours checking out our onward travel options, we ventured downstairs again. We'd told the truth; a stroll around the lake was our only goal, with perhaps a bit of casual shopping en route. Nothing Jimmy could really help us with, but I knew that wouldn't stop him trying.

We couldn't sneak past him, because the entire hotel was less than three metres wide. There was no vast lobby across which to scoot while he was looking the other way; we had to go right out past him, physically stepping around him if he didn't move first.

"Hello Mister Tony! Where you go now?"

"To the lake, Jimmy. To the lake."

And with that we were around him, and out into the chaos of the Old Quarter.

Ah, the Old Quarter! I loved the place. The streets were a mess, both in their reason-defying medieval layout, and in the more conventional sense. Hundreds of tiny shop fronts crowded the narrow alleyways, spilling out into the street with shelves of merchandise from food to shoes to engine parts. Scooters whipped to and fro, their riders dodging through the crowds of pedestrians without feeling the need to slow down. Junctions were a crucible of high-speed near misses, as everyone simply went whichever way they felt offered them the best route; left, right, middle of the road, or sometimes all of the above in quick succession. Very occasionally a car would slice through the melee, scattering all before it; the cars were no more inclined to stop than anyone else. The incessant beeping of the scooters became a background din, over which groups of friends shouted to hear one another, cars revved for attention and no-one cared either way. If you were to build a shrine to the concept of 'accident waiting to happen', the Old Quarter would be it.

There was a pavement, or sidewalk of sorts, but it was crammed with parked scooters, stalls, and pavement cafés which were literally that – a few blokes barbequing what looked like off-cuts from more promising restaurants, on griddles homemade from tin cans and wire mesh. Each of these entrepreneurs crouched in the gutter, surrounded by dozens of enthusiastic diners – all of whom were perched on tiny plastic stools of the kind you might buy for a toddler. The smell and the heat from these places followed us wherever we went, as we strayed down roads barely wide enough for us to walk side-by-side. It was a labyrinth; a smelly, noisy, dangerous labyrinth that distilled every ounce of Vietnamese weirdness and excitement into a single constant stream of sensory overload.

I couldn't remember the last time I'd felt so alive.

Of course, it wasn't hard to feel alive when the probability of not being alive was increasing on a second-by-second basis.

The walk around the lake took us three hours.

It wasn't a big lake. The walk would have taken us about an hour under normal circumstances, but the locals were out in force. I wouldn't say we queued around the lake, because that would suggest some form of organisation; rather, I'll say we fell in with the crowd. We didn't fall into the lake, as that was the one thing no-one was doing – the water colour alone suggested it would be a bad idea.

But people were here in droves, working out, shopping, taking a stroll. All facets of life were available to glimpse on that single circumnavigation, from the couples posing for their wedding photos at several points around the shore, to the tourist-packed bridge to the tiny island and its (closed) fort, to the young boys optimistically trying to fish with lengths of string. All ages from ten weeks to eighty years were represented, and the single most common activity (after staring at the rest of the activity) was exercise. People were jogging. Doing star jumps. Walking backwards, for no immediately apparent reason. Playing badminton, in possibly the least-conducive circumstances I have ever seen for playing badminton; some of the games looked set to end up as water polo if the players weren't careful.

We bought sausages on sticks, followed by a polythene bag of donuts, and just went with the flow.

And tried to forget about how the donut lady had ripped us off.

A hundred-thousand *dong,* that was... *Five dollars* for a bag of donuts? *Whoops...*

I was determined to find a mini-market we'd looked up on Google. With the vast number of micro-grocery stores lining every street, big supermarket chains were a demon that had yet to cast their shadow over Vietnam. But the little shops were tiny almost to the point of being ridiculous, and none of them stocked anything I fancied putting on a sandwich. There was meant to be a bigger store of some kind, somewhere near here, if only I could find it...

I never did.

But we did find a huge gothic cathedral, surprising us with its presence inside an officially atheist state. It also surprised us by being closed. As we wandered the backstreets, taking a break from the throngs around the lake, we were treated to another bizarre phenomenon: the seed bar. The district surrounding the church appeared to bristle with pavement cafés, but closer inspection revealed the young people squatting on their toy stools were actually scoffing sunflower seeds from little bowls! Here and there someone was drinking a beer, and of course everyone had one eye on their smartphone, but no other food was in evidence. I really wanted to sit down and scoff some seeds myself, by way of a cultural experience, but there wasn't a spare stool in sight. We must have passed a dozen of these places, and they all had one thing in common (apart from the ubiquitous bowls of seeds) – every one of them was rammed out with customers!

By the time we found our way back to the main road, the traffic was getting stupid. I mean, borderline farcical. The road was three lanes wide, but the scooters using it were at least twenty deep. Somehow we'd ended up on the wrong side of it, and had to cross – along with about sixty or seventy other poor souls, although none of them seemed as nervous about the prospect. We clustered together at a pedestrian crossing, and then just went – a surge of people, much like I imagine the storming of a castle breach, where countless heroes lay down their lives so that others may crawl across their bodies to victory. It happened like this: the crowd, swelling rapidly, reached critical mass; the leading people, presumably recognising that they were about to be forced into the road anyway, simply spilled into a gap between two scooters, and then everyone else followed, flowing across the road one strand of traffic at a time.

Neither people, nor bikes, stopped moving. They became sort of interwoven, picking their own paths like two intersecting flocks of birds – only without any sort of natural instinct guiding the process. A scooter bounced off the woman directly in front of me, and she didn't even flinch; merely pressed on regardless, presumably with a substantial bruise on her thigh to show for it.

The press of people carried us across the road, and we had little choice but to stay with them as they flooded along the edge of the lake back towards the main junction.

It was only when we reached this junction that we started to realise this was not a typical day in this part of Hanoi.

The junction had become a parking lot. Hundreds of scooters sat there, most still occupied by their owners, sitting as though they were safely ensconced in a drive-in movie theatre. Except that traffic was still struggling to flow – here and there a truck or a bike was forcing its way through, aggressively pounding the horn whilst creeping inexorably onwards. This was a six-lane-wide arterial ring road, but nobody seemed to care about that.

The streets were crammed with people, occupying every inch of ground that didn't already have a bike on it. And all of them seemed to be focusing their attention on the centre of the roundabout, where a small stage had been erected and a group of contortionists were going through their routines.

"This is nuts," I said to Roo.

She clung to me by way of reply, fearful of being swept away by the human tide we were caught in.

Noticing the closest vehicle was a small truck with a flatbed, I decided to get a better angle on proceedings. "I'll find out what's going on," I said, and pulled myself up onto the bed of the truck.

This was definitely a show of some sorts, though quite why everyone had been allowed to just stop their bikes in the middle of the road and sit on them to watch it was beyond me.

"Now it's just a few chicks in headdresses, doing some crummy dance," I shouted down to Roo.

"Get down!" she called back to me.

"No, you should come up here! The view's much better. The whole place is chocka-block, it's like a rock concert."

"No, get down *now*," Roo hissed.

No view was worth causing her concern, so I waved my intention to the crowd around her and leapt down into their midst. "Are you okay?" I asked Roo, once I had swum back to her side.

"This lady next to me said you had to get down," she explained, pulling me away from the vehicle. "She seemed quite worried."

"Ah well, I do tend to have that effect on people."

We pushed through the wall of bodies and came around the front of the truck.

"That's probably why!" Roo said, pointing.

Two uniformed officers were sitting in the cab of the vehicle.

'POLICE' was emblazoned across the bonnet.

"Ah. Right. We should probably go…"

High-Jinks

After another lacklustre breakfast at the Asia Star, we made Jimmy's day by asking him to book us a taxi to the bus station. Our internet research had thrown up an interesting possibility. Not far from Hanoi is *Ha Long Bay*, a legendarily beautiful cluster of almost 2,000 limestone-karst islands. The bay was declared a UNESCO World Heritage Site in 1994, and it's the number one tourist attraction in all Vietnam for both local and international tourists.

We couldn't wait to go there.

In fact, we'd booked an overnight boat trip to Ha Long Bay, with a visit to a beach and a spot of kayaking thrown in for good measure...

But not for another three weeks.

Roo's sister Vicky was coming out to meet us in Vietnam, and we'd all decided to do the Ha Long trip together as a treat. Still, that didn't mean we couldn't explore the area a *little* bit.

Apparently there was good rock climbing to be had on *Cat Ba* - the biggest island in Ha Long Bay, delightfully named after three mystery women who washed up dead on the beaches there (Cat Ba means 'Women Island').

Buying a bus ticket was refreshingly easy, after Borneo – we simply rocked up to the bus station, checked the timetable, paid the correct price and boarded the next bus.

Just like that! No haggling, no interminable waiting for the bus to fill, and ideally no obese woman flicking stinky fish sauce all over me...

I dunno, maybe I was setting my standards a bit high.

The bus stopped without warning in a place we later discovered was called Hai Phong. Everyone was ordered off the bus and told to collect our luggage, and then we waited – hoping this was all part of the plan rather than some hideous miscommunication, and that another bus, or boat, was en route to collect us. But we'd been dumped outside a shop that sold ice cream, so I bought us one each. The idea caught on, and pretty soon there were thirty backpackers of all different nationalities standing around nervously slurping Magnums. Another bus did arrive half an hour later, and drove us through a landscape dominated by miles of container-filled freight-yards. Eventually the bus performed the craziest of three-point turns and reversed onto a strip of jetty barely wider than its wheels. The ferry to Cat Ba Island awaited, and beyond that another bus – this one to take us clear across the island, over the central mountain range, and down through lush green forests to a sliver of town on the opposite coast.

It started to rain the second we pulled our backpacks from the last bus, so our first order of business was to find shelter. We got directions to Asia Outdoors, a climbing company that operated from the second floor of a double-width hotel called The Noble House. The hotel looked kind of posh, but we asked about the room rate purely out of interest and were delighted to find we could afford it. We'd turned up just before the start of the holiday season, and scored an impressive sea-view room for an equally impressive $15 per night.

Within an hour of being dumped in the rain, we'd booked in for a climbing/kayaking trip the following day and were free to explore the town.

There wasn't a lot of it. Most of the buildings fronting the sea backed up against a cliff face that was taller than any of them. These were eight and ten storey buildings – they had to be, as they were all only one room wide. I'd solved the riddle of the bizarrely skinny buildings whilst hiding from Jimmy in Hanoi. Much as England once had a 'window tax', designed to ensure that owners of larger homes paid a bigger bill, Vietnam once had a tax based on the width of its buildings. Hence, the tradition developed to build deep, tall houses with the absolute minimum frontage – proving that the age-old urge to screw the taxman transcends all cultural barriers.

Amusingly enough, it's become a self-sustaining situation. With all the land still divided up into these ridiculously slender lots, if you want to build anything wider you'd have to buy and flatten the houses either side of you.

Or in this case, the hotels either side of you.

Unsurprisingly, it doesn't happen much.

Saving those tax dollars had made the architecture way more interesting, but it was a crap design for hotels. It tickled me no end that I could tell exactly how many rooms each one had by counting the floors. Where else in the world could you come across an eight-storey hotel with only seven rooms available? This entire strip, running the length of the seafront with almost every building a high-rise hotel, could still only accommodate a few hundred people.

In a narrow gap between two hotels we watched a bunch of workers attacking the cliff face with jackhammers. They were at least fifty feet up, not fastened on to anything, and were literally drilling the ground out from under their own feet.

Clearly the trade unions still had a few battles to fight in Vietnam.

Next morning, we piled aboard a repurposed old fishing boat for the trip out to the islands. As well as one English and one Vietnamese guide, we had six other companions on our climbing experience: an English couple, who would be climbing on their own as they'd done a lot of it, and a pair of French blokes who, like us, were beginners.

Oh, and each of the French blokes had brought a hooker.
Seriously.

Two pretty Vietnamese girls, each beginning the trip

entwined around their respective 'boyfriend', they tried talking to me when they realised I spoke English. They were sisters. They both worked in the same bar in Sapa, northern Vietnam, which was where the French guys had picked them up. One of the girls spoke patchy English. Neither of them spoke a word of French.

Having lived in Thailand, I knew that a lot of western guys tried to save money by hiring a long term hooker/girlfriend. From a purely financial standpoint, it made sense – like buying a box of Mars Bars rather than forking out for them individually. And I guess, from an STD standpoint, you're at least limiting yourself to one particular can of worms…

Ugh! Anyway, it happens – and I've seen enough to let it pass without comment.

Which is probably for the best, as most blokes don't take too kindly to you calling their girlfriend a whore. Even when that is quite *literally* the case.

What blew me away was not just that these guys had the audacity to bring their professional body-slaves out in public – but that they had *paid for them both to go climbing!*

Ouch.

Obviously their bank balance was bigger than mine. I'd blown half a week's budget to bring Roo climbing with me – but at least she wasn't going to charge me for anything else…

Although I love to climb, I haven't really done much with ropes and harnesses and all that jazz. It's not that I disdain such things, it's just that half a ton of rope and metal connecty bits never seems to be around when I want to climb something. I guess what I do is called 'free climbing'. Unless you're talking to Roo; she calls it 'stupidity'. (Incidentally, my mum calls it 'please God stop that, you're going to die!'). But this proper climbing was great fun. The ropes gave me confidence to push on well past the height where my legs usually turned to rubber. I made it quite easily to the top ring, where the rope from my harness doubled back and disappeared down to the hands of our guide Russell. I was trembling with the excitement of getting so high so quickly, and wished there was another section to climb above this one. Swinging out from the rock on my way back down, I took it all in – the beach of shells, the turbulent water, the scant patches of blue sky. This was an elemental place to be, with the wind whipping past and the rain coming in squalls. I was having the time of my life, and I couldn't wait to get back on the rock again.

Roo and I managed four good climbs apiece. Everyone else had given up after three attempts, apart from the hookers – they'd had one half-assed go each, squealing when they found themselves a handful of metres off the ground, and then spent the rest of the afternoon sitting on the beach, looking sullen.

The adrenaline rush from climbing was so strong it carried me all the way home and right up to the bar above Asia Outdoors, where it was happy hour on cocktails. Roo and I sat on the balcony nursing $2 mojitos, chatting about climbing spots with the English couple. It was warm, and the sun was sinking into the ocean directly opposite us. Our room was only a couple of floors above, and shared this dramatic view from its own private balcony. I was exhausted, exhilarated, and starting to feel the effects of my third delicious cocktail.

This place had a lot to recommend it, I thought.

Breakage

We had to leave the Noble House the next day, as the manager unapologetically doubled the price on us.

"Weekend," he shrugged, by way of an explanation. This short-sighted customer service ethic turned out to be a national standard. Every business owner we came across, from motorbike touts to stall holders to hotel managers, seemed to be chasing the quick buck, as though their strategy had never evolved into a long-term game plan. Word of mouth, customer loyalty and win/win transactions didn't interest them once they got the dollar signs in their eyes. When we nipped back later on for a cheap cocktail, the manager begged us to take our room back at a heavy discount, as the flurry of expected weekend bookings hadn't materialised. His loss, unfortunately.

We moved two blocks down the main drag, into a guest house recommended by our climbing guide. A tiny old man took a break from his ear-cleaning business to lead us to the back of his shop, and up eight flights of incredibly narrow stairs. We had to duck to get up the first set, which resulted in us getting wedged by our backpacks against the roof, but we persevered and finally made it. The room he showed us opened straight off the stairs, and took up the entire floor plan of the building. A wall of glass dominated the far end, offering unrestricted views out over the bay. The rest of the room was in good repair, with a big bed, TV and shower room – and he wanted just $8 a night for it.

We could hardly believe our luck!

I actually felt quite bad, as though we were ripping the bloke off, so I agreed to rent his motor scooter, and promised to let his wife give me a shoulder massage later on. He took my money, handed me the bike keys and quietly resumed his ear-cleaning. His current customer, a young man in a business suit, had patiently sat there with dental tools protruding from his ear the whole time.

It took me a while to convince Roo she would be safe on the back of the scooter. For starters, she'd been in cars with me driving – a nerve-racking experience by anyone's standards.

And that was with doors, seat belts and airbags for protection.

"I rode one of these things every day for a year in Thailand," I protested.

"Yes, and how many serious accidents did you have?"

"Well, three. But I was drunk every time!"

Whether or not that comforted her she didn't say, but she climbed on the back and clung tightly to two things: me, and her camera. I didn't know which was more precious to her, but I knew which one she'd rather see damaged.

We drove twice around the island, looking for a cave that had been used as a hospital during the war. So clearly was it marked on our map that we didn't realise we'd missed it until we found ourselves back in town. We fared no better on our second attempt, keeping our eyes peeled for signs, but finding none. We did find great clouds of butterflies though, and Roo delightfully snapped them as they swarmed around us. Giving up on the hospital we decided to visit a French hillfort which was more visibly sign-posted. Turning onto the steep mountain road, I changed down a gear and gunned the engine.

Mistake!

The bike reared up, the front wheel coming up in front of

my eyes – and Roo was unceremoniously ditched off the back. Three things broke her fall: her left bum-cheek, her right bum-cheek – and her camera.

"SHIT! Sorry love!" I got off the bike as soon as I could, and ran over to help her up. "Are you okay?"

"I won't be sitting down for a while," she said, rubbing her ass.

"Is the camera okay?"

She held it up, checking it out from different angles. "Looks okay. I think it'll live."

"I'm so sorry," I told her, "there was too much torque."

She fixed me with a glare. "Too much talk is what got me into this mess."

Understandably, she was a little nervous about getting back on behind me.

She had no choice, of course, because we were halfway up a mountain, miles from anywhere.

And the road leading up to the French fort was *far* too steep to walk up.

"I'll go slow," I promised, though I don't think it reassured her much; I'd been doing less than five miles per hour when she'd been so violently ejected.

But Roo is a survivor, and she's learned how to cope with me screwing things up.

Well, she's had plenty of practice, anyway.

Somewhat reluctantly she climbed back onto the bike and let me drive her very cautiously up to the fortress. The views from the top were amazing, and I'd almost forgotten about our little accident by the time we headed down again.

Roo, not so much.

As a direct result of my motorbike mishandling, she suffered two rather impressive bruises – one on each buttock – and her fiendishly expensive zoom lens developed a slight attitude problem. She took it all in good cheer, as is her way, but I had a horrible feeling that come Christmas time, I had $600 worth of penance to do.

Roo never rode on a bike with me again.

It was starting to go dark when I returned the scooter to our landlord. He was still busy plying his trade, and I considered getting him to clean my ears out. It's something I've never had done, at least not that I'm aware of. There was bound to be plenty of stuff in there that shouldn't be, and my hearing isn't wonderful – perhaps the two were connected? But right now there was a queue for his services. Obviously, it was a popular pastime here.

Meanwhile, I needed a massage to assuage my guilt.

Sometimes, life is hard.

The tiny bloke's wife was even tinier. She also looked even older – so much so that I started to wonder if she was actually his mum. She also didn't seem super-keen on doing a massage, so I confirmed that I only wanted my back and shoulders worked on. She sat me down in an oversized hairdresser's chair, content to let me keep my t-shirt on, and took up position behind me on the back of the chair.

Then she dug both knees into pressure points either side of my spine, gripped my neck in some kind of wrestling hold, and twisted.

The massage was on.

Now, I suffer from an affliction common amongst men.

It goes like this: no matter how much something hurts, we are only allowed to admit to feeling pain under two specific circumstances.

Emotional pain (and only emotional pain) can be admitted to your wife, or a particularly trusted girlfriend – but *only* if they ask about it first.

Actual pain – physical, agonizing, I'm-going-to-scream-and-pass-out-at-any-minute-type pain – can only ever be admitted to a qualified ER doctor. And even then it must be downplayed, with judicious use of phrases like 'not too bad,' and 'a bit sore'.

And you have to at least *offer* to drive yourself to the hospital. Even if you've lost an arm and are bleeding to death through your eyeballs.

So it goes without saying that I could not admit to this miniscule octogenarian that she was inflicting excruciating pain on me. As she hauled backwards on my arms with all her might, and my shoulders bulged and threatened to dislocate,

I ground my teeth and forced out complimentary noises through my nose.

"MMmmmnnnmmnn!"

She pulled tighter.

Either she genuinely thought I was enjoying myself, or she knew what game I was playing, and was hell-bent on making me crack. I had my suspicions about which. We were locked into a spiral of denial which could only end in tears – my tears, specifically.

Sitting fully in the chair behind me, she placed both heels between each vertebra, wrenching my arms so far backwards I could hear the tendons ping like plucked guitar strings. It was too much; a low moan escaped me, and I was horrified to realize it was the precursor to a scream.

My torso was like an elastic band stretched well past the point of no return. Five more seconds and she was going to be slapped in the face with the bloody stumps of my arms.

I opened my mouth to unleash a wail of agony – when she stopped.

Abruptly, without warning, she relaxed her grip.

"Is finis," she croaked.

Was there was a note of defeat in her voice, or was it just my imagination?

Slowly I swung my arms back into normal alignment, hyper-sensitive to every click and twinge. Satisfied they still worked, but not daring to trust my weight to them, I leapt out of the chair with probably too much enthusiasm.

The old man at the other end of the shop glanced up from his work.

Still embedded in the ear of his latest customer, a metal implement halfway between a scalpel and a lock pick moved slightly of its own accord.

I decided against getting my ears cleaned.

Upstairs, Roo was sitting cross-legged on the bed, trying to coax her camera lens into full extension. She looked up as I came in, sweating, anxious, and breathing heavily.

"Hi love! How was your massage?" she asked.

"It was... okay. Not too bad."

"Not good, though?"

"Ah, well, you know. Average."

"Oh! That's a shame. Hey, would you like to massage me instead? I've been very lonely up here…"

"Uh… not right now, thanks."

That got her attention. "Why not? Are you okay? What's wrong?"

"Nothing, nothing. I'm just a bit… sore."

"Sore?" Suddenly, her brow furrowed and her mouth formed a circle of mock sympathy. "Awww! Did de widdle owd lady hurt you?"

And that is why men don't admit to pain.

Things That Go Bump In The Night

The route we planned to take around Vietnam was somewhat unconventional, because halfway through our stay we had to meet Roo's sister Vicky at the airport.

Not the airport in Hanoi; *Tan Son Nhat* International, in Ho Chi Minh City – formerly Saigon – which was a little over 1,000 miles south of us, at the opposite end of the country.

We had ten days to cover that distance and collect Vicky, after which we would simply turn around and repeat the trip in the opposite direction.

Now, you'd think we could go down one side and up the other, to add a bit of variety to our experience – but Vietnam is borderline anorexic, much like its houses. At its narrowest point the entire country is a sickening 31 miles wide, causing fat countries everywhere to throw chips at it and mumble about Photoshop.

With every plane, train and hotel of our return journey booked and locked-in since before leaving Perth, we knew exactly which bits we were going to miss. There were precisely two of them.

To the north of Hanoi rose the hill country. This was

hiking territory, where remote villages could be reached on epic and arduous treks through the mountains. The city of Sapa, built in the shadow of Vietnam's highest peak, was known as the gateway to the mighty (if rather daft-sounding) Tonkinese Alps.

It was also in exactly the wrong direction.

Roo did the calculations, lying on our bed in Cat Ba Island.

It would take a few days to book and travel back to Hanoi and on up to the north, giving us less than a week to do a circular hike of some sort. Then we'd have to put on a serious burst of speed and leg it down south if we were to meet Vicky in time.

"And we haven't got much hiking gear with us," she lamented. "We'll have to rent a tent, sleeping bags... hell, cooking gear, pots and pans... and find somewhere to ditch all our other stuff."

It didn't look promising.

Which left us with *Nha Trang*.

It had been my job to read up on this place, and now I had to break the news to Roo.

"I'm sorry, love." I sighed for dramatic emphasis. "I'm afraid, there's nothing at all to do in Nha Trang. Not a single thing. Just acres of golden sand, lined with dozens of bars selling cheap cocktails."

"Sounds awful," she said, shaking her head.

"I know. I mean, for hardcore adventure travellers like ourselves, it'll be hell."

It was Roo's turn to sigh. "Sometimes, sacrifices have to be made..."

"I know. I have faith in us. We'll cope, somehow."

"Still, lying on the beach, sipping ice-cold piña coladas..." she was counting on her fingers. "How many days will we have to put up with that?"

"A week. If we leave tomorrow."

"I'll start packing."

Our return to Hanoi was memorable only for the crowd of taxi drivers that mobbed the bus, barely moving aside to let it pull into the station. They were scrabbling around peering into windows, obviously marking their targets amongst the tourists. Roo and I pushed through the melee, using our height to our advantage, and made it to the fringe of the crowd. We were followed out onto the road by a few more persistent guys, but they must have realised we'd escaped when we flagged down a green Mah Linh cab and jumped in.

The word on the travel forums was that *Sinh Tourist Café* was the most reputable long-distance bus company, as they used their own fleet of well-maintained vehicles. Apparently ticket-scamming was another huge problem in Vietnam, with dodgy tour operators selling overpriced seats on decrepit old buses, double or triple booking them, and then vanishing without a trace. We were about to spend the best part of two days and two nights on a succession of sleeper buses, so I wanted to be sure we got the real deal.

The taxi dropped us off outside the Sinh Tourist Café, and the driver pointed up at the blue sign above our destination. "That one," he explained, helpfully.

"Okay. Thanks for that…"

Then, as he drove off, I shouldered my rucksack, straightened up, and realised I was looking at another Sinh Café, directly opposite.

"That's weird…" I pointed it out to Roo.

"Maybe that's why he said 'this one'. There might be two different branches…"

The two businesses looked the same, but the address I'd taken from their website agreed with the taxi driver. That's when I remembered all the warnings I'd read about imitation travel companies. "It's a fake!" I told Roo.

The lady in the genuine Sinh Tourist confirmed it. "Very bad," she said, "but there are so many!"

I've bought plenty of knock-offs in my time, especially clothing – the ridiculous mark-up big brands charge, purely for putting their logo on a t-shirt made in a Bangladeshi sweat-shop, winds me up a bit. But I'd never heard of knocking off an entire business! And then setting up shop in full view of the original…

"I can't believe they're so audacious," I said to Roo, as we sat on plastic chairs in the tiny booking office. "If it was my business, I think I'd be inclined to put a brick through their window. And I'd keep putting bricks through their windows, every night until they buggered off!"

With the bus still a couple of hours away, we went for a stroll to loosen our limbs. It would be the last chance we had to move around for quite some time. Walking down the street, I realised why the good people of the Sinh Tourist didn't spend their evenings throwing bricks through their neighbour's windows; they were outnumbered! Within a hundred metres of the shop, three more Sinh Tourist Café's had sprouted, all proudly displaying the same blue and white sign as the original. It was the most blatant display of copyright infringement I'd ever seen – clearly the rules were different in Vietnam. If I opened a shop selling bootleg action figures, called myself Toys'R'us and borrowed that company's branding for my shop front, it wouldn't be long before I had an army of lawyers camped outside. Not to mention the cops. By imitating a legitimate business, surely these others were declaring their intentions as anything but? They might as well advertise to the Vietnamese authorities that they planned to steal money from tourists! But then again, as we were to discover, that wasn't a crime either, in Vietnam – it was closer to a commandment.

When the night bus arrived, I was blown away. I'd braced myself for the worst, and was privately afraid we'd be sleeping on a pile of rust barely held together by its own paintwork. But not so! A bright blue modern coach swung into the narrow alleyway, clearing the imitation Sinh Café by inches. On board was another surprise – or rather, a series of them. Firstly, the bus was clean, as evidenced by the driver making us take our shoes off as we got on. We were each given a plastic bag for our outdoor shoes and the option of disposable paper slippers! But the interior layout of the bus was the most impressive thing; it contained three rows of bunk beds, left, right and centre, creating two tight aisles between them. Stacked two high, the bunks didn't have a lot of headroom, but looked comfy enough – moulded plastic frames with reclining car-seats in navy blue. Your feet went into a triangular box which formed the headrest of the bunk in front. Each bed was equipped with a blanket and a pillow, and a hook from which your shoe-bag could be dangled. We both chose to keep our carry-on bags in bed with us, as we'd stuffed them with snacks and drinks to keep us going. And so, as the bus lurched off towards our first stop in *Hoi An*, we settled back on our front-top bunks and got ready for some enforced relaxation. I fired up my laptop and began to open files of what would eventually become Kamikaze Kangaroos, while Roo was avidly watching an episode of Australia's Next Top Model on her tablet.

Travelling can be tough at times, but you just have to roll with the punches.

We changed buses twice, in towns I could hardly remember. We'd be seeing them both later on with Vicky, so it didn't really matter; each time we stumbled from the bus, bleary-eyed, clutching our belongings, trying to make sense of what had just happened. Impressive though the buses were, getting any kind of quality sleep was precluded by the less impressive condition of Vietnam's roads. Also by the headlights of oncoming traffic strobing through the windscreen, and by the driver's use of the horn as his primary method of communication. Thus, we were unleashed onto the streets of *Hué* (pronounced 'Huay'), dazed, confused, and surprisingly hungry. We found a café, propped each other up long enough to consume the first thing we recognised on the menu, and then forced ourselves to 'explore' the surrounding area. I recall none of it, though Roo assures me we bought ice creams and were offered trousers at prices only a sleep-deprived backpacker would consider reasonable.

(As a side note, I sometimes read Roo's journals to help me write about certain places and events. Her entry for Hué consists solely of the phrase 'expensive trousers', followed by three exclamation marks – which says something about her sense of priorities.)

Our arrival in Nha Trang was a huge relief. At some time in

the previous twenty hours I'd started to question the nature of reality, and whether I was really trapped inside this slender tube of steel at all. I could be dreaming on a beach somewhere, or tangled in the wreckage of an accident, or frozen in time as I fell from the last cliff I would ever climb. What was life, really, I asked myself, other than a series of electrical impulses recorded by my brain? Who was to say what was real, and what was only in my head, when in reality, everything I perceive exists solely in my head?

It was a long bus trip.

Surviving it, and bursting out into the morning sunshine in Vietnam's premier seaside resort, was a breath of fresh air both figuratively and literally; my seat on the last bus had been a cramped booth above the toilet compartment. Getting in or out required several minutes of extreme contortion, and I could only fit into it in the foetal position. The banging of the toilet door, inches from my head, did little to promote a state of restful sleep, so instead I lay awake and passed the time trying to guess the last thing each passenger had eaten by the smell of their shit.

So.

Nha Trang!

We'd made it.

As expected, a handful of touts had turned up to prey on those of us who had no prior bookings. As Roo and I fell into this category, and as we were both so tired we couldn't face an extended hike around town with our backpacks, I just shrugged at the first tout who approached me and climbed on the back of his scooter.

"Is it a nice hotel?" I asked him.

"Yes, yes! Nice hotel!"

"I'll check it out," I told Roo, and left her in the Sinh Tourist office with our bags.

The tout drove me a few blocks over, then ducked into the kind of alleyway in which murders are committed. Too narrow for a car, squashed between high-rise buildings so that daylight was reduced to a blue stripe far above, I was already mentally crossing this place off my list as he pulled up behind a pair of pot plants. Opposite me there was a wooden façade, glass doors, and a faded sign.

'Nice Hotel', it read.

So at least he'd been telling the truth on that score.

Five minutes later I was back with Roo, grinning ear to ear. "You should see this place!"

Our new friend on the scooter earned his commission that morning, taking first me, then me plus backpack, then coming back for Roo. The Nice Hotel was a gem. The scooter guy had promised me a double room for $10, but the hotel receptionist, when questioned, apologised profusely. The room rate was actually $12. But this did include air-con, WiFi, an en-suite shower room, a private balcony – and a lift!

Which matters a whole lot more when you consider that our air-con, en-suite, private balcony was located on the ninth floor.

We stood there for a moment, admiring our new domain. The room was small but clean, with a tiled floor, a large bed, fluffy white towels and satellite TV.

Twelve. Dollars.

You can't buy a pizza for that in England.

"So, here, we are!" I said to Roo. "New city, full of opportunities! Bars, and cafés, and beaches as far as the eye can see. *Lonely Planet* says there's a crazy old theme park on its own private island, and a cable car that takes you up a mountain, and every kind of water sport known to man can be found within five minutes of this spot!"

She nodded wearily. "So. Bed, then?"

"Absolutely."

Paradise City

Ahhh, Nha Trang!

The beach was every bit as good as we'd hoped. The weather left a lot to be desired, but you can't have everything, eh? It rained on and off pretty much the entire time we were there, but Roo developed a clever strategy to deal with this. Being Australian, she'd been brought up to fear the sun, and even on the brightest days she'd only dare spend half an hour out in it. So we kept our sunbathing gear on standby, and whenever the clouds parted we leapt into action – typically getting just enough exposure on the beach to satisfy Roo before the rain began again. At which point we retreated back into our hotel, and back into bed.

There were certain, ah... *things...* that we wouldn't be able to do very often, once Vicky showed up. By way of saving money, we'd booked all three of us into one room for most of the time.

So we didn't mind the rain one bit.

In fact, so blissfully happy were we, it took us two days to notice that my wallet was gone.

The fault was entirely mine; well, unless you count the thief who'd actually stolen the damn thing, as I lay sleeping on the night bus. Roo had taken her valuables into the bunk with her, even going so far as to wrap her bag strap around her as she slept. I was kind of pushed for space as it was, so I'd been content to hang my bag from the hook provided. It was right by my head, so I figured no-one would dare get close enough to open it, even if I seemed to be sleeping. And I didn't sleep a lot. But the wallet was gone from the pouch it usually occupied, and there wasn't anything we could do about it. I went back and asked at the Nha Trang branch of Sinh Tourist if they'd had a wallet full of cash and credit cards handed in, but it did sound like a bit of a futile request.

"And you don't know who really killed Kennedy, do you?" I added. Hell, it was worth a shot.

"No," came the answer. I didn't bother asking which question was being replied to.

I handled it rather well, I thought.

No tantrums, no prophecies of doom, no wailing and gnashing of teeth. Let's face it, gnashing of teeth is *so* last century. Almost no-one does that any more.

Instead of my usual state of panic, I calmly listed everything that had been in the wallet, then sat listening to elevator music on hold with two banks in two different countries, two credit card companies, and my mum. It took most of the morning, but it was sorted; bank accounts frozen, cards re-ordered, and instructions left with my family to forward them on to the Hanoi Asia Star as soon as they arrived. *Maybe I'm growing up,* I mused, as I packed my bag for the beach. Or maybe it was just the deliciously relaxed atmosphere of Nha Trang, that feeling of unrufflability that comes with being in paradise.

Or maybe it was the $3 bottle of vodka I'd bought next door to Sinh Tourist.

It was surprisingly mellow, which coincidentally was also how I was feeling.

However, it did not change the fact that we now had precisely *one* bank card between us. It accessed only Roo's Australian account, into which we quickly transferred all our remaining funds. It couldn't be used online, so we'd made our last internet booking for a while...

"If we lose this card, we're screwed," Roo informed me,

"so I think it's best if I keep hold of it for now."

She got no argument on that.

Our holiday continued fairly smoothly after that; neither poor weather nor financial difficulties could faze me. In fact, there was only one thing I *was* nervous about – and that was meeting Tim and Charlotte.

Tim and Charlotte were (and are) a young English couple, who had both quit very respectable jobs in the financial sector to travel the world. By all accounts they were doing a much better job of it than I was, having clocked up an impressive tally of countries visited in well over a year on the road.

They were also avid readers, which is where I came into the picture. They'd both read my books, and they wanted to meet me – either to congratulate me, or to punch me in the testicles for wasting hours of their time.

Either way, it was going to be a first.

A few months earlier, I'd managed to meet an idol of mine – best-selling author and all-round legend Paul Carter (if you get chance, check out his book 'Don't Tell Mum I Work On The Rigs, She Thinks I'm A Piano Player In A Whorehouse' – it's absolutely hilarious, and was the book that inspired me to write my own adventures). Mr Carter came to do a book signing at a small shopping centre south of Perth, and I jumped at the chance to meet him. I thought about nothing else for days, but when I was finally there in front of the man, all I could do was grin like an idiot and stammer out, "I love you! Err, I mean, your books…"

Cringe.

I get ridiculously star-struck when meeting famous people.

And as it turns out, I get just as star-struck when meeting fans.

So when they rocked up at the Why Not Bar, I was delighted to find they were as refreshingly not-normal as both Roo and myself.

"Toonaaay!" Tim shouted, pulling me in for a man-hug.

And that was all the introduction we needed.

"I was worried you wouldn't recognise me," I admitted.

"Mate, you've got a website with about a thousand photos of you on it. And you're sitting here next to a hot chick with rainbow-coloured hair."

"Ah! Fair enough, then."

"But you should really change your publicity shot. It looks like you're auditioning for a boy-band."

Before long the drink was flowing, and we were swapping horror stories from years of adventures. Tim and Charlotte had narrowly escaped natural disasters, political coups and terrorist attacks, seemingly stalked by ordeals which had thankfully left them unscathed. I regaled them with the stories I'd left out of my books, the ones I'd thought too weird or too risqué to publish. It was a great night, with good food and drink flowing freely.

And that's when it all went a bit pear-shaped. There's a reason that western tourists flood to bars like this, in resorts like this. In the UK you get the occasional free drink if you find the right coupon, or if it's your birthday, or if you're sleeping with the barmaid – but it's a fairly rare occurrence. In Australia, where booze is expensive, it's practically unheard of.

Not so Nha Trang.

There was a young German bloke at the entrance, enticing people to come in with the offer of a free drink. I'd joked with him that free booze must be dangerous for the staff, and he'd agreed. After a particularly enthusiastic night of 'work', he told me, he'd fallen over and smashed his head on the kerb outside. It had taken three surgical procedures to get him able to work again, with more to come. "And still, I've completely lost my sense of smell, and taste," he finished.

Which sounded like a pretty shitty end to a night out, and should have served as a cautionary tale. But he saw no irony in being an enabler. He was going from table to table, pouring shots and daring people to take his challenge. Now, I may have mentioned that I like a challenge. Add a couple of drinks and, well...

"This guy'll have a go!" Tim shouted, pointing at me.

The German was there in a flash, holding up a bottle of bright blue liquid with a pouring spout. He'd been giving out free shots, but had yet to tempt anyone into anything more serious. Now he loomed over me, the bottle poised enticingly.

"You ready for this?" he asked.

"I dunno. What are we doing?"

"We're seeing how much of this stuff you can take. I pour, you drink, I count. The record is thirty-three *Mississippis*."

"Thirty-three?" I scoffed. "Pah! That's the record? That's rubbish!"

"Oh, really? You think you can do better?"

"Of *course* I can do better," I told him, "I'm a *diver*."

"Oh yeah?" He looked amused. "Let's do it, then!"

And he poured the drink.

Now, I've been to university. I can down a pint. I can open my throat and just let the stuff pour straight into my stomach, filling it up like a water balloon. Which is exactly what I did.

"One Mississippi…"

Gulp! I had to gulp, because that's how it works. I was secretly proud of this skill, but I rarely get to boast about it. At least since I took it off my CV.

"Five Mississippi…"

I was chugging the stuff down, and loving it. Blue sugar water, it was obviously alcoholic, but tasted like pop.

"Twelve Mississipi…"

There was a note of panic in his voice, as though he recognised me as a serious contender. I hadn't flinched yet, and he was already approaching the halfway point. So he tipped the bottle a bit further over, and that's when shit started to get real. My mouth was filling up faster than I could swallow, and the stuff was spilling out, trickling down my cheeks as he tipped the bottle further and further.

"Nineteen Mississippi…"

I was drowning. I coughed, spluttered, and splattered everyone at the table in bright blue liquor.

"That's it!" cried my tormentor, "No win! Twenty-three *Mississipis* – not even close!" And with that he was off towards the next table, where a trio of scantily-clad women had been eyeing the procedures with interest.

The rest of my table were laughing, shaking their heads, pointing at me.

"If one *Mississipi* is one shot, then I've just had twenty-three free shots!" I declared. "In what way is that not a win?"

And that's the last thing I remember about that night.

Roo tells a slightly more elaborate story. Apparently I spent the rest of the night stumbling around the Why Not Bar, picking up and downing any drink I found unaccompanied. A bunch of rowdy lads had bought a vat the size of a beer keg full of something bright yellow. They thought it was hilarious to watch me guzzling cup after cup of the stuff, so either I was doing something particularly amusing, or the yellow stuff was very cheap and/or horrible. Or perhaps the vat had already been emptied of booze, and they'd been using it as a toilet?

It had taken Roo a long while to extricate me from the bar and lead me home. Then, in the middle of the night, she'd woken up to find me building a sculpture of some sort on the floor, out of towels. There had been a foul stink, which she'd quickly identified as coming from me.

"Have you been sick?" she yawned.

"Indeed!" I replied. "But do not fear! The vomit is contained by these towels! The situation is entirely under control!"

I like to think she found this endearing.

But she sat me in the shower and hosed me down before she'd let me come back to bed.

Nha Trang was a very forgiving place. The toughest thing I had to do the following day was lay on a beach, and stroll around town looking for somewhere to eat. There were dozens of possibilities, but all the posh restaurants had their menu displayed in two languages: Vietnamese, and Russian. From this, we concluded that a lot of Russians came here, at least compared with the number of English-speaking tourists. There were other strange indicators; caviar featured on almost every menu, and vodka was available in every grocery store. But possibly the weirdest evidence of Russian influence were the fur shops; legions of the things, as though anyone in their right minds would come to a subtropical beach resort and want to buy a fur coat as a souvenir?

Regardless, our search for a potential dinner venue went well.

We'd enjoyed sampling all the different Asian cuisines – when in Rome, as the saying goes (though I have to admit that, had I been in Rome, I'd have been stuffing my face with pizzas the size of dustbin lids). But recently we'd been starting to crave some comfort food; a little bit of something familiar, to remind us of home. Believe it or not, rice and noodles start to seem bland when you eat them three times a day for over a month.

So the sight of an English Café, right by where the night bus had dropped us off, set a little bubble of excitement rising through our day. We could hardly wait for dinner – and real, *Western* food!

Roo had been lusting after pie for weeks. Don't ask – it's an Australian thing. Sometimes, as we lay awake and sweating in some dingy hostel bedroom, I'd ask Roo what she was thinking about. "Pie," was almost always the answer.

And now, with pie on the menu and a full day of fantasising about it, we prepared to drown our sorrows in the taste of rich gravy and – in my case – baked beans! A full English breakfast was what I'd been craving, so that is what I was going to eat.

Or so I thought.

When the food arrived, my face fell a bit. In place of bacon, there was a sliver of sandwich ham; in place of sausages, there was a single bright red frankfurter. The fried egg was present, as were the beans – about eight of them, in a tiny pot designed for serving ketchup.

And it was cold.

All of it.

I was a little disappointed to be honest, but if I felt the urge to bitch about it, I'd have to get in line. Because Roo was devastated.

"Pie...?" she asked, forlornly. "This is my... pie?"

Poor girl.

What sat in front of her was about as far removed from a pie as it was from a badger playing the trumpet.

A ceramic cereal bowl had been half-filled with pieces of rubbery, boiled chicken. Several slices of raw mushroom also decorated the interior of the bowl, but that was it – no pastry, no sauce – nothing. It was a bowl of steamed chicken.

For a lid, they had beaten a slice of bread so flat it became rigid, and then cut it into a rough circle. This was presumably in lieu of the crust, which any confirmed pie eater knows is pointless and dispensable anyway. I mean, one way to look at it was like modernist architecture; they had distilled the essence of a pie down to its simplest, most minimal form. They'd removed all that fattening pastry, and done away with that calorie-laden, gravy-filled interior. Perhaps they'd succeeded in creating the world's first genuinely healthy pie?

They'd also succeeded in reducing Roo to tears.

"All I wanted was a pie," she moaned, as I moved around to comfort her. My breakfast, as uneaten as it was Full English, remained where it was.

"Come on," I said to Roo, "let's go and get an ice cream."

On our day of departure, a power cut rounded out our good luck in Nha Trang. The Nice Hotel's lift stopped working, which allowed me to get a bit of exercise, and afforded me the opportunity to make possibly the world's most boring video. I thought it would be a great idea to film myself climbing all eighteen flights of stairs from the lobby to our room – just to prove how stupidly far it was. You'll be happy to know I resisted the urge to keep the camera rolling for the trip back down. I blame the limitations of the technology at our disposal for the video's shortcomings; on reviewing the footage, it seemed to consist mostly of the view up my left nostril, set against a background blur of passing steps.

"Ideas like this," Roo explained to me, "are why you're not allowed near the cameras."

"Do you want me to try it again?" I offered.

She just rolled her eyes.

We never posted this video on our blog.

Somehow, I doubt it would have gone viral.

Market Forces

The night bus from Nha Trang dropped us off in *Ho Chi Minh City*, formerly *Saigon*, at 6am.

A week of relaxing on the beach left us feeling a bit guilty, as though we'd been squandering the opportunities presented to us. I mean, travel is all about absorbing cultural experiences, right? Just... sometimes that seems a lot like hard work. But now the holiday was over, we had no excuse – so we booked ourselves onto a tour of the world-famous floating markets, leaving at 7am.

That we hadn't slept since Nha Trang may have been partially to blame for this decision.

With an hour to kill, we stumbled a few doors up the street and into the *Gon* café – which was quite lucky, as it turned out to be the best place we ate in Vietnam. I can't even remember what I ordered – eggplant stuffed with something cheesy, according to Roo. It was amazing, and less than half the price of the cheapest meal I'd bought in Hanoi.

Then we boarded the minibus for the trip, and spent the next two hours sitting in traffic as the driver screeched, honked and cursed his way out of the city.

In fairness, we both felt like crap, so we probably weren't

in the best mood to appreciate the trip. But the floating markets were high on Roo's list of priorities, and I was determined to make the most of it. And anyway, we couldn't check into our hotel until midday – taking an excursion had seemed more productive than spending five hours in the nearest bar.

Staring out of the bus windows at the ceaseless flock of scooters swerving every which way around us, I felt compelled to ask the tour guide about it.

"No-one follows any of the normal road rules," I pointed out, "they just go wherever they want."

"Yes," he said, "big problem. Ten years ago, no scooters. No cars! No traffic at all. Now, Saigon have 6 million persons, population. And have 9 million motorbikes!"

"But isn't there some kind of driving test?"

"Of course," he said, "but it's not compulsory."

When we reached the mighty *Mekong* river, we transferred to a motorised narrow boat with wooden benches and a canvas roof. As we motored out past a strip of shanty shacks built on stilts, the guide laid out the bad news he'd been saving for us.

What they don't really mention in the brochure is that the Floating Markets only sell fruit and vegetables. This being the case, they are also seasonal – and this was not the season. What bit of trade did go on at this time of year was conducted very early in the morning – even before we'd boarded the bus back in Saigon, so we had no chance of seeing it. And we wouldn't have been allowed to buy anything anyway, because the Floating Markets were wholesale only.

I'm paraphrasing here, but what he basically said was, the floating market is crap at the best of times – and these are not those times.

Roo was seriously unimpressed.

The boat laboured up and down a filthy stretch of river, past the sunken remains of a giant fishing trawler. Our poorly-timed visit did show us a different side of the market; a handful of the decrepit trading barges were anchored close to the water's edge, allowing us to scrutinise them as we passed. They were all large, open-topped boats, laden with mountains of produce hidden under tarps. A single piece of fruit hanging from each bow confirmed what she was hauling, and the only bit of the boat not piled high with goods was the living quarters; a Portaloo-sized square hut at the stern, in which the owner lived, cooked, and ate. And watched TV, judging by the battered satellite dishes tacked onto some of the cabin roofs. An open-air hammock provided the only sleeping arrangements, and one trader was demonstrating his washing facilities as we passed – squatting on a shelf at the back of the boat and pouring buckets of river water over himself.

I didn't want to think about where he went to the toilet.

But I stopped dragging my hand in the water right away.

The 'Floating Market Visit' was followed by series of thinly-disguised sales pitches, as we were taken to a variety of workshops lining the banks of the Mekong. First up was a family of beekeepers, displaying their honey and honeycomb-based wares.

Their prize product was undoubtedly their Royal Jelly. According to leaflets they distributed, it had a truly impressive range of qualities. Obviously it was good for skin, and helped prevent wrinkles, but I was surprised to find it could actually slow down aging. Even more surprising was the fact that it 'reinforced vision and had good eyesight'. And if that didn't persuade you to buy a pot, it could also restore sexual ability and desire to both genders, was a cure for hepatitis A, B, C *and* D – and sterility – and the menopause.

Oh, and it was also a tranquilizer.

So, pretty much an all-rounder.

We got to watch traditional sweets being made (buy our sweets!), and wooden spoons being carved (buy our spoons!), and got to handle an enormous python at a place where they were selling – wait for it – pickled pythons. In bottles. No, *seriously!*

Finally, we were ditched at a real market somewhere inland, and left to our own devices. Jeez, our tour guide really had his work cut out today! We marvelled at the variety of rice on offer (over 20 kinds on one stall), and scratched our heads at the stalls selling scarves. Their stock was piled a metre deep, tens or even hundreds of thousands of carefully folded lengths of silk. And the next stall held exactly the same thing. As did the next one. Whoever their customers were, they must have had a powerful need for scarves. Shit, they must have wanted to wrap their whole bodies in them. And their houses.

As tours go, it wasn't the most successful; basically a traffic jam followed by an extended infomercial followed by a traffic jam. We arrived back in Ho Chi Minh City (hereafter referred to as HCMC), reclaimed our luggage, checked into our hotel, and collapsed.

But not for long.

Vicky was arriving that afternoon, so we scrubbed the Mekong off our skin and jumped in a taxi to the airport.

It wasn't until we were in the taxi to the airport that we realised we couldn't pay for it. We'd spent the last of our cash on sweets, scarves and wooden spoons, and were in dire need of an ATM. We tried to explain this to the taxi driver, and he grudgingly agreed to let us pay on the return trip. As soon as we arrived I went on a scouting mission, while Roo waited by the Arrivals door for Vicky.

It didn't take me long. I came back grinning.

"Guess what! Not only did I find the ATMs, I found one you'll recognise!"

I took Roo's hand and led her along the concourse, taking a left turn around the edge of the terminal building. There were two cash machines, nestled together in a niche opposite a row of bins.

"Look, see!" I pointed out the Commonwealth Bank of Australia logo above one of the machines.

"Well done, love." Roo had the grace not to sound patronising.

She took out the bank card – our one and only bank card, that precious, fragile lifeline on which our entire world hung suspended – and passed it to me.

I inserted it into the ATM.

The instructions were in English, so I keyed in Roo's PIN, followed by a sensible amount of cash to withdraw – *one million dongs,* or something equally ridiculous.

And then I saw something that I have never seen before in my life.

And something that, God willing, I hope never to see again.

'Shutting Down...' said the screen on the ATM.

"Wha? B—?"

In shock, my mind takes note of the strangest things. Right now it was fascinated to discover that this cash machine was running Windows XP. I recognised the swirly graphics on the shutdown screen from my sister's first laptop.

And then the screen went black.

Roo had been watching over my shoulder (in case I did something wrong), and we exchanged incredulous glances.

"Did that just...?" she asked.

"It did! It's got the card. It's... IT'S GOT OUR FUCKING CARD!"

'OFF LINE' flashed the ATM, in green on an otherwise blank screen.

"Oh dear," said Roo.

"Oh DEAR?"

"Shh! Look, it's booting up again."

And we watched as Windows XP ran through its loading screens, scrolling lists of programs to open and finally coming to rest on the familiar green graphics of an ATM open for business.

A chilling message was flashing on the screen.

'INSERT CARD,' it read.

But there was no sign of the card.

No sign of our money.

No record of the transaction.

"Oh my God," I said to Roo, "I think we're screwed."

"Yes," she agreed, "I think you're right."

There was a contact phone number printed on the side of the console, so in desperation I dialled it. Against all my suspicions, the lady who answered switched to English as soon as I started babbling. She very calmly explained the situation, that this sort of thing was not unheard of, and that I had no need to worry. A maintenance guy would be around at some point over the weekend, and he would bring any trapped cards to the bank, from where I would be able to claim it back. On Monday, because that was the next time they were open.

Today was Friday.

"Must be fate," I said to Roo, as we sat on the floor outside the Arrivals building, our backs against a giant column supporting the roof. "If we were leaving here on Sunday evening instead of Monday evening, we'd be utterly buggered."

"Yes, it's pretty lucky…"

That's one of the things I love most about Roo. She's relentlessly positive. Not many people would consider the sequence of events we'd just been through as lucky.

"What the hell are we going to do if this happens again?" she asked.

"What the hell are we going to do this weekend?" I countered – just as the glass doors slid open, and a nervous looking Vicky pushed her trolley out into the sunlight.

Taller than Roo and even slimmer, Vicky is the youngest of Roo's three sisters. A proud 'ranga', she has the classic complexion of a redhead – alabaster skin and shoulder-length curly locks. I have it on good authority that when she was about five, she bore a striking resemblance to the orphan Annie.

"There you are!" Roo leapt to her feet and grabbed her sister in a hug, while I stabilised the rickety trolley.

"Sorry I'm so late," Vicky started, "the first plane was delayed, and then the queue for visas was insane. They kept my passport for so long, I didn't think they were going to accept that dodgy letter…"

"Never mind," said Roo, hugging her again. "You're here now, safe and sound. We'll look after you!"

"Yes, of course we will!" I agreed. "Welcome to Vietnam!" I paused for a second, to let that sink in. Then added, "Have you got any money we can borrow?"

It was a nerve-wracking moment, watching Vicky insert her

bank card. She hadn't bothered to bring any *dong*, quite rightly figuring that the airport would have cash machines – and quite wrongly assuming that we'd have a bit of cash to tide her over if it didn't.

We led her around the corner whilst telling the story of our misfortune, before pointing her towards the *other* ATM.

"Will this one swallow my card then?" she asked. Understandably a bit nervous.

"I really, *really* hope not," I said.

It wasn't the answer she wanted to hear.

"What happens if it does?" She was sounding less sure by the second.

"Ah, well... that's a good question."

"We're fucked," Roo supplied, helpfully.

"Oh crap," said Vicky. And she pushed the card into the slot.

Later, back at the hotel, we laughed about the whole ridiculous situation. Now that Vicky was here, and she was safe, and she had enough cash to feed us all over the weekend, things didn't seem as threatening. It was just another minor inconvenience along the road, of the kind that somehow always seem to happen to me.

"Sorry," I said to Vicky, as we sat in the *Gon* café waiting for our dinner, "but you'll have to get used to this when you're travelling with us. Stuff tends to go wrong when I'm around. I don't know why."

"It'll be fine," she said, still riding the wave of enthusiasm from having successfully made the thousand-mile trip to a new and exotic country. "What else can go wrong?"

I thought about suggesting she not tempt Fate, but the moment passed; then our food arrived, and all we wanted to talk about was how delicious it tasted.

It was only much later that I looked back on this first act of defiance, this callous disregard for potential disaster, this challenge to whatever powers govern Fate, and realised; it was all her fault.

Tunnelling Out

Our first excursion all together was every bit as good as the Floating Markets had been crap.

We'd read about the Cu Chi tunnels back when we were planning this trip, and all agreed we had to visit. A hand-dug warren of tiny tunnels and hidey-holes, they had been used by the Viet Cong to counter the superior technology of the US ground troops. You can't really go to Vietnam without finding out *something* about the Vietnam War, so this, plus a trip to HCMC's War Remnant Museum, would fulfil that obligation.

It was a popular trip; the minibus was full of backpackers. We faced the usual gridlock, but had come prepared this time – Vicky and Roo watched shows on her tablet while I read *Lonely Planet* on my Kindle.

Beyond the city, the countryside glowed a vibrant green. Lone farmers in conical hats worked infinite rice paddies, slogging through ankle-deep water like their ancestors had for hundreds of years.

It was a beautiful day with clear blue skies; or, damn hot and ridiculously humid, as we discovered on leaving the air-conditioned confines of the minibus. We were now in the jungle near Cu Chi village, where some of the most vicious fighting of the Vietnam War had taken place.

Our group was led straight into a thatched shack, where rows of plastic chairs awaited. We filed in and took our seats – and were treated to the most hilariously awful propaganda video ever made.

I mean, it was mind-bogglingly bad.

In a world of ultra high-definition, they were using a 1980s TV set to show a video from the 1960s. And I'm not just referring to the footage – I mean the actual video cassette was from the 1960s! The black and white film was so grainy and blurred with age that it was hard to make out what was happening on the screen. Fortunately, an audio commentary kicked in after the strident screech of Soviet intro music. A female voice kept pace with the action in halting, monotone Chinglish...

And it was superb.

"*Ban Yi* is only fourteen years old, cute and gentle of the fields, but she has killed many American soldiers. Sometime she use rifles, sometime she use grenades. After her first battle, *Ban Yi* was awarded the title 'American Killer Hero'."

It was very nearly too much. I was trying really hard not to laugh, and I wasn't being entirely successful. I had a horrible feeling that the Cu Chi staff took this kind of thing seriously, and wouldn't appreciate me collapsing in hysterics at the death-struggles of their ancestors.

We listened on, spellbound both by the audacity of the propaganda and by the unbelievable crappiness of the video. We heard how brave the Cu Chi people were, following their fathers' teachings: a rifle in one hand and a plough in the other. We heard how otherwise peaceful villages had been "completely destroyed by the bombs and bullets of Washington DC" – and we heard the tale of several more individuals who received the award 'American Killer Hero'.

But what the tape had to say about those American soldiers was priceless.

"Like a crazy batch of devils, they fired into woman and children. They fired into schools and Buddha statues, into pots and pans, and roadside chickens."

Roo let out a peal of laughter, quickly stifled.

"They fired into...?"

"Roadside chickens!" I confirmed.

"And pots and pans, too," Vicky whispered, "the brutes!"

Sadly, none of the chickens rose to become American Killer Heroes as a result of their ordeal. At least, none that we know of.

Revenge, unlike chicken, is a dish best served cold.

After the video, the tour got serious. We had a lecture about the ingenious three-level tunnels constructed by the peasant farmers, with scores of cunningly concealed entrances, mile-long air vents that carried smoke from underground cooking fires far away, and deadly traps for defence. The tunnels were so small that the US troops couldn't physically fit into them, and so extensive that they proved impossible to map. One US base was even built directly over part of the tunnel system! The GIs had no idea why they were getting shot at in their tents at night, and never figured out that enemy fighters were living only a few metres beneath their feet.

We were directed to a hidden tunnel entrance, utterly invisible to our untrained eyes. A few leaves were brushed back and a tiny plug of wood the size of a piece of A4 paper was removed, revealing a hole only a child would be able to climb through. One of the guides leapt in, pulling the hole shut after himself, and once again it disappeared completely. It was a terrifying thought, that you could walk right past dozens, or even hundreds of these escape hatches without ever knowing it. And any one, or all of them, could conceal a skinny Vietnamese youth with a Chinese-made AK47.

The traps the Cu Chi fighters set in their villages and on paths were horrific. Pit traps with bamboo spikes, bladed weights swinging down to impale anyone who opened certain hut doors – it was easy to see why fighting against them would be so demoralising. The traps were meant to maim, rather than kill, a tactic common in guerrilla warfare. Troops move at the speed of their slowest man, so chop the legs off a few of them and the whole group slows to a crawl – giving their attackers plenty of time to pick the rest of them off.

Next, we were offered a chance to go down into one of the

remaining tunnels. Now, I love this sort of thing, but it wasn't for everyone – over half the group got as far as the entrance before developing a sudden case of claustrophobia.

We went in. The tunnel was about waist height on me, so I was bent double, following the ass in front.

It wasn't a bad ass, really, belonging as it did to a slender Swedish chick in short shorts. I mean, if you're going to squeeze through a tiny, barely-lit tunnel, there are worse things to be forced to look at.

Unbeknownst to me, Vicky had discovered a much better form of locomotion; crouched down, she was frog-bopping along behind me. Roo giggled at her, and it distracted me just enough that I didn't notice the ass in front of me had stopped moving. Consequently, I face-planted right into it.

Which was awkward.

Being inside the tunnel was at once creepy and exciting. I loved it, and begged our tour guide to ask if there were any more sections I could try. At first the answer was no, but the staff must have liked my enthusiasm. One grabbed my hand and led me off to another part of the system, one that wasn't open to the public because it was considered unsafe; even smaller than the last one, sloping downwards and completely unlit. I crawled in, thrilled, and two other lads followed me. There were bits where I had to twist my shoulders sideways to get through, and the bare earth walls seemed to invite collapse at any moment; it was, hands down, my favourite part of the trip.

Finally, after posing for photos with a tank, we were given the chance to fire a variety of Vietnam War-era machine guns. All three of us opted not to, based solely on the fact that the bullets cost $1.50 each. The M-16 rifles on offer could chew through up to 950 rounds per minute on fully automatic – that's over 15 shots per second! Plenty of the other tourists had a go, though, while we stood drinking cans of Coke. It was deafening.

RAT-A-TAT-ATAT!

There goes twenty dollars, I thought.

RAT-A-TAT-ATAT-ATAT-TAT!

And another thirty-five. I had to wonder if any of the

participants were good at mental arithmetic.

CRACK-CRACK CHAGUNG!

Holy crap! If that's the heavy machine gun, someone's blown a hundred bucks right there...

No-one threw any grenades.

Quite cleverly, the staff only accepted credit cards for this activity, and all prices were listed solely in Vietnamese Dong. Perhaps it was some small measure of revenge on the Western world, that half our tour group would be getting home to credit card bills scarier than any Viet Cong hidey-hole.

The following day we moved hotels, finding a much cheaper place to stay in the heart of HCMC's backpacker district. A veritable labyrinth of alleyways crisscrossed the area, all bursting with life and commerce. We spent most of the day exploring, browsing the open-fronted shops that dominated the alleys, and stopping for crazily cheap snacks and drinks at the cafés in between.

The day after that, we finally reclaimed Roo's bank card.

It was far less hassle than I'd anticipated, and we did a good job of navigating our way around the city proper. The hassle came from a group of local teenagers, though it was good-natured; one girl, dressed in a floor-length white satin robe, shyly asked Vicky if she could have a photo taken with her. Vicky didn't know quite what to say, so she nodded – and before long both she and Roo were posing with an entire college class, while their mates took it in turns to take pictures from every angle. It took half an hour for them all to get the shots they wanted, and it left us bemused. Surely they'd seen plenty of Caucasian chicks before? They'd been fascinated by the girls' height, their pale skin and their colourful hair – Vicky's being a rich, vibrant red, and Roo's being pretty much every other colour.

No-one wanted to have their photo taken with me.

But there were stranger things than Roo's hair going on in Ho Chi Minh City.

We found an impressive French cathedral, rising like an

atoll from a sea of speeding vehicles. Getting over to it seemed impossible, so we contented ourselves with the view from afar – but this wasn't good enough for the wedding parties, several of which we noticed dotted around the building. They were all determined to take their wedding photos, despite the fact that the cathedral had three lanes of traffic blasting around it at high velocity. It was madness. Each group hovered near one of the useless pedestrian crossings, and whenever there was a slight gap in the traffic the bride would leg it out into the road, fluff up her dress and beam at the camera for three or four shots before scooting back to safety.

Later that day we paid our visit to the War Remnant Museum. This was another experience I'll not quickly forget; on the one hand there were displays so tragic they moved me to tears, and so shocking I couldn't get them out of my head. Like a glass case of aborted foetuses, each showing signs of mutation caused by notorious chemical defoliant Agent Orange. On the other hand, the whole place was drowning in over-the-top propaganda so ridiculously biased it would have been funny, were it not being used to indoctrinate every generation born since 1975.

'The American War Of Terror In Vietnam', they called it.

Now, I'm no historian, but I feel that is distorting the truth just a tad.

Here's my super-brief recap on the Vietnam War:

Once there were two countries; North Vietnam and South Vietnam.

North Vietnam was communist, and so had allies in Russia and China; South Vietnam was a Republic supported by the US.

When the North Vietnamese invaded the South, the US stepped in with weapons and supplies, leading eventually to almost half a million troops on the ground. China and Russia trained and equipped the Communist forces of the North, and the unfamiliar territory and vicious guerrilla tactics of the Viet Cong wreaked havoc with the American war machine. The death toll started to mount, and the American people pressurised their government to pull its troops out. In

1973 it did, signing a series of peace agreements with the North Vietnamese, none of which were subsequently honoured. In 1975 the North Vietnamese army took Saigon, winning the war and conquering South Vietnam completely.

At which point there officially ceased to be two warring countries, each supported by their own allies; instead there was only one Vietnam, an oppressive, Soviet-backed Communist regime. America was repainted as the enemy of the entire nation, as though it had decided to rain destruction on all of Vietnam purely for the hell of it.

And that is the legacy we read about in the halls of the War Remnant Museum.

Not an accurate, historical recounting of the deeds of both sides, but rather a shameless tirade against the evil and merciless attacks by America.

It was a shock to read, as it seemed so childishly one-sided, so unsubtle and amateurish in its blatant perversion of the truth.

And yet…

We never really had the chance to befriend any locals in Saigon, so I never got to find out what they believe. Whether they all swallow the party line, or whether there is a widespread understanding that the 'history' they're taught contains a substantial dose of BS. If the former is true, it would be a terrifying testament to the power of propaganda. They do say that history is written by the victor, but never before have I come across such a potent example of this.

Everywhere we went in Vietnam, we were asked if we were American.

To which we replied, "No, we're Australian!" And were rewarded with smiles, and "Ahhh, Corocodire Dundee! G'day mate!"

I got the feeling we'd have received a very different reaction if we'd replied, "Yes."

Crazytown

We left HCMC the next day, following our pre-planned route north to *Da Lat*.

The clock was now ticking on our time in Vietnam; we had a week to get back to Hanoi, from where we'd booked a two-day boat tour of Ha Long Bay.

After that, we'd be leaving the country for Mongolia...

No matter how many times I said it, I still couldn't get used to the idea.

The flight to Da Lat was the shortest I've ever experienced. There was barely time to unfasten our seat belts before we were descending again, this time into the central highlands of Vietnam. Blanketed in temperate pine forest and wreathed in fog, it was reputed to be much cooler than the more low-lying areas of the (east) coast and (southern) jungles. Da Lat had an architecture all of its own, replacing the slender, high-rise stack-of-boxes look with a scattering of French-style villas. Having started life as a resort, the town had a tranquillity that differed completely from the chaos of Hanoi and HCMC.

The airport shuttle bus took us on a round trip of every hotel in Da Lat, dropping a few people off at each one. As the number of passengers dwindled it became apparent that we'd picked the furthest-out, most seldom-visited hotel. By the time we reached it, the bus driver squeezing down a series of tight alleyways, we were starting to get a little nervous. But the hotel was fine – clean and quiet, the manager attentive – hardly surprising, given we were the only people staying there.

The next morning, we went our separate ways. With only one full day in Da Lat, Vicky and Roo had opted to see as much of the place as possible, booking themselves onto an extensive sightseeing tour of the surrounding area.

Whereas I'd said bollocks to that, and decided to spend the day canyoning.

Canyoning is all about getting down a river canyon from top to bottom, by climbing, abseiling and jumping off waterfalls. It's a rapidly growing sport (there's a joke in there, if you know where to look), but it's still not available in many places because you need a canyon to do it in.

Da Lat was blessed with just such a place, and I'd been looking forward to having a crack at it ever since we'd put Da Lat on the itinerary.

I think canyoning is classed as an adventure sport – probably an extreme sport if you ask your travel insurance company. Of course, I hadn't bothered buying travel insurance, which is one of the reasons I could afford to do things like canyoning.

Sometimes you can gauge how hardcore an activity is going to be by the other people in your group. For example, the first time I'd done canyoning, in New Zealand, I'd taken my Mum. So I introduced myself to the two guys already in the minibus, and found out they were a pair of Israeli blokes who had just completed their stint in the army. Next we picked up a couple of professional climbers who ran a gear shop… and that was it.

No convenient octogenarians to hide behind.

It was shaping up to be a tough trip.

The first stage was getting life jackets and harnesses on, after which we were offered a brief instruction in abseiling.

"Have you abseiled before?" the guides asked.

"Uh, yeah, I've done a bit," I said. Which was exactly what I had done – *a bit*.

The climbers didn't feel the need to practice, because they were climbers. And the Israeli guys declined as well.

"Did loads of that in Parachute Training," one explained.

I didn't want to be the squeaky wheel, so it was decided that no practice was necessary.

Which meant our first abseil, sixteen metres down a 'dry' cliff, was rather nerve-wracking. Luckily it all came back to me, because the next abseil was a doozy – twenty-five metres down the middle of a waterfall. I went first; by now adrenaline was pumping through me, spurring me on into the river. The pressure of the water was intense, as it crashed into me at waist-height. Once over the edge, the torrent engulfed me, making it hard to breathe without getting a mouthful. It was like ice-skating upside-down; the rock was so slippery, and the force of the water so great, I spent a fair bit of time abseiling on my arse.

A few metres off the bottom we'd been instructed to kick away from the cliff, let go of the rope, and drop into a pool at the base of the waterfall. It all happened so fast, I didn't realise that our second guide was perched on a rock halfway down, using hand signals to tell us when to jump. No matter – I landed in the right place, plunged a good way underwater, and came up yelling in triumph. There are few feelings like this; the exhilaration that comes from conquering a perfectly sensible fear, the rush of excitement, and the sudden irrational desire to do it all over again.

Next we slid down rapids – some feet first, some head first – and then we came to the cliff jumps.

Now, I've always wanted to do this, but it's surprisingly hard to achieve. Anywhere remotely suitable in the UK would be barricaded off, plastered with warning signs and threats of big fines. Likewise, it's a rare tour operator that includes jumping off cliffs in their itinerary. I mean, it's perfectly safe, if done right…

Tell you what though, standing at the top of a twenty-metre cliff, looking a long way down into the water below, it did seem perhaps *a tad* dangerous. There were all these intervening protrusions one could so easily bounce off, or catch a foot on...

It was almost enough to stop me doing it.

But then, after both the Israeli guys had charged over the edge and emerged from the pool howling with delight, the male half of the climbing couple asked the guides if he'd be okay to try a somersault. They shrugged, so he went for it – a short run-up, a huge leap, and one and a half rotations on the way down. Which unfortunately meant that he hit the water flat-on, in possibly the biggest belly-flop the world has ever seen.

It was an agonizing wait for him to surface, and when he did his face was streaming with blood. His life jacket dangled open – we later discovered that the force of his impact had shattered all three quick-release toggles, as well as splitting his nose and lip.

For me, still at the top, it was a call to man up. This dude had tried something so crazily dangerous that I had to admire him – even though he'd ballsed it up royally.

So I retreated a few paces from the cliff edge and screamed my war cry (which probably didn't sound nearly as manly as it did in my head).

And I jumped.

The sensation as my feet left the edge was like someone reaching a hand into me and squeezing their fist around my stomach. The microseconds of free fall lasted long enough for me to notice my entire body had pins and needles. It wasn't my life that flashed before my eyes, it was my death; half a dozen grizzly images of my soft body contacting the surrounding rock with extreme violence.

And then I hit the water, feet together to protect my delicate bits, and carried on going right down to the bottom. I kicked off towards the surface, rising for what seemed like an age, then burst out of the water and screamed again.

It was an incredibly beautiful part of the world, but not a good place to live if screaming bothers you.

I arrived back at the hotel only moments before Roo and Vicky.

They'd enjoyed their trip too, though it sounded rather

sedate to me.

They'd been all over the city, visiting 'Love Valley', which turned out to be a park with weird, concrete animal statues that they'd sat on and burnt their bums. Lesson learned; concrete gets hot in full sunlight, even in the highlands. They hadn't been impressed by a bizarre cowboy show, or by some knackered bumper cars. They'd taken a cable-car ride up to a Buddhist temple, and sampled coffee made from beans that had passed through the digestive tract of a certain species of weasel. The beans were apparently quite difficult to get back afterwards, so they retail at around $100 per bag.

"What it taste like?" I asked Roo.

"Shit," she replied.

But then, Roo's not really a fan of coffee, so it was probably wasted on her.

Next they'd narrowly avoided being robbed by the tour bus driver, catching him red-handed rifling through all the bags that had been left on the bus! And then they'd been taken to the Crazy House, which had been so good they immediately dragged me back out and into a taxi to see it for myself.

Ah, the Crazy House! It defied any rational explanation. The closest I can get is to say, imagine if someone with absolutely zero knowledge of construction decided to recreate the set from a Disney cartoon – after taking a fistful of acid.

The result was nothing short of spectacular. Towering up to five stories in places, it was supposedly meant to look like a giant *banyan* tree. With dozens of structures connected by curving walkways, bridges, tunnels and twisting staircases, the Crazy House was a riot of colour, curves and construction debris. Mere words could never do justice to this kind of weirdness. Seriously – go right now to Google, type in 'Crazy House Da Lat', and you'll see what I mean.

We spent a good couple of hours lost in that place, exploring the web of corridors and stairways, finding several *very* unique animal-themed bedrooms, plus countless random spaces, landings, look-outs and balconies, all with curving, organic shapes and brightly-painted render.

According to the guide from Roo and Vicky's trip, when the lady who owned the place first started building in this bizarre, free-form fashion, local opposition had been fierce. Planning consent in an area of architectural distinction like Da Lat would have been impossible to obtain but for one small fact; the lady in question happened to be the daughter of the General Secretary of the Communist Party, the second-most powerful man in all Vietnam.

Which must have helped smooth things over with the neighbours, too.

After more than twenty years of continuous construction the place was still a work in progress, as I discovered when I ducked underneath a plank of wood blocking a doorway. I found myself high up in a cavernous, three-story ball-room (in the sense that, it was in the shape of a ball). Everything was rough concrete, with huge gaps in the floor and walls. A person could quite easily fall fifty feet to their death in there, which was probably why they'd gone to the extraordinary lengths of placing a plank across the entrance. Mind you, the safety standards were delightfully non-existent throughout the Crazy House. Some of the stairways looped high above the buildings for no immediately apparent reason, descending again to meet an exposed balcony with nary a bannister or balustrade in sight. My advice: if you want to go and see this place, do it now, before some toddler gets pancaked and they start making everyone wear harnesses.

It had been an exciting day, and to top it all off we decided to walk back to our hostel from the centre of town. We figured it couldn't take more than an hour, and it didn't – despite an unexpected stop en-route.

We'd been secretly hoping to find some trace of nightlife, which had so far eluded us in Vietnam. Hanoi had been home to many pavement cafés which served beer, and the occasional tiny, secluded bar. Hardly party central, and even though the traffic never slept, the eating and drinking establishments were licensed till midnight and not a second more. Beyond that, the only options for drinking were posh bars in exclusive hotels – hardly the scene we were looking for, even if we could afford it. Which we couldn't.

My one attempt at discovering the night life in HCMC had ended with a crowd of hookers chasing me through the streets of the backpacker district.

So not exactly a rip-roaring success.

Da Lat, as far as I could tell, had no large crowds of hookers.

Da Lat had no night life at all; not a shred of it.

Or so we thought.

And then, in the middle of our walk home, along quiet and otherwise empty streets, we came across a bakery.

Not just any bakery; this was a brand-new bakery. And tonight was their opening night.

Disco lights were blazing and dance tunes blared from man-sized speakers outside the front door. The management was trying hard to create a buzz, and they were succeeding. Scooters were stacked in the tiny car park; a phalanx of security guards were picking them up and moving them closer together, allowing more vehicles into the space. The shoe-box-sized bakery was rammed with customers, all enthusiastically buying bread and cakes and bread-buns, and... well, that's all they were selling, really. But man, they were selling a lot of them.

We joined the mob-scene, pushing our way through the crowd to buy cupcakes and bread rolls for breakfast. Then we left, as there was naff all else to do – bemused and bewildered, as behind us the locals arrived in droves to get a slice of the action.

You have no idea how badly Da Lat needed a TGI Friday.

Stitched Up

The next stop on our crusade north was Hoi An – forever lodged in my memory as the home of expensive trousers. Surely there was more to the place than that?
    We nearly didn't get to find out.
    The manager of our hotel in Da Lat had assured me he would be awake early in the morning to let us out.
    He wasn't. I stood pounding on the door to his room, as the airport taxi driver sat outside, unable to reach us. The problem was that, in common with most of the hotels we'd stayed at in Vietnam, this place had a heavy steel security shutter which they locked at night. Once it was shut, which could occur anytime between 9pm and midnight, no-one could get in or out until morning.
    Obviously this wasn't usually an issue, because no-one ever ventured out after dark. Why would they? Unless the disco-bakery had extended its opening hours?
    As far as I could tell, in case of fire, the evacuation strategy was to assemble in the lobby and burn to death.

We just about made the flight. It was another short one, this time to *Da Nang*. We'd found nothing interesting to do or see in Da Nang, so we did what most visitors to the city had been doing since the 1500s – buggered off straight away to Hoi An.

We took a taxi from the airport. It was parked directly under a sign which said (in English) 'FIXED PRICE TO HOI AN – 400,000 DONG' (US$20).

Predictably, our driver asked me to pay the airport tax he'd been charged, waving a receipt in my face as he accelerated down the main road. I ignored him for about ten minutes, until he finally gave up. It was irritating, but inevitable; we'd heard so much about taxi driver scams, but had dodged the bullet so far. That wasn't what was bothering me.

Doing nearly double the speed limit didn't bother me either, at least as long as we stayed on the road.

What bothered me was our driver's rather extreme form of nervous tick.

Every few seconds he'd run a hand through his hair, then flick the hand violently towards the windscreen as though trying to dislodge whatever he'd found in there. Then he'd do it again, several times in a row, culminating in a sudden, exorcist-style snapping of his neck from side to side.

If he'd been walking down the road in front of me I'd have pointed at him and laughed, saying, "Look, that guy's high as a kite!"

Being in a taxi with him driving was an entirely different experience.

We made Hoi An in record time, but our driver ignored the sign for our hotel despite all of us spotting it and pointing it out to him. He made a quick phone call in between flicks, then pulled up in the middle of the road. A scooter stopped next to us and the passenger, a Vietnamese girl, leapt off. She climbed into the back of our taxi next to Roo and Vicky, and spent the next ten minutes trying to convince them to buy her tailoring services, while the taxi did laps of Hoi An town centre. Eventually we persuaded her to give up, and we all ended up outside the Sunshine Hotel. Then I had a stand-up row with the driver when I tried to pay him the fixed-price fare.

He screamed in my face, threatened to call the police, and demanded I pay more because he had a "big car". In the end we solved the problem by carrying our luggage into the hotel. He followed us in and ranted at the receptionist for a while, but she was inclined to take our side, what with us checking into her hotel and all.

"Sorry," she said, when he was gone, "him bad taxi!"

No shit! I was starting to get that idea.

The Sunshine Hotel was a little ray of... um... luxury. It was the most expensive of the hotels we'd booked from Perth, but there hadn't been much else available in Hoi An. Now, looking down from our balcony into the pool, I could appreciate the benefits of the higher price bracket. Mostly, I was looking forward to the all-you-can-eat breakfast.

Man, I can eat a lot of breakfast.

First though, we had to see the sights of Hoi An, so shamelessly neglected the last time Roo and I passed through. *Lonely Planet* informed us that Hoi An was a town of tailors, first and foremost. Well, we'd already met one of those. It was also known for its traditional yellow buildings, lanterns, and had one monument of interest – an historical Japanese bridge called – wait for it – The Japanese Bridge.

So we set off to see that.

The bridge itself was quaint and charming, a wood-roofed structure covered in ornamental carving, standing on stone arches across a canal. It divided the town in two, as most other streets stopped at the water, and it was officially closed to vehicular traffic. Not that that stopped people on scooters using it, but no-one else seemed to care.

On the other side of the bridge, a long street showcased the local vernacular; ivy-covered walls, flaking yellow buildings and roofs covered in thousands of semi-circular tiles. Lanterns hung everywhere, trees lined the street and flowers cascaded from window boxes. It was gorgeous. Definitely a restored-for-the-tourists gimmick, but a lovely one. We passed a pleasant few hours exploring the surrounding alleys, buying even more colourful silk scarves, and visiting an art gallery – purely because it had displays upstairs, and I was fascinated to see what these buildings were like on the top floor. The answer: hot, creaky, and not tall enough for me to stand up in.

We returned that evening, and became seduced by the idea of having clothes tailor-made for us. Vicky ordered a dress, and Roo and I both bought lightweight, zip-off trekking trousers, of the kind outdoors companies sell for upwards of $200. The amusing thing is, all that stuff is made in Vietnam – only ours would be handmade individually, instead of mass produced in a sweat shop. And we were paying less than twenty bucks a pair. The staff took our measurements and told us to come back by close of business the following day to collect our garments. We were all quite excited by this, especially Roo and me. After a month of hard use, some of our travel clothes were starting to lose their appeal – along with their zippers and buttons, and in certain cases holes were developing around the testicular area. Quite why that always happens to me, I've never figured out.

*   *   *

The following afternoon we hired bicycles for a trip to the beach.

The beach was called *An Bang* – presumably named after a popular activity that went on there.

The Sunshine Hotel's rental bikes were in surprisingly good condition, and had fetching baskets on the front in case any of us wanted to smuggle ET out of the area. And they had bells, which delighted the girls.

The map provided by the hotel was rather simplistic, but there was only one straight road to the beach, and our hotel was on it. So.

Off we set.

It was a glorious ride, through glistening rice paddies where farmers pushed rusty steel contraptions designed by Leonardo Da Vinci, and water buffalo did whatever the hell it is that water buffalo do all day. Stare and chew, as far as I can tell.

The beach was an easy 2km away. We made it mostly without incident. We crossed over the main coast road, and found a little area of stalls leading down to the beach. An old woman leapt out in front of me shouting "PARKING!" – my reflexes aren't the best, so I rode straight over her. She was still clinging onto my bike, screaming, "PARKING!" at full volume when I came to a stop.

"Uh... parking?" I asked her.

Apparently they don't allow bikes on the beach.

The beach was postcard-perfect, and dozens of locals were taking full advantage, sitting around in big groups of family and friends. We mucked about for a bit, swimming, sunbathing, trying handstands, before deciding to move on to another beach marked on our map. The stream of locals arriving had become a flood, and we hoped to find *Cua Dai* beach a bit less crowded.

It was not to be.

Cua Dai was packed with people, all come to view the sunset. Maybe they were tourists from other parts of Vietnam, or perhaps they all lived locally and they did this every day? I can't say I'd blame them; sunset was spectacular, the air and sea turning shades of orange and pink, and both still deliciously warm.

But we had to go.

Mostly because we had to pick up our clothes from the tailor shop.

But also because it was getting dark, and we had no lights on our bikes.

Looking at the map, we'd ridden straight up the main road and hit An Bang beach at the 12 o'clock point. The road we'd followed to Cua Dai banana'd round to the 3 o'clock point, from where there was another long, straight road, right back into the centre of town.

Too easy, as the Aussies would say.

Too easy indeed.

We set off to cycle that banana, with no greater plan than to look for the big-ish road leading off to the right. I'm fairly sure it was the right – I have slight issues around the whole left/right thing, which makes me spectacularly unsuited to being a navigator. But this wasn't the time for that kind of revelation. We had a nice easy route to cycle... if only it would appear. Minutes passed. A lot of them.

Our first clue that we might not be exactly where we thought we were was when we passed a signpost pointing straight ahead. 'Cua Dai Beach' it read – together with the legend '23km'.

Now, something was obviously wrong here. And it had to be the sign, since we'd just spent an hour on Cua Dai beach, and it was quite a way behind us…

Or so we thought.

Of course, that could have been any old beach, it's just that there were only two marked on our map. Just as there were only two main roads…

Hm. I was starting to sense a pattern here.

Cycling another 20-odd kilometres, potentially in the wrong direction, was not really an option, so I led the girls through a car park and across a bridge, both of which belonged to a restaurant rather than being part of the road system. I figured that we had to head towards town, which was on our right, by any means necessary. We'd walked all over the centre of Hoi An, so if we travelled straight towards it we were bound to recognise something eventually.

Neither of the girls were particularly happy with this leap of logic, but if we were to get back in time to pick up our clothes, we had little choice.

We turned down lanes, riding alongside canals, past farmsteads, and occasionally stopped a passing scooter for directions. These were almost always contradictory, both to the direction we were taking, and to each other, but we pressed on as best we could in the rapidly failing light.

Full darkness found us around the same time the main road did – well, some main road, at any rate. It seemed to happen all at once; I started noticing street lights, which I considered a good sign until we'd been following them for half an hour. By then the traffic had picked up substantially, and we were suddenly cycling in between buses, trucks, monstrous four-wheel-drives, and hundreds of swerving, honking scooters.

I remembered back in Hanoi, when I'd shuddered at the thought of driving in that insane traffic. "Certain Death," I'd called it, and Roo had agreed. Now we were in it – only on push-bikes instead of scooters – with no lights, no hooters, and no bloody clue about where we were going.

It was enough to make me laugh, but I restrained myself for the girls' sake. Somehow, I don't think they were appreciating the comedy of the situation.

Vicky was powering on ahead, determined to get to her dress fitting. Vehicles whizzed all around us as we gritted our teeth and prayed for survival. Stopping wasn't an option now, not unless we wanted to get driven over by the stream of cars behind us, who were already trying their best to do just that.

The closer we got to town, the more chaotic the traffic became. Cars and bikes nipped in and out of any opening they could see, or predict, undertaking, overtaking, swerving right across in front of us to nab a gap through the opposing carriageway. Bikes came at us from all sides, even heading directly towards us on the wrong side of the road! This was common practice it seems – presumably because, for short distances, crossing and then re-crossing the stream of traffic was not worth the effort. To avoid collisions, anyone trying this trick would drive down the edge of the road – which is exactly where we were riding. The first time I looked up to see a motorbike barrelling straight towards me, I shit myself and swerved out to avoid him – just as a deafening 'MEEEEEAAARRP!' from behind me announced that a huge bus was coming around me at top speed...

It was a bit stressful, at times.

We knew we were home safe when we saw the Japanese Bridge. There was no mistaking the structure, lit up as it was by dozens of lanterns. Only... we were on the wrong side of it!? Somehow, and to this day I cannot figure out how, we had managed to circumvent the town centre, before finally entering it from the opposite side – the nine o'clock position, to use my earlier analogy. Not only should this not have been possible, it also meant we would have had to cross over the road leading to our hotel *twice* – which we were all adamant we had not done.

I blamed the map.

I never dared ask the girls who they blamed.

Anyway. From the bridge we could easily navigate back

to the tailor's shop, which was just about to close. It was 9pm – we'd been fighting our way back here for two whole hours! No wonder we felt like shit. Sweat glistened on every part of me, yet my head pounded from dehydration. Both girls' t-shirts were plastered to them, the heat, humidity and exertion proving no kinder to them.

"Not *ideal* for trying on a new dress," Vicky admitted, as we entered the shop. "But I can't believe we made it in time!"

She went straight in for her fitting, while Roo and I tried on our trousers. They were flimsy things, ill-fitting, with loose threads everywhere.

"They're too short," Roo moaned, "after all that! My skinny ankles stick out the bottom!"

Vicky re-emerged, smiling, and paid for her dress. We left the shop in mixed spirits, or so it seemed.

"Did you like it?" Roo asked Vicky, when we got outside.

"It's hideous," she replied.

"Really? What's wrong?"

"It's too short, it's too baggy, it looks cheap and it doesn't fit *at all*. It's going straight in the bin."

"Shit," said Roo, "what a waste of time. And money."

"Never mind," I said, "at least we had a nice bike ride…"

Hué Too Close

As we wound our way inexorably northwards, our next stop was Hué (pronounced 'Hu-ay'), a city that had been the capital of Vietnam for 150 years. Sadly, Hué had the living snot beaten out of it during one of the most brutal engagements of the Vietnam War, with eighty percent of the city, and ninety percent of its historical and culturally significant buildings being destroyed by aerial bombardment.

We arrived on the train from Da Nang, with high hopes of seeing the remaining 10% – but our first stop, after checking into the hotel, was for cocktails. Because that stuff is important, too.

The next morning, we began our own assault on the Citadel – the heart of Imperial Hué, and the scene of the most vicious wartime fighting. It was certainly an impressive target; two-metre-wide stone walls bounded a square two kilometres across, and they in turn were surrounded by an enormous moat. Water for the moat came via sluice gates from the Perfume River, and giant lilies floated on the surface. A middle aged Vietnamese bloke was wading around in there up to his chest – quite possibly tending the lilies, but as far as we could tell he was stealing them.

Walking around the front wall to reach the entrance took

half an hour, and the staggering amount of stone needed to build the place put me in awe. Once within the walls, the halls and pavilions were all wood, heavily carved, decorated and gilded. Another two-and-a-half kilometre-long wall enclosed the Imperial City (which wasn't a city), and within that yet more walls contained the Purple Forbidden City (which was neither purple nor a city). All this to house one family and a bunch of their servants... and you thought Bill Gates had a big house! I hear he can park 23 cars in it. Emperor Nguyễn could park *Heathrow Airport*, bitch!

We passed a pleasant morning, posing for photos, dressing up in the Emperor's golden robes and posing for more pictures. We spent most of the afternoon trying to get out of the place, as it went on forever; wooden-columned walkways, temples beyond temples, square after paved square, giant gatehouses and pagodas and yet more temples. Vicky was delighted when she spotted the international sign of the moustache incorporated extensively into the architecture – definitive evidence that the war-like Nguyễn Emperors were really a bunch of hipsters.

Overall, the Citadel looked quite dilapidated, with grass starting to dominate some of the courtyards and many of the outlying buildings still in ruins. I guess we weren't seeing the place in its best light; less than a year after we left, the Vietnamese Government initiated their Imperial City Renovation Programme – spending sixty-one *million* dollars in the process! So, you know, it might have had a lick of paint.

We finally navigated back to the entrance and begged to be let out – but no. The staff were enforcing a strict one-way policy, despite the almost non-existent influx of tourists. The only exit was through the gatehouse in the adjacent wall, ninety degrees from our current location – and about two kilometres away.

By the time we found our way out, we had nothing left to sweat. I reckoned we'd walked at least five miles, to the Citadel, around it and out again.

I was suddenly glad that only a tenth of Hué's ancient

buildings were left; bollocks to doing this nine more times!

It was 35 degrees Celsius and almost ninety-percent humidity, and we still had to walk back to the hotel. Where I felt reasonably sure it was beer o' clock.

That evening, we were joined for dinner by Tim and Charlotte. Like us, they were passing through Hué on the way to Hanoi – we'd even be on the same train, though at opposite ends according to our tickets. Wandering back through the streets behind our hotel, we noticed little bowls of incense outside every business, most burning fake banknotes. Roo asked the hotel manager about this, and he brushed it aside; some Buddhist celebration, he explained with disinterest.

We'd ordered a taxi to take us to the station, from where we'd booked an overnight sleeper train to Hanoi. We'd bought all our train tickets months earlier and posted them to the Hanoi Asia Star, where Jimmy had reluctantly turned them over to me and Roo. Understandably a bit paranoid, we asked the manager to call the taxi straight away, rather than waiting the twenty minutes we'd intended. He wasn't keen, and tried to convince us we had plenty of time, but I insisted and the taxi collected us only a few minutes later.

We loaded our luggage into the boot, and he set off – turning the corner into gridlock.

After sitting there for a while, going nowhere, the driver reversed down the road and took the next one, only to find the same thing. He edged forwards enough to find a back route he liked, but that too ground to a halt. Roo and Vicky were exchanging nervous glances in the back, while I rechecked my watch. We'd left three quarters of an hour early, for a journey I could have walked in twenty minutes. But now, as cars honked and drivers swore all around us, we started to realise we were in trouble. Time was running out.

The bridge over the *Song An Cuu* canal still separated us from the station end of town, but the driver knew our concerns, and wormed his way through the traffic to try a different tack. Eventually, after a long and agonising detour, he came to the bridge from an entirely different direction – or at least, he would have, if there hadn't been half a mile of standing traffic between us.

"What do we do?" I yelled.

"Go, go!" the driver shouted, waving us out of the car. It was a desperate tactic; I'd been trusting to Fate, gambling on him finding a last-minute way through. Consequently, we were now down to the last minute. Unless the station was right outside the car, we were screwed.

"There!" the driver pointed, straight ahead. A wall of cars screened everything else from view. Roo and Vicky were struggling to pull their luggage from the boot. I looked at my watch again; less than four minutes, and the station wasn't even in sight.

There was no chance.

"We can't make it," Roo called to me, panic in her voice.

I hate to hear panic in Roo's voice.

This time it wasn't even my fault.

There was no way I was going to let it go unanswered.

"Don't worry about anything else," I told her, "just get yourselves to the station. I'm going to stop that train."

I strapped twenty kilos of rucksack onto my back, dangled the lead weight of my daysack around my chest – and ran.

I ran like the Hounds of Hell were at my heels; like the ground was opening up beneath me; like there was a cliché I hadn't used just in front of me, and it was getting away. I pounded down the side of the road, dodging car doors and groups of bystanders. The further I got down the road, the more obvious it became that our taxi wasn't going anywhere.

As I drew nearer to the bridge, I started to get an idea of what we were up against… and then I ran straight into it.

Not the bridge, I hasten to add – into a parade.

Now, as every movie-going audience knows, parades happen all the time. If you're being chased by the FBI for a crime you didn't commit, nine times out of ten you'll run smack bang into a parade, where you'll be able to lose the pursuing agents with ease.

But in real life, I can count on the fingers of one hand the number of parades I've seen.

And this was one of them.

It was huge. Both sides of the road were thronged with onlookers, while the middle of the carriageway contained some kind of colourful religious procession. Gongs were being struck, cymbals were clashing – it's quite possible that dancers were twirling somewhere beyond my immediate field of vision, but none of that mattered, because I couldn't stop to admire the view.

I couldn't stop at all.

Coming to a halt gracefully when running full tilt with a heavy rucksack is kind of like landing a light aircraft. It takes space, and it takes time. I had neither.

What I did have was the frantic realisation that this parade represented the end of any hope I had of making the train. With only minutes to spare, and only seconds to make the choice, I went with base instinct.

Fuck it.

The girls were counting on me.

I would make that train, or I would die trying.

The line of gawkers barring my path never knew what hit them.

"MOVE!" I bawled, somewhat belatedly.

The next barrier was the parade itself, gapless, advancing, cutting me off completely from my destination.

Oh Buddha…

Scattering orange-clad monks like bowling pins, I crashed through the throng. I didn't look back to see what carnage I'd left in my wake, or how it was being dealt with. I only knew I had to get to the other side of the bridge…

And then?

"STATION!" I screamed, casting around me frantically for any sort of clue. "TRAIN!"

It was at this point I realised I was at the head of the parade, alone in the middle of the road, facing a row of armed policemen. Quite what they thought of me I don't know, but the violence of my arrival left them only two options; shoot me, or tell me where to go.

"There," called an officer, pointing off the bridge. A pair of his comrades took up the gesture, so I barrelled on, turning towards what would ordinarily have been a decent-sized street.

However.

Unlike spy films, Vietnam has relatively few parades, and her citizens were out in force to see this one. Rather ingeniously, knowing the roads would be closed, instead of bringing chairs and a picnic blanket, they'd simply driven their scooters as close as they could get to the action, then turned them off and sat on them. Facing me across the road was a wall of scooters, crammed in so close together their pedals were touching. On the far side I spied a slim gap, where people on foot were straining to catch a glimpse of the monks I'd flattened.

There was only one thing for it.

I charged towards the opening, my backpack heaving from side to side. It didn't make me a particularly agile target, and as I approached some of the people I was facing started to realised what was about to happen. They sprang back out of the way, dragging friends and relatives with them – but not everyone was quick enough.

I crashed through the gap, sending several people flying. A slow-moving old woman bounced off the front of me; my backpack absorbed the return blow of her handbag as I plunged onwards. Vietnamese went down in droves on all sides of me; I'd have made one hell of a weapon in the American War Of Aggression.

And then I burst through into empty space, like the Millennium Falcon rocketing out of the Death Star's fiery doom. I screeched to a halt and glanced around for any sign – and there it was.

The sign.

Hué Gar (station).

So close…

But time was up. My heart was hammering the countdown. I didn't even pause to wipe away the sweat, which was sheeting down my face and drenching my shirt. I turned towards the station doors and sprinted the last few metres to the turnstile.

"Calm down!" the ticket checker shouted, when I was still a few steps away.

"No, my train—" I began.

"Calm! Down!" he repeated.

Shave My Spider!

"Listen, I'm on the Hué to Hanoi, there are two more people coming for it, you have to let me in so I can hold it!"

"Sir, please, calm down," said the guard. It was clear he wasn't even going to listen to me until I'd stopped raving. But I'd been quick. Maybe there was still time.

I took a deep breath.

"I'm sorry." *Breathe.* "I have a ticket." *Breathe. Dig ticket from back pocket.* "I HAVE to be on the train to Hanoi." *Breathe. Extend ticket. Ticket is... moist.* "My wife is coming too. PLEASE let me get on that train, so I can hold it for her."

His answer was direct. "No," he said, shaking his head, "you cannot get on this train."

Shit-shit-shit! Try again.

"Please, listen to me, I HAVE to get on that train!"

"No, SIR. You CANNOT get on that train."

Faced with dwindling options, I drew myself up to my full height and advanced on the bloke. No bureaucratic box-ticking bullshit was going to wreck my plans. I was a stinking, panting, sweaty mess, and I was majorly pissed off. And I was probably wanted for GBH on half the population of Hué. The guard suddenly looked very small as he stared up at me.

"I am getting on that train," I growled.

"Sir! You cannot get on that train!"

"Why not?" I demanded.

"Because that train is not here yet. That train is late."

Getting Hanoi'd

We caught the train.

Vicky and Roo charged up, panting, a few minutes after I did.

Following my trail of carnage, they'd managed to add to the devastation themselves – even taking it to the next level.

"I hit one scooter," Vicky explained, "and it fell over onto the next one. It was in this long row, and the whole lot tipped over one after another, like dominoes!"

Wow. Epic destruction! We'd been the worst thing to hit Vietnam since napalm.

"Sorry," I said to Vicky, "I thought I'd made a big enough gap for you guys."

"You did make an impressive Tony-shaped hole," Roo admitted, "but you're forgetting one thing." She pointed to Vicky's luggage, now resting innocently in the corner of the carriage.

"Vicky brought a suitcase…"

We saw Tim and Charlotte briefly on the platform. They'd also struggled through the parade, though I think they managed it with a modicum more class and substantially less violence. The festival we'd so rudely violated turned out to be nothing special – only *Buddha's frikkin' Birthday!* I had a nasty feeling I'd accrued a smidgen of bad karma in there somewhere...

The train journey itself was mostly unremarkable. At some point in the night we were joined in our cabin by a quiet Japanese man, who kept to himself. He had with him a large polystyrene box, of the kind I once used to transport the decapitated head of a dog. I had no idea what was in the box, and it surely wasn't as bad as what had been in mine... but it leaked. When he got off, a sizeable puddle of something vaguely fishy stayed behind. But we were lucky; an English couple in the cabin next to us told an entirely different story. They'd also arrived just in time, and settled into their carriage. At which point a local lady, who was in there already, stood up – vomited copiously, over the beds and the floor – and then left.

I was rather glad we'd got the leaky box.

Arriving in Hanoi, things got weirder.

It goes without saying that we were met at the entrance to the train station by a mob of taxi drivers, shouting at us, pulling us... but we were prepared. We shoved our way through the crowd, ignoring the looks and calls and hands that came our way, and emerged on the pavement by the main road. Rumour has it there was a taxi rank here, where the honest drivers sat patiently waiting for anyone brave enough to escape that melee. We knew to look for a *Mah Linh* taxi, but I must have forgotten to impart that piece of wisdom on Tim and Charlotte – they'd plunged right into the mob-scene alongside us, and then been hustled away by the first driver to latch on to them. I could only hope that, experienced travellers as they were, they'd sense a scam coming and be ready for it.

But we had a stroke of luck; an empty green *Mah Linh* taxi was passing right at that moment. I flagged him down, and he pulled up and popped the boot.

I loaded our bags in, while Vicky climbed into the back seat.

And just then, the taxi surged forward. He must have been aiming for a spot in the taxi rank or something. I shouted "Woah!", and jogged a few steps to catch up. But the car jolted forwards again, just as I reached it.

And suddenly, I realised that something was very, very wrong.

This wasn't a simple misunderstanding.

This wasn't an accident.

This guy was trying to rob our stuff.

And he was trying to abduct Vicky.

The shock of realisation hit me like a slap in the face. I was stunned for a fraction of a second – then instinct kicked in.

My instincts are rarely the most reliable – or the most predictable. In this instance they computed the situation and came up with only one course of action – so I flung myself into the trunk, on top of our luggage, and clung to the bags as the taxi swerved out into traffic.

It was chaos.

Roo was screaming. Vicky, inside the car, was pounding on the driver's headrest. Traffic was gridlocked, as it always seemed to be, which did not make for a fast getaway. In a few steps Roo caught up with the taxi, swung open the back door that had never closed properly, and threw herself inside.

With the taxi barely moving, I stood up in the boot and began hammering on the back windscreen. I pummelled the glass with all my strength, hoping to smash it. I've no idea what this would have achieved, other than covering both Vicky and myself in broken glass, but in the heat of the moment it seemed my only option.

Oh, well, there was one other thing I could do.

"HEEEEEEEEEEELLLLLP!" I yelled, bellowing above the noise of the traffic with every cubic inch of those diver's lungs.

No-one heard me, of course.

And if they did, no-one gave a shit.

But things were moving now. Cars were moving in fact, all around us. The lights must have changed, because traffic was starting to flow – but our taxi sat stubbornly still. Not for want of trying – tyres screeched and squealed, smoke and smell rose from the burning rubber – but Roo was inside the car, and her instincts, as always were much better than mine.

Landing on the back seat, Roo had taken stock of the

situation. We were being robbed; Vicky, at least, was being abducted. We had to escape, and that meant we had to stop the car. The driver was ignoring Vicky's frantic attacks, and Roo isn't psychologically equipped for hand-to-hand combat. But she thinks on her feet, even when she isn't standing on them.

Lunging through the gap between the front seats, she'd grabbed hold of the handbrake and yanked it upwards with all her might.

Hence, the car – suddenly in motion – was suddenly not.

The driver tried to shove Roo away, and kept his foot on the gas, pedal to the metal. The tyres shrieked, the car shook, the engine howled – and we went precisely nowhere.

In the boot, I was still screaming for help, beating pointlessly on the glass. I daren't get out – no matter how much I wanted to throw myself into the taxi and sort this situation out, I couldn't risk being left behind if it took off the second I got out of the boot. So I hammered on the glass again and again, powerless to help the girls, and all the while I was bawling at the top of my voice.

And finally, someone began to take notice.

Sitting behind us, parked on the curb we'd recently vacated, was a green, canvas-covered truck.

Full of soldiers.

Several uniformed figures were milling around outside the truck, and a few of them were looking my way. So I took a chance and stood up, waving to them as emphatically as I could without falling out of the boot.

"HELP US!"

And they did.

There were shouts and gestures, and one soldier seemed to be ordering the others to come and get me. Normally this is exactly the kind of situation I try to avoid, but in this case I was so glad to see them approach that I nearly peed myself in relief. I carried on shouting and raving, trying to make it obvious that I was in trouble, rather than some madman attacking a taxi.

With rifles at the ready the soldiers surrounded the vehicle. Then their commander strode up and stood in front of the taxi, pointing a stern finger at the driver – and it was all over.

Well, mostly.

One soldier opened the far-side back door and extracted a furious Vicky; likewise, Roo climbed out of the car, visibly shaking with the stress of the ordeal. I jumped out of the boot, but kept hold of it just in case. I pulled our backpacks out and piled them on the road, while the captain of the soldiers had words with the taxi driver. Neither of them looked very happy about it.

But none of them paid us any attention after that. A few minutes later, we were back in the station car park, surrounded by a crowd of slightly-less boisterous taxi drivers. As I watched, our driver shook his head, and went to sit back in his car. Apparently satisfied, the army guys dispersed, and that appeared to be the end of it.

I couldn't believe he hadn't been arrested, or at least detained until the police could be called.

"Him bad man," one of the onlookers said to me, by way of explanation. "Him Mafia."

The other drivers around us had begun touting again, and I glanced at them in despair. The anger was draining out of me, and I realised that we were back to square one. "Taxi to the Old Town?" I asked, dejectedly, and received a flurry of ridiculous quotes in return.

These guys were all as bad, I realised – perhaps not as far as kidnaping was concerned, but none of them was going to offer us any decency. The rules of the game hadn't changed, and they were still playing 'Screw the Tourist'.

I traded glances with the girls. Honestly, I didn't know what to do.

Then there was a shout.

I looked up. The crowd parted. Our friendly neighbourhood kidnapper was out of his car, pointing at us angrily. His taxi hadn't moved an inch, in spite of his attempts to flee the scene. Traffic was flowing around it on both sides, but his car was going nowhere – smoke still lingered in the air above it, trickling from the underside. Whatever Roo had done to the car had immobilised it for good.

And the driver wasn't happy about it.

He stalked towards us, parting the crowd like Moses at the Red Sea.

He was swearing vehemently, shaking his fist, presumably demanding something from us, or threatening us...

Which was a mistake.

Fury surged back into me. Ignoring Roo's warning look, I stormed over to meet the bloke, bringing him up short between two parked cars.

"WHAT?" I bellowed. I pushed up against him in full attack mode, aggression pouring out of me.

He shouted something defiant back at me, which probably wasn't the best thing he could have done.

I slammed him back against the car behind him and pushed my face against his.

"I will fucking tear you apart!" I slapped the car roof beside him, pressing him back. Suddenly he seemed very small. The top of his head barely came up to my nose; he was skinny as a rail, and must have weighed about half what I did. But he was the enemy; he had threatened the people I cared about, in the most serious of ways, and I was coursing with adrenaline. The rational part of me held sway, keeping my body in check – but only just.

"Fucking HIT ME!" I screamed, point blank into his face, tapping my cheek. "Hit me you bastard! Start something. Right here – I'll let you fucking hit me!"

He didn't hit me.

Luckily, or I'd probably be rotting in a Vietnamese prison for manslaughter.

I haven't fought anyone for as long as I can remember, as the prospect of it terrifies me. Not because I'm afraid of getting hurt, but because I'm afraid of what I'm capable of. A decade of kung fu taught me that violence is always a last resort; that if there is any other conceivable option, I should never, ever fight anyone.

Of the four possible outcomes, three are a lose: either I get seriously hurt, or we both get seriously hurt; or I seriously hurt him, then feel terrible about it (and quite possibly go to jail). The only way to win a fight is if no-one gets hurt – in other words, there isn't a fight. So generally, I do anything I can to avoid them.

But it's not always that easy.

The taxi driver shrunk back, eyes shut, and I think he knew that if he fought me, I'd kill him. I knew it too, but I couldn't help myself; I roared at him, swore at him, unleashed as much rage as I could without actually giving in to the urge to smash his head through the car window.

I think he shit himself.

Eventually I let him go, and he slunk back to sit motionless in his inoperable car.

Both Roo and Vicky were staring at me, eyes wide in shock and probably a decent dose of fear. It was the first time, and hopefully the last, that either of them will ever see me in that state.

I swung back towards the crowd of taxi drivers, who had been watching the whole thing.

"Taxi," I said, unable to keep the menace from my tone, "I want a taxi to the Old Quarter."

None of them volunteered.

"You." I pointed at the closest driver. He was wearing a red Manchester United t-shirt. "Old Quarter. Three people." I waved at Roo and Vicky. "We pay forty-thousand dong, *only.*"

He opened his mouth as though to protest, then thought better of it. He picked up my backpack and led us off to his taxi.

He was strangely quiet, during the journey, and didn't quibble when I handed him a pair of 20,000 dong notes – the going rate for the journey, but less than a tenth of what he was used to scamming people out of.

And then we were safe, back in the lobby of the Asia Star Hotel.

Jimmy was there, his freakish teeth beaming a welcome; against all my expectations, I was genuinely pleased to see him.

Jimmy allocated us a triple room at the front of the hotel, overlooking the road. I paced up and down, still wired from the confrontation, while the girls collapsed on their beds in shock. It had been an interesting morning, that's for sure.

Then Tim called. He and Charlotte had made it safely to their hotel across town. "But we got majorly stung by the taxi driver, mate!" he said. "The meter was just spinning and spinning as we drove, I thought it was a bit crazy, and then he tried to charge us half a million dong! I told him to fuck right off, and he threatened to call the cops... it was a right mess. I haggled with him, and in the end I gave him a hundred thousand, and he buggered off. But you were right mate! What a bunch of scamming bastards. Did you have any trouble?"

I thought about this for a couple of seconds.

"Yeah mate," I told him, "a bit."

Roo had been re-thinking the experience, and had a concern she wanted to share with me. "We totally wrecked that guy's car, you know. Like, it's going to cost a fortune to get it fixed. And towed. And the other drivers all said he was mafia. They all knew him."

"Yeah, true enough."

"You don't think he'll come back for us, do you? Or... send someone else after us? We're fairly easy to spot." She toyed with a bright pink strand of hair for emphasis.

"Oh." I thought about this for a few seconds. "Nah, probably not. I mean, his car is knackered, and anyway, we never told him where we were staying. We're safe."

"Yeah..." Roo didn't sound convinced. "So long as he doesn't know the driver who just brought us here..."

I had no answer for that.

Culture Shock

We couldn't sit inside all day, waiting for the mafia to send someone to kill us.

Where's the fun in that?

A bit later we'd all calmed down, and the ordeal seemed a thing of the past.

We wouldn't need to risk a taxi again until our trip to the airport on the way out of the country, but we didn't feel like staying in our hotel room – just in case.

The Ha Long Bay cruise, which we'd been looking forward to for weeks, was set to depart the following morning. I'd even managed to convince Tim and Charlotte to join us – they'd sensed my enthusiasm for the trip, and had booked onto the exact same one themselves. It was a bit more expensive than the standard backpacker tours, but at least we knew what we were getting: safety and comfort, on the tour company's own boat.

But first, Tim and Charlotte had invited us to go and watch the Water Puppet show with them. This thousand-year-old art, originating when peasants entertained each other with puppets in the flooded rice paddies, offered us a chance at a genuinely cultural experience. Plus, it sounded far too weird

Shave My Spider!

to resist.

We filed into the theatre, and sat on benches so narrow I could rest my chin on my knees. Before us lay a shallow square pool filled with murky brown water. This was where the action would take place, and it was backed with a red velvet curtain to hide the puppeteers. The show began, with a burst of noise from the accompanying musicians. They were playing a variety of traditional Vietnamese flutes, guitars, and ornate wooden pegboards with strings they plucked like a harp. Or at least they appeared to; closer inspection revealed them to be miming, as all their string instruments had no strings! Speakers crackled and warbled with the operatic accompaniment; apparently the story would be sung at us in ear-piercing, out-of-tune, badly-recorded Vietnamese. Nevertheless, the show we'd signed up to was some kind of creation myth – and it was everything I hoped it would be.

Bizarre. Surreal. Absolutely hilarious, and utterly unintelligible.

The first puppets emerged from the water – an old man wearing speedos, playing a flute, sitting astride a water buffalo. And that was about the last thing we recognised. Suddenly, soldiers marched, dancing girls twirled, and fairies erupted from the murk with alarming regularity. At one point, what looked like rows of babies turned synchronised backflips for several minutes; even the flat screen TV, thoughtfully provided to show a running commentary in Chinglish, gave no clue as to what was happening. 'They were menaced by the evil beats,' it read.

Wha...?

There followed a fairly graphic scene in which a dragon vigorously pursued what appeared to be a peacock, before capturing it, mounting it, and giving it a damn good rogering. We were in tears of laughter, and must have come close to getting kicked out. Only the deafening cacophony of drums saved us, as the show drew to a close and the puppeteers received their applause.

Fleeing the scene, we decided to take a City Tour on an electric golf cart. This gave us a chance to look around a bit –

something not possible when walking unless you want to end up wrapped around the front wheel of a scooter. We briefly visited the posh district of Hanoi. I could tell we couldn't afford to buy anything here, because the shops had doors and windows. Stores like Gucci and Prada had outlets here, whilst only a few blocks away whole rows of shops were devoted to selling fake versions of exactly the same stuff. It brought into question the whole idea of fakes, being as how the real stuff was made here anyway – quite possibly in the same factory as the fakes.

Then the golf cart plunged back into the madness of the Old Quarter.

Tim and Charlotte hadn't been to this part of Hanoi yet, and I was eager to show them my favourite bits of Vietnamese weirdness. Masking Tape Street was one; a street where almost every shop sold nothing but sticky tape, in a bewildering array of shapes and sizes, and a handful of other packaging supplies. It was like driving through the same scene again and again, as every shop spilled out onto the pavement with hundreds of giant stacks of tape rolls, taller than a person. Who, in what universe, could ever have a need for so much tape? And if they did – perhaps a rugby team was in town, determined to cocoon their entire bodies in the stuff for a fancy dress party – how gutted would you be when they bought everything they needed from the shop next-door?

And then we turned onto the next street, where the madness continued – only this time, in string.

The main tourist drag was lined with shops selling North Face branded waterproof jackets, with oversized Gore-Tex labels dangling prominently from every lapel. They also sold backpacks, again bearing The North Face logos, ranging in size from bum-bags up to rucksacks big enough to hide a body in.

And the next shop had exactly the same products in the same range of colours, positioned the same way in a shop-front that was completely indistinguishable from the last one.

As did the next.

I'd walked this street of clones, as I actually wanted to

buy a North Face jacket. I sure as hell couldn't afford one in Australia. But in every shop I met the same response: "Is real, is genuine!" This was used to justify the prices, which bore remarkable resemblance to those back home. Try as I might, I couldn't convince them I knew the truth; they were selling fakes, and I was happy to buy a fake – but not at the price of a real one. I got the impression that the shop keepers honestly believed all tourists were stupid – like we would fall for the most ridiculously obvious of scams, as though we're a race of great white simpletons sent out into the world for them to exploit with their superior cunning and trickery. In this case, they'd slapped a North Face logo onto anything they could get their hands on, whilst adamantly denying that they weren't real.

Yet the company's official website didn't have nearly the same range of colours, or products, as these places were offering. And I know for a fact that North Face don't make pink and yellow spotted bum-bags.

We left Tim and Charlotte at the golf cart depot, and headed back to our respective hotels to pack for Ha Long Bay. We'd had an amusing afternoon, and Roo rounded it off beautifully when a young woman brought fresh towels to our room. Roo took the towels, but the lady was staring at her in something like awe. "You are very beautiful," she said.

Roo was taken by surprise, and her response was priceless. "Oh!" she said, "Thanks! You're... um... small and cute."

Oh boy did I laugh.

That evening, we introduced Vicky to the delights of walking in the Old Quarter. As always, it was a total immersion experience – if they'd shown it on one of those old-school IMAX dome-cinemas, people would be ducking and flinching and shrieking all over the place. We got to practice our road-crossing technique again, strolling casually out into the heaviest traffic and allowing the scooters to weave their way around us. There were plenty of zebra-striped pedestrian crossings scattered around, but they were just prettily-decorated bits of road with no significance at all.

Likewise, there were traffic lights, but as far as the vehicles were concerned they only had two phases: 'Go', and 'Oh fuck it, go anyway!'

We were looking for a nice restaurant, and the choice was made for us when I spotted a place that had frog on the menu – no less than three different frog-based dishes!

Settling on fried frog, I took pity on Vicky and convinced her to try Bun Cha. This was a traditional Vietnamese dish which I'd eaten at the Handspan Café, on our first visit to Hanoi. Little patties of pork on a bed of white rice noodles, served with a sweet and sour broth for dipping – it was absolutely delicious, and hands down the tastiest thing I ate in Vietnam. Roo ordered the same, and when it came, both girls devoured it.

But I had ordered frog, and I was in for a treat.

Once, back in England, whilst playing tug-of-war with my dog, I got a bit too enthusiastic and ended up with half a rubber frog in my mouth. I didn't really take the opportunity to savour the taste at the time, but what I remember of it (apart from the second-hand slobber) was that it tasted like nothing at all; just bland rubber. I'm not quite sure what I expected, but there you go.

And now I know that real frog tastes exactly the same.

The consistency was the same, too; rubbery. And judging by the amount of meat on those bones, I'm guessing the nutritional value was also quite similar. The fact that it had bones at all was quite a surprise. I'm not sure what I thought a frog was made of – solid jelly, perhaps – but it turns out that they are built like most creatures; out of slender bones and joints. Which comprised the lion's share of my meal. Because they were tiny, I'd been given five of them; I had a think about this, and decided I would prefer to eat five small frogs than one very large frog. Somehow, that would seem... froggier. Their skin was still on, of course; make no mistake, this was the whole-frog experience. On the upside, they were coated with deep-fried batter and garlic butter. Which was very nice indeed, even if it did make the frogs themselves rather slippery. It made for a fairly interactive dining experience. I treated it like a puzzle; how to get the maximum amount of meat with the minimum amount of mess sprayed over nearby diners. Not all of them had ordered frog you see, in fact none of them had. I didn't think they'd be too pleased if they got some anyway. Especially not if they were wearing it.

Vicky, amused and repulsed in equal measure, started filming my efforts – just as I cracked a leg, firing a piece of frog directly down Roo's cleavage.

"Aaaaaaah!" she shrieked, "I've got frog in my boobies!"

"Don't worry love," I said, diving to her aid, "I'll get it out!"

"You will *not*," she replied.

*   *   *

I'd say we slept well, but it would be a lie.

Worried that nervousness about the upcoming boat trip would keep us awake, instead our roller coaster of a day had left us exhausted.

But we still couldn't sleep, because Hanoi had another surprise in store for us.

The power went out around 10pm, which made our final bits of packing quite tricky. But then it stayed off, meaning no air-con – meaning it rapidly reached thirty-five degrees C in the room, and we lay in matching puddles of sweat. I could tell from the noise on the street that something was going on, and by about 2am I was pissed off enough to climb up to the roof for a look.

In the cramped junction next to the Asia Star, a team of workmen with a brace of forklifts were replacing the electricity substation. Not just a component of it – the whole bloody thing! It sat precariously on the prongs of a woefully inadequate forklift, a complex hunk of machinery the size of a small car. Right next to it sat another forklift, vainly struggling to raise the new substation. Neither truck could manoeuvre, because with their loads attached they were both longer than the space was wide. Each had boxed the other in neatly, with no chance at all of them getting out. Half their team was yelling at one driver or the other, whilst the rest of them stood around smoking and making phone calls. It was absurd, as though the boss had let his kids plan the entire operation for a laugh. It was civil engineering in farce.

It was exactly what I'd expect of Hanoi.

Looking up and down the street, I could see that power was out for the whole area. *These guys had better sort their shit out before the cafes started to open,* I thought.

They didn't. Two hours later I watched, incredulous, as they reinstalled the original, presumably faulty, substation. Neither forklift had moved.

Due to the continuing power outage, breakfast at the Asia Star was even more lacklustre than before. Toast was off the menu, which was a problem as up until that point toast had *been* the menu. Instead, we could dip slices of stale bread in puddles of what had once been butter... and wash it down with fresh orange juice, served at a temperature more readily associated with coffee.

I made to down a glass of the stuff anyway, when Vicky laid a warning hand on my arm. She was sitting facing me, and the breakfast bar behind me. "Don't drink it," she said, "I just watched that woman picking dead ants out of it before she brought it over."

I drank it anyway, because I'm not adverse to a bit of extra protein. And dead ants were certainly not the least appetising thing I'd consumed in Hanoi.

Ha Long Awaited Trip

We'd been looking forward to the Ha Long Bay cruise ever since we'd booked it, back in Perth. It was set to be the highlight of our time in Vietnam. The bay, with its limestone karst formations, was meant to be spectacular. According to our brochure we could jump off the boat and swim in the crystal clear waters; kayaking around the inside of a cave was on the itinerary, as well as a trip to one of Ha Long's famous island beaches. The accommodation would be comparatively luxurious, as a key part of the Kangaroo Café's marketing was pointing out that they had their own boat, fitted out to Western standards of safety and comfort. That was why we'd picked them as tour operator of choice; all the other companies in their price bracket simply ditched their customers in whatever boat was next on the list, resulting in a profusion of horror stories about filthy cabins and thieving crew. Overloading, boat crashes and even sinking were frighteningly common in the Ha Long Bay area – demand for trips was so high that many an unscrupulous operator had decided to take a piece of the pie.

But they wouldn't get a piece of us.
We were on a good boat.

We had a proper breakfast at the café, before meeting our

guide, 'Kong', and heading off on a minibus to the docks.

There were nine of us on the trip; us three plus Tim and Charlotte, another young English couple, and a pair of Chinese girls from Hong Kong.

We were surprised to arrive at the main docks, as the Kangaroo Café brochure said their boat went from a smaller, much less busy pier. But that made no real difference; after a bit of kerfuffle with the tickets, we were soon in a tender being taken out to our boat.

"How can you tell which is ours?" I asked Kong, marvelling at the sheer quantity of identical Hua Bin Tourism boats.

It had been a rhetorical question; these boats were the hit-and-miss ones chartered by more dubious companies, and at any moment I expected to round the fleet and see the much nicer boat advertised on the KC website. Instead, Kong replied, "I tell by the number."

And sure enough he spotted the one he was looking for, and we were led aboard Hua Bin Tourism Company's boat no.36.

It wasn't too bad. Remembering that Roo and I had recently been married, Kong offered us the honeymoon suite – a grand room taking up the entire back of the boat. It had a walk-in shower and sliding doors that led to a private balcony. Result! The English couple, Ollie and Kaleigh, were quick and nabbed a matching suite next-door to ours. I felt bad for Tim and Charlotte, as they ended up with a cramped cabin on the deck below us, with two single beds, a single tiny window and a broken toilet. They were paying more than us, too, as they'd opted to spend an extra day on the boat to visit Cat Ba island; understandably, they weren't too thrilled about this.

I expected a safety briefing, as that used to be part of my job back when I worked on a dive boat. Instead, Kong gathered us together and told us to give all our spare money and valuables to him for safekeeping. I asked why, and was told it was to make sure the boat crew couldn't steal anything. It wasn't the best news to start the trip with, but I handed over our spare cash and got a receipt for it, so it was all good.

And then we got underway.

Lunch was a grand affair, with all of us seated around a huge rectangular dining table.

It took an aeon. Dishes were brought out one at a time, with about fifteen minutes between them. We laughed and joked, while poor Charlotte, who was a vegetarian, eyed the parade of food reluctantly and ate none of it.

A meaty broth was followed by fish, still with its eyes, which Ollie and I dared each other to slurp up. Then a chicken dish came out, followed eventually by another bit of seafood.

Charlotte ate some bits of cucumber garnish, and by the time the rice was served, last and alone, she was famished. But we were all stuffed by then, so she could eat her fill. It had been a fun meal, if a bit frustrating, but I was concerned that hours had passed. We had a lot to do today, and not a lot of time left to do it in.

Our itinerary said we'd be visiting the 'Amazing Cave' on the second day, thereby avoiding some of the crowds, so I was quite surprised when we made it our first stop – at 4pm on the first day.

"Are we swimming here?" one of the group asked, "or can we take cameras?"

"No, no, cave is dry, okay to take cameras," Kong replied.

So we set off into the Amazing Cave.

Now, I love the natural world, and usually I adore caving. But the Amazing Cave was shit. I should have known, with a name like 'Amazing' that it would be an anticlimax, but I honestly think the bloke who called it that was being a tad sarcastic. The key attraction was a stalagmite which, growing up from the floor like stalagmites do, was meant to resemble a penis. Oh, and a corresponding hole in the cave roof – no prize for guessing what that was meant to represent. There were several Asian tour groups milling around in there, and all of them seemed to find this hilarious.

It's sad to say, the thing I found most amusing were the rubbish bins. There were dozens of them, all shaped like cheerful cartoon penguins. Presumably because... well, because... um... nope. I got nothing.

I will admit though, that it *was* amazing how fast we got through the place. Up the steps to it, around the cave, back down and back on the boat in a little over twenty minutes. I don't know how we'd have managed it without Kong chiding us constantly to keep moving, and not to stop for photographs. I wasn't crushed though, as I've got plenty of photos of caves that weren't shit, and I was in need of a good sprint. And anyway, this cave wasn't the tour's main selling point. The selling point was a different cave, that we were supposed to be kayaking around – and the fantastic beach we were going to be visiting afterwards.

Speaking of which, our next stop was what they call a 'kayak farm' – a little complex of buildings built on floating pontoons, miles from land. They had hundreds of kayaks, tied together in vast, bobbing rafts – the only trouble was, we'd gone straight there by tender from the Amazing Cave, never returning to the main boat.

Consequently, the group was festooned with expensive digital SLR cameras, and all wearing our regular day clothes.

"But... you said it was dry!" one of the girls protested, "You said we didn't need swimwear!"

"Yes, *cave* dry. *Now,* need swimwear."

"But that's not what you said on the boat..."

Luckily, we all had clothes for tomorrow on the boat, so there'd be something for us to change into later. With great reluctance, Kong agreed to take the camera gear back to the boat. Tim and Charlotte had to accompany him, as they didn't want to ruin what they were wearing, so they each took a neckful of camera straps, and the rest of us queued up to collect our kayaks.

Instruction was non-existent, so Roo went with Vicky, who had never been in a kayak before.

"See that island, with temple on top?" Kong said. "Go there."

That was our only direction, and I was embarrassed to find I couldn't achieve it. No matter what I did, my kayak swung me back around in a circle. I was going nowhere.

"You're in the wrong bit," Roo called out (when she stopped laughing at me). "You have to be in the back seat if you're on your own, or you can't steer!"

"Ah! Thanks, love. Glad someone knows what they're doing!"

She paddled back and held my kayak steady while I transferred to the back seat, and we all set off with a vengeance.

"So much for leisurely kayaking around inside a cave," I said, as we aimed ourselves towards the island. The bow waves from larger boats were pushing us around, and our group was scattered all over the place. "This is hard work!"

The island with the temple on top was deceptively close. It took ten minutes to get there, across a fairly busy stretch of water. Half our group had arrived before us, and were drifting aimlessly outside a netted-off swimming area. We'd been told to wait here to be picked up, so that's what we did.

The next ten minutes were spent being sworn at violently in Vietnamese by the drivers of dozens of tender boats that were criss-crossing that stretch of water, ferrying happy beach-goers back to their tour boats. I was nearly hit by a few of them, as they didn't seem all that keen to avoid me. "Fuck off!" I yelled at the captain of yet another boat, as he screamed "MOVE, MOVE!" and ploughed his tender straight towards me.

Another twenty minutes passed. I was getting a bit annoyed, as I'd paid extra for an hour's kayaking in a cave. So far it had consisted mostly of dragging myself out of the path of belligerent tender-boat pilots, whilst waiting to be picked up.

The group rafted up for a conference, and I offered to ask at the docks if we could get out. Staying in that stretch of water was dangerous, and getting more so – the number of boats ploughing back and forth was increasing by the minute. I approached the docks, only to be screamed at by an irate dock worker, whose emphatic gestures made it pretty clear I wasn't welcome there, either.

By the time Kong showed up, the whole group was scared – a bit panicked even – and mightily pissed off.

At first, he told us to try climbing from our kayaks into his tender, which I was preparing to do when he suddenly changed his mind. "New rules," he explained, "Cannot stop here! You must go back."

"What? Where?"

"Go back, where you come."

"To the kayak farm?"

"Yes."

"You've got to be kidding me."

I looked at the rest of the group, all of whom were tired and stressed from spending the last half hour dodging boats. I looked at the expanse of water we'd crossed, which was busier than ever. The kayak farm was an invisible landmark, impossible to see until you got very close, and I had no confidence in finding it again.

"No," I said to Kong.

"Eh?"

"There's too many boats," I told him. "Too dangerous!"

"No, must go back!"

No-one seemed keen. In the least. And it was starting to get quite late.

"Bollocks to it," I said. "I'm getting out."

"No! Cannot!"

"Watch me! This ain't my first rodeo."

So I paddled up to the docks, and one by one the others followed me. We helped each other out of our kayaks, and left them with Kong. I narrowly avoided leaving a few four-letter words with him, too, but I managed to remain civil.

Because at long last we were headed towards the second-most important venue of the day: the beach!

The beach was fenced off from the docks, with a little admission booth and a turnstyle. We marched up, fully expecting we'd have to explain that we'd already paid, and that our guides must have our tickets. But it was not to be; a burly security guard barred the way, palm thrust outwards. "No," he said.

"But…" I began.

"NO!" he told me again.

"But why?" I had a horrible feeling he'd seen us climb out at the docks, and was punishing us for that transgression.

"No entry," he said, instead waving at a big sign next to the booth. "Is closed."

I looked at the sign and did a double-take.

This beach had *opening hours.*

And they ended at 5:30pm.

Which was exactly the time it said on my watch.

Coincidentally.

By now, every one of us was fuming. Even if everything else had gone to plan, there was no way we'd have managed more than half an hour on this beach. If we'd kayaked back to the starting point, it would have been dark before we arrived. This was the last in a succession of fuck-ups, which had essentially reduced our day to one agonizingly-long lunch, and one rapid-fire tour of the Amazing Cave.

Kong was still tying kayaks to the tender when we got back to him.

"Kong, the beach is closed," I said.

"No… why?"

"Because, Kong, the beach shuts at 5:30pm."

"This must be a new rule!" he declared.

So I pointed out the sign, which was visible from the docks, and was quite obviously *not* new.

"Ah, sorry," Kong relented, "My fault."

Yes, quite, I thought. But never mind. It only cost us a hundred bucks each to come here.

"I'd like to make a complaint," I said to him.

"Oh! You complain, you have to talk to Mr Max."

"Fair enough. Please give me his phone number."

"On boat, I give."

So we returned to the boat.

The sun was going down now, but the heat was still intense. Only three of the loungers on the deck had cushions, and the rest had missing slats, or were broken altogether. But if I couldn't relax, at least I could swim.

I climbed up on the railing and looked down. I was on

the top deck, so the sea was about four metres below me.

It looked inviting.

But there was a shout from Kong. "No! Cannot swim."

"Why not? It's on the brochure."

"Is illegal."

"But I swam here two weeks ago, with Asia Outdoors!"

"Rules change. Now, is illegal."

"But people are swimming from that boat, there." I pointed to one of the three boats moored less than fifty metres behind us. Actually, now that I looked, people were swimming from all three boats.

"No. Not allowed."

"Look, Kong, if I swim are you going to get in trouble?"

"No, not me. You."

"Are you going to report me?"

"Ah... no..."

"Then I'll take my chances."

"Me too," said Kaleigh, climbing up beside me. She jumped, and I jumped, and the water was blessedly cool and calm.

We swum around the bow of the boat, looking for a ladder, only to find the captain, irate, screaming at us in Vietnamese. "OUT, OUT!" he finally added – but he carried on haranguing us, and the crew made no move to fetch a swim-ladder. In the end I had to climb up the side of the tender, which was moored alongside. I helped Kaleigh out of the water, and she cut her leg on the rough hull of the boat. Then we had to confront the captain.

"NO swim," he shouted at us.

"But why?" I asked, making the question clear with my body language.

The captain thought about this for a minute. "Jellyfish!" he declared. Then stalked off.

It was nearly too much. The others fell about laughing when I told them. If I had to guess, I'd say the truth was the boat didn't have a swim ladder. The crew almost certainly couldn't swim, as most Vietnamese are terrified of the water, so they'd invented a raft of reasons to stop us going in. Which was a shitter, as that was the bit I'd been looking forward to most of all. So far, 'illegal' activity aside, we hadn't swum once.

Things went from bad to worse on the boat. Kong was refusing to let us call Max to complain. He said he was afraid of losing his job. We tried to set his mind to rest, promising not to mention him in person. The truth was, he was a nice guy – he just had a bad habit of trying to cover up his mistakes with BS. Judging by how scared he seemed of getting fired, I couldn't really hold that against him.

But try as we might, we couldn't convince him to let us complain. "Later, later," he said – yet he spent most of the next two hours on the phone himself.

We compiled a list of complaints, worded carefully to avoid laying any responsibility with Kong. We showed it to him, offering to email it instead, but this only made him more cagey. Finally, Tim and I threatened to call Max ourselves, using the number from the Kangaroo Café literature. At this he relented, promising he would call Max himself, and ask him to call us back.

As complaint procedures go it was bizarre, and a far cry from what it said in the brochure; 'Beer not cold? Coffee not hot? Tell us immediately, don't wait till you get back to Hanoi!'

And then Max called.

Tim answered, as I'm pathetic at making complaints. I'm English; I usually start by apologising for having to complain, and by the time I'm done I've offered to solve the problem myself, pay for the damages, and buy the other person a beer.

Tim was much more suitable for this role because, unlike me, he actually has a spine. Despite being English.

But nothing could have prepared him for what came next.

The phone call from Max began with him demanding to know who had jumped off the boat. Obviously he'd been prepared with a few complaints of his own, and he unleashed them in a fashion that none of us were capable of.

Tim's end of the conversation went like this: "Well, yes that's... No, we didn't mean... No, that's not what was said. But we... Max, look, I... No, I'm not trying to scam you!

But… If you'd just… I'm sorry, did you just tell me to fuck off? But… what I mean is… Eh? I don't want to see your financial records! Whaddaya mean I…?"

I caught a lot of it, such was the venom with which it spewed out of Tim's phone. It was a torrent of abuse, and after about twenty minutes, during which time he hardly got a word in, Tim hung up on him.

"Holy shit. That went well," he said.

"You okay, mate?" I asked him. "That sounded pretty tense."

"Yeah, it was. He kept threatening to fuck us all up!"

"Shit, what?"

"Yeah. He said, "You don't know who I am, I'm a one-percenter, I own boats and hotels, and I know people who will fuck you all up!"."

"Oh."

"And he kept going on about how we were trying to scam him, and he wasn't falling for it, and it was the oldest trick in the book. He said we can fuck right off if we think we're getting a single penny back."

"Oh."

"Yeah. And then he said he'd have his gang waiting for us when we got back to the docks."

"Oh my God!"

"Yeah. To be honest, I've had more successful phone calls."

Where Complaining Gets You

Dinner that evening was subdued, sullen, and very weird.
    Kong spent most of the meal taking surreptitious photos of each of us, moving around when one of us turned away. Several times he was asked to stop, but he just laughed it off and carried on. Tim and Charlotte hid their faces for a while, but it was obvious he wasn't going to stop until he had what he wanted. Afterwards, we sat up on deck, huddled on the three unbroken sun loungers. The topic of conversation: 'What the hell was all that photo-taking about?'. None of us could think of any rational reason. Not once 'so Max's associates can identify us' was suggested.

It was a tense night on board.
    Being threatened, verbally, very aggressively, and repeatedly, is not something I'm great at dealing with. But because my wife and her younger sister were amongst the passengers on the boat, I tried to laugh it off as empty posturing – perhaps Max had had a bit too much to drink before making that phone call?
    I was, however, more than a little scared. Being a writer, I have a depressingly fertile imagination at times. I couldn't help but think how we were totally at the mercy of this man. Floating in a quiet lagoon, at night, miles from anywhere.

Outnumbered by the ship's Vietnamese crew, our only neighbours a handful of other boats belonging to the same company...

We had no allies, no language skills, and none of our mobile phones worked in the lagoon. Not that there was anyone we could have called. It was slowly dawning on us just how precarious our position was, what with the mega-rich boss of the whole tour company personally threatening to have his gang attack us.

What if they came now? I thought. By tender, from one of the other boats?

What if he called a dodgy mate and asked him to send some guys to raid our boat? My traitorous mind kept imagining the conversation: "Yeah, only nine of 'em. Six are chicks. No, the boat crew won't stop you, I've told 'em to let you in. Yeah, just fuck them over, take all their shit and give 'em a bloody good kicking, then bugger off. I'll get the crew to report a random robbery by no-one they recognised..."

This was, after all, Vietnam.

Shit.

When our own tender fired up its engine and left our boat for no immediately apparent reason around 11pm, and was gone for an hour, some of us were close to tears.

I was amongst them. But internally, of course. I had to be strong in front of the ladies...

When dawn came, and we were still un-fucked-up, I have to say I was overjoyed. Maybe it *had* been empty posturing. Or drunkenness. But the tension aboard was still so strong that only two people dared stay aboard for the remaining day and night of the cruise they'd booked. The rest of us demanded to be taken back to Hanoi as soon as we made landfall for lunch.

I was rather pleased to be back on dry land.

Tim took a photo of me lying down in the road, kissing the tarmac, just to prove it.

I hadn't realised until then how nervous I'd been. Suddenly, back on land, where escape was as simple as walking across the road and jumping on a bus, I felt much safer. I felt lighter, looser, like I could relax. Our guides took us back to the Kangaroo Café in their bus, and for the first time I thought there might actually NOT be a bunch of Vietnamese gangsters waiting for us when we got there.

And there wasn't.

Just Max; a wiry Australian bloke in his fifties, with a moustache – and a video camera. Max had clearly spent his day preparing for our return, and rather than turning on the charm he had decided to *film* us as we made our complaints in person! He stood behind the café counter, panning around us whilst ranting on about how we had no integrity and couldn't be trusted. It was an essay in defensive, passive-aggressive behaviour, but I still preferred it to the actual aggressive behaviour we'd spent the bus ride back anticipating. Max seemed obsessed with irrelevant details, demanding to know who'd been making poo jokes and criticising Tim and Charlotte for leaving their tour early. At one point I managed to explain, calmly and rationally, what the real nature of our complaint had been – that by trying to combine a two-day and a three-day itinerary, our trip had been screwed up and had managed to achieve none of it. I described the day-ruining issues with the kayaking, the closed beach, and the ridiculous lengths we had to go to just to complain. But then I came to his abusive phone call, which he flat out denied. Even though all of us had been present, and had witnessed Tim's reaction to the abuse he was receiving. After this, and another twenty minutes of him talking over us, it was clear we were getting nowhere. Max didn't even want to hear about the genuine issues we'd faced, and far from apologising for anything, spent the entire time twisting our words, misquoting things he'd obviously heard from Kong, and complaining about our behaviour. None of which he'd actually witnessed. He told us that the email we'd managed to send from the boat, listing all our complaints, which was a collaborative effort and had been read and signed by all of us, was a pack of lies. He based this on the fact that I'd mistakenly said we'd spent eleven minutes in the Amazing Cave, rather than twenty, and that the English couple, who had stayed on the boat, had apparently called him to deny the whole story. Oh, and to tell him just how awful we were, and how appalled they had been by our behaviour. I was later to email them, and find that Max had twisted their words, too – they'd had fun with us, hadn't said anything negative about us, and were shocked to find that Max had used them to get at us.

Max argued about the boat we were on, and about how Kong had felt bullied – totally ignoring the actual complaint, about the quality of the tour. No mention was ever made of Kong taking those mysterious photos the night before – there simply wasn't any chance – so I had to assume they were still out there, somewhere. Hopefully not in the hands of people who meant to do us harm.

"This video is going straight up on YouTube," Max warned us.

Which seemed a bit odd, because as far as I could tell the video was showing him up in a pretty bad light. If nothing else, it highlighted a serious flaw in his customer service ethic. I couldn't imagine floods of people suddenly wanting to book tours with him after watching a video of how he handled complaints…

Then Roo, who hadn't spoken much so far – hadn't had the chance, even if she'd wanted to – piped up. "Well, Tony is a travel writer, so you'll probably end up in his next book!"

"So? I'm a travel writer too," Max replied.

I couldn't resist this. "Really?" I asked. "So where have you been published?"

"Oh, you'll find out…" he replied with menace.

It was definitely the most cryptic threat he issued.

And that was it.

We gave up and left, shaking our heads. Outside, Charlotte burst into tears, the stress and the embarrassment of it all catching up with her.

I just looked at Roo. "Maybe we shouldn't have told him I'm a travel writer. Nothing good ever comes of that."

"Yes," she replied, "but did you see his face? I bet everyone who tries to complain to him says something like that. Only, in your case, it's true!"

This did make me feel a little better about the situation.

"And he's a travel writer too, eh? Only, he's published somewhere so secret he's not allowed to tell us about it. Ha! I think he just isn't quick enough to come up with a reasonable lie."

And that was the last I thought about Max's shadowy, publication-based threat.

Sometimes I wonder if, looking back, I should have been able to see what was coming.

But no. I couldn't possibly have anticipated what he had planned...

Whilst collecting our luggage, I had one last chance to check with Jimmy at the Hanoi Asia Star, to see if my replacement bank cards had arrived. I didn't hold out much hope, and in that way I was not disappointed. My cards had not arrived, and I would be leaving the country without them. I couldn't cancel them again though – not yet, anyway. Mum had emailed me the card numbers, and they were still the only method we had for booking things online. And we were heading to Mongolia, where there would be plenty of things needing booking. To say nothing of China...

I just had to leave my cards drifting in the ether – or in the Vietnamese Postal Service – and trust to Fate that they would come to no harm.

The odds weren't great.

Particularly when you consider just how kind Fate had been to me recently.

We left Hanoi later that day.

I'd really enjoyed the place, and Vietnam as a whole. Sure, there'd been the odd little hiccup...

"Is this the sort of thing that always happens to you, then?" Vicky asked.

"Ah... yes, I'm afraid it is. Sorry."

"No offence or anything, but I don't think I'll come travelling with you again."

"Understood – none taken!"

"I mean, none of it was really your fault, but somehow we're fleeing Vietnam, wanted by the mafia, and quite possibly targeted by whatever gang Max is part of. You have to admit, that's pretty extreme."

"Yeah, true enough. On the upside, we're getting out at

just the right time."

"Oh really? Why is that?"

"Well, none of us is dead yet. That seems like a pretty good time to leave."

"Is that how you usually decide when to leave a country?"

"Not always…"

MONGOLIA

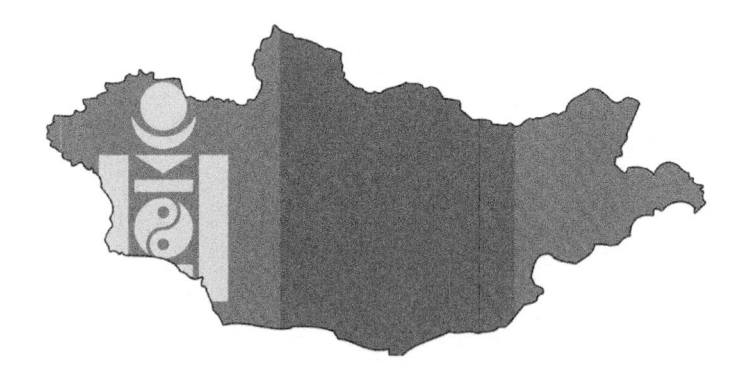

Mongolia By Night

You can't fly direct from Hanoi to *Ulaanbaatar,* the capital city of Mongolia.

For some strange reason.

I mean, there must be *dozens* of people wanting to make this trip each year. Well okay, maybe not dozens...

Unsurprisingly, it had not been the simplest of journeys to book. In fact it took a week; luckily Vicky, Roo and I had all been back in Perth at the time, three people using high-speed internet in two different locations to ferret out all the alternatives.

Where we'd ended up is Incheon Airport in Seoul, South Korea, where we had a barely-noticeable fourteen-hour layover between our allegedly 'connecting' flights. Korean Air made the six-and-a-half hour trip to Ulaanbaatar at least once a week – maybe more, if there was enough interest.

Which there wasn't.

But still, this left us with a fat chunk of time to kill in one of the best airports in the world. We used it to do what everyone wishes they could do in every airport they ever visit; we found a quiet corner, and we slept.

At least, we planned to.

First we tracked down the special reclined chaises, which are free to use for as long as you want. They were full, of course; it was 5am, after all. So we settled into a quiet corner near the top of an escalator that had been turned off, pulled our sleeping bags over us, and relaxed. For a good five minutes.

That's when we discovered that the escalator wasn't out of order – it was motion-activated. People were still using it sporadically, and every time it whirred into life it broadcast one of those ridiculously over-the-top safety warnings: "Please be aware that your child will be decapitated by this escalator," or something similar. This was followed by the same thing (presumably) in Korean, by which time the decapitated children had reached the top and lay sprawled in a pile of corpses (or possibly went on about their business). Either way, the warning was triggered roughly every three minutes. By the time I'd lain there for an hour, I was reasonably sure I knew the Korean for 'decapitated child', which was bound to come in useful some day.

Not quite as useful as sleep, however, so we grabbed a trio of the chaises as soon as we could, and managed to catch a few precious hours of shut-eye.

Hanoi had been an assault on the senses, and whilst I'd loved every minute of it – okay, *most* of the minutes – I was the first to admit exhaustion. The heat, the emotional turmoil, the lack of sleep and the constant need to be aware of my surroundings had all taken their toll. Consequently, we never made it as far as the indoor ice rink.

Mongolia, when we got there, was a breath of fresh air.

Or freezing air, if you want to get technical.

It was night-time, and after subtropical Vietnam, Mongolia's positively polar climate was going to challenge us in different ways. In truth, it already had; packing for six months on the beach is relatively easy, until you decide to stop off next-door to Siberia. For the last two months we'd been hauling around bags crammed with jumpers, knee-length socks, woolly hats and thermal knickers. It had earned us a few strange looks as we repacked our rucksacks in Borneo. Added to this was the smaller burden of presents I'd bought for the local children – sweets and pens, which I hoped would brighten their lives a little as we passed through. The largely nomadic population of the open steppes lived a fairly meagre existence, and we would be arriving amongst them as comparatively wealthy foreigners.

Despite the fact that, on our budget, pens and sweets were the only gifts I could afford.

Now, there is a phenomenon known as the 'Mongolian Scramble'. Reading about it, in the comfort of our Hanoi hotel, it seemed an exaggeration of the typical crush we'd experienced at many train and bus stations. Asians aren't overly fond of queuing, which came as quite a shock to my delicate British sensibilities.

Back in England I've been in the awkward situation of approaching a turnstile at exactly the same time as someone else; it's a nightmare scenario that most English people dread, and both of us spent the next five minutes insisting the other person go first. The Asian alternative had taken some getting used to. Instead of waiting patiently in an orderly line, most people simply mobbed the entrance to the bus/train/ticket booth and shoved their way in wherever they saw a gap. Come to think of it, that's how they drive, too.

So, this Mongolian Scramble sounded like business as usual – at least until we saw it.

Baggage Claim at the airport is normally where people are on their best behaviour. No-one wants to risk looking suspicious when all that stands between them and their destination are the rubber-gloved hands of the Customs Inspectors.

Not so the Mongolians.

They attacked the carousel with enthusiasm and ferocity in equal parts. Flinging themselves forward, arms and legs flailing out at anyone who got in their way, our entire planeload of passengers fought their way to their bags tooth and claw. Even though most of them hadn't arrived yet. As the solitary suitcase became a train of them, the surrounding frenzy grew too; we decided to hang back and take our time at this point.

Vicky's giant suitcase and my tatty red backpack started circling the conveyor belt quite early on, not that we could get anywhere near them. Between us, a seething mass of

Mongolian limbs churned and waggled as their owners vied for position. Being the tallest people there by a good foot, all three of us stared across a sea of scalp; our heads, protruding from the morass like three confused giraffes, were probably visible from the other side of the building.

It wasn't until Roo's bag hove into view that I decided to make my move.

And that was only because a dumpy chick in a woollen overcoat grabbed it off the conveyor.

"Woah!" I yelled, doing a passable impression of the scramble myself as I dove through the crowd and snatched it off her. She barely seemed to notice, which was odd; I'd expected either an argument over ownership, or admission of an honest mistake. But Roo's bag is fairly distinctive – a bright blue rucksack, it bears the scars of many adventures, and has 'I Walked 1,000 Kilometres!' painted across the front. Chances are, we'd just seen the reason for the intensity of the scramble; *get to your bags before any other bugger does...*

Our contact was waiting for us in the Arrivals Hall. Manlai, the founder of auspiciously-named Brilliant Holidays, was big for a Mongolian – maybe 5'8, and heavyset. In a society that still considers girth an indicator of wealth, Manlai looked quite prosperous for a tour guide.

I apologised to him for being late; not only was the plane itself an hour overdue, but we'd been amongst the last to emerge from the scrum of the baggage claim.

"Hey, no problems," he drawled, his strong American accent a welcome relief. "My driver's out front."

His driver was, in fact, out front. Literally – Manlai's Land Cruiser was sitting in the loading zone right outside the airport doors. It must have been there for almost two hours, but no-one seemed to care, including Manlai.

The journey from the airport was nothing like I'd expected.

I've visited plenty of rural airports, and I guess I'd imagined it like landing in Bali or Mulu – surrounded by nature, with shacks built of sticks and livestock on the road.

Instead, we spent two hours in the back of Manlai's car – in a solid traffic jam the entire way. Honestly, I could have got out and walked faster.

"Why so much traffic?" I asked him.

He waved a hand dismissively. "It's always like this."

"But… it's midnight!"

"Yeah," he agreed, "busy."

Ulaanbaatar, it turns out, is one of the most congested, most polluted cities in the world. Almost half of Mongolia's population lives there, and the younger generation is still flocking to the capital, abandoning centuries of nomadic tradition for the thrills and spills of city life.

That night, we didn't see much of it. Streetlights were even less prevalent here than in Borneo and Vietnam; I didn't see a single one, making for a long, dark, featureless journey.

When we arrived at the Lotus Guesthouse, I realised that perhaps this was a mercy. We were all tired and a little nervous, and if the city we'd passed through looked anything like where we ended up, there's a good chance one of us would have had a full blown panic attack.

In the light of Manlai's headlamps, he led us over to a huge steel door. It looked like something I'd expect to find sealing the gas chamber in a concentration camp. The buildings surrounding us looked derelict, and the alley we were parked in kept me scanning the darkness behind us, expecting gangs armed with chains and bits of pipe to emerge at any moment.

When no-one answered the door in spite of Manlai giving it a prolonged beating, he resorted to calling the hostel and persuading the staff to come and let us in.

"Probably shouldn't stay out late partying," I told the girls, but any reply was obliterated by a screech of reluctant steel. That door was even less keen to open up than its owners, and it made damn sure the whole neighbourhood knew about it.

I winced, and was to wince every single time I opened or closed that door – which was quite a lot, as the Lotus Guesthouse turned out to be the best hostel in Ulaanbaatar.

At first glance, it didn't look too promising.

The stairwell we entered looked like it had seen better

days.

Actually it looked like it had seen heavy fighting in a civil war of some kind. The potholes in the concrete floor matched the ones in the road outside, and the walls and stairs were all the same; painted concrete, cracked and crumbling, with a lingering smell that I'd didn't want to analyse. If someone had shown me a picture of that stairwell and asked where it was, I'd have guessed it was the remains of a multi-storey car park in downtown Baghdad.

We climbed the steps, which were weirdly uneven, and entered the hostel proper through another huge steel door. *At least they take security seriously,* I thought.

Once inside, there was a more homey feel to the place; cheery blue walls, vinyl on the floors, and, as we were shown into our room, a proliferation of bright orange wooden furniture.

In miniature.

The beds, of which there were four, were raised atop rows of drawers. Narrow cupboards formed the head and foot, and each was decorated with intricate designs like Celtic knotwork, done in blue and green. Under the window, two orange chairs and a table matched perfectly, both in décor and scale. It was like we'd wandered into a rather gaudy oriental hobbit-hole.

We were too tired to care.

Even when we discovered that the traditional Mongolian beds were sized to fit Mongolians, and thus were too short for us by a head.

We had less than five hours before Manlai would be back, picking us up to begin a tour we'd booked with him – which we still knew next to nothing about.

Well, I knew it was called 'Central Mongolian Beauties' – and as far as I was aware, the beauties being referred to were scenic vistas, rather than porn stars. Although I could be wrong. Either way, horses were also involved...

"You know," Roo said, as she curled up on her garish sleeping platform, "sometimes I worry about our organisational technique."

Into The Wild

I woke only inches from disaster. I was curled up in the foetal position, having smacked both head and feet on the bed's built-in cupboards several times during the night. My knees were so far over the edge that the slightest wriggle would have spilled me onto the floor, where the vinyl covering might look like wood, but had something rather less forgiving underneath it.

Tired and stiff, we decanted most of our belongings into Vicky's suitcase, which we stored in the Lotus Guesthouse's office. Then, after a quick piece of toast in the kitchen, it was downstairs to meet our tour group.

I should mention that we'd been very fortunate in this instance. When I'd contacted Manlai, on Tim and Charlotte's recommendation, he'd mentioned he had a group already doing the same trip we were interested in, at almost the same time. He'd convinced them to let us join their group, bringing the price per-person down to $65 – an unexpected bonus for them, and for us it brought the trip within the bounds of affordability. It was still technically out of our budget, but the serendipity was too good an omen to pass up.

Otherwise, it would have cost Roo and me $180.

Per day.

And that was *definitely* out of our budget.

That was why we hustled out of the hostel at 7am, rather than having a relaxing lie-in followed by a day to acclimatize to the country. It was cold on the street – it had been snowing the day before – but Manlai was waiting for us, and with him was our ride.

The Russian-built UAZ van looked like the love child of a VW kombi and a WWII tank. It was clearly a museum piece. With a rounded body in battleship grey, perched on wheels the size of a BMX's, it was the least likely tour vehicle I could imagine.

"It's quite cute," said Roo, "in a 'this'll never work' kind of way."

I was inclined to agree.

But hell, this was Mongolia. Stuff was bound to get weird here; I was counting on it. What's the point of traveling, if you don't get to experience strange and unusual things?

Honestly, if I Googled 'Strange and Unusual Things', this van would show up in the first page of results.

In we climbed, after stowing our luggage in the boot.

Three seventeen-year-old girls were already sitting across the back, so Vicky squeezed in next to them. Roo and I sat facing them, on separate seats either side of a tiny table. Beneath the table, rumbling ominously, was the engine, protected by a steel cover that was hot enough to singe my leg hairs. Through my trousers.

Manlai introduced us to Soyol, our guide, cook and translator. She looked every inch the youth of Mongolia – tiny, with close-cropped dark hair, coffee-coloured skin, a round face and smiling eyes. The driver was her opposite number; a hunched, weather-beaten old man who looked like he needed a damn good ironing.

Between them, this duo would be getting us into, across and out of, the vast Mongolian wilderness. They would be our lifeline; food, shelter, transport and protection would all be down to them. They looked perfectly suited to it.

The van, not so much.

Especially when the driver crunched into first gear on the eighth attempt, and we shuddered slowly out into the traffic.

Ulaanbaatar is a bloody ugly city. Built almost entirely by the

Soviets along the lines of Russia's finest post-war block-of-flats aesthetic, its suburbs are decayed and depressing. There are none of the beautifying features you'd find in capital cities, like... well, everything. Architecture. Urban planning. Green spaces.

The road system was a nightmare; woefully inadequate to the point where our entire journey out of the city was spent in standing traffic.

It took us four hours.

The van didn't cope well in town. Soyol kept up a constant stream of chatter with the driver as he cursed and cajoled the vehicle into gear, but every shift from first to second and back again was a struggle. The van bucked, the gears ground, the driver cursed; then he stomped on the pedals, smacked the gear lever, swore again and managed to force it into gear against its better judgement.

"Sorry!" Soyol explained, "The car does not like this kind of driving!"

By which she meant, 'the car is fucked; it can only drive when we don't need to change gear'.

It didn't bode terribly well for the six days we would be spending inside the thing.

After battling our way through miles of dirty, featureless apartment blocks circa 1945, we finally hit the open road.

And then we saw the real Mongolia.

'Open road' is an interesting term. Most of the roads in Western nations are anything but. This road, however, was the very definition of open.

On the outskirts of Ulaanbaatar was a sprawl of canvas tents, the homes of nomads who'd felt the need to visit the city for some reason. In a place the size of Mongolia, with no public transport options and journeys measured in days rather than hours, it made sense; if you're going on an extended trip, bring your house with you. And your goats, and your horses... we passed large numbers of both of these, some corralled in pens, most simply roaming wherever they wanted.

And beyond the scattering of *gers* (the Mongolian word for their circular, yurt-like homes), there was just... nothing.

Grass. Hillsides. The occasional tree.

Hundreds – no, *thousands* of miles of it.

There are only two sealed roads in Mongolia, outside the capital, and we were on one of them – pushing the van to a speed where every surface vibrated evenly. It was oddly soothing, and I wasn't the only one who nodded off occasionally, as vast tracts of empty grassland slid by on both sides of the bus. The sky was pure and clear out here. Although an arctic wind cut through the landscape, the temperature inside the van bordered on cosy. Muddled together, we exchanged notes with our tour-mates, a blonde Norwegian chick and two Chinese girls, all of whom had just graduated from a prestigious high school in Hong Kong.

We stopped for lunch in a spot as picturesque as any we'd passed. Just ahead the road bridged a small river, and to either side rose steep hills. The driver slowed slightly, did something with the gears, and then swerved off the road and down the embankment. Suddenly we were bouncing all over the place, heads and elbows smacking off the roof, the walls and each other. We rattled to a stop in the middle of a field... except, a field would have had boundaries. This patch of land pressed north to the river, and beyond it faded into the horizon. Between us, and the ghosts of mountains at the furthest edge of sight, there was nothing but grass and rocks.

It was breathtaking.

Further up the river a herd of wild horses was crossing, forging their way through the water with the stallion in the lead. All the girls in the group (which was everyone except me) were spellbound, and immediately chased off along the river bank, festooned with cameras.

Our driver crawled underneath the van to make a few repairs, something he felt compelled to do every time we stopped. I tried not to let this worry me. Instead, I helped Soyol unload our luggage from the back of the van, scattering it around on the grass. She needed the space; the wooden floorboard in the boot of the van was her kitchen. Pretty soon she had a portable gas stove set up and was sitting cross-legged in the grass, chopping vegetables on her knee with a cleaver.

This was to become the pattern for our meals. Soyol prepared everything we ate on that trip, from supplies she kept in a stack of cardboard boxes. She was a wizard, that woman; pasta and pancakes, sauces and stews, she cooked completely from scratch, starting out with raw ingredients like flour and water.

And mutton, which featured heavily.

Every meal she made was delicious, and every one of them was extremely well-received. They also took over an hour to prepare, which made us wish on quite a few occasions that we'd thought to bring some snacks with us.

What with my culinary expertise being somewhat lacking, I decided to leave lunch to Soyol while I climbed the exposed rock face of the nearest hill. I pulled off my socks and shoes and waded through the icy river, losing all feeling in my feet long before I made it across.

The climb was simple enough, and exhilarating. I've always loved being up high, and getting there myself only adds to the thrill. On top of the hill was a big pile of rocks like a cairn, only this one was draped with dozens of lengths of blue materiel, like silk scarves. We'd seen a few such monuments dotted around the countryside; called 'Ovoo's, they were shrines after a fashion, used by the locals to ask for good luck and blessings on their journeys. Soyol had mentioned that the correct way to make an offering was to walk three times clockwise around the Ovoo, and then place milk, sweets or vodka on the rocks. If I'd had any milk, sweets or vodka at that point they'd have gone straight into my belly, but I made my three circuits of the rock pile because it felt like the right thing to do.

The view, with the horse herds and the river and the endless expanse of grass, was almost prehistoric; the only sign of the modern era was the road, stretched out towards Ulan Bator like an old leather belt, pocked and scarred and crumbling at the edges.

I tried to film the panorama to show the others, but the battery in my video camera chose that moment to surrender its life. Looking around me, I had a feeling it would be a long time before I could charge it up again.

I made the climb back down, discovering a very worried Soyol cooking noodles. "Please be careful," she said, in a tone which suggested her tour groups didn't normally run off and climb cliffs.

"I'm always careful," I said.

Which was not entirely true, but she didn't need to know that.

The girls had returned from photographing the horses. They were out of breath and excited, much like I was. "Hey Roo, can I borrow your camera?" I asked, hoping the heat of the moment would work to my advantage.

"Where are you going with it?"

"Well, I was going to go back up that rock pile. The view from the top is unbelievable."

"So, you want to wade through that stream and climb the cliff face over there?"

"Yes."

"Then no."

"Aw! What about the bomb-proof camera?"

"The bomb-proof camera hasn't worked since you took it canyoning in Da Lat. I don't know what the hell you did to it, but it obviously wasn't Tony-proof."

"I didn't do anything to it..."

"My point precisely."

"I'll take the phone, then," I decided. "That's no good out here anyway."

There were some advantages to being overburdened with technology.

Roo sighed. "Okay, but please be careful."

I rolled my eyes at her. "Why do people keep telling me that?"

"I can't imagine."

"Lunch is nearly ready," Soyol chipped in, concerned for a different reason. "I think, not enough time."

"Don't worry," I promised her, "I'll leg it."

Both women were shaking their heads as I took off at top speed.

Women, eh? Sometimes there's just no pleasing them.

In Tents Workout

After lunch we returned to the road, though by this point it had deteriorated so dramatically that it was barely worthy of the name. Soyol explained that we were heading for *Kharkhorin,* the ancient capital of Mongolia. That was as far as the road went, a paltry two-hundred and twenty miles from the modern capital.

Allowing for lunch, and the rather poor condition of that road, it was a mind-boggling ten-hour drive.

We stopped several times to break up the journey. Seeing mounds of snow on the verge was cause for one stop, and the incredible emptiness of the surrounding landscape inspired us to take turns dancing in the middle of the road. It had been an hour since we'd sighted another vehicle; a shuddering bus similar to ours, only in an even worse state of repair.

The next stop was for a more pressing concern; the jiggling of the van was starting to have an effect on our bladders, so we requested a toilet break.

"Where's the bathroom?" Vicky asked, as we pulled up in a disused summer camp.

"All of nature is your bathroom!" Soyol replied, grandly. "Is the biggest bathroom in the world!"

Which meant there wasn't one.

It was a phrase we would be hearing a lot on this trip,

Shave My Spider!

and it heralded a certain amount of dread. Especially for the women; privacy for a man in the wilderness is as easy as turning his back on whoever he's with, whereas the ladies had slightly more delicate sensibilities.

They also had no choice.

Poor Vicky struggled the most, and couldn't bring herself to go no matter how well she hid herself. After a lifetime of civilization, peeing on the floor just didn't come naturally to her, and she returned to the van unrelieved.

We stopped twice more to use nature as our toilet, and each time Vicky failed to go. She was in quite a bit of pain by the end of that first day, and was starting to panic when we arrived at our lodgings for the night.

Kharkhorin was the Mongolian capital for just twenty-five years, shortly after the death of Genghis Khan (or Chinggis Khan, as he is known in his homeland). As a modern city in a modern world, it had to be unique; not only were all the buildings tents, there were no roads, no running water, no sewage system and no amenities of any kind. Properties were divided by sagging plank fences, or in the case of more affluent owners, bare concrete block walls. There were a handful of brick buildings scattered around, including one very charming attempt at an English cottage – but over ninety percent of Kharkhorin's population lived in *gers.*

One such enclosure was our destination, and the van bumped and bounced over the rough, rocky ground between fences. In the past, a half-hearted attempt had been made to scatter gravel over this area – presumably for the tourists, as few of the locals had cars.

Two skinny lads in tracksuits hauled a rusty gate open. We entered the compound, parked the van, and Vicky sprinted for a shack at the far end of the enclosure. It *did* look like a toilet, though I was half expecting our hosts to start bawling at her for pissing in their tool shed.

She emerged much happier, and limped slowly back to the group.

The toilet, when I tried it, was not a vast improvement on nature. Travelling through Asia had accustomed us to squat toilets, and Roo and I had experienced long-drop toilets in the Australian outback. This was like the best of both worlds; a long-drop-squat toilet, consisting of a pair of knackered planks over a deep hole in the ground. Peeing accuracy never being a strong point amongst the men of the world, it wasn't the sort of place you'd want to go barefoot. Still, the door closed, which provided a welcome dash of privacy for the ladies, and there was rarely a queue – the sheer quantity of insects in residence persuaded most people not to linger.

As did the smell.

Definitely not the kind of facility in which one sits to read the paper.

"Welcome to Tourist *Ger* Camp!" Soyol said, proudly. "You like?"

I glanced around, taking in the rectangle of fenced-off wasteland. Scrappy grass grew on most of it, and the family who owned the place stood watching us admire their property.

Two *ger* tents had been erected beside a small concrete-block hut. The tents were for the tourists of course, while the family squeezed into one side of the hut. The amount of smoke coming out of the other side revealed it to be the kitchen. It was hard to decide if they felt they were getting the better end of the deal; was a permanent structure of any kind seen as a status symbol here? Or had our arrival kicked them out of their nice comfy *ger* and into the bare-block hut?

"I do like it," I told her. "I like it very much."

"Oh! That is good!"

"They have space for more *gers*?" I asked, pointing at a circular concrete pad next to the second tent.

Soyol redirected this to the weary-looking woman in front of us.

"Yes!" came the translated reply, "this lady's husband, he is making a *ger* now. You want to help?"

"Of course! I'd love to!"

The husband was rummaging around in a larger shed just beyond the kitchen. He didn't seem thrilled that I was being apprenticed to him at short notice, but a few curt words from his wife settled the matter. Then she rounded up her offspring – the willowy young lads, who looked about twelve and fifteen but were probably at least five years older than that – and ordered them to help out too.

Clearly the lads had done this many, many times, and to them it was a chore of the most menial kind. They were teenagers, but I was well over twice their bodyweight, and whilst I was shivering in the evening chill, they weren't even bothering to fasten their ragged jackets, as though the cold had no effect on them.

Between us, we emptied the front of the shed, carefully carrying rather than dragging the heavy bundles of wood and cloth components. It was a lot of stuff, but not more than a pair of stout horses would be able to transport. Most precious of all was a carved wooden ring the size of a cartwheel, which was raised on two sturdy posts; painted bright orange, with identical designs to the beds at the Lotus Guesthouse, it was both sacred and practical, in that it held the roof up.

Stage One of the build involved the older lad bullying the younger into standing on a stool in the middle of the concrete circle, holding the wheel-on-stilts upright. Then everyone else made to walk away, as though they were going to get a nice cuppa while they pondered the next step. A snarl from the lad, which was instantly translatable as 'That's NOT funny!' brought shrieks of mirth all round.

I could tell this wasn't the first time he'd been left holding his ring.

The main structure of the *ger* was made of that folding wooden lattice stuff they sell in garden centres for people to grow roses up. Sections of the lattice were tied together with string, forming a fence about four feet high that encircled the concrete pad. This was Stage Two – and it took about five minutes, most of which was spent cursing whoever had tied the knots last time.

Next, bundles of painted orange poles were unwrapped. These gaily decorated struts formed the rafters, and like the door and the centrepiece they had to be bought from a specialist *ger* manufacturer. Perhaps because of this, every set I ever saw was identical, and all were treated as precious objects.

The poles rested on the lattice, and from there were slid up until their tips poked through slots on the edge of the central roof-wheel. There were sixty of them, and it took only a few seconds to place each one. They rested loosely in place, not fastened to anything, but their support was enough that the younger lad could come out to help with Stage Three: the covering.

The heaviest things we'd hauled out of the shed had been huge parcels of thick grey materiel. These were now unfolded, revealing misshapen sheets of coarse, homespun felt. Each one was cut to fit either the sides or the roof, and they had ropes on all corners to secure them to the lattice walls. Pulling them tight not only ensured a snug, chink-less barrier against the night-time air – it also squeezed the wooden structure, holding it together in a way that was both strong and easily reversible. Well, depending on who was tying the knots.

Another round of good-natured cursing was required as we unrolled enormous sheets of canvas and bound them around the entire structure, covering the insulating felt with a final, waterproof layer. Lastly, a pair of long ropes added to the *ger's* tension, hauled tight and secured to the cheerful orange door frame.

And just like that, the *ger* was done.

Time to erect: less than twenty minutes.

It would have been much quicker if I hadn't been there, grabbing the bits of felt in the wrong order, upside-down and back to front, and then tripping over them when someone else tried to turn them. These guys knew every move in the dance, and for me it was kind of magical to be involved.

The youngest lad was now scurrying around on the roof, tugging on various bits of canvas as his dad directed him. The older lad had found a splintered rafter pole and was trying to pull off a trick – holding it in both hands in front of him, then trying to take it over his head, behind his back, and step through to bring it back in front of him without letting go. I gave it a go, and earned a round of applause when I managed it first time, owing to me having unnaturally bendy wrists. It was a bonding moment, and one of the highlights of the trip so far. I picked up the pole again and showed off a few moves, half-remembered bits of a kung fu staff form I hadn't practiced in years. The lads howled with laughter when I smacked myself in the face, and had a few goes themselves. I felt like I'd made some new friends.

Suddenly, I had a brainwave. The pens we'd bought in Vietnam were still in my backpack, and I was on the lookout for someone to give them to. Perhaps a small gift would be the perfect way to cement our friendship. I didn't know if these lads did much in the way of schoolwork, but they were bound to have some use for them. Their living conditions looked so poor, so basic, and I was already feeling a little guilty about the posh labels all over my trekking clothes. Here I was, flaunting my Western riches; they weren't to know I'd bought them all second hand in a string of charity shops.

Roo was standing off to one side admiring our handiwork, so I strolled over with the suggestion. "Hey, love, do you know where those pens are? I want to give some to these lads. I bet they'd love that, and I'm getting on really well with them."

"Yeah, alright, I'll go dig them out."

Then there was a musical beep from behind me. I turned to look just as the older of the two lads reached around into his back pocket – and pulled out an iPhone. He frowned at it for a couple of seconds, then barked a laugh and tilted the screen towards his brother.

I looked back at Roo. She was suppressing a smirk.

"Maybe we'll leave the pens for now," I said.

Follow The Yellow Dirt Road

We slept well that night.

For all that this was a city – and I use that word in the loosest way possible – to all intents and purposes, it was the middle of nowhere.

There was no noise, beyond the rhythmic drumming of rain on the canvas roof.

There was no light pollution, which made the stars a spectacle to be savoured. For about two minutes, which was the longest we could brave the cold to look at them. This lack of light made the toilet more of a challenge, as did the temperature; squatting and aiming are even harder in pitch darkness when you can't see the hole. As for maintaining one's balance whilst shivering so hard it looks like you're having an epileptic fit...

Let's just say, what happens in a Mongolian pit toilet stays in a Mongolian pit toilet.

Unless it sticks to your trousers, and gets carried back inside the *ger* for all to see.

Soyol had cooked mutton and vegetable stew for dinner, taking over the family's kitchen for an hour to do so. It tasted a lot better than it sounds.

Then the stove in the centre of the *ger*, a black steel

firebox the size of a pirate's treasure chest, was filled with wood to keep us warm overnight, and we turned in early. Six single beds lined the walls – a low coffee table and a storage chest were the only other pieces of furniture present. It goes without saying they were both bright orange.

As far as I could tell, Soyol and our driver slept on the floor in the family's hut.

Breakfast was a simple affair, consisting of bread and jam, tea and coffee, and some hard biscuits Soyol had made to go with dinner last night. She also offered us a kind of butter, which the local family produced. "Yak butter!" she explained, which was enough to convince me. The others all declined, but I'm nothing if not experimental. The butter was rich and creamy, and utterly delicious – but I still couldn't persuade anyone else to try it. I've no idea why.

Piling back into the van, we had only a short drive across 'town' to our first stop of the day. The monastery of *Erdene Zuu* is all that's left of the ancient city. It consists of an impressive two-towered gateway with a pagoda on top, and colossal brick walls enclosing an area four-hundred metres square.

Outside the walls, the land is nothing but acres of coarse, scrubby grass.

Inside the walls, it's exactly the same.

Scattered here and there were a handful of brick-built shrines and temples. There was no real order to them, and for the most part no paths connecting them. More than anything though, this monastery was famed for its vast number of Mongolia's most common religious sculpture, known as a 'stupor'.

Yes – a dumb name, and a fairly appropriate one. Stupors, which look like giant chess pawns, have to be the least impressive and most pointless religious monuments I've ever encountered. They aren't gilded or encrusted with precious stones – they aren't even carved or decorated. Just white, pawn-shaped lumps of plaster, ranging in size from slightly bigger than a garden gnome to slightly smaller than a double-decker bus.

This place had thousands of them – mostly atop the walls – and the overall effect was spectacularly unspectacular.

It made you sort of stand there and say, "But... why?"

I guess it's possible I've become a little jaded when it comes to ancient monuments. I mean, once you've visited the pyramids of Egypt and the rock-tombs of Petra, pretty much anything else pales into comparison. But still, Erdene Zuu was a bit rubbish. In fairness, it *was* created by a bunch of nomadic horse-warriors, whose knowledge and ambition of advanced construction techniques were perhaps somewhat lacking. Then again, the Mongol Empire, at its height, was the largest the world has ever known. The monastery was built after their power declined, but without any of the grandeur they must have seen in the lands they'd conquered. I can only assume the descendants of Genghis Khan had better things to do with their loot than invest in religious architecture.

In one of the temple buildings within the walls, we were treated to a chanting session by the Buddhist monks. Not a staged, tourist demonstration, but a genuine chance to observe them as they performed their mid-morning prayers. It was fascinating, as a row of boys and young men sat on wooden benches either side of a table, reading aloud from a series of scripture sheets. They weren't even trying to chant in unison, and the resulting discord formed a constant drone of voices rising and falling. It felt private, and secret. It felt spiritual.

I was even inspired, on the way out, to give the prayer wheels a spin. What the prayers inside the cylindrical tins said, I had no idea, but I was doing well at the moment – I had a feeling that someone up there was on my side.

Outside the temple, stalls had been set up to catch the bustling tourist business. From the excitement displayed by the stall holders, it wasn't hard to tell that we were the only ones doing any bustling recently. They eagerly pointed out their wares, most of which were handicrafts, beads and necklaces, wood carvings and incense braziers. But each stall had a cache of antique metal work, from tin lanterns to horseshoes to... knives!

I love knives.

I have a fetish about them, to be perfectly honest. I don't know why, but I love to hold them and collect them. And these were absolutely incredible. One stall holder, noticing my admiring glances, ducked under his table and brought forth an old Japanese samurai sword. After our time in Vietnam I'd become pretty well inured to fakes, but there was something *different* about this stuff. Then I put my finger on it – this stuff was real! None of this 'made in China' crap here – it was far too costly and difficult to import cheap manufactured shit designed to look old. Here, the stuff that looked old, was old. The knife I was holding in my hand, for example, could well have existed for a hundred years or more. Its edge had been sharpened numerous times, its bone handle worn smooth with usage. The patina of the metalwork showed it had been handmade, by someone who had the time, and the skill, to put into it.

I had to have it – and after a few minutes of tense negotiation, I did.

For less than ten dollars.

Bargain!

Vicky and Roo were snapping up treasures too, buying lockets and bits of old jewellery as presents for their sisters. My gaze lingered on the katana, but the old man knew his market; he held out for fifty dollars, which was more than I could spend.

"And even if you did buy it," Roo pointed out, "how the hell are you going to fit a sword in your backpack?"

Alas, she spoke the truth. We left there with more than a few trinkets between us, the impromptu market proving a far more exciting experience than the hour spent wandering amongst the stupors.

At the end of the row of stalls, an old man in battered riding boots and a knee-length woollen jacket was offering up his pet for photographs. A magnificent golden eagle, with a wingspan that had to be approaching two metres, was handed over to us to pose with for the price of a cup of coffee. I held the glove high, and the eagle responded by flaring her wings out. Vicky got the best picture though, being far more photogenic than me, and the eagle conspired to produce an image that was destined to win contests. The Mongol man seemed to have a good rapport with the bird, and one beauty of traveling this part of the world was that tourists were few and far between; this was unlikely to be his regular job. That bird would be off hunting wolves come the evening.

It's a different world up there.

Kharkhorin was the last time we saw road.

Leaving behind all vestiges of civilization, we rattled off into the wilderness. Now the van came into its own, powering up steep inclines and ploughing down rocky slopes, bouncing along rutted goat-tracks or forging new paths through the endless expanses of grass. It was, just as Soyol had said, "good for the countryside." Roo and I had done a four-wheel-drive course back in Perth, purely for the fun of it. We'd learnt all about correct tyre pressure, bridging angles, and how to steer in sand *et cetera*. Our Mongolian driver, on the other hand, looked like he'd been doing this for at least a hundred years.

Faced with a tricky ascent that would have had our instructors climbing out to investigate, then standing around debating optimum approach angles and gear ratios, he simply pointed us towards the hill and floored it. The van roared, powering up with the kind of lean you expect on racing yachts. Several times we flung ourselves to one side or the other, in desperate attempts to balance the van before it rolled. But the driver knew his stuff, and cackling triumphantly he conquered terrain features that I was sure would send us all tumbling to a messy end.

And almost to prove a point, he did it all at a speed he couldn't even manage on the road.

We made our lunch stop at a pair of *gers* owned by a nomad family. This was the real deal; horse tack hung from the central support poles, decorative rugs had been used to line the inside of the walls, and opposite the entrance was a tiny TV connected to a car battery. Tools like handsaws had been slipped between the rafters and the felt covering for storage, a miniature Buddhist shrine sat on the now-familiar orange chest of drawers, and a sofa occupied the gap between the two single beds. The couple invited us to take tea with them, which we did – discovering in the process that Mongolians don't make tea with sugar. They make it with salt. The couple had six young children, cute as buttons in their miniature riding boots, so we managed to distribute our stash of sweets amongst them. They were delighted with the Yan Yans – a Japanese snack of biscuit fingers and flavoured dipping chocolate in a pot. Vicky had become addicted to them in Vietnam – not because they were good (they were) but because the biscuits had bizarre slogans written on them in English – like "Whale: Biggesy Mammal" and "Stag Beetle: Love It".

A couple of hours later we passed through a herd of yaks. Huge, shaggy beasts with humped shoulders covered in coarse, patchy hair, they looked misshapen – and to be honest, bloody ugly. Vicky was delighted, however; seeing a yak in the wild had been one of her main priorities, though as I was forced to point out, another hour inside that van and she'd be seeing me yak in the wild.

As the herd moved down towards a river, we approached a bridge that had to be seen to be believed. Made of logs stacked in layers and crumbling in several areas, it looked like it pre-dated the invention of motorised transport. Perhaps it did. But we had to cross it anyway; the river below was swift, the water clear as glass and colder than a penguin's nadgers. Soyol recommended we get out of the van before it made the attempt, just in case, and we were happy to oblige. I filmed the crossing, half expecting the bridge to collapse under the weight, but in a shower of splinters the van racked up yet another inadvisable victory.

I tell you what, it might sound at this point like I'm complaining, but I bloody loved that trip. *This* was adventure – about as extreme as someone like me can realistically attain. I mean, Bear Grylls is obviously off somewhere shaving his pubic hair with a live piranha, whilst other daredevils are throwing themselves off skyscrapers strapped to a frame tent. But for me, living in some approximation of the real world, this was as good as it could get.

At least until I get a Red Bull sponsorship.

I mentioned these musings to Roo, as we jounced and jangled on towards our destination for the night – the biggest waterfall in Mongolia, apparently, and a famously beautiful one.

"Don't Red Bull sponsor the X-Games?" Roo asked me.

"Yup."

"Hm. You *might* be setting your hopes a bit high, there. You need to find something closer to your level. Something with a message that reflects what you're all about. You could always try Dr Pepper…"

Nature Calling

Our camp that night was a cluster of *ger* tents set up in the shelter of a small rocky outcrop. Technically it was a tourist camp, as evidenced by the fact that there were four *gers*, all showing signs of age, and a battered Russian ex-army jeep parked amongst them. But again I remembered that tourism was a scarce commodity in these parts, and the people running the camp would never be able to rely exclusively on it for their livelihood. Consequently, it was more like a homestay than purpose-built tourist accommodation. Animals roamed freely around the area; scrawny goats, towering yaks and dogs whose size fell somewhere in between. *Lonely Planet* sagely informed us that the traditional countryside greeting, *"Nokhoi Khori!"*, usually called out on the approach to a stranger's *ger,* literally translates as "Hold the dog!"

As always, the first order of business upon arriving was to locate the toilet. Roughly half the time this proved impossible, because there wasn't one.

This time, however, we were in luck. This being a semi-permanent residence, at least for half the year, the owners had dug a loo, so we went in search of it straight away. It was much farther than we expected, and took some finding even with directions. Presumably to keep unpleasant odours away from the camp they'd dug their pit a good few minutes' walk from the tents. By way of compensation, they'd picked an incredible spot; if ever there was a loo with a view, this was it. Surrounded by a waist-high log fence, it faced the mountains across the vast, undulating plains.

"Worth making the trip," Roo commented, as she squatted behind the privacy screen. "This thing works as a windbreak, too!"

Now, it's not often that wind direction is a factor in urination – but out here on the steppe, the buffeting breeze could have serious implications for one's aim.

When the nomads were good enough to provide us with boards over their hole to stand on, it did seem rather rude to piss all over them.

Of course, this wasn't a problem for Roo. She was more concerned with the bum-chill factor.

It was a beautiful walk back though.

The matriarch of the family was milking a yak, which by that point seemed completely normal. She crouched on a tiny plastic stool, and had mastered an interesting milking technique. Holding a baby yak under one arm, she let it reach out and take its mother's teat in its mouth. Once the baby started to suckle she pulled it away, fastening her gnarled hands on the teats and squeezing them for all she was worth.

The baby yak moaned in dismay, and received a clip around the ears with the woman's free hand as she adjusted her grip.

"Poor little thing," said Roo.

"She might regret doing that, when it's the size of a pickup truck."

Next we explored Mongolia's biggest waterfall, which the lateness of the season had reduced to a trickle. It was still impressive though – a sudden stab wound in the heart of the grasslands, the much-reduced Orkhon River spilling twenty-six metres into a basin far below us. The sheer-sided gorge was filled with the tallest trees I'd seen in the country. They grew exactly as high as the gorge was deep, stopping abruptly level with our feet; even they knew better than to mess with the fierce winds of the steppe.

That evening Soyol invited us to help her cook dinner. She was making *khuushuur*, a popular snack pastry eaten mainly during *Naadam*, a countrywide festival of wrestling, horse racing and archery that we were sadly going to miss. Soyol made dough balls and rolled them out into small circles, working on a round (orange) table near the central stove. She put a teaspoon of mince in the centre, folded the circle over it to create a pocket, and pinched it closed, creating a distinctive crimped edge. My own attempts were significantly less uniform, looking kind of like Soyol's would have if they'd been driven over by a jeep. The girls, unsurprisingly, excelled at khuushuur-crimping, and Soyol fried our creations in batches, serving them hot from the pan. They were delicious, like savoury donuts, and very moreish. The minced meat in them was, of course, mutton; I had a strong suspicion that Soyol had half a dead sheep stashed in one of her cardboard boxes, and was slowly working her way through it.

By way of a treat, the local family invited us to sample *tarag*. I accepted before I knew what it was, and was shown into their home *ger* next door. I was presented with a big bowl of yoghurt, which I took with my right hand as tradition demanded. The yoghurt was fresh – still warm, in fact – and slightly fizzy. It had a vaguely sour taste, but was not unpleasant.

"Made from horse milk," Soyol translated, "you like?"

"Yes, very good," I replied, making enthusiastic "Mmm!" noises to convey my appreciation.

This was a mistake, as my empty bowl was immediately swapped for another full one. Which of course I had to eat for politeness, though I learned my lesson and finished it quietly.

"It's good you only eat two bowls," Soyol told me afterwards, me with a wink.

I found out later that tarag is a powerful laxative.

That night I felt the dreaded clench in my stomach, a sure-fire indication that the yoghurt had done its evil work. It hit me with an urgency that brooked no argument, so I sprinted out of the tent and into the frigid darkness.

I remembered to grab a head torch on the way out, which got me as far as the dirt road we'd driven in on. I knew the loo was over the road, so I crossed it – and was faced with the endless, trackless grasslands in front of me.

Only it was all pitch black.

"Okay, I can do this," I told myself.

Whilst it's true that my sense of direction isn't the greatest, I knew I only had a short distance to go. I was fairly sure of the rough direction, and of course I was heading for the only structure between me and the mountains. If I reached them without finding the toilet, well, I'd have covered at least a hundred miles on foot, so I'd probably have shit myself.

There was a rise in the ground, an embankment running parallel to the road. This I also remembered, and I jogged up it and down the other side. *Keep walking straight,* I thought, because my trajectory on leaving the road had seemed about right.

Until I'd been stumbling through the darkness for several long minutes without coming across anything. My stomach gurgled audibly, and I stopped to consider my options. I could retrace my steps and try a slightly different angle from the road. Or I could carry on this way, and hope. Or I could walk in a spiral, like divers do when searching for something... Hm. Perhaps that was a bit ambitious. Plus, it was kind of hard to concentrate with my arse about to explode.

Walk back, I decided, *try again.* So I turned around, and behind me there was nothing but darkness. No road. No bus. No sign of the camp at all. There was a ridge between here and there, and it prevented even the tiniest trickle of light from reaching me. Then I made a huge mistake; I turned around again. It was automatic, a reflex action to see if I could spot any other clues. And just like that, I no longer knew which direction I'd been facing to start with.

The night extended seamlessly in all directions.

It made me want to cry.

I had no frame of reference. The ground rose and fell at random intervals, making walking difficult, but none of these features worked as a landmark. I swept the torch around me, but its beam failed to penetrate the darkness. It was good for showing up the grass at my feet, and not much else.

Shit!

I couldn't risk doing a wild poo, only to discover that in full light of day it was clearly visible, ten feet from the camp, leading to awkward breakfast conversations along the lines of "Who put that turd there?"

I had no choice but to keep walking...

About forty minutes later, I crested a rise and saw the ghost of a log fence.

Thank the Gods!

I daren't run, because breaking an ankle whilst going to the toilet and freezing to death in the sub-zero wilderness five minutes from my tent would be a shitty way to go.

So I moseyed.

Within the confines of the logs, the torch-light was far more useful, and allowed me to position myself without sticking a leg down the toilet. Then I took hold of the fence and squatted, praying that my arse was aimed correctly, and that my frozen fingers would retain their grip.

And, relax...

But not too much.

Finally, with my business done, I stood eyeing the route back to camp.

From here it should be a fairly simple trip. My sense of direction was restored, and sooner or later there should be some light leakage to help guide me.

By which I mean, leakage of actual light, not, you know, the other stuff.

So I set off.

Ten minutes later, hopelessly lost again, I was starting to despair. Why the bloody hell did they have to build the bog in such a ridiculous location? They were a tourist camp, for crying out loud! Surely this problem had arisen before?

Or was everyone else escorted by a guide on their way to lay cable?

Maybe it was my fault. Obviously I lacked the basic ability to walk in a straight line, otherwise I'd have hit at least some part of the camp by now.

I stopped, and stared around me.

Nothing.

Then it dawned on me: the head torch was screwing me over!

Its beam was too weak to pick out anything more than a few metres away, but it was ruining any chance of developing night vision. I reached up and switched it off, and stood there with my eyes closed for a couple of minutes. Sure enough, when I opened them the world had taken on a tiny bit more definition. Everything was still black, but there were shades to it now – so, following my nose (because it juts out quite a way in front of me), I headed off in what seemed like the right direction.

I could tell when I crossed the road, because the hard-packed earth underfoot felt different from the grass. It was flat and hard and rocky, rather than uneven and hard and rocky; a small distinction, but it meant I was on the right track. Literally.

Then, out of the inky blackness loomed a shadowy form, a structure perhaps. I walked towards it, one hand extended before me… and recoiled as it made contact with something warm and hairy.

"YAK!" I yelled, as what I'd hoped was a wall suddenly moved beneath my fingers. "Hairy yak!"

I backed away – not in revulsion, because even unexpected animals are my friends – but because the yak might not share this sentiment, and might instead choose to stick his horns into my belly.

I edged around the beast at a safe distance, and there it was – a tiny sliver of yellow light, spilling out from under the door of our *ger*. Somehow I'd approached from entirely the wrong direction, and the yak had been blocking my line of sight.

Which, you know, happens sometimes.

Cold and weary, I strode up to the door and let myself back in.

"There you are!" said Roo. "We were about to send out a search party!"

"I could have used them about half an hour ago," I said,

"but you'd never have found me. I was beyond the yak."

"Oh," said Roo, "that's... unfortunate."

"Tell me about it!"

"I'm glad you're back though."

"Yeah, me too."

"I've been waiting for you, because I need you to help me with something."

"Oh, right? No worries. What is it?"

"Er... I'm busting for the toilet, and it's a bit dark outside... Will you go with me?"

One Small Steppe For Man

The following morning, immediately after breakfast, we were introduced to our horses. A small herd of them had arrived with the dawn, led by a taciturn Mongolian herdsman and his teenage son.

This was the part of the tour we'd all been looking forward to; the next two days were to be spent in the saddle, exploring the steppes the way the Mongols had for many hundreds of years.

In agony.

Because the saddles we'd be spending those days in were made of wood.

Two short planks joined lengthways, they were wrapped in a thin sheet of leather. Stirrups dangled on loops of rope, and the whole thing rested on a scrap of carpet thrown over the horse's back.

That was bound to make it more comfortable.

But this is how the Mongols rode, how they'd been riding for hundreds – nay, thousands, of years. Chinggis Khan had created the greatest empire the world has ever known from one of these things, though how he went on to father hundreds of children afterwards was a mystery. Obviously the Supreme Warlord of the Eastern Steppe had sturdier bollocks.

The horses were cute; scruffy, miniature beasts, with the look of real horses but about half the size. With the diminutive Mongolian horse-herder mounted atop one, it still looked undersized. With a six-foot white guy on, it looked ridiculous. My feet almost touched the ground on both sides.

But I'm getting ahead of myself. Before he let us mount, the horse guide made us line up in front of the horses. Not too close, mind, in case we startled them.

He inspected us like we were troops in his army, looking us up and down before making what I assumed were scathing comments about our dress sense.

"No," he said, tugging on Vicky's scarf. Perplexed, she took it off, and looked to Soyol for an explanation.

"Nothing loose," she translated, "because it could flap and scare the horse."

"No," the horse man said again, pointing to a dangling camera.

"No taking pictures," Soyol explained, "because it may startle the horse."

"I could turn the flash off?" Roo offered.

"No. The sound of it, and the movement, could scare her. Don't make sudden movements while on the horse."

"Are we allowed to fall off?" I joked.

"No. Nearest hospital is Ulaanbaatar, so please don't fall off!"

Now there was a sobering thought. In case of emergency, an airlift didn't seem likely. Especially since we didn't have any insurance.

Well, Vicky did.

"Only Vicky is allowed to fall off then," I said, "because they'll send a helicopter for her!"

Vicky didn't look too thrilled at the prospect.

When it came time to mount, we were helped into the saddles by the horse guide's son. Honestly, I think I could have thrown one leg over without difficulty, but the guide seemed to think it was very important that we be helped on and off.

"You have ridden before?" Soyol asked me.

"Yes," I said. I didn't bother telling her exactly how long it had been since I'd last ridden, as there was no point in worrying her. I felt sure I could control this pint-sized beast – and if it wouldn't behave, well, I could always get off and carry it.

"That's good," Soyol told me, "because the man says your horse is nervous."

"Oh. Well, I can handle it."

"Good! You are like a proper Mongol!"

I had the feeling she was mocking me, just slightly.

"He told me my horse is nervous, too," Roo said, nudging it closer.

"Oh? Funny, that..."

With everyone mounted and struggling to find a comfy position, it was time for the off. Soyol guided her tiny pony to the head of the line for a last conference with the guides.

"Can you ask him what my horse is called?" I asked her as she went passed.

"Has no name," she replied.

"Why is that?"

"All Mongolian horses have no name. Because... so many!"

"Ah! Fair enough. But these horses *have* been ridden before?"

"Oh yes," she replied, "some of them."

Soyol mounted her horse, looking far more appropriately scaled for it, and we moved off. The van, with all our gear in the back of it, would meet us at our destination – which for today was the *Khujirt* hot springs, which are famed for their healing waters. Like pretty much every hot springs on the planet.

By the time we got there, I'd be needing them.

It wasn't long before that saddle started to take its toll. Half an hour into our first day on horseback, my arse began to sing. The rhythmic back and forth motion, with the saddle rising and falling in time with the horse's gait, was easy enough to master. I let my hips do most of the work, keeping them loose enough to absorb the movement, and for the most part, that was okay.

But sitting on a plank for any length of time isn't pleasant – that's why we invented upholstery. Sitting on a moving plank that spanks you every time your horse takes a misstep, well, that's worse. And Mongolian grasslands aren't known for being smooth.

A pair of thick steel rings protruded up from the front and back of the saddle, and the space in between them was clearly Mongolian-sized. My buttocks were being ground against the metal with every step, until I shifted slightly forwards – at which point the same thing started happening to my testicles.

There really was no way to win here.

I'm not saying I have a big ass, but Kim Kardashian, if you're reading this, *do not* book yourself a horse tour of the Orkhon Valley. Seriously.

By the time we'd gone an hour, my thighs were on fire. I could feel blisters developing in some of the more tender areas of my anatomy – you know, the ones where you hope never to have blisters. The heat of the sun and the effort of riding conspired to make me sweat quite a bit, and the sweatiest part of me was the bit stuck to the saddle.

Oh man, did it chafe.

But pain is a mental thing. I could ignore most of it. I knew, intellectually, that no permanent damage was being done – well, except to my chance of having children – so I managed to tune out some of the discomfort, and instead became enthralled in the surrounding scenery. It was epic. The grasslands were as flat and empty as they had been since the last ice age. Occasionally I'd catch a glimpse of the van, trailing us at a discreet distance on some invisible goat-track.

The ground was rocky, with sharp edges protruding from the stubborn grass. Passing a tree was an event; some had blue scarves tied around them, as though to thank the gods for providing something more interesting to look at.

The scale of that place, and the complete lack of anything between the scrub and the sky, dwarfed all my concepts of open spaces. I'd hiked through the wilderness in several countries, but nowhere else did it seem quite so wild, and so impossibly isolated. The steppe felt eternal and unchanging, as though humans made no difference here; neither the wind nor the grass cared one whit about them.

They were somebody else's problem.

The guide led Vicky's horse by the nose for the first few miles, until she felt brave enough to take control herself. But control was mostly an illusion; the horses followed their herd, as they must have done their whole lives, moving from place to place with their owner and his family. In his battered trilby and crumbling leather boots, this guy was the real deal – not gimmicked up for the public, because why bother? Everyone out here was the real deal. Here the nomadic herders followed the grazing, followed ancient migration patterns – hell, they followed I-Ching for all I knew. Their lives were simple, and their needs basic. It was a hard life, for a tough people.

But at least they didn't get stopped five times a day and asked if they'd accepted Jesus.

The blonde girl from Norway had the least control over her horse. Head down, munching grass, it ignored the rest of the group until we'd all filed past. Then it would look up, think, 'Shit, they're getting away!' and bolt back to the front of the column. Once there it would chill out and start grazing again, waiting until the last horse plodded in front of it, before repeating its burst of energy. The blonde girl was carried along for the ride, bouncing around with a white-knuckled grip on her saddle ring – and then she sat there grinning sheepishly as we all rode past her again.

The horse kept this up all day.

When I spotted the van parked beside a river, and realised we were about to stop for lunch, I could have cried.

"Is this enough adventure for you?" Roo asked, as she munched on a sandwich.

I thought about this for a moment. "Love, next time I suggest doing something adventurous, I want you to kick me as hard as you can in the testicles, and keep kicking me until I remember this moment. It'll be safer, a lot cheaper, and at least one of us will get to have fun."

"So you're not thinking of wearing the J-Lo Pants then?"

"The…?"

Then a bulb pinged on in my head. *The J-Lo Pants!*

I'd found them in a tiny supermarket in Hanoi, and tried them on for a laugh. They were women's knickers, flesh-coloured and satin-smooth. Only, for no reason any of us could figure out, they had thick padding on each bum cheek – like a wonder-bra for your butt. I could only guess the Vietnamese had discovered reality TV.

After wearing the pants all around the shop just to watch people's reactions, I thought I'd probably better buy them. They were a steal at $3, and they'd been buried in my rucksack ever since. No matter what anyone says.

Now I dug them out, and pulled them on over my jeans. At 3XL, they were a snug fit – who knew?

I instantly felt more attractive, and my twerking confidence increased a hundredfold. Roo filmed me whilst Vicky, Soyol and the three girls pissed themselves laughing.

Our horse guide just looked confused.

Within minutes of climbing back on the horse, my arse was in agony again. Unsurprisingly, the J-Lo Pants did absolutely nothing to protect my delicate buttocks – I felt like I'd been kicked from Kharkhorin to here, without being allowed to touch the ground.

Get to the hot springs, get to the hot springs, became my mantra.

As each bruised bum-cheek bounced off the instrument of my torture, I gritted my teeth and sounded it out in my mind;

Just.

Get.

To.

The.

Hot.

Springs!

"I tell you what," I said to Roo, in a rare moment of riding next to each other, "these hot springs had better be worth it."

The Hot Springs

Five hours later, the guides led us up to a *ger* and dismounted, waving at us to do the same.

Swinging my leg up and over was so painful I nearly passed out and toppled right off the beast. Which would have been embarrassing, as when my head hit the ground my legs would still have been wrapped around him.

But once on my feet, I found I could still walk. Blood flow returned to some parts of me that had been denied recently, and with it came the realisation that I might still be capable of having children one day.

The whole group tottered around like kids trying to walk in their mum's tallest heels, and there were gasps and grimaces of pain from all quarters.

"That wasn't too bad," I said, trying to lighten the mood.

I received a number of black stares.

Soyol seemed completely unaffected by the ride. After conferring with the guides she came over to make us an offer. "If you want, we can go the rest of the way in the van. Because we go too slow with the horses."

All eyes looked up. Hope flickered in every one of them.

"If you want," Soyol continued, "say now, and we all go in the van."

Shave My Spider!

There was a chorus of agreement.

But then, as we were clustered around the bus repacking our things, an idea came to me.

We'd been going slow on the horses because of the inexperienced riders. So if I stayed with the horses on my own, while the others rode in the van... I might get to do some real riding!

And just like that, the switch in my brain was flicked to adventure. So what if my backside felt like Rocky's punching bag? This could be the experience that made Mongolia for me – galloping across the wild steppe like one of Chinggis's riders, only without the butchery, rape and pillage at the end of it.

"I think I'll take my horse," I said, eliciting shocked responses from all around me.

"Aren't you in pain yet?" Roo demanded, clearly upset that I wasn't.

"I am," I admitted, "but this could be my one chance to go fast!"

She shook her head and climbed into the bus. "Suit yourself. But you'll regret it."

I headed back over to the horses, brimming with enthusiasm. I knew this was going to hurt – but that didn't matter, because it was also going to be *awesome*.

Unfortunately, such acts of bravery are often contagious.

"Yeah! I think I'll go on my horse, too," said the blonde girl.

"Hey, why not?" said her friend.

And within seconds, my plan was in tatters. All three girls had decided to join me, ruining any possibility of going for a gallop. Even worse, I couldn't back out now; after inspiring them with my bravado, I couldn't just chicken out and bugger off back to the bus.

So, one by one, we remounted – and I felt my mistake in every shriek of tortured flesh.

Vicky and Roo sat in the bus, looking smug.

Absolute bastards, I thought.

But it was not directed at my wife and her sister, nor at the girls who had unintentionally scuppered my scheme. This epithet was reserved for the Gods of Fate – which is who I choose to blame when I know, deep down inside, that it was really my fault.

The bus led the way, speeding off down a dirt road in a fashion which Roo later told me was even less fun than being on the horses. We plodded along afterwards, each lost in our own private torment.

Then my horse, which had been following the narrow strip of grass beside the road, climbed a few steps as the grass became a bank. The girls stayed in formation, riding single file down the middle of the road, but I've always liked to be different – and anyway the horse had made the decision to be up here, not me. I could live with it.

But then the ridge I was on and the road began to part company. In a few strides I was no longer walking with the pack; I was walking above them.

I hauled on the reigns, but already my horse's hooves were as high as the saddle of the horse next to me. Which admittedly wasn't that high, but it was getting higher all the time.

The guide called out to me, something that Soyol translated as, "Tony, come down from there!"

I bit back a savagely sarcastic response in favour of, "I'm trying!"

A tree was growing on the edge of the hill, and the guide was urging me to jump down before we reached it. The horse had other ideas though, and took the opportunity to climb further up the hill. By now the guide was shouting at me, presumably swearing, and I was starting to get worried. I wasn't in nearly as much control as I'd thought, and this horse was more than half wild. I didn't dare try to punish it, as I was now at its mercy; a fall from here was suddenly a much more dangerous prospect.

Fighting with the reins, I managed to drag the horse's head back towards the others. Ahead I could see a dip, where the ridge came within a metre of the road again. After that the slope rose dramatically, and I'd be on my own. Flapping my legs ineffectually, I hauled on the reins. It wasn't the kindest way to treat the horse, and not something I would usually do, but I was getting desperate. Gradually the horse came around, and I pointed him at a spot where the lip of the ridge had crumbled. I'd have to let him figure out how to negotiate it. *Oh shit, here goes,* I thought – and the horse sprang down onto the road, trotting a few steps as though in triumph.

'*Look what I did!*' he was saying, as he pranced past the others.

I clung to his back and waited while the guide caught us up. He rode around the front of my horse, leaned out of his saddle, and punched the horse squarely in the face.

Soyol trotted up to translate his advice to me; "Be careful with this one. He's trouble."

Great, I thought. This is exactly the right time to tell me that.

An hour down that road, we came to a fence. The van was parked in a nearby clearing, and Roo and Vicky were waiting for us.

This was it!

I dismounted eagerly, if a little stiffly, and we all piled through the gate, along a path, and up the hill.

And finally, we saw it.

The famous hot spring.

Vicky gave voice to the words that were on everyone's mind;

"You have got to be fucking kidding me!"

There, right before us, was a barely discernable puncture in the Earth's skin. From beneath a small pile of stones, steaming water trickled out into a depression the size and depth of a dinner plate. Well okay, maybe not *quite* that big.

I believe the technical term for this natural phenomenon is 'a puddle'.

It has to be said that, as tourist attractions go, it was a bit of a disappointment.

Although it was more of a hot dribble than a spring, I guess it fulfilled the dictionary definition. Water, heated by geothermal activity inside the ground, came out of it at precisely this point. Only, it came at a rate that, had it been a leaky tap in your bathroom, you wouldn't even bother to call a plumber.

Suddenly, the ridiculousness of the situation caught up with me.

"Don't think we'll be taking a bath in it," I said, and chuckled.

The van driver was similarly unimpressed. He'd brought a plastic coke bottle to fill with these supposedly healing waters – but the puddle was too shallow to get the neck of the bottle into.

We'd struggled so hard to get here, and our expectations had grown alongside the pain. For the last few hours I'd been fantasising about total body immersion; sliding into a pool of hot, mineral-infused water and letting the heat and the bubbles massage the ache from my muscles. An actual massage wouldn't have gone amiss either, and I'd strongly considered the possibility of paying for one, were it on offer.

Now, it all seemed so silly. This was Mongolia for gawd's sake! What on Earth made me think that after days of grass, goats and canvas-covered tents, there would be some kind of luxury resort? A health spa, with fluffy white towels and maybe even a steam room? Exotic fragrances in the air and natural salts in the huge stone baths…

I'd been thinking of England. The Roman baths at Bath.

Or New Zealand, where they had a modern-day version near Rotorua.

Not Mongolia. Where the concept of any kind of bath had yet to catch on.

Hell, the concept of running water had yet to catch on everywhere outside the capital. I should have known. We later discovered there was only one public swimming pool in the entire country, in central Ulaanbaatar.

And it was closed.

Soyol, bless her, tried hard to mitigate our disappointment. It only occurred to me now that neither she, nor our driver, had been here before either. There was an element of the blind leading the blind at work here, but I didn't want to think too hard about that. Instead I focussed on the conversation between Soyol and an extremely reticent old man, who turned out to be the owner of the spring.

It took her a long time to coax the information out of him, but as it turned out he was planning to build something similar to what we'd expected. On a more appropriate scale no doubt, but he'd already built a wooden chalet, which was to be a hotel of sorts. He'd also erected a narrow concrete hut – the first use of a solid building material I'd seen since the sporadic walls in Kharkhorin. Inside the hut were the old man's pride and joy: a row of modern shower cubicles not unlike my high school changing rooms. The water for these was supplied by a huge steel tank, which was raised on stilts behind the chalet – and it was spring water, slowly siphoned from the lowest puddle at a rate that would take it a decade to fill.

After a good ten minutes of terse negotiation, Soyol broke the good news. "You want to try?"

Hardly able to contain my excitement, I volunteered to be the first person to test the showers. The owner had given them a go of course, to check they were working – but I don't think he'd actually stripped off for it. Mongolians are quite strange when it comes to water touching their bodies, and until the place opened for tourists – sometime in the next millennium, judging by demand – no-one else was going to get near it.

I raced back to the bus for my towel, and took a quick shower in the warm, sulphur-smelling water. Roo waited patiently for me, and let me out when I was done; bizarrely, the doors locks had been fitted the wrong way around, and could only be opened from the outside.

Roo and Vicky took their turn next, and having been raised in Australia, with their uber-conscious attitude to water wastage, they were both done inside three minutes.

The three younger girls returned from the bus laden with bags of toiletries and cosmetics. They looked like they would be taking full advantage of this opportunity, so the rest of us regrouped at the bus and waited for them.

And waited. And waited.

We took bets on how long they'd be. The landowner was obviously reluctant to let us use his brand new facilities, and Soyol had needed to do some fast (and extensive) talking to convince him. So of course, the right thing to do was justify all his fears by spending half a day in there, draining all his precious water.

Not.

The girls seemed oblivious to this though, and by the time they returned – having changed into their pyjamas – Vicky's guess of forty-five minutes was closest. But only because none of us had guessed higher.

Soyol was annoyed, for a number of reasons. For one, it was getting quite late, and we still had a lot of ground to cover. For two, the girls were now inappropriately dressed, as that ground had to be covered on horseback.

Even I was surprised about this, although I should have seen it coming.

"Too many horses for the guide to take on his own," Soyol explained.

Of course; his son had stayed with Vicky and Roo's horses while the rest of us rode here. It was my fault the horses had been brought at all, instead of being left at the *ger*, but if the girls hadn't decided to spoil my fun by accompanying me, there'd only be my horse to take back anyway.

And if I could have ridden at a decent speed, I'd have been more than happy to take it back myself.

But no. Instead, and with much complaining, the girls returned to the shower block and changed back into their stinking horse-clothes. Then, at the same agonising pace, we plodded back the way we'd come.

The only point of interest on this last hour of torment came when I guided my horse along the track beneath the ridge he'd tried to climb earlier.

Apparently he 'saw' a stick in the path, and thought it was a snake – so he tried to climb the ridge again.

Only backwards, this time.

I pretty much shit myself at that point, I can tell you.

A Steppe Too Far?

We plodded into camp, utterly exhausted, just as the light began to fail.

Now, before anyone scoffs at our lack of endurance, I should point out that in Mongolia, at that time of year, dusk comes around 10:30pm.

A few breaks aside, we'd been in the saddle for almost twelve hours at this point.

It was late, and it was dark.

We were starving.

And Soyol had just started mixing flour and water to make dough.

I guessed it was dumplings for dinner, then. And it looked like it was going to be a midnight feast.

After eating I went out to brush my teeth, and spent a few minutes marvelling at the stars. There were so many of them out here, they were almost bright enough to see by. I'd stopped using the head torch for my night-time ablutions, as it generally did more harm than good. Without it, I was treated to the full brilliance of the night sky, a spectacle at once awe-inspiring and utterly humbling. I bet the nomads never got bored of it; I know I never would.

I finished brushing my teeth, starting to feel the cold, and spat a mouthful of toothpaste over the nearby fence. Too late, I glanced down and noticed a large shadow directly in the line of fire. I clicked on my head torch and its beam revealed our horse guide's saddle, neatly arranged on the ground – and now liberally splattered with white foam.

Direct hit! What were the chances?

I wiped it away as best I could, and hoped it wasn't some kind of omen.

Day Two of the horse ride very nearly didn't happen.

I woke up stiff – and not in the way I usually wake up stiff.

Sorry, was that too much information?

Anyway, I was not alone in feeling the effects of the previous day's exertions. Soyol had explained that our first day in the saddle was a practice run, and that we'd be covering nearly twice as much ground on the second day.

I couldn't tell if she was joking or not, but had a horrible feeling she wasn't.

So when she announced, over breakfast, that we'd only be riding until lunch, she earned a special place in my heart. Suddenly, the whole day was looking up; stale bread and jam had never tasted so good.

Mounting up was still accompanied by groans of pain, but having a clear end in sight made the discomfort more bearable. I felt more in control as well, with my horse responding to my use of the reins. Perhaps he'd thought he was rid of me, and seeing me come back for more had taken the fight out of him.

Or maybe he was starting to like me.

Either way, I decided to play around with my newfound confidence, letting the others get a fair way ahead of me and then persuading my steed into a light canter to catch up. For his part, he seemed to enjoy the change of pace, so I kept it up.

After a few hours the landscape grew rockier, with dagger-like points of stone protruding from the ground. Caution, rather than speed, was needed here, so I let my horse pick his own route again, and went back to admiring the view.

I could tell we were nearing the end of our trek when Soyol, after a few words with the horse guide, asked us if we'd like to try a bit of a trot.

Everyone seemed keen, having all gained in confidence over the last couple of days. So Soyol told the horse guide, and he gave a sharp cry.

The horses weren't entirely convinced, but I wasn't having any of it. I pressed my calves into him (as my heels were much too far away) and he sprang away at full tilt.

Unfortunately, he chose to full tilt straight into Vicky's horse, which had also started running. The two beasts crashed into each other, rearing up and flailing with their hooves. When my horse came down, I was still on top of it – just.

Not so, Vicky. She'd been thrown violently from the saddle, landing heavily on the rocky ground. But that wasn't all. Her horse, suddenly free from the burden of its rider, decided to celebrate by doing a victory lap.

And Vicky's foot was still caught in the stirrup.

It was a terrifying scene as the horse bolted, dragging Vicky around like a rag doll. The guide raced to grab the horse, while I leapt down and ran to where Vicky lay, her foot having finally twisted free.

She wasn't moving.

Her eyes were open but she was just lying there, trembling in shock, as tears ran down her face.

Oh fuck, I thought. Time to call the air ambulance.

If Mongolia even had one.

But Vicky was made of sterner stuff. After a few minutes we helped her up, and she hobbled around to prove nothing was broken. It had been a lucky escape. Although Soyol had deliberately waited for less rocky ground before suggesting a run, there were still plenty of large outcroppings littered around. Vicky's head had bounced around like a basketball, and of course none of us were wearing helmets. She wound up having a truly impressive series of bruises on her back and legs, but it could have been so, so much worse. It was a timely reminder that the steppe, though seemingly benign, was not to be fucked with.

Chinggis Khan had conquered three-quarters of the known world on the back of his trusty Mongolian steed, campaigning constantly from the saddle for almost fifty years.

And falling off his horse had killed him.

Vicky bravely remounted, and a sedate half-hour brought us to a shallow river, which we splashed across towards the van on the other side.

And lunch.

It was such an arbitrary place to stop. There was nothing to mark it as significant, beyond the wide sweep of river we'd just crossed; nothing that gave a sense of 'here is the end', or a feeling of closure.

"A shame, really, that we're not riding on after lunch," I observed to Roo.

The look she gave me was filled with horror. "Don't even *think* about it," she warned.

The secret to my more relaxed attitude was a small orange towel, which I'd rolled up and stuffed down my trousers. It had provided significantly more protection than the J-Lo Pants, though at considerable cost to its use as a towel; Vicky filmed me as I pulled it out from between my thighs, warm, moist, and somewhat fragrant. I was tempted to chase her around the van with it, but even the towel hadn't absorbed all the punishment. My bollocks had taken a beating ten football hooligans couldn't have inflicted in a week, and had finally given up. All I could feel now was a spreading numbness that reached to my knees. I wasn't entirely sure I could walk, let alone run.

I settled for delivering a piece of wisdom to the camera; "When they warned you in The Hitchhiker's Guide To The Galaxy, that you should always know where your towel was," I said, "this is *exactly* what they were talking about."

While Soyol got to work on our lunch, we took a few photos of each other with the horses. It was hard to believe so much pain and discomfort had come from such unassuming beasts. The guide and his son went around the herd, tying them all to a long lead rope, and they left without another word.

Just like that, the horse-borne part of our adventure was over. Out of the advertised six-day horse trek, we'd been prepared to spend only two of them actually riding. We'd ended up with one and a half – but you know what? I didn't see a single person complaining.

Safely back in the van, we made much better time, arriving at our next destination substantially quicker than we would have done on horseback. I had to admit though, the van was *so* much more comfortable, even with my head bouncing off the roof every time we hit a pothole.

Our original goal for the second day's ride would had been impossibly ambitious. The remote *Tövkhön Monastery* was perched atop a heavily forested mountain, towering some 2,600 metres above the steppe. Established by a fourteen-year-old Tibetan Buddhist from Outer Mongolia, it had survived attacks from savage tribesmen and from Chinese-backed Communists. Well, it hadn't; it had been destroyed by both of them. But each time it had been restored and re-consecrated, and now we had arrived to invade its sanctuary once more.

Our driver decided he wasn't up to tackling the trail up the mountain, so we left him with the van and went up on foot. In truth it was a rough old route, great crevices opening across the road and the path twisting and turning upwards at a crazy angle. Poor Vicky hobbled bravely along, her ankle now swollen to three times its normal size. It wasn't until we reached the top that we realised there must be a back way up there; in a clearing just below the peak, there was a bloody car boot sale! At least twenty vehicles, some of them not even four-wheel-drives, sat in a row while their occupants milled around, sharing out food and drinks.

We lumbered out from the trees, sweating and panting from our exertions, still walking like we had a horse between our thighs, and waded into the midst of a family picnic.

It made us feel rather daft, to be honest.

We climbed up to the monastery, which in typical Buddhist

tradition had been built in the least accessible place possible. I've never quite understood why. I mean, I'm all for communing with nature, and getting away from the distractions of modern life, but in Mongolia? What the hell were they trying to escape from, yak attacks?

Soyol led us around an exposed precipice right by the tip of the mountain. There, a tiny cave had been walled in with bricks, creating a refuge so far removed from this world it was almost in the next. The view, though, was also heavenly; from this height, as I looked out to the horizon, I swear I could see the curvature of the earth. And all that lay before me, from the foot of the mountain to the next range over, and beyond until the haze of atmosphere clouded my vision – was grass.

No wonder they had so many horses.

We got lost on the walk back down the mountain, spending a good hour stumbling through the forest looking for clues. We never found our way back to the path we'd come up on, but we did stumble over some unexpected ruins, including great blocks of chiselled stone which lay almost completely buried in the undergrowth. It could have been anything; the remains of an earlier monastery perhaps, or something even earlier still? We had no way of knowing, and Soyol was marching onwards, obviously a bit embarrassed at getting us so completely lost. But I couldn't help wondering, just what we'd discovered back there. So much of Mongolia is still wild and unexplored, at least by Westerners, and so much of their history is still shrouded in mystery.

"We should remember this place, and come back one day to explore it properly," Roo suggested.

"Hell yeah!" Vicky agreed. "Only… not on horses," she added.

Understandably.

The Kindness of Strangers

The drive to camp seemed to take forever that night. We roamed across the hills, stopping to ask directions whenever we saw a *ger*. After getting so lost in the forest, I was starting to worry that we were even more lost now, and would simply miss our destination altogether. It wasn't too hard to imagine; there only had to be a single hillside between them and us, and we'd drive right past without knowing. Soyol was starting to look anxious, when we came to a pair of *gers* with a sturdy-looking log barn behind them. Goats were everywhere, roaming freely around the tents. Soyol got out once more, and started chatting to the camp's owners. They seemed rather surprised to see us.

"Oh man, I don't think this is the place," I said, as I saw Soyol pointing back the way we'd come.

I was trying to figure out what she was asking the couple, and what they were saying back to her, based solely on the body language. It was only then, as I squinted out of the window at Soyol's negotiations, that I had a moment of clarity.

"Oh my God. These places we're staying at, they're not arranged in advance. They're not even arranged at all! It's not directions she's asking for – we're just rocking up at random *gers* and asking if we can stay for the night!"

Recognition dawned on every face. Of course that's what we were doing! Relying on the legendary hospitality of the Mongolian nomads. Which is why, as Soyol shook hands with the man she was talking to, his sons emerged and carried their beds from one *ger* to the other. They were being so hospitable, to a van load of strangers on holiday, that they were booting their own children out of the house!

We watched aghast as the family made room for us, removing a goodly amount of furniture and possessions from the *ger* we'd be sleeping in. I could only hope that some money was changing hands for the inconvenience – especially as every one of us was paying sixty-five dollars per day for this trip. I'd assumed that included the price of accommodation; I had no idea we'd be begging for it en route.

But when I thought about it, it made perfect sense. The kind of multi-day excursions we were used to went from point to point, with all stops pre-arranged; this simply wasn't possible in a nomadic society. The physical terrain features, like waterfalls and hot springs, would stay the same from one tour to the next – but the people who lived by them would be different every time. And it's not like Manlai could just call these guys and warn them we were coming, or jump on the internet and book us a bed each. *He'd never met them either!*

I was suddenly reminded of a story Tim and Charlotte had told us, from their own experiences in Mongolia. They'd been on the same tour as us, staying at a random *ger*, when the son of the house, aged at least eight, had felt hungry. The lad had come running into the tent, pulled up his mother's tunic, and started suckling away on her breast.

It had been quite awkward, or so they'd told me.

And that was just it. This wasn't your standard tourist experience, rehearsed and sanitised. This was real life for these people, and we were voyeurs; invited in, after a fashion, but only because they were too nice to turn us away. And so, inadvertently, we'd been having an experience even more genuine, more *real*, than we'd realised.

A little too real, in Tim and Charlotte's case.

I felt quite guilty as I hauled my backpack into the tent.

The fire in the stove had been left burning, and on it a large iron pan was bubbling with something noxious. A viscous white liquid was boiling away, leaving a crust of oily scum floating on the surface.

"What the hell is that?" I asked.

It's *urum*," said Soyol, "like you try on the first night, remember? Mongol butter. They make it this way. The yak milk is boiled, then they scrape the *urum* off the top and store it in a stomach."

The way she said it, so matter-of-fact, suggested that this was considered a fairly normal practice. I felt a bit queasy, thinking back to the rich, greasy texture of the stuff. I could tell from the looks the girls were exchanging that they were quite relieved they hadn't tried it.

"If you want some, I can ask the family?" Soyol suggested.

"Ahhh.... Maybe not right now. But we could go and hang out with them for a bit?"

"Yes! We should go have tea!" Soyol was happy to take me over there, and delighted that I was showing an interest. I'd been struggling to keep track of all the customs I'd read about, mostly on the long driving days to and from Kharkhorin. Armed with my recent revelation, this seemed like the perfect time to test them out.

We didn't knock. I was careful not to touch the two central supports of the family *ger* as we entered, and I made sure to progress around them to the left, going clockwise, rather than walking between them. I sat down on one of the beds, and took my baseball cap off, making sure to place it open-side down.

"*Sain banu?*" (How are you?) I asked my host, and he nodded his response.

I took the offered bowl of salty tea with my right hand, but didn't need to worry about accidentally exposing my wrists as I was wearing two jumpers.

"*Bayarcla,*" I said, which means thank-you.

I racked my brain for the next phrase in the formal greeting process. Seeing as how I was already inside the *ger*, it seemed a bit late for 'hold the dog!'

"*Tanaikhan sain uu?*" I said, tripping a fair amount over

the guttural pronunciation. 'How are your family?' I'd asked him, or tried to. Soyol corrected for me, and translated his answer: "Good. How are yours?"

I thought about my parents back in England, and my sister Gill and her husband Chris, who were newly pregnant and halfway through emigrating to New Zealand. They all seemed to be doing quite well, to be honest. *"Sain,"* I replied – Mongolian for 'good'.

With three-quarters of my conversational abilities already exhausted, I had no choice but to pull out the third phrase I'd been learning. It was, at any rate, the third thing you were supposed to say to a Mongolian, after asking about his own health and that of his family.

"How are your animals?" I asked.

There was a pause, and a look of disbelief crossed the face of my host. Then he erupted with laughter, delivering his response between guffaws.

"He says they're fattening nicely, thank-you," Soyol translated, "and he asked, how are yours?"

I shrugged, thinking of Vicky and Roo, folded double on their narrow cots next door. "Too skinny," I told him.

They would never know.

The next morning, we spent a few moments admiring our surroundings. The owners of this camp had picked an exquisite spot; encircled by low hills, the area was table-top flat for miles in every direction. A small lake lay only a few minutes' walk from their front doors, providing adequate water for themselves and their animals, and their nearest neighbours were mere specks of white canvas halfway to the horizon. Their concessions to the modern world included a solar panel, a satellite dish, and a dusty workhorse of a motorbike that looked older than I am.

As we left, a herd of goats were playing king of the castle, taking it in turns to scramble on top of an ageing tractor. Life amongst the nomads had its compensations, but it was no real wonder that the younger generations were flocking to the city in search of excitement. The irony was, those of us who lived in cities were paying big bucks to come out here in search of exactly the same thing. It's Mongolia's national crisis; in fifty years there might not be any nomads left, and all the *gers* will be tourist camps.

It's a tragic situation, but what could possibly be done about it?

The grass was certainly greener on the Mongolian steppe, but not everyone wants to spend their whole life surrounded by it. We'd been out here less than a week, and despite being bewitched by the beauty of the place we were craving showers, flushing toilets, cheeseburgers and the internet as much as anyone.

I put it to Roo; "Would you live here? As a nomad, I mean?"

Roo thought about it. She'd always wanted to be a farmer, and had spent years at agricultural school studying animal husbandry. She was an accomplished rider, liked to make her own clothes, loved camping and preferred to cook and eat unprocessed foods as much as possible. She was definitely a contender.

"I think I could manage," she said at last. "But you'd be dead within a month."

Our path now led back to Ulaanbaatar, and comparative civilization. We still had a long way to go to get there though, and plenty of stops to make on the way. Our first was in a small town we'd ridden past the previous day. It rose abruptly out of the grass, nestled into the foothills of a mountain range. No road led to or from the place; only the wheel ruts of previous vehicles scarred the grassland, showing which was the most popular route into town.

We drove through a familiar scene of *ger* camps divided by rough-plank fences, and ended up at a market on the outskirts of town.

Of course, it wasn't just any old market.

In place of stalls there were shipping containers, lined up next to each other with their heavy steel doors open for business. Some were kitted out like grocery shops, with shelves of tins and packets and a counter at the back. Most held tools, motorbike parts, horse tack and animal feed. The last two we saw were selling brand new *gers* – complete packages or individual components, rolls of fresh white canvas and stacks of orange-lacquered wooden rafter poles. It was a one-stop shopping centre for everything a nomad needs, and it was buzzing – we hadn't seen so many people in one place since leaving the airport. The contrast between young and old was never so apparent; the wrinkled herdsmen wore their traditional knee-length gowns, belted with bright silk sashes, and leather riding boots that almost never left their feet. The young, predictably, were rebelling, opting instead for Western-inspired fashion – skinny jeans, shiny leather jackets and brand-name trainers. Every one of them looked groomed and manicured, as though expecting their dates to show up at any moment for a night on the town. No wonder they were all so anxious to gravitate towards the capital – the only nightclubs in the whole country were in Ulaanbaatar.

Both of them.

Our next stop was in the Gobi desert. Not the actual Gobi desert of course, which was hundreds of miles to the south; this was the Mini Gobi, an inexplicable sea of sand dunes seemingly plonked at random into the middle of the steppe. Soyol couldn't tell us how big it was, as the powerful winds pushed the sand around a lot; on a good day, the Mini Gobi probably moved further than we did.

We got out and climbed the dunes, marvelling at yet another weirdness in this country full of contrasts. Just for the hell of it I sprinted off into the 'desert', and managed to make it about halfway across. The whole thing couldn't have been wider than four or five kilometres, yet standing in the gully between a couple of big dunes, you would swear you were in the Sahara.

Finally, we rocked up at the *ger* of a family who were happy to provide us with a place to kip. We'd become accustomed to sleeping on the floor, in our sleeping bags on large embroidered rugs, as not many places had six beds to offer us. But this place had something even better – a tame camel!

The two-humped, or 'Bactrian' camel, is critically endangered in the wild, with less than 800 of them left. The few we'd seen on our travels were almost certainly domesticated, like this one. But that had its advantages. Namely, that we could ride it!

The three young girls went first, taking turns at squealing when the camel lurched to its feet. They each took a short stroll around the camp, the camel's owner leading the shaggy beast on a length of rope. The rope was tied directly to a wooden peg which pierced the camel's nose; plastic bottle caps had been added to keep the peg in place.

When it was my turn, Soyol said something to the dude which must have had something to do with my enthusiasm for speed, as he set off at a run, the camel trotting happily along behind him.

Then it was Vicky's go, and she requested a more sedate experience. Roo was taking photos as the camel completed its circuit, bringing Vicky back to us. Well-versed in its duties, it knelt down on its front legs as though to let her off – only, it stayed there. Its back legs were still standing, its body sloping down in the most unnatural position, but the camel seemed quite comfortable there. Vicky was stuck, lying backwards across the hump behind her, and clinging with both hands to the hump in front.

The camel honked and brayed, as its owner smacked it ineffectually with a stick. It didn't seem inclined to move an inch further.

We all fell about laughing as Vicky stared into the sky, her voice containing a tremor of alarm as she asked, "Is this supposed to happen?"

Back To The Future

The next morning, we began the long drive back to Ulaanbaatar.

We re-joined the tarmac road near Kharkhorin, noticing as we did that the Erdene Zuu Monastery was closed, the giant gateway shrouded in scaffolding, the trinket stalls gone. We'd been lucky with our visit.

I was sad to leave the magnificent wilderness of the steppe, but looking forward to a soft bed, a chance to check my emails, and a meal that wasn't mutton.

Not that there's anything wrong with mutton, but even Soyol was running out of ways to make it interesting after eating almost nothing else for six days.

We'd been saved by the three young girls. One of their pieces of luggage was a large holdall full of packets of biscuits, which they'd munched on more or less continuously throughout the entire trip. They'd been happy to share; consequently, the bag was now empty.

We hit the outskirts of the city and ground to a halt, the driver fighting the gears again as we queued through the honking, revving gridlock for the next couple of hours. It made me wonder if the waves of youngsters in search of new lives ever got this far and thought, *Hang on! This wasn't on the brochure…*

The van dropped us off in the ghetto outside Lotus Guesthouse, and rattled off to wherever the girls were staying. I was going to miss that crazy old vehicle. We'd had a few hair-raising moments in the back of it, but it had taken more punishment than any vehicle had a right to, and brought us safely home. Mostly, I'd miss laughing at its face. The spacing of the grill and big round headlights made it look like its eyes and mouth were wide in terror – like it had just seen the state of the road ahead, and was about to shit itself.

We reclaimed Vicky's suitcase from the Lotus staff and checked back in to their 'traditional room', with its scale-model orange furniture. There were three items on our to-do list; clean ourselves thoroughly, lie down until the room stopped shaking, and then venture out into the city in search of food. Ulaanbaatar, which the locals just call 'UB', was ripe for exploration. It seemed like we'd been in Mongolia for weeks, but this was only our seventh night there; we hadn't been out into the city at all.

The Lotus Guesthouse was set to become our base for most of our stay in Mongolia. Only two other places in our price bracket were reviewed online, neither favourably. We could have roamed the city looking for alternatives, but that seemed like an awful lot of effort. And the Lotus was a great place. It had a few little… idiosyncrasies, of course.

Like how the toilets in the one shared bathroom were right at the front of their stalls. There was a big gap behind them, but not enough room for your legs if you needed to sit on them. This meant you either had to leave the door open, or shit side-saddle. I had a nasty surprise once, walking in to see one of the old ladies from the room next door propping the door open with one leg while she was peeing.

The showers were another source of amusement. Hot water is supplied centrally in Ulaanbaatar, meaning there are times – pretty much every day – when there isn't any. Maintenance work is carried out on the system overnight, so we daren't even consider taking a late (or early) shower. But that was just business as usual in UB; the showers at the Lotus were something else. They were cylindrical, space-age capsules, complete with disco lights, speakers, and multiple motorised moving jets – each wedged into tiny tiled alcoves that must have been the previous shower cubicles. Of course, none of the massage jets worked. The speakers and lights ended in dangling wires, and the deluxe thermostatically controlled experience the factory labels promised was a joke, as more than half the time there was no hot water at all. I could only assume they were a cheap Chinese knock-off of a very high-end shower, which had proved cheaper to install than repairing whatever they'd had before. But there was one slight problem; the plastic-fantastic capsules only fitted into the previous shower cubicles sideways, requiring a feat of contortion to actually get into the buggers. And once you'd finished showering, the only place to towel yourself dry was the middle of the bathroom – which, as I might have mentioned, was used by everyone in the guesthouse.

Having successfully cleaned ourselves, we went in search of dinner.

A few minutes of internet research had informed us that Ulaanbaatar's food scene was what they called 'nascent'. Which, translated for anyone who doesn't speak guidebook, means 'they only serve mutton'.

Or horse, apparently.

But neither of the girls seemed keen to experiment with this.

So we headed out, strolling down the main road towards the city centre.

The hordes of cars queuing alongside us weren't at all what I expected. Gleaming Hummers jostled for position with brand new Land Cruisers; nowhere in sight were the battered Ladas and other dusty vehicles we'd been fighting through on the way in. Clearly, there was money in UB, and clearly most of it had been spent on gas-guzzling four-wheel-drives. Which was a pity, really, as none of them were going anywhere.

We crossed Peace Avenue, which runs east to west right through the middle of the city. All the important buildings were on it – the post office (there's just the one in UB), the Palace of Culture, and the massive State Department Store, which is the closest thing they have to a shopping centre.

Suddenly, Vicky pointed and shrieked in triumph; "KFC!"

We looked where she was pointing. Hunger had sharpened her eyes; she'd spotted the familiar red logo from three blocks away, through the hole in another sign! We made a bee-line towards it, crossing the broken wasteland of a park, six lanes of traffic, and several blocks containing the National Library of Mongolia and the National Theatre. Oh yes – this was prime real estate all right!

The Colonel has done a pretty good job of conquering Asia, with over eight thousand restaurants covering every major city on the continent. Compared to, say, McDonalds' paltry 3,500 establishments (of which 2,000 are in China), it's an impressive achievement. It stems from the popularity of chicken in the Asian diet; most countries in the region don't have the land for large-scale cattle farms, so historically, beef products have been off the menu for the vast majority of people.

Mongolians, however, don't eat a lot of chicken.

Probably because chickens aren't easily compatible with a nomadic lifestyle – they're notoriously bad on leads, for example.

But Western culture is booming in UB, the wealthy citizens importing anything and everything they perceive to be a status symbol.

And so fast food had come to Ulaanbaatar.

Yesterday, as far as I could tell.

The KFC parking lot on Chinggis Avenue (Mongolia's most powerful address), contained the kind of vehicles you'd expect to see in the valet parking section of a swanky New York restaurant. Hummers (x2), a Bentley, a badgeless handmade sports car and a host of lesser vehicles, like BMWs.

The queue was out of the door.

Undeterred, we joined it, feeling rather out of place – not only were we significantly taller than everyone else present, we were appallingly under-dressed. The rich and powerful of UB were impressively turned out. Sharp suits and cocktail dresses abounded; it was a line more appropriate outside a Soho nightclub. Women tottered on absurdly high heels, there were hats and fascinators, Gucci and Prada handbags, coats of every fur imaginable from mink to abominable snowman, and labels, labels, labels.

It almost made me wish I'd washed my jeans.

But they were shredded anyway, so it wouldn't have made much difference.

We spent over an hour in that queue.

It was nothing your average KFC couldn't handle, but this was not your average KFC. Mongolia had imported the franchise, but not the skills, and they hadn't quite figured it all out yet.

The woman in front of me ordered six meals. Whether this was a status thing I couldn't tell, but she appeared to be there just with her husband. The couple waited about ten minutes for their food, as it was inspected and signed off on by three different managers at various stages of preparation. The last item to come through was the drinks – six large cups brimming with cola.

The worker on the counter very carefully teased the plastic tops onto each cup. Then, equally carefully, she loaded them all into a plastic carrier bag and offered the handles to the lady.

It took precisely two steps for the tops to pop off her drinks, flooding the floor with two litres of Coke. She looked utterly amazed at the accident, staring in shock as the liquid lapped her stilettos, whereas I'd been predicting it since the cashier began placing drinks into a bag. Idiots! Had they no clue?

Obviously not; the same worker was already bagging up drinks for the next customer.

Our food, when we got it, was delicious, in that guilty,

pleasure-heavy way that fast food is. It was cold, apart from the bread buns which were steaming hot and soggy from being microwaved, but it still tasted vaguely like KFC should taste – and that, after a week of mutton dumplings, was enough.

We made the trek back to the hostel, marvelling at the effort involved in nipping out for a burger. From start to finish the endeavour had taken us over two hours, but it had given me an insight into the psyche of Ulaanbaatar, if not Mongolia in general. These people were desperate to prove their worth, their status – to themselves, to each other, and more than anything, to the outside world.

Sadly, I don't think the outside world gives a toss whether you've got a KFC or not.

That night we slept the deep sleep of the exhausted, hardly even noticing when we bashed bits of ourselves on the wooden bed frames. The following morning brought good news, however; a regular-sized bed in a regular dorm had come free for Vicky, whilst the Lotus' only double room was now available for Roo and I. Vicky eagerly dragged her suitcase across the landing, while I took Roo to inspect our new accommodation.

The room was perfect.

A four poster bed almost filled it, leaving just enough room to walk around it and to stand our rucksacks in the corner. Entry was via a sliding glass door to the shared balcony, which meant we had to walk through the dormitory whenever we wanted to leave, or go to the toilet. But that didn't matter at all.

This room was private, isolated, and compared to what we'd experienced so far, it was pure luxury.

I took off my shoes, and immediately knew that something was wrong.

"Erm, love... the floor's wet."
"What? Like, how wet?"
"Soaking."
"Ohhhh... does that mean we have to move again?"
"Oh hell no. I can live with a wet carpet. I'm just worried that the roof might be leaking."

Roo mulled this over. "So long as it doesn't leak on the bed, we'll be fine," she decided.

Still, it was a puzzling thing, as there were no other signs of rain getting in – no cracks or stains on the roof, and the whole carpet was saturated, rather than having specific wet patches.

The answer came to us a few hours later, as we walked through the city in search of dinner.

"Look!" Roo exclaimed. "That's it!"

A few doors up, a tiny, wizened old lady was going about her household chores. She had dragged several thick, woven rugs out onto the pavement, and was vigorously mopping them.

"No way..."

But it was true. The Lotus cleaning lady mopped every floor in the place, every day. There weren't that many of them, and all except ours were covered in vinyl.

But no matter how hard we tried to convince her that our room didn't need cleaning, that determined old woman forced her way in there every morning with her bucket of water, and thoroughly mopped the carpet.

City Of The Lost

Ulaanbaatar is an interesting place.

Or perhaps 'anachronistic' would be a better word for it.

Guide books harp on about a fusion of cultures, how the ancient and modern collide and contrast here – but that's just a fancy way of saying it's been built too damn fast, and it's sodding ugly as a result.

Two-hundred years ago, UB wasn't even a permanent settlement. A tent-village that came and went, housing Mongolia's most prominent monastery in the process, it began to linger in the rough vicinity of the modern city because it was a popular spot for trading.

A hundred years ago, the population of the 'city' (then called *Urga*) was just 60,000 – a third of whom were monks. Apart from their Chinese overseers, they were all still living in tents. It was around this time that Mongolia decided to throw off the yoke of Chinese oppression; the Chinese disagreed, naturally, and carried on oppressing the citizens of Urga until the Russians invaded in 1921. The Russians managed to conquer Urga twice in the same year – once in the name of Imperial Russia, and then again in the name of the Communists. They renamed the place 'Ulaanbaatar' (meaning 'Red Hero') in 1924, and spent the next 50 years building a whole city of identikit Soviet apartment blocks on top of the old *ger* districts.

In keeping with most of Russia, not much changed until 1990 – at which point Western culture exploded onto their scene, the population skyrocketed to over a million inhabitants, and the city traded all its old problems for new ones.

Like traffic jams, and smog, and foreign investors wanting to build multi-million dollar sky-scraping hotels.

Where presumably tiny, wrinkled old ladies still mop the carpets.

UB is the very definition of the phrase 'victim of its own success'. With no clue how to handle the sudden influx of people and wealth, the city's planners seemed to have shrugged their shoulders and copied everyone else – buying Hummers and driving them straight into gridlock, there to spend the remainder of their natural lives.

We had one more day before Vicky was due to fly home.

Understandably, she wanted to see as much of the city as was possible.

Now, you can spend a week in London, or Paris, or New York, and not even come close to seeing everything. But Ulaanbaatar is a bit different.

On our first exploration we came across the huge square at the centre of the city, flanked by the Government Palace, the Central Cultural Palace, the Mongolian Stock Exchange and the HQ buildings of both national banks.

Sitting proudly in the centre of the square is an imposing statue of revolutionary hero *Damdin Sükhbaatar* (literally 'Axe Hero'), astride his horse.

Trip Advisor had a list of the Top Ten Things To See In Ulaanbaatar. Three of them were this statue.

The next four were the square surrounding the statue, and the government building fronting the square – twice each.

It made the sightseeing tour quite efficient.

Number Eight on the list was a traditional operatic performance called *Tumen Ekh*; Number Nine was the railway station.

We decided to go to the opera.

Reviews of the Tumen Ekh show pretty much all agreed on two points; that it was absolutely brilliant, and that it was an absolute bastard to find.

For starters, the guidebook couldn't give us an address, because most buildings in Ulaanbaatar don't have one. It's one of those trifling conventions of the outside world which Mongolians couldn't be bothered with. I guess in a society where most of the older generation grew up as nomads, having fixed points of reference for each house was too alien a concept. So a typical address in UB is something like 'the third building with a blue door going east on the street behind the history museum'.

It made me awfully glad I hadn't asked Mum to post my bank cards here.

We asked in the Tourist Info office for directions, and the conversation went like this:

"Hello! We'd like to go to Tumen Ekh."

"Oh! Tumen Ekh very good!"

"That's great. Where is it, exactly?"

"Oh… Tumen Ekh very hard to find…"

Which begged the question, why the bloody hell don't they sign-post it then?

The Tourist Info girls tried to show us the location on an outsized cartoon map – which, we later discovered, was not to scale. Nevertheless, we followed their dubious directions, wandering away from the main streets and past the skeletal remains of a multi-storey car park that had been abandoned either mid construction or mid demolition.

After an hour we found ourselves in yet another random backstreet, which was unremarkable apart from a round road sign which had a picture of a trumpet with a line though it, crossing it out.

No trumpets.

Presumably unruly trumpet playing had been a major problem in the past? I wondered if real estate agents put it in their small print; *'Warning – this street carries harsh penalties for trumpet violators…'* It would make more sense if we'd spotted this sign in other areas, but we never saw it anywhere else. It seemed a trifle unfair that residents of this street weren't allowed to play their trumpets, when the rest of the city could do it as often as they liked.

A few streets further on we came to a fenced-off patch of wasteland. The gate was open, so we strolled in to investigate. We found an empty car park and a low brick building which seemed to have some activity going on inside. I went in, discovering that it was a pub with a handful of old men propping up the bar. My simple question of "Tumen Ekh?" was met with wide, sweeping arm movements which could have meant anything from 'round the back' to 'take the ring road north of the city'.

"I think it's round the back," I said confidently to the girls, when I emerged.

So we went round the back, and I immediately reversed my opinion. Round the back was some sort of dumping ground for old sea containers. About a dozen of them were stacked here and there, rusting away, the rough ground between them littered with broken glass and bits of household waste.

"Okay, this *might not* be the way," I admitted.

"No shit," said Roo.

A gap between two stacks of containers led back into the surrounding wasteland, so we picked our way through to see if there were any clues.

And there, suddenly appearing beyond a straggle of unruly bushes, was another low building.

It was Tumen Ekh.

And it had certainly lived up to its reputation; it had been an absolute bastard to find.

Perhaps the craziest thing was that this deserted stretch of rubble-strewn no-man's land was, according to the map, Mongolia's National Children's Park.

I had already figured out that Mongolian children were a lot tougher than their Western counterparts, most of them competing in extreme horse races and wrestling tournaments by the age of five. But still... I've seen derelict industrial estates that looked safer to play in. This was meant to be the biggest park in the country. Obviously their ideas of what constitutes a park differ slightly from ours. I guess when you've got the wild beauty of the steppe right outside town, a green space within the city does seem a tad redundant.

So! Onto the performance. We'd given ourselves plenty of getting lost time, so we were amongst the first to arrive and buy tickets. We hung around while the audience grew, then filed inside to take our seats.

And that's when we discovered why the Tumen Ekh ensemble was happy to remain hard to find. The venue was an intimate, low-ceilinged lounge not much bigger than your average high school classroom. It had rows of benches on three sides, surrounding a large carpet; no stage, no grand lighting rig, just the performers doing their thing within easy reach of our front-row seats. The place was full without being uncomfortable. A group of older French tourists filed in after us and squeezed onto the end of our bench. They instinctively dropped their chatter to a whisper, such was the atmosphere of expectation in the room.

A troupe of dancers were up first. In white skirts and jackets they twirled enthusiastically, perfectly in time, performing a series of energetic dances that had obvious Russian and Chinese influences. They were great, and being so close to the action really drew me in.

Next up were the contortionists, and they had to be seen to be believed.

Two slender women in black bodysuits, they started off sitting on their own heads – and it only got crazier from there. Their grace, skill and synchronisation was incredible. I winced as their backs bent further and further, sure to snap at any moment, one lady-pretzel balanced impossibly atop another. When they both took one arm off, there was a collective gasp from the benches.

"C'est formidable," the bloke next to me breathed, momentarily forgetting that I didn't speak French.

"Je suis un lapin," I agreed, momentarily forgetting the same thing.

The final act was the domain of the throat singer.

This bizarre tradition has its roots in the wide open

countryside, where nomadic herders could project their voice for miles to honour the elemental spirits of the grasslands.

I had a friend at university who referred to vomiting as 'calling Ralph on the great white phone' – because you inevitably end up with your head in the bowl, going, "RAAAAAAAAAALLFF!"

Tonight's performer had taken that RALPH sound and weaponised it.

His eyes half closed, his head shook like he was fighting off demonic possession, while sounds I swear can only be made with an electronic synthesiser pulsed out of him. The room throbbed. His ululations rode up and down the scale, from a nasal whistle to a deep, earth-tremor-inducing vibration. If you took what they did to Mel Gibson at the end of *Braveheart*, and did it to the balrog from The Lord Of The Rings – you'd get a close approximation of what we were hearing.

In a word, it was unearthly.

Tumen Ekh had therefore fulfilled the second part of its legend, in that it was absolutely bloody brilliant. If you ever find yourself in Ulaanbaatar with nothing to do (presumably because you've already seen the statue of the guy on a horse) – go and see Tumen Ekh. Honestly, you won't regret it.

Well, assuming you can find it.

For us, it had been well worth the hour we'd spent getting lost in the backstreets. It was now getting dark, however, and it was time to head home.

"Ah... which way *is* home?" Vicky asked.

We peered around ourselves, into the rambling ruination of the Children's Park before us, and the unlit streets beyond.

"That," I said, "is a very good question."

End Of An Era

The day of Vicky's departure dawned warm and clear.

Her flight wasn't until that evening, so she packed her gear and left her suitcase on our soggy carpet while we went out to absorb a last snippet of Mongolian culture.

The central square seemed the obvious destination, so we strolled over there and spent half an hour admiring the lack of people admiring the monuments. It was an ordinary work day for most of the population, and still just outside the peak tourist season of late June to early September. I didn't know if there would be a torrent of international sightseers or a trickle, but either way I was happy to be there before them. Although hot in the daytime it wasn't unbearable; the 'shoulder season' of late May to June had proved the perfect time to visit.

Finally, we paused for a lingering look at the famous mounted statue of Damdin Sükhbaatar. A skilled soldier and tactician, Sükhbaatar led a life straight out of a pre-war spy film. Negotiating in secret he convinced the Russians to help drive the Chinese out of his beloved country, personally leading the Mongolian resistance fighters to victory and establishing a new independent government.

Interestingly, the location of Sükhbaatar's birth is marked

by a small stone plaque. He died in his bed, and was buried and dug up again three times over the intervening years, finally being cremated and put back into his first grave in the National Cemetery.

The enormous statue marks none of those events.

Instead, it was constructed in 1946 on the exact spot where, during a parade following his ousting of the Chinese in the People's Revolution, Sükhbaatar's horse was seen to piss.

Apparently, that's a lucky sign.

Mongolians are delightfully weird.

We left the Square, heading back towards our guesthouse on a road between the big bank HQs. There was a small museum there, which looked about as welcoming as any other building in the area – which was to say, not very. We passed on the other side of the street, and narrowly avoided walking straight through a patch of wet cement. Someone had thoughtfully decided to repair one of the ever-present potholes – a bit like trying to stem the blood flow from a bullet hole in a body riddled with them, but I guess if every one of the city's one-point-three million inhabitants fixed one, they'd get nearly half of the buggers. Leaving the concrete completely unprotected in an area of high foot-traffic was a bit of a mistake, though. It was too much temptation to resist, even for the girls. And so, if you ever visit Ulaanbaatar, on a small side street leading away from Sükhbaatar Square, if you look very closely at a small patch of pavement opposite the National Museum of Mongolian History – you might just notice three names, inscribed for posterity near the heart of Mongolia's capital.

It's not quite the Hollywood Walk of Fame, but for travellers like us it was the peak of notoriety. It made UB the second place in the world that my name is enshrined in fresh concrete; the first being television's Coronation Street, which I worked on for years as an extra.

Feeling delightfully rebellious, we nipped back into the Tourist Information office – which I should point out (for the sake of completion) serves a perfectly-poured Chinggis beer. Chinggis (Genghis) Khan has lent his name to pretty much everything in Mongolia; shops, streets, banks, the currency, the airport... Even Sükhbaatar Square was renamed Chinggis Square shortly after we left. Chinggis beer, unlike most of the great Khan's recent namesakes, is actually rather good.

It was kind of odd that they served it at the Tourist Info, though. Not that I was complaining! The ice-cold beer gave us a refreshing break from the blanket of exhaust fumes which lay over the city. It was so pervasive on the main streets that I could taste it, and I didn't like to think how many minutes each breath was shaving off my life expectancy. Still, it was great to have a valid medical reason for drinking beer at 10am. It was crisp and delicious, and served in glasses so ornate I was tempted to keep one as a souvenir – until I found out they only had four of them.

After this, and a picnic lunch back at the Lotus Guesthouse, Vicky and Roo decided to visit a museum of traditional Mongolian costume that they'd read about in *Lonely Planet*. I bowed out of this one, letting the girls spend a last bit of time together while I caught up on my journal.

They weren't gone long.

"Did you find it?" I asked Roo, as she flopped onto the bed next to me.

"I think so."

"You... think so?"

"Yes. It was really weird. I'm pretty sure we found the right place, but it was just a doorway that led upstairs. We went in, and there was no-one around. It was only one room. There was one case with, like, four mannequins dressed in gowns, and the rest of the room was just full of cardboard boxes with costumes in them. We picked a few out, tried them on, put them back, and left."

"Were you supposed to be trying things on?"

"Dunno. It's a museum, so probably not. But we'd gone all that way, so..."

"Fair enough."

For a celebratory dinner that evening we splurged, going into an expensive Western-styled restaurant and ordering hamburgers.

They weren't half bad, as it happens.

I'm pretty sure they were mutton, though.

Sated, we strolled back to the hotel, where I manhandled Vicky's giant suitcase down Sarajevo Staircase. We'd ordered a posh taxi to take her to the airport, and weren't disappointed when a shiny black Land Cruiser showed up to collect her.

Hugs were exchanged and more than a few tears were shed, as this phase of our travels came to an end. Being three had never felt like a crowd, and having Vicky around had made us all more chatty and excitable. Left to our own devices Roo and I tend to be quite lazy, but Vicky's energy and enthusiasm had turned the trip into a whirlwind of new experiences.

We'd miss her a lot; Roo, more than anything, was bereft.

We waved at the car as it turned out of our alleyway, and then she was gone.

Tears streamed down Roo's face; sadness tinged with a healthy dose of worry.

Vicky had quite an odyssey ahead of her.

First up, she would use the return half of her ticket to UB, flying back to Hanoi via (inevitably) a substantial layover in Seoul. Unfortunately, you can't get directly from Hanoi to Perth (you can't get direct to Perth from bloody anywhere, but I won't get into that right now) – so she'd had to fly home via Kuala Lumpur. That made four international flights with three different airlines, with hotels booked for overnight stops in both Vietnam and Malaysia. Roo was understandably concerned. It had the potential to become a nightmare journey, with disaster lurking around every corner. Vicky hadn't done much solo travel, which is why she'd come along with us. Now she was staring down the barrel of three full days in confusing foreign airports, with time differences, currency differences and language barriers – to say nothing of tyrannical Hanoi taxi drivers and predatory hotel clerks.

"She'll be fine," I told Roo, placing a consoling arm around her.

"I hope so," she sniffed.

"Do you think she'll come traveling with us again?"

That brought out a crooked smile. "Ahh... probably not."

Fair to say, Vicky had been through quite a lot in the four short weeks she'd spent in our company. It's possible she was actually safer on her own.

"You never know. Maybe she'll develop a taste for adventure."

Roo gave me a sympathetic look. "Tony, I love that you call it 'adventure' when everything falls apart and we're left shitting ourselves in blind panic, but that doesn't mean it actually *is* an adventure. Vicky might develop a taste for travel, but unless she develops a death-wish I think she'll be steering well clear of us."

I had to agree with that. "Still, it gives me something to write about."

Roo tightened her arm around my waist. "Just don't write about Vicky, whatever you do! She'll die of embarrassment."

"Ha! Yeah... True enough."

Sorry, Vicky.

The next event worth writing about happened only a day later.

Our lovely double room had been booked by someone else, forcing us to move out into the dorm. We'd spent the day catching up on our internet chores – or rather, we'd wanted to, but Roo's precious tablet couldn't find the hostel's wireless signal. Despite working perfectly until now, it threw itself into an endless loop of trying to connect and failing. I turned it off and on again, thereby exhausting my repertoire of computer-repair skills, but it didn't help.

So I took it upon myself to find a solution.

We still had the tiny laptop, so the internet was my first port of call. A few hours of intensive research revealed someone having a similar problem which was solved in a surprising way. He'd discovered that his modem had a hidden list of devices it wouldn't allow to connect, and his tablet, identical to Roo's, had somehow added itself to that list.

I'd tried everything so far, with no results – either the tablet was knackered, or this mysterious blacklist was to blame.

It took me no time at all to log into the modem, using the hostel's computer, and to find the list I'd read about.

Roo's tablet wasn't on the list. Nothing was. But then I noticed an interesting option. Whilst the unique MAC address of the tablet wasn't currently listed, I could manually add it – and then force the modem to recognise it as the default device to connect to. While this was happening, it would be the only device that could connect, so nothing else could interfere.

It was a sure-fire way to re-establish a wireless connection – or so I thought at the time. It was late; I'd had a long, frustrating day, made worse by a small boy that had been hanging around the place since 10am. He belonged to one of the women that ran the place; she'd ditched him in the dorm, and all day he'd alternated playing games on the computer with half-hour bursts of running around screaming. It was after midnight, and he was still pestering me to let him back on the computer.

Anyway, I figured it was worth one last ditch attempt to get the tablet working again.

I entered its MAC Address into the modem software, and selected the option to 'Connect only with this device'.

My fingers hovered, while I considered this course of action.

Yup – everything seemed to be in order.

It wasn't until I clicked 'apply' that a slight snag in the plan occurred to me. The instant my finger lifted from the mouse button, an icy dread slid down my spine as a thought barrelled in too late for the party. *If the tablet is now the only thing that can access the modem, it's also the only thing that can undo what I just did. What if it still doesn't work?*

Well, then I'd be screwed.

And you know what?

Roo's tablet still didn't work.

And just like that, I had single-handedly destroyed the internet for the entire hostel.

It was nearly 5am when I gave up. I'd figured out how to reset the modem, with a paperclip stuffed into the tiny reset hole. Not having a paperclip amongst my traveling gear, I'd tried everything from pencils to kitchen knives, and had finally achieved success with a sterile needle from the first aid kit.

Resetting the device should, in theory, have worked – only, instead of doing what I'd expected it to do – ie, start working again – it was now asking for passwords and account numbers. At least, it looked like that was what it was doing. I couldn't be a hundred percent sure, because it was asking for them in Mongolian. Far too many 'X's in that language for it to make sense.

So.

I cursed myself. I cursed Fate. And I cursed myself again, for good measure.

"Did you fix it?" Roo murmured, as I slipped into the bunk below her.

"No."

"Oh. What are we going to do?"

"Well, I'm thinking we've stayed here long enough. Let's move out."

"Okay then."

There was a pause, during which I thought she'd fallen asleep.

"What are you going to tell them if they ask about the internet?" she asked, finally.

I thought long and hard about this. No two ways about it – I'd stuffed up royally. There was zero chance the two women in the office would be able to fix this. They'd have to call a telecoms engineer. And even back home, getting one of those guys to solve your internet connection problems is pretty much a euphemism for 'bastard impossible'.

I'd made one hell of a mess. Realistically, there was only one course of action.

"I'll blame the boy," I told her.

Red Tape

The next morning, we had breakfast at the Lotus – and fled.

The UB Guesthouse was the only other hostel we could find reviews of. It was a short walk across town, in a district that looked remarkably similar to the one we'd just left.

We checked in, scoring a private room, and surveyed our new domain.

It wasn't a vast improvement. In fact, it was a fair step down from the quirky charm of the Lotus. For starters, it didn't have a lounge, just a TV and a sofa in the lobby. It did have a kitchen, but it looked like someone had pissed off a yak and let it loose in there; everything was broken, doors hung off cupboards, taps stuck out at odd angles and the window had been painted shut.

"Don't even *think* about trying to fix anything," Roo hissed.

Now that we were here, we arranged to meet a man called Ganban. Word on the street said that Ganban, who hung out at the UB Guesthouse, was the right person to talk to about onward travel. We planned on leaving Mongolia by train, and booking tickets would be much easier with the help of a local agent. We were also hoping Ganban could help us with another small matter...

You see, we had some chores to take care of. You know, those tiny administrative details that build up inevitably when you travel.

For example, the next country we planned to visit was China.

Assuming all went well with the ticket booking process, we'd be heading there in less than two weeks.

And we still didn't have visas.

Now, China is a hard country to get into. (It's an even harder country to get out of, but we'll get to that later.) Recent internet research had taught us a variety of things; chief of which was that we should have done more research. The Chinese take a dim view of... everything that isn't China. Or Chinese. They're especially not keen on this new phenomenon called 'tourism', where suddenly any old bugger can come into your country and traipse all around the place, discovering things like how the local people live, and where all those nuclear weapons silos are buried. If it wasn't for the fact that tourism drags billions of dollars away from foreign nations, and deposits them kicking and screaming into Chairman Mao's pocket, there wouldn't be any tourism at all in China.

As it is, strict controls are enforced to ensure that undesirables and dissidents aren't allowed into the country.

Especially not those dreaded deviants known as *writers*.

Imagine – not only would they go and tell everyone about their experiences in China, it's actually their job!

It may sound ridiculous in this day and age, but as a person who likes to share my adventures with readers all around the world, in China I would be public enemy number one.

"So, we don't tell them you're a travel writer," Roo reminded me for the fiftieth time.

"Given what happens when we do tell people I'm a travel writer, I'm thinking we should make that a general rule from now on."

"I see your point."

We were stood in a queue inside the Chinese Embassy,

having entered through a small, unremarkable door. The door was so unremarkable, tucked away on the side of the building, that it had taken us a while to discover it. We'd shown up at the time listed on the embassy website, and waited outside the formidable main gates. We'd been debating whether or not we dared press the intercom buzzer, when the steel gate rolled smoothly open and a shiny black limousine with flags on the bonnet pulled out. The gate guards, on seeing us stood there clueless in front of the car, kindly gestured with the barrels of their machine guns that we should consider exiting the area.

"Let's try the other side," Roo had said, and I'd been quick to agree.

This had led us past the long white perimeter wall, around the corner, and past more of the same – until we spotted a back door hidden behind a bush. A tiny sign graced that entrance, giving the times that the Visa Office was open – and we were in luck.

Mobile phones had to be turned off, but beyond that there were none of the anticipated draconian security measures; just a head-to-toe x-ray and body-cavity search before proceeding.

No, seriously – there was nothing. We wandered in and joined the queue, patiently awaiting our turn to see the solitary visa officer behind her wall of glass.

A young Chinese man in a sharp suit loitered in the corner of the room, his presence just subtle enough to make me nervous. Secret Service, or whatever their equivalent was, he must have pissed someone off to end up with this gig – probably the least exciting post it was possible to have.

Stand there. Look unobtrusive, whilst quietly menacing the queue of tourists. Do nothing else.

At least until the older German bloke at the front of the queue started arguing with the lady behind the glass. There was some problem with the documents he was being asked for – he didn't have them, I think, and was demanding they process his visa without them. Then the suit-man stepped in, silent as a blade, and escorted the unkempt German out of the room.

To his death, presumably.

"This is a bad idea," Roo whispered.

"Don't whisper!" I whispered back. "It'll make us look suspicious!"

It was paranoia, pure and simple. We had absolutely nothing to worry about. True, we were attempting to enter China with false documents under false pretences, but as far as I was aware, that sort of thing was fairly common in backpacker circles.

Still. It did have me a little concerned.

Amongst the mass of contradictory information we'd read online, there was a suggestion that interviews were sometimes conducted. Separate interviews, in the case of couples, where questions were asked of both parties and their results compared. It seemed very unlikely, but then I'd been in these situations before.

For some reason, they *always* pick on me.

Or Roo; having tie-dyed rainbow hair does seem to set off alarm bells in certain quarters.

In order to enter China, you need to have flights booked both in and out.

Not normally a problem for most people – I can't imagine one-way tickets to Beijing are a big seller in the rest of the world. But we didn't want to fly, and couldn't afford to anyway, so we were going in by train. Which is perfectly fine and above board, except that to do so legally, we would have had to get our visas back home.

We had no idea how we would actually be leaving the country – "let's worry about getting in, first," had been Roo's advice on the matter. This was because every attempt we'd made to research a way out of China had fizzled into hearsay and conjecture – there simply weren't enough facts available online to make a solid plan. Hence, our decision to wing it.

Which is what led us to buy fake plane tickets.

Ganban had friends who ran a travel agency, and for five dollars a pop he'd rigged up fake bookings on the flights which best suited our intended travel dates. As we stood there in that visa queue, I was clutching a plastic wallet containing a print-out of our phoney flight details on the travel agency's headed paper. Honestly, if I'd been wanting to mock up some fake flight tickets, I could have done a better job aged 10 on the Sinclair ZX Spectrum I'd had at that age. They were printed on a dot matrix printer anyway, so the difference would be negligible.

Also in that wallet was our fake itinerary. This was a masterpiece of deception, which had taken me most of the previous day to concoct. Following a rough travel plan given to me by Tim and Charlotte, I'd booked hostels and hotels in every city they'd visited, staying for a few nights in each, and printed out a stack of booking confirmations. Then I'd cancelled the lot of them, seeing as how we had no intention of using them; this was only possible because of Booking.com, and their wonderfully generous free cancellation policy.

I'd drawn up an elaborate itinerary, listing everything we wanted to see in each location, museums, landmarks, attractions etc. I'd even allowed for travel time between each place, although hindsight has since revealed this to be the most impossibly optimistic part of the plan – getting anywhere in China as easily as I had allowed for, would have been grounds for belief in angels.

Fulfilling the required trifecta of documents, along with our fake flight tickets and my fake itinerary, was a fake letter of invitation. Possibly the weirdest requirement for getting a tourist visa, the letter had to be an invitation to visit the country from either a Chinese relation, a friend, or a registered tour company.

No problem, if you're travelling with a registered tour company! Booking and paying for things in a package, like the two-grand-for-two-weeks deals we'd seen advertised back in Perth.

For those of us on a more modest budget, this presented a real problem. Luckily, Ganban had stepped forward again, giving us the email address of a friendly hostel owner in Beijing. This bloke had 'invited' us to come and stay at his hostel – something we had no intention of doing, because his rooms were three times the price of the place we *were* going to.

But it's the thought that counts. Or in this case, the print-out of the email, written mostly in Chinese, which (I sincerely hoped) read the same in that intricate language as it had said in the accompanying English message.

Other than that, our visa application was entirely above board. I mean, our application forms were filled out with *mostly* true things, and our passports were real. It was only everything else in the wallet that was a lie.

Crazy, eh! But what could you do?

Our intentions in visiting China were completely honest (apart from the fact that Roo was planning on photographing everything in sight, and I was going to write about it). But they'd made it so difficult...

Almost as though they didn't want us there.

Our turn came. We stepped over the line on the floor and approached the desk. The vast expanse of glass separated us from the slender Chinese woman, forcing us to bend down and try to speak through the slot we pushed our documents through.

"Tourist visas, please, thirty days."

She barely glanced up, shuffling my lie-filled papers into a folder and punching numbers on a concealed cash register.

"We both work as cleaners," I explained through the slot, in case she'd forgotten to ask.

Roo stood on my foot, in a polite-but-firm way she has. It roughly translates as "Shut the fuck up before you get us into trouble."

It's way more discreet than, say, an elbow in the ribs, and consequently it gets much more use.

I took the hint, paid the bill, and we left by the same door – clutching a receipt with our application number printed on it.

"That was easy," Roo said, once we were back outside.

"Yeah. Almost *too* easy," I replied – and I was only half-joking.

"Pah! They won't even look at those papers, I bet," Roo scoffed.

"Yeah... still, I wish we'd kept a copy of it all."

"Why? So we can apply again?"

"No, to read next week. In case they ask us anything..."

"How do you mean?"

I showed her the receipt. Printed ominously across the bottom was the legend, 'Return Appointment:' and a time and date next Monday morning.

"Ohhh…"

"Yeah."

It was a quiet, thoughtful walk home to the UB Guesthouse.

Best Served Cold

We only lasted a couple of days at the UB Guesthouse.

The place felt so small and cramped compared to the wide lounge and spacious dorms at the Lotus, and being slightly cheaper, it was constantly full to capacity. Well, it was full beyond any sensible measure of capacity – like living in a two-bedroom terrace house with eighteen sweaty backpackers and no hot showers for days at a time.

So, cap in hand, we headed back to the Lotus Guesthouse, hoping they wouldn't hold a grudge.

To our eternal delight they offered us the 'traditional room' – all other beds being occupied at that point. We took it as penance, and braced ourselves for a night of bracing ourselves.

The good news was, they had internet. Whatever I'd done to the old network had proved irrevocable, so they'd found a way to extend the separate office wireless to reach most of the hostel. This meant we could pass a pleasant afternoon catching up on Facebook, and trying to find something interesting to do with the rest of our time in Mongolia. With Roo's tablet still out of action in terms of internet capacity, it was left to our tiny laptop to do the donkey work.

"Oh, hang on, the battery's about to die!" I pointed at the

message that had just appeared on screen. "Don't worry, I'll get the power thingumy."

I dug through the gear in my daysack and pulled out the charging cable. Roo's dad had done a great job on it, splicing the absurdly small components together. I had a feeling his handiwork would be the only part of the laptop to survive this trip.

I found a wall socket and pushed the plug into it.

Or tried to.

There was an almighty BANG! and I was thrown across the room in a shower of sparks. Roo screamed as a flash lit the room, and there was terror in her voice as she ran over to me.

"TONY? Are you okay?"

I was fine. A little… shocked, perhaps.

Alas, the same could not be said of the charger. The socket was blackened, with a streak of burnt paint running up the wall from it. Of the three pins on the computer's plug, two were black and one was twisted, with a small notch taken out where presumably the power surge had melted the metal clear off the thing.

"You could have been killed," Roo said, still holding me, the fear not leaving her eyes.

"Nah, I'm fine," I said, trying to downplay the same fear in my own eyes.

I could have been killed.

It was a sobering thought.

I mean, I've always been pretty sure I'll never make it past forty, but there are good ways of going – rescuing orphans from a burning building, for example – that sit quite well with me. I'm not particularly afraid of dying, but I'd prefer there to be some kind of *point* to it. I know that's a lot to ask, but really – losing my life to a dodgy plug socket? In some crummy hostel in Ulaanbaatar?

That would have been a crap way to die.

But the real casualty in this was our laptop.

Luckily, Roo hadn't connected it to the power supply before my disastrous attempt to plug it in, so it was still alive. Just.

"Less than five minutes' battery," Roo confirmed.

"Shit. Everything is on there."

I dug out the hard drive, used for back-ups in case of emergencies.

I was fairly sure this qualified.

"Take everything you can get," Roo pleaded, reminding me without saying so that the laptop contained the last of our entertainment. Movies, TV shows... they would have to wait.

I dragged the files containing my most recent writing efforts across to the hard drive, and that was as much as I managed. The computer powered down, for what could very well be the last time on this trip. Quite where we'd find a matching power cable I had no idea, but it was a fair bet there wasn't one to be had in Mongolia.

"Shit," said Roo.

"Yes," I said. "Indeed."

"But you're really okay?" she asked.

"I am. Sort of a silver lining really, if you think about it. The laptop may be dead, but at least I'm not!"

I mentioned this slight issue to the women in the office.

They nodded sagely throughout my description of the event, and didn't seem the least bit perturbed. After I'd finished they debated the situation amongst themselves for a while, and came up with the following piece of advice: "Don't use that socket."

"Should I at least put a warning label on it, or something?" I asked.

My response was a matching pair of shrugs, which I assumed meant, 'if you want.'

One positive result was, they checked the circuit breakers and flipped one back on. Following the explosion we'd lost power to the whole room, but now the other sockets came back to life. And the laptop – when gingerly introduced to such a socket – started charging as normal.

Roo's relief was evident. Even more so when she checked her email.

Vicky had made it home safe and sound, had spent the obligatory entire day in bed, had resurfaced, and was ready for a chat.

Roo arranged to called her using Skype, another marvel

of this modern age we live in. These days all phones can use it, but back in the day we'd had one of the first. Well, until Roo dropped it down the toilet and peed on it.

Anyway, Vicky was quick to get back to us, and we set up a call.

"Oh, you're still at the Lotus," she said, when she could see us.

"We left for a bit, but we're back now," Roo explained. "We kind of had to leave, because Tony destroyed the internet here."

"What? How is that even possible?"

"I have no idea. But it's okay – Tony blamed it on a small boy."

Vicky took that in her stride. Perhaps a little too easily – I dunno, had I blamed too many things on small boys recently?

"So, I tried to see Jimmy at the Hanoi Asia Star," Vicky continued.

"Oh right?"

"Yeah. It's been closed down."

"What, the whole hotel?"

"Yep."

"Oh."

I guess that meant my bank cards weren't going to be discovered anytime soon.

"But you got home safely?" Roo asked.

"Yeah, no worries."

"Whew! I was so nervous, thinking of all the flights and connections and airports and taxis..."

"It all went fine," Vicky confirmed, "in fact, since I left you guys, everything went smoothly."

Roo shot me a look.

I knew that look.

"It's not my fault," I protested.

Even though the Skype image was grainy as hell, I could tell from Vicky's expression that she didn't believe a word of it.

"So, how's it going there?" she asked, changing the subject.

"Oh, great," Roo said. "Except, Tony just electrocuted himself. He was trying to plug the laptop in, and there was this massive *BANG...*"

At that point, I decided to bow out gracefully. Clearly the girls had lots to discuss, and they didn't need me around to get in their way. I left to the tune of a lively debate on the wisdom of faking all our documentation for China.

Some people just aren't suited for travel, I thought, shaking my head.

Evidently I was one of them.

Trying to turn it into a career might not have been the greatest choice.

When I came back in, Roo had something to show me.

"It's the video," she said, "the one Max took of us while we tried to complain about the Ha Long Bay tour. He wasn't lying – he's put it up on YouTube."

Max had posted the video in two sections – neatly editing out the bit where I calmly, rationally explained our complaint in full. The first clip ended as I finally got a word in edgeways, and started to describe the kayaking debacle. Then it cut off, inexplicably, mid-sentence. The second video started with Max telling me he understood what I was saying. "Put like that how could anyone doubt you?" he admitted.

But it went rapidly downhill from there. Eventually, we watched ourselves leave in disgust, and the video wrapped up with Max's claim of being published in some mysterious, unspecified place.

It was nearly as biased as the Cu Chi tunnels film.

What I couldn't figure out, and still can't to this day, is what on earth he thought he could achieve by posting it?

I mean, he runs a tourism business. So anyone watching that video, no matter whose side they end up on, would be left with one overwhelming opinion of Max: 'Jeez, I wouldn't want to complain to him!'

So, is that *more* likely to make them book a tour with him? Or less?

I'm thinking that, in the whole wide spectrum of customer service, no-one has ever fired an own goal quite so spectacularly. Especially as the links he posted on his website referred to us as 'backpacker scum'. And the vast majority of his customers were, what, exactly? Oh, that's right – backpackers. I jumped on the horn to *Lonely Planet,* and was informed that the Kangaroo Café had already been removed from the latest edition of their guide, due to bad reports. No wonder Max's homepage referred to them as 'Lying Planet'! I contacted the Rough Guide, and they said they hadn't included him since 2008. But that 2008 review was obviously a proud moment for Max, as it still featured prominently on his website five years later.

But, weird as it was, that was just the beginning.

My first inkling that it was about to get weirder was when I received a message on Facebook from a large-breasted woman who'd just added me. Back then I accepted every friend request that came my way; it simply never occurred to me that someone would create a fake account and use it to stalk me, sending out malicious messages to my friends and readers. I mean, *why?* Who would bother? Who could ever want to hurt me so badly that they would go to that amount of effort?

Well, as it turns out, there was just such a person, sitting in his café in Hanoi, and he was far from finished with me.

The message I got from the dubious account led me to a website called The Hanoi Watchdog. And it was there, on a blog that had been taken down by Google several times before, that the rest of this drama unfolded.

Max, writing under the pseudonym 'Watchdog', had created a blog post entitled 'Tony James Slater is a little pussy-bitch coward!'

And it got worse from there.

What followed was an obscene rant about me, punctuated with pictures of hardcore gay porn onto which my face had been carefully Photoshopped.

This was the link the fake Facebook account had been sending out to my friends and family.

I stared at the screen in disbelief – and would continue to do so, as every few days from then on another post would appear. All followed a similar theme; all featured photos of me culled from my website – and there was a cock in my mouth every time.

And that's when I remembered Max's cryptic threat, now immortalised on the video he'd posted to YouTube: *Where was he published?* I'd asked. "Oh, you'll see..." came his reply.

And he was right. Now I saw.

It was rather graphic, if mostly harmless. At first, I was so shocked that I told everyone. I found it funny, in a rather pathetic way, that anyone would go to such lengths to get back at me. For trying – and failing – to make a complaint. For leaving a bad review on Trip Advisor...

Wow.

But after commenting on the blog, explaining what had originally transpired for anyone who cared to read it, I realised that my best tactic would have been to starve the site of any attention. Instead, a war erupted in the comments, with both my readers and random strangers rallying to my defence. Max typed messages back and forth between himself and his 'Watchdog' alter-ego, tearing into my defenders, making the kind of comments that, had they been written in America, would have resulted in me owning his family for the next ten generations.

Vietnam, not so much. I can only assume that's one of the reasons he'd chosen to settle there. Although, the food was also good.

It took weeks for things to die down. I stopped looking at the site when Max used our wedding photos, creating photoshopped versions to illustrate a story about us getting married in a male-only sauna amidst an orgy.

This upset Roo, and in turn I began to lose my sense of humour. So I reported Max to whatever agencies I felt might care, mostly cyber-bullying taskforces, and decided to ignore it.

And I succeeded. Mostly.

The posts persisted for months, before someone else pissed Max off enough for him to target his rants elsewhere. And for now, that was the last of it.

At least until this book comes out...

Ever get that feeling, when you're doing something, that this is not going to end well?

Like when you intentionally piss off someone who is

quite possibly unhinged?
    Yeah.
    I totally just got that feeling.

Double Dutch

To be honest, we were getting a bit sick of Ulaanbaatar.

We'd explored the local markets, noticing they had for sale every single item we'd seen in any of the gers we'd visited. Mostly carpets, horse tack, leather boots, and the kind of mundane farming and domestic supplies that made for pretty crummy gifts. We browsed tourist shops, which sold mostly carpets, horse tack and leather boots – but slightly more decorative versions, at four times the price.

We visited some shabby temples, explored all six floors of the State Department Store, and fretted over our Chinese visas.

Part of the problem was, we were kind of stranded. On the one hand, we dearly wanted to explore the rest of the country; on the other hand, there wasn't anything in it. We had neither the time nor the money for an expedition to the far north or the even farther west, but we couldn't simply mooch around closer to home, as once outside the city there was nothing but grass.

Roo had wanted to visit the reindeer herding country surrounding *Khövsgöl Nuur*, a vast lake which contains 2% of all the world's fresh water. But that would take several days of driving each way, and the complete absence of public transport would require us to book an expensive private tour.

Then a pair of older American ladies moved into the Lotus guesthouse. They'd just returned from a *ger* camp not far from UB, run by a Dutch bloke called Bert and his Mongolian wife. Eager to get out of the city, I gave Bert a call and arranged to spend the rest of the week at his camp. Then we'd have to come back to UB to collect our Chinese visas.

Well, hopefully.

Because we'd already spent $500 on train tickets to *Beijing*.

Here are the directions to Bert's Eco Ger:

Take the bus to Terelj National Park. It leaves from the south side of Peace Avenue, 150 metres east of the junction with the road that runs south from Gandan Khiid Monastery. The bus stand has a large "Pepsi" sign on it.

The bus takes 3.5 hours to reach Terelj village.

It's 40 miles.

Get off at UB2 Hotel, turn right and wade across the river. After that, turn east along the track that follows the electricity poles. When you reach pole number 40, turn 90 degrees right and go straight on to find the camp.

Yeah… We got Bert to pick us up.

Bert was a large, loud, Dutch bloke. He was understandably a bit grumpy, as we sat in his silver 4x4 queuing out of the city. He'd found a pristine patch of wilderness to escape the rat race, and built his little dream of an environmentally friendly tourist haven. Only, five times a week he still had to fight his way into Ulaanbaatar, and back out again – either to pick up supplies, or to pick up customers.

This time he was killing two birds with one stone, so we stopped at a couple of stores on the way out of town and filled the back of his car with industrial-sized bags of flour and rice, giant tubs of chicken feed, and every single piece of fresh fruit and every vegetable on sale. Which amounted to one small carrier bag.

It took the obligatory two hours to clear the centre of UB, after which we passed through miles of *ger* districts. Ragged fence boards divided roughly rectangular patches of wasteland, each with a tent or two set up and a scatter of children and animals roaming around inside. It was fascinating to see this medieval lifestyle maintained within a few miles of where concrete high-rises clad in glass were having their fibre-optic broadband upgraded.

By the time we reached the *Terelj* National Park, the scenery had changed dramatically. Whereas UB was built on the plain, this part of Mongolia actually had *trees*. I hadn't seen one since visiting the mountaintop monastery, and getting lost in the forest on the way down. That was nearly two weeks ago. *Two weeks without trees?* How was that even possible?

We left the road at a barely-there town, carefully fording a series of rivers. Horses grazed on the banks; only the power lines reminded us we were still in comparative civilization.

We'd picked up a tail; a Dutch couple were following us on a gigantic BMW motorbike. Bert stopped for a few words, and they introduced themselves as Bart and Anita. Anita climbed into the back of Bert's car as Bart tackled the next ford, driving the big bike along in our wake. Powering through the metre-deep water was exciting in the car; on the bike, Bart must have been brown-trousering it all the way.

And with that we arrived at Bert's little slice of paradise.

Nestled into a sheltered valley, Bert's camp consisted of half a dozen spotless white *gers* and a log cabin that housed the kitchen. Roo and I would have a *ger* to ourselves, with two single beds either side of the central stove.

Anita and Bart were in the next *ger* over. The big bike looked ridiculous parked outside the round canvas tent – for starters it was taller than the door. Big steel pannier boxes held the couple's belongings, and glued to the sides was a map of their journey. Unbelievably, the sixty-year-old couple had ridden the bike here from their home in The Netherlands – crossing Eastern Europe, several countries ending in 'stan', Russia, Siberia, and then driving down through Mongolia from the far north. According to Bart, the scariest part of the whole trip was crossing that river outside Bert's camp. At well over five-thousand miles it was an epic journey, but they brushed it off with typical Dutch honesty. "We do something like this every year," Bart explained.

Holy. Shit.

These two were more adventurous in their sixties than I'd been my entire life.

I again felt a moment of doubt about my chosen career.

A travel writer that doesn't dare tell anyone he's a travel writer!

Well, if nothing else, that was very... me.

And it's always good to have something to aspire to.

We passed a lazy few days at Bert's place, drinking in the tranquillity of the location.

We watched his wife make cheese, in a delightfully low-tech process. She milked the cows, churned the milk, heated and mixed and heated and mixed the stuff, finally pressing the solids in cloth sacks under a stack of house bricks. It was fascinating to watch, but it took hours. The cheese then had to cure for two months in a special cellar Bert had created underneath the kitchen. "But it's either that, or eat Mongolian cheese!" he explained.

We all paused for a collective shudder at that point.

Meals there were was delicious – after such a bland diet, we tore into the rich Dutch foods like meatballs, sauerkraut, salads, homemade bread and creamy white sauce. Everyone had brought booze of some kind with them, so we sat up late into the night, telling jokes and swapping stories. And for breakfast? Bacon and eggs.

I was in heaven.

We spent a leisurely afternoon on horseback, riding to a sacred grove surrounded by ovoo rock piles. It was an enchanting spot. Once again I was struck by the scale of the countryside; we rode out from Bert's *ger*, stopped after a certain distance, and went back. But what if we'd carried on? Would we have blundered into another camp, or would we have continued, completely uninterrupted, for a hundred miles or more? The primeval landscape was as beautiful as it was vast, and very nearly as empty.

Another day we hiked into Terelj village, crossing rivers on fallen tree trunks and bundles of sticks. Aside from the hotel there was only a handful of buildings, and no roads to speak of. There was a bar, with a pair of horses tied up outside it; it's what the Wild West would have looked like if it had been built in 1950s Russia. Anita and Bart arrived in town and bought us a beer, before we made our way back over the log bridges and turned right at power pole number 40.

The only thing Bert couldn't provide us with was a shower.

I didn't mind at all, as I'd been planning on taking a dip in one of the little rivers.

"It's freezing!" Roo pointed out.

But I knew that. It was cold and pure, snow melt from the mountains, and I was determined to plunge myself into it for as long as I could cope.

"Did you bring shorts?" Roo asked.

"No, of course not."

"Are you going in your underpants, then?"

I gave her a look. "I'm not wearing pants."

Roo sighed. "I brought the towel, at least."

She held up one of our micro travel towels. It was not substantially bigger than a placemat.

I glanced around, but I'd picked a stretch far enough away from the camp to avoid detection. The river spilled into a small pool here, which looked idyllic, if a tad on the chilly side.

I stripped off, and leapt in.

And nearly passed out when the frigid water hit my delicate parts.

Roo took a few pictures of me howling and thrashing, before deciding it was time to help me out.

And that was when Bert's oldest son rode up on his bike. Two younger lads, who both looked about eight, trailed happily along behind him.

Suddenly, I had a dilemma. I was rapidly reaching the point of no return – I *had* to get out, while I still could. But my private bathing spot was suddenly a lot less private...

I made a panicked face at Roo. "What do I do?"

"Use the towel, love!" And she held the pathetic scrap of fabric out towards me.

Luckily, this was Mongolia. Rather than call the police and report me as a pervert, the kids raced around collecting fallen branches, and in minutes had a fire blazing on the riverbank. I sat there in the buff, on a log, warming my frozen bits and pieces by the fire. It was only then, satisfied with having helped us out, that the kids carried on with their errand. They went a few metres downstream, to where the water spread out even further, and the older lad rode his bike across the shallows.

"Oh, you picked the perfect place to strip naked, didn't you!" Roo crowed. "That bit of river, there? It's a ford!"

Farewell To Mongolia

Leaving Bert's camp was bittersweet; amazing as it had been, our time in Mongolia was drawing to a close.

To complete the Mongolian experience, our journey back to UB was in two distinct halves. We rode out of the camp on a flatbed wagon pulled by a white horse. The driver, a gnarled old herder, drove the horse through the river as I tried to film it; Roo kept a tight grip on me, otherwise one of us would have ended up in the drink.

In Terelj Village we caught the bus – a nine-seater minibus, which somehow managed to cram in seventeen men, women and children. I tried to film that, too, but there was barely room to turn my head. If the pony-and-trap was symbolic of the country life, then the crowded, urgent minibus was all UB. A few hours later we were back in the smog-wreathed capital, checking into the Lotus guesthouse one last time.

We picked up our Chinese visas without a hitch. No alarms sounded, no Secret Service men came running to surround us – it was a bit of an anti-climax, really.

For which Roo was rather grateful.

On the walk back I noticed a haughty-looking woman glaring at us from the passenger seat of a vast black Hummer.

Probably Russian, I thought, and turned to look at her surreptitiously. Ten minutes later, the reason for her attitude became obvious – we were all progressing down the same street, only Roo and I were on foot, and she was driving.

And we were beating her.

We stopped in a café to celebrate our visa victory with an iced beverage. I took out the laptop to see if there was WiFi, and Roo pulled out her tablet on reflex.

"Don't suppose that gets any signal?" I joked.

"I've had it on Flight Mode to save the battery," Roo said, "but I'll try it."

She flicked the device into wireless mode, and a few seconds later her jaw dropped. "Tony! It's *working!*"

Well, shit.

We had one day left in the city, and we'd saved UB's last monument to give us something interesting to see.

Gandantegchinlen Khiid, or the Gandan Monastary, was the only religious structure in Mongolia to escape destruction by the Communists. A handful of extremely lucky monks survived the Stalinist purge of over 15,000 lamas, and were allowed to reopen the monastery when the US Vice President asked to visit one in 1944.

The route there was an interesting one.

First we walked clear across UB, passing from the glittering Blue Sky Tower to more humble suburban shops in districts that could do with a lick of paint.

Or, demolition to be quite honest.

Then we crossed a road, crossed an open sewage ditch on a plank of wood, scrambled up a muddy hillside and found ourselves in a *ger* district. We followed a bare-earth path between ragged wooden fences, waving to barefoot children who peered at us through gaps where boards were missing.

And then, without warning, we came out into the temple complex – right in front of the main *Stupor.*

Gandantegchinlen Khiid consisted of several smaller temples, leading up to a square in front of a much more ornate building. All were Tibetan-Buddhist in style, though mostly brick-built and showing proof their 180 years had been hard ones.

The square contained one large stupor – and about a million pigeons.

Roo dug out the guidebook, trying to decide which temple to go into.

"Oh, it says here about the pigeons. The monks won't kill them, you see, so they keep on multiplying."

Ouch. There must have been thousands of the little buggers. As we watched, a young girl on the edge of the square threw a handful of breadcrumbs into the seething mass of birds. It was like an electric current ran through them – instantly they flocked to the girl, mobbing her in seconds. We lost sight of her for a while, such was the turmoil of beating wings.

"I bet when they fly away, she'll just be a skeleton," I told Roo.

She laughed – but it was a nervous laugh.

"Come on," she said, "there's a massive pair of feet over there. And they're covered in gold."

I turned to look. She was right.

We had to figure out what this was all about, so we dodged through the cloud of predatory pigeons and stood in the shadow of a massive golden toenail. Unsurprisingly, it turned out to be the start of a giant statue of Buddha – standing, rather than sitting, for the sake of variety.

There was a series of information boards opposite, which were unfortunately all in Mongolian. However, one particular graphic stood out as needing no explanation; it was a size comparison, showing the completed figure of this statue towering over the Statue of Liberty and Brazil's Christ the Redeemer.

Which certainly would have been a spectacle, were it even remotely possible. I had to snigger, as I climbed onto the big toe to get a better view of our surroundings. They'd made the feet – which was the logical place to start of course, though building it from the ground up would give them one hell of a bill for scaffolding when they came to shape Buddha's eyebrows. But would it ever rise beyond ankle height? It seemed doubtful. Almost as much as the planned mega-temple complex illustrated on the next board over. If the scale was accurate, it would be bigger than half of Ulaanbaatar. A clear case of the architects letting their imagination run away with them; it would cost the GDP of the entire country for a decade to get this thing built. As it was, I half expected to see a rusty collection bucket wedged between the toes with a sticker on it; 'Donate your loose change to the Big Buddha Project! Help us hit our target of five-hundred-million dollars...'

Beyond the great golden feet, the monastery's main temple (called *Migjid Janraisig*) was indeed impressive. Towering six stories high, it had the tiered, pagoda-like roofs of ancient Chinese architecture and was a staggering achievement for a population as sparse and scattered as Mongolia in the 1900s. The ground floor entryway had been opened up with a wall of glass, so we strolled inside to take a look. Technically there was an admission fee to be in here, but no-one else seemed to be bothering with it so we followed suit. It would only be a quick visit. I knew we wouldn't be allowed into the upper levels – we never had been, in any of the temples we'd visited so far.

And Migjid Janraisig was no different.

We weren't allowed into the upper levels, because there weren't any.

Beyond the modern foyer we passed through another, much older set of wooden doors, and found ourselves in the strangest room I've ever been in. A titanic statue of Buddha towered up through where the ceiling should be – all of the ceilings! There simply weren't any; the full height of this gigantic temple was hollow. The whole thing was just one huge, ornate box which housed precisely one thing: the tallest, gaudiest golden Buddha statue you could ever wish to lay eyes on.

Which made the project outside seem a bit redundant.

Especially since this 26 metre high, 20-tonne statue had only been completed in 1994.

What were those crazy monks thinking?

"At last! Our temple contains one of the biggest Buddha's in the world!"

"Great! So what do we need now?"

"AN EVEN BIGGER BUDDHA!"

Yes. Quite.

We goggled at the statue for the requisite amount of time, then went back outside to watch the girl being mauled by pigeons.

That night we treated ourselves to a feast of traditional Mongolian cuisine. Restaurants in UB were surprisingly expensive, given the fact that most of them served mutton and horsemeat. So we'd had a lot of picnics, buying bread, cheese and salami from a small supermarket we discovered. The supermarket (which had cute miniature versions of the trolleys we were used to seeing back home), also featured an entire aisle of vodka; more bottles and brands than I knew existed.

So of course we tried some of that, too.

And we ate a lot of pot noodles. Green ones, which Roo was in charge of buying after I came home one evening with two red ones. I've always maintained that being colour-blind is not a huge disadvantage, but it was that night. When Roo refused to eat hers, I put a post on Facebook asking if I'd made a mistake. A Korean girl replied, telling me the writing on the red noodles said (in Korean) 'super-fiery-hot!'

Good job I had plenty of vodka to douse them in.

We walked past a funky-looking restaurant called Modern Nomads on our way to the supermarket, and it always looked enticing – perhaps because we were on our way to buy pot noodles and vodka. Tonight we decided to take the plunge, and sample their traditional offerings.

This meant a variety-plate of dumplings to share, which came divided by contents in a wheel-shaped dish. There was mutton, obviously, plus, beef... and horse. Rather cleverly, the dish wasn't actually labelled in any way, so we had no way of telling which section contained the old sheep, and which contained Black Beauty.

They were all equally delicious.

Roo decided not to share my other choice, however. I do love to push her boundaries sometimes, and nothing achieves this better than sitting opposite her making slurping noises as

I consume something she considers a tad unsavoury.

'Five Organ Soup', in this case.

It was surprisingly chewy.

*   *   *

We were sad to leave the Lotus Guesthouse. It had come to feel like home; a refuge from the noise and choking exhaust fumes of the surrounding city. It was a cheerful little place, once you got beyond the forbidding steel doors. It was clean and spacious and, dodgy wiring aside, safe. I could only hope we'd do as well in China.

We took a taxi to the train station, booking it an hour early to allow for traffic on the 3.5km drive.

The sun shone brightly as we boarded our train; dusty brown carriages that had already completed the journey across Siberia to arrive here. They would now be carrying us all the way to Beijing, 4736 miles from their starting point in Moscow, making it the second-longest train journey in the world.

As we settled into our four-berth, second class sleeper carriage, I reflected on our time here.

I was going to miss Mongolia. Although UB was polluted to all hell and could be seriously frustrating, I loved the rough edge to the place, the frontier-style atmosphere. I got a sense that we were here right at the beginning of something, some great new era in which Mongolia would transform itself utterly into something unrecognisable. People were coming, with new ideas and big dreams. It seemed like the kind of place you might share a beer with a scruffy German backpacker, only to recognise him in a suit five years later and discover he's been appointed Minister for the Environment.

A good example of this was a 30-something Canadian bloke we'd hung out with on our last night in the Lotus. When we mentioned we were leaving by train, he got very excited and told us to watch out for Mongolia's first ever wind farm, which we'd pass about an hour outside of UB. "It had to be close to the train line," he explained, "that was the only way we could get anything in or out. Half the government turned up to watch us switch it on last week. Thirty-one turbines – that's a hundred million dollars worth! That one site is going to generate five percent of all Mongolia's energy needs."

"You worked on it then?" I asked him.

"You could say that, yeah," he laughed. "I ran the project."

CHINA

A Change Of Track

The Gobi desert dominates the border between China and Mongolia. Already Asia's largest desert, at over half a million square miles, the Gobi is expanding southwards at up to 1,400 square miles each year. It's generally referred to as a cold desert, although temperatures can fluctuate wildly between -50 and +50 degrees centigrade. Despite this alarming characteristic, some life survives there; more interestingly, the first dinosaur eggs were found there, along with a fantastic variety of fossils and prehistoric artefacts.

It's a fascinating place.

Alas, being a desert, it has relatively few street lights.

So as it was night-time when we passed through, we didn't see a bit of it.

At some ungodly hour of the morning, we were shaken from our bunks by what felt like a collision. A series of collisions, in fact, working their way up the whole length of the train. I was only pretending to sleep, anyway, and I knew straight away what this was, so I grabbed Roo's camera and headed for the end of our carriage.

Because something truly bizarre was about to happen.

The thing is, Chinese train tracks are about three inches narrower than their Mongolian counterparts. You'd think that, in the interest of facilitating more efficient transit between the two countries, some bright spark would have come up with a decent work-around for this problem?

No.

What was about to happen bordered on parody. It was the most ridiculous, most illogical, most impossibly labour-intensive solution to the problem.

Put another way, it was the *Chinese* solution.

Rather than building a big shed, then pulling everybody off the train and making them walk through and get back on a different train on the other side – or you know, *inventing* a train with adjustable wheels (something that has been achieved in places like Spain, Sweden and Poland) – the Chinese had tackled the problem in their own inimitable fashion.

So we watched with mounting excitement as our train was drawn into a gigantic hanger and, one carriage at a time, was *lifted up* by dozens of hydraulic rams – still full of passengers and their luggage. The carriage's wheels, which had been unfastened, remained on the rails. They slid out from under us and clanged away, whilst another set of wheels – slightly wider – were coaxed underneath. The hydraulics then reversed, lowering us very, *very* slowly onto the new rolling stock – and that was that.

Only another twenty or thirty carriages to go…

The whole process took around four hours.

This solution could only have been brought to you by the people who built a 4,000 mile wall across their entire country just to keep the northerners out.

It was dawn by the time we were back underway. We made an epic journey of about eight or nine minutes, before we stopped again for the border crossing. At this point a guard came down the train collecting passports, and we got to sit and wait for another two hours while some shadowy official in an unmarked office nearby scrutinized and stamped every one of the buggers. Why it hadn't occurred to anyone to unify this process with the previous one was quite beyond me. I know that efficiency and bureaucracy rarely go hand-in-hand, but there are occasions when it completely takes the piss. This was one of those occasions.

On the upside, no-one called us out on any aspect of our travel documents. We hadn't even been searched, which was a surprise – recent reports said that Chinese border guards were finding and confiscating copies of *Lonely Planet: China* at all entry points, due to an unfavourable write-up about their handling of Tibet. Our copy was safely buried in the Kindle files on Roo's tablet, but you could bet there were a few physical copies scattered around that train. Still, no-one asked, and we sure as hell weren't going to mention anything.

Which I guess made us smugglers. Of digital information.

The name's Bond. James Bond.

As we set off again, in the full grey light of day, we fastened our eyes on the scenery outside – and could hardly believe our eyes.

The contrast was staggering. Crossing over from a remote part of southern Mongolia to a remote part of northern China via a desert they both share, I hadn't expected to notice much change.

How wrong I was.

The Gobi notwithstanding, Mongolia as a whole had been characterised by its emptiness. Almost since the outskirts of Ulaanbaatar, vast, untamed landscapes stretched as far as the eye could see, with rarely any sign of human presence.

China, on the other hand, was *inhabited*.

It came as quite a shock at first. This was still the frontier; the wild extreme, as far from mainstream civilization as it was possible to be. Mountains rose up, the train flowing through tunnel after tunnel as it wormed its way beneath the peaks.

And yet everywhere there were villages, snuggled into niches in the rocks, clinging to ledges, spilling down gorges and straggling across the lowlands. Every inch of space between them was cultivated; vibrant fields glowed green, dominating the view from the train with ingeniously sculpted terraces that squeezed maximum growing room out of the steepest slopes.

Huts appeared in the most inaccessible of spaces, almost like a challenge to the precipitous landscape.

Ancient mud-brick buildings stood side-by-side with modern houses in villages still surrounded by ramparts of crumbling earth. Power lines snaked across the fields, and as the mountains gave way to more hospitable, level ground, enormous electricity pylons appeared, marching across the fields into infinity.

The pylons themselves made me smile. Whilst they did blemish the almost medieval view, they were of a comical design clearly modelled on Space Invaders. It was like the concept of minimalist design had been turned on its head.

"Why settle for a spindly tower with cables on either side?" the lead engineer must have said. "What we need is massive great square things, with the cables running through the middle! We'll be able to squeeze five times the steel into those puppies. Imagine how many more jobs we'll create!"

It took most of the day to reach Beijing.

The sky remained grey and unwelcoming, but once clear of the mountains the fields spread out, pristine and glistening. Towns became more frequent, and the roads around them became bigger and in better repair. Then we transitioned from the countryside into the urban environment, and Beijing began in earnest. It's a vertical place, with more skyscrapers than anywhere else on earth. From the train they formed a wall on both sides, tall and unrelenting. From street level I could well imagine them blotting out the sun – well, had there been any sun to blot out.

It always amuses me when I see a Chinese couple walking the streets of Perth wearing those little white surgical masks over their mouths and noses. I can't help but think, *Jeez, if you think the air is bad here, how the hell do you cope at home?* They must walk around wearing full Hazmat suits with breathing apparatus.

But now, in Beijing, I was starting to appreciate the reality behind that affectation.

It wasn't just the weather that was grey – it was smog.

A teenage Chinese girl who spoke English with a strong American accent had spent the day chatting loudly to pretty much anybody who would listen. So far we'd managed to avoid her for exactly this reason, but as we approached Beijing we started to wonder what our first move would be. And we started to get just a little bit nervous about it. So I made eye contact with the girl, and that gave her all the opening she needed. Within minutes we knew all about her life in China and her studies in the US. But more interestingly, she was assembling a group of clueless passengers from the train, and would be doing her good deed of the day by orientating us on arrival. She had barely paused for breath by the time the train arrived, pulling up beside the longest station platform I'd ever seen.

At last! We were here.

A feeling, in equal parts excitement and anxiety, washed over me.

This. Is. China!

Trains the world over are exited in a scrum – even in England there's a spot of mild pushing – but the sheer scale of Beijing station, and of the crowds inside it, made me want to run and hide.

Somehow we made it through the one-way system, past the ticket inspectors stationed, oddly, at the exit. Imagine having successfully scammed your way across the entire country, only to find you couldn't get out of the station without a ticket... gutted!

Our little group assembled outside, and were led from the concourse over a footbridge above eight lanes of swirling traffic. Here, on the far side of the road, lay a bank with an ATM machine that accepted foreign cards.

Cash had been the first item on everyone's agenda.

I let Roo do the honours for us.

Having survived Mongolia without incident, it would suck to lose our only bank card when we were so close to receiving the replacements. I'd asked Mum to post them to our hotel here in Beijing, and I was very much looking forward to the extra financial security.

And to not shitting my pants every time we had to use a cash machine.

Roo was triumphant. With plenty of Chinese *Yuan* in hand, our next step was simple; grab a taxi, and head to our hotel. The heat was intense, and we were both dripping with sweat already. Even ten minutes walking with all our bags on had us gasping, though perhaps the lack of oxygen in the atmosphere was partially to blame. Our new friend had calculated that most of the group would be able to come with her, but our hotel was, predictably, a long way off in the opposite direction. She found a taxi, chatted briefly with the driver, then asked us if 100 Yaun ($20) was an okay price.

I think she could tell from our reaction that it wasn't, at which point she pretty much washed her hands of us, wishing us good luck and leading the rest of her posse away.

We retraced our steps to the station concourse, found a queue of about two hundred people, figured it had to be for taxis, and joined the back of it. It was a well-oiled system, and ten minutes later we were in a metered taxi on our way to the Beijing Dreams hotel.

It was a short trip, and we stared out of the windows as massive buildings flew past on all sides, largely indistinguishable from one another. The multi-lane roads, the vast junctions, the profusion of signs covered in Mandarin glyphs; it all looked the same. This was no kitschy tourist town, this was the Big City – as big as they come, and as foreign – and to be honest, it was more than a little intimidating.

Oh, but the taxi fare wasn't – that trip cost us $4.

Which, I felt, represented a significant saving.

Because along with marking the halfway point of our six-month trip, the epic 29-hour train ride from Mongolia into China had also crossed another important milestone: $9,000 spent, from our original $8,000 budget.

And we only had three countries to go…

Beijing Dreamin'

I probably shouldn't admit this, being as how I'm trying to portray myself as a professional travelly-type person, but the first meal I ate in China was McDonald's.

I take full responsibility. I can't help it! I am a fast food addict.

So far, we'd eaten KFC once in Borneo (for breakfast), and had no fast food at all in Vietnam (it doesn't exist – either because it's a product of evil American capitalist society, or because the real food in Vietnam is so good and so damn cheap that it wouldn't stand a chance). We'd succumbed to the lure of KFC again in Mongolia, but given the transitional state of lifestyles there I considered this a bona fide cultural experience. Especially because it was crap. Now, faced with the kind of juicy, preservative-laden cheeseburgers we hadn't seen since Seoul Airport, I found myself standing in a puddle of my own drool.

I still fought my urge to cheat, and ordered something not available in Western outlets; the 'Spicy Pork McRib', with McSticky Rice.

Roo had a Big Mac.

Man, was I jealous.

We were to spend quite a lot of time in various McDonald's

restaurants, in China.

If that makes you want to stop reading this book right now, I completely understand.

The sad truth is, those Golden Arches were to become a beacon of hope for us in our darkest moments, when food options shrunk and our desire to seek out exciting new culinary challenges had been eroded to zero.

In hindsight, it's possible to say that we were a little naïve about the food in China.

Both Roo and I love Chinese food – who doesn't? I'd prefer to eat it over any other kind of food in the world. Throughout most of our time in Mongolia we'd been fantasising about reaching China, for exactly this reason. As we tucked into yet another stringy mutton stew we'd talk about our cravings for sweet-and-sour sauce, for chicken *chow mein*, for no.87 with chips and a free bag of prawn crackers.

And somehow we'd let those dreams blind us to the inevitable truth; the Chinese, as a people, don't eat Chinese food.

At all.

What we in the West have come to know as Chinese food was largely developed in America, in the nineteenth century, by Chinese immigrants. Unable to get any but the most back-breaking of jobs due to (legal) ethnic discrimination, many immigrants turned to food selling, using their self-taught cooking skills and adapting meals from back home to suit the American palate. Sweeter, richer, more fatty foods, with less emphasis on vegetables and (eventually) bucketfulls of added MSG became a staple of the US food scene, pioneering the 'take-out' system that we have come to know and love. However, somewhere in the middle of that process, the form of Chinese cuisine that we in the West were becoming addicted to ceased to bear any resemblance to the actual food eaten by Chinese people in China.

Unfortunately.

And no, in case you're wondering – fortune cookies also do not exist there.

With dinner accomplished in the easiest, most stress-free

manner possible, we crossed the road back to the Beijing Dreams Hotel, took the lift up to our 8th floor room, fell into bed and slept for thirty hours straight.

Prolonged travel does this to you sometimes, or at least, it does it to us; every once in a while all the mental stresses, the sleep deprivation, the physical exhaustion and the lack of nutrition combine to create such an epic tiredness that only a day or two in bed can fix it. This had been our first major slump of the trip, and with that out of the way, we could begin to explore our immediate surroundings.

The Beijing Dreams was a fairly accurate name for the place, in that it was in Beijing, and I do sometimes dream of cockroaches. It was neither the cleanest, nor the dirtiest room we had stayed in so far, but it was the only one (as far as I know) with an inhabited ceiling. Every night we were treated to a frantic scratching, as something – presumably a rat – tried to burrow its way into the room. This also influenced my dreams, further reinforcing their choice of name.

I daily expected to wake up as the thing plummeted from the ceiling to land, voracious, on my chest, but it never happened. I guess whoever got the room after us had that to look forward to.

Unsurprisingly, the place was a treasure trove of Chinglish. Roo delightedly took photos of a sign on the back of the door, warning us that: 'We do not take any responsibility for your lost in your room.'

I figured this one was aimed at me, as if there's anyone who could conceivably get lost in their own hotel room, it's me.

Perhaps more disturbingly there was a 'CCTV' logo on the toilet seat. I never determined if this was just a conveniently-named manufacturer of conveniences, or if Big Brother was actually watching me take a shit.

After all, this was China – nothing could be taken for granted.

Our main difficulty with the Beijing Dreams was that, despite it being advertised as an international youth hostel, most of the staff spoke only Chinese.

Asking them if my replacement bank cards had arrived from England was, therefore, an essay in frustration. I eventually convinced the girl at the desk to check the shelf where they put the day's post, but couldn't convince her to delve any deeper. So the package, which could have arrived days or even weeks ago, could be sitting in someone's desk drawer with a Post-it note on it saying 'URGENT! FAO Mr Tony Slater!' – and we would never know.

Ah well. I would have to keep trying.

Having established our base, our first thought was for supplies. This reminded me of a joke about a Chinese worker who was sent to get supplies, and ended up jumping out at the other workers shouting "Supplies!" But that's probably not considered politically correct these days, so I won't tell it.

Roo and I bravely ventured past McDonald's, discovering that the shop next-door to it sold live turtles in plastic bags – I couldn't decide if it was a pet shop, or another fast food outlet. And next-door to that was the joyous sight of a supermarket.

Ahhh!

Supermarkets are a dream for travellers like us. By which I mean that, Roo and I are exceptionally lazy travellers. In order to have as 'authentic' and 'immersive' an experience as possible, the guidebooks all advise spending your days frequenting the local markets, browsing the bewildering array of goods on offer, taking in the foreign sights and smells and engaging with the local people on their own turf.

Which all sounds very poetic, when you're reading it in a comfy armchair in your air-conditioned flat in Perth.

The reality is thirty-five-degree heat, humidity off the scale, sweat pooling around your feet as you stare in horror at the swarm of flies battling over the bleeding stump of a freshly decapitated chicken. All the while being jostled by locals and shrieked at by every stall-holder in a half-mile radius, all of whom are determined to behead one of their chickens just for you. The smells range from spices to offal to sewage, and if you're anything over five feet tall your sight is invariably compromised by walking into one or more awnings and getting poked in the eye by the supporting broom handle.

So we were kind of glad to see a supermarket.

Don't get me wrong; I love exploring a good market. I already had more scarves than I knew what to do with. It's just that, from a food-shopping perspective, I'm that wussy kind of person who prefers not to look his dinner in the eye before eating it. Or step in its entrails.

The shop was exactly what we needed. We could browse the shelves at our leisure without being hassled, which meant we could actually find some kinds of food that we recognised. And the smell of sewage was kept to a minimum.

We left the place with an impressive haul of bread, butter, soft cheese, a sausage-like cooked meat that may have been salami, milk, cucumbers, a bag of crisps and a big bottle of fizzy pop.

"Party at our place," I joked to Roo.

That afternoon, over unspecified meat and Laughing Cow sandwiches, I committed my first crime in China.

Well, unless you count entering the country under false pretences, with travel documents obtained by fraud.

I was definitely going through a naughty patch.

But it was kind of hard not to commit crime in China, because practically everything we wanted to do was a crime.

Take Facebook, for instance.

ILLEGAL!

Oh yes, the Chinese leadership, in their infinite wisdom, still feel the need to censor the outside world. It's well-known that we in the West only see of China what they allow us to see, but I hadn't really thought about it being the other way around. To keep out all those evil Western influences, Facebook was banned – along with Twitter, YouTube, Hotmail, and Google. Even my blog, which runs on Wordpress, was inaccessible; blocked centrally by the 'Great Firewall of China'.

Reportedly anywhere between thirty and fifty *thousand* cyber-police men and women sat at their desks, monitoring and filtering the internet content, and restricting anything deemed to be 'Harmful to public order, social stability, or Chinese morality'.

Come to think of it, I'm not surprised my blog was blocked.

Along with anything even remotely pornographic.

Which begs the question: without access to porn – and all those other sites, of course – what the hell do the Chinese *do* on the internet? I was hard-pressed to think of a single thing.

Luckily, I'd come prepared. Vietnam had also made visiting some sites (specifically Facebook) problematic, though it was usually down to stingy hotel owners wanting to conserve their bandwidth rather than mass government censorship. Regardless, I'd downloaded stealth software to keep us online – kind of like a layman's version of what the bad guys use in spy thrillers, it did that thing where it bounced our signal all over a map. Presumably whilst rooms full of FBI agents and army generals looked on in despair.

And so, having been in China for less than two days, I was able to flout their draconian censorship laws by posting a Facebook status telling everyone I was flouting their draconian censorship laws.

That was bound to end well.

"Are you sure you should have posted that?" Roo asked me.

"Of course! It can't come back to us. They can't even get to Facebook here, so how is anyone going to know what I've written?"

"Love, they have CCTV *in our toilet* for crying out loud! I dread to think what they have in their interrogation rooms. Please be careful, okay?"

"Of course, darling. Careful is my middle name."

And that was the last thing I posted on Facebook, from China. Not because Roo's caution had swayed me, but because my miraculous stealth software suddenly stopped working shortly after this, for no apparent reason.

Strange, that.

Dying to Explore

Now that we were rested, and had located adequate provisions, there was one more vitally important task we had to complete, before we dared venture out into the city proper.

I imagine it's an issue that most travellers face, sooner or later.

We had to dye Roo's hair.

It was starting to go brown in places. Not like fruit; it wasn't rotting or anything – just, her natural colour was starting to reassert itself, and Roo wouldn't leave the room until this situation was remedied.

So. She dug through her rucksack and produced a bottle of purple hair dye, which she had been hauling around since Perth. I know, I know! Just... don't get me started.

Anyway, the first stage of the process involved bleaching her roots, because otherwise the colour wouldn't take.

"They might sell bleach in that supermarket," I said doubtfully, "but I'm not really sure I'd trust it on your head. I mean, we won't be able to read the packet or anything. And I doubt it would be hair-specific..."

"Don't worry! I have some here in my bag. I got Vicky to bring it over when she came to Vietnam."

"Oh, right! That's good."

Roo pulled out a bag of suspicious-looking white powder.

"That's it?" I asked.

"Yes. We just mix it into a paste..."

"So, Vicky brought that with her, on a plane, from Perth?"

"Yes."

"And she didn't get stopped at customs?"

"No, of course not. It was in a box that said 'bleach' on it."

"Riiiight, well, that's sure to fool anyone. And where is this box?"

"Oh, I threw it away. It was way too big to fit in my bag."

"Okay. And since then we've crossed... how many international borders?"

"Oh! Yeah. I never really thought about that."

I had to laugh.

Inwardly, my mind was reeling with the shock of disaster so narrowly averted. The staff at Perth airport might have found it funny, with their trained sniffer dogs and sophisticated chemical analysis machines. But in a remote customs office on the Chinese/Mongolian border? We could have been sat in a cell for days waiting for the all-clear to come from a lab in Beijing.

It's not like we could have just eaten the stuff.

We spent a good few hours in the bathroom, transforming Roo from shrinking violet into purple personified.

After a little while, I noticed her watching me intently through the shower screen.

"Why are you staring at me like that?" I asked.

"I'm only following the instructions," she replied.

She pointed to something printed on the shower screen at shoulder height; 'Please look out the glasses' it said.

"Oh. Fair enough."

It's easy to make fun of Chinglish. We probably do exactly the same back home, writing ridiculous labels in bad Chinese on all our buses and trains. Or do we? There are plenty of Chinese people working in the UK, so presumably anyone needing a sign in Chinese at least gets it proofread before spending money on having it made... or, say, etching it onto hundreds of panes of toughened glass for an international hotel's shower screens! I mean, really? They run an international youth hostel! And they didn't have a single English-speaking backpacker there to ask?

Anyway. Beijing was now on our doorstep, and we had procrastinated long enough. It was our first afternoon in China – well, the first one that we spent awake – so we resolved to visit the infamous Tiananmen Square.

History fascinates me, and I was an avid student at school. When it came time to choose the subjects we would pursue for our GCSE exams (at 16 years old), I chose History without a second thought. It was only after those decisions were irrevocably cast that they revealed the topic I would spend most of my last two years at high school studying; for History, it was a module called 'The Rise of Communist China'. I don't think I'd been as disappointed since Mum told the Air Force recruiter I was colour-blind, ending my dreams of being a fighter pilot in a single sentence. I mean, there's history, and there's *History*. Seriously? In terms of real-world relevance, not to mention personal interest, The Rise of Communist China was about as far off the mark as it was possible to be.

It was an incredibly boring and intensely depressing topic, which could be summarised like this: in China, an abusive regime was killing lots of people. So they decided to become Communists, killing lots of people in the process. Then the Communists became an abusive regime, killing even more people.

The End.

In the time-honoured tradition of students in the UK, I did naff all for two years, memorized as much information as I possibly could in the 48 hours before the exam, passed with a halfway decent grade, and then promptly forgot every last bit of it. And until now, I can't say I've ever felt disadvantaged by my lack of knowledge of Communist China and its Rise. But my one abiding memory of that course was drawn from the accounts of students who survived the 1989 massacre, where forces of the ironically-named 'People's Liberation Army' unleashed their military power on unarmed protestors in Tiananmen Square. Specifically, I remember one man's graphic description of the sound a live human head makes when a tank drives over it – it goes 'poc!' apparently.

So it was with a mix of dread, curiosity, and remembered boredom that I set out to visit the site of the massacre. Interesting note: the Chinese government still denies it was anything other than an uprising of radicals, and had never released an official account, or a death toll (which some international sources project to be in the thousands). You cannot search the internet for 'Tiananmen Square Massacre', or any similar search string, from within China. And if you're stupid enough to try, well, losing your stealth software is probably the least that would happen.

We took the underground, which was refreshingly easy to navigate as the station names were written in English – a throwback to the Beijing Olympic Games in 2008. The map was the familiar web of tangled lines, although (being colour-blind) I had to get Roo to read it. It was also huge, mostly because the subway was huge; the second biggest in the world in fact, after – can you guess?
Nope, you're all wrong! It's Shanghai.
In terms of sheer scale, China was already shaping up to be an eye-opener. Putting it in perspective, the London Underground carries up to three million passengers every day; the New York Metro manages a staggering five and a half million. The Beijing subway? Between *nine and eleven million passengers,* every single day. It's a monster.
But the trains were modern and surprisingly clean, given the general filthiness of the streets above, and the tickets – once we figured out how to buy them – were incredibly cheap, at just 20p (30c) no matter how far you went.

We made it to Tiananmen Square without incident. Well, almost – we made it to the subway station, but it took us the best part of an hour to figure out how to cross the road.

Tiananmen Square is absolutely vast, and the road that surrounds it is appropriately impressive. Traffic can't be stopped at all there, or the whole city would grind to a halt, so there's a series of underground passages leading to the square itself.

Which is huge. Insanely huge – walking a diagonal line from one corner to the other would take you over a kilometre. In that time you wouldn't pass a single bench, tree, or ornamental flowerbed – just flat, endless paving, punctuated by lampposts which bristle with CCTV cameras. Oh, and you'd also pass at least a hundred policemen, most of whom are in plain clothes.

For me, Tiananmen Square was that rare contradiction; the kind of wide open space that is just *begging* for you to turn cartwheels in it, whilst simultaneously being one of the worst places in the world to attempt any kind of unorthodox behaviour. I settled for a few handstands, and planned a quick getaway – at least until a Chinese tourist caught sight of Roo's hair.

Roo posed politely for photos with the man and his wife, individually then together, and by this point other people were starting to show an interest. We were in serious danger of violating the 'no gathering' laws, so we slipped away towards a towering, colonnaded palace on the far side of the square.

But this was no palace.

This was a tomb.

A massive mausoleum, in fact, where beloved Chairman Mao, the People's Hero and the Founding Father of Communist China, was interred. 700,000 people voluntarily laboured to complete the structure, which houses Mao's perfectly-preserved body in an earthquake-proof crystal coffin. Now the building is visited by more Chinese tourists than any other place on the planet, in blind pilgrimage to their fabled *Great Helmsman*.

It's the kind of bare-faced, blatant re-writing of history that could only occur in the heart of Communism; Mao Zedong, poet and visionary, killed more people than Hitler; in fact, between his military campaigns and his schemes to modernise China, which resulted in widespread famine, he was personally responsible for more deaths than the entire Second World War.

Estimates put the fatalities directly attributable to him at around 70 million.

Seventy. Million.

This makes Chairman Mao the single biggest killer the world has ever known.

I suspected that little factoid might have been omitted from the information plaques around the mausoleum, but I wasn't paying to find out. I didn't fancy queuing past the embalmed corpse of a tyrannical mass-murderer, whilst watching his besotted countrymen overcome with love, laying floral tributes to a man they all believed was the Father of modern China.

Communism, eh?

Who'd have it?

Monumental Mission

Now, rumour has it there's a big wall knocking around in China somewhere; you might even have heard of it. It can't be seen from space, as is often said (by people who haven't been to space), but it *can* be seen on reasonably-priced day trips from Beijing. Which was much more convenient, as we were already there.

On the advice of Tim and Charlotte, we decided to visit a section of the Wall near *Jinshanling*. There's a closer section called *Badaling*, but it's the number one spot for tourists, both foreign and domestic, in the entire country. It's served by its own railway line, its own motorway (the 'Badaling Expressway') – and a cable car. I briefly considered going there and trying to crowd-surf all the way to *Mutianyu*, where some bright spark has built not just a cable car to get up the Wall, but a toboggan ride to get down.

I felt this might not provide the most authentic Great Wall experience.

Kind of like touring the Tower of London on space-hoppers.

Actually, scratch that – touring the Tower of London on space-hoppers sounds *awesome*. I'm totally patenting that.

The first stage of our journey involved finding a certain *hutong* (alleyway) that contained the Downtown Backpackers. Beijing's *hutongs* have graduated from low-rent backstreets full of vendors selling cheap street food, to trendy hotspots full of vendors selling dramatically overpriced street food. Celebrated for their old-world charm, the narrow alleys have been reinvented for tourism – ironically at the price of their old-world charm. This was a somewhat depressing trend we were to observe throughout China. Anything with historical interest was being ruthlessly replaced with old-looking modern equivalents, in a process I began to refer to as 'Disneyfication'. At first glance, the buildings lining the alleyway appeared to be built from thousands of tiny, flat bricks. But closer inspection – plus the occasional missing tile – revealed them to be poured concrete structures, clad in tiny-brick-effect tiling. Still, the atmosphere couldn't be faked. It felt like a permanent carnival was going on in the *hutong*, with strings of paper lanterns overhead and crowds of well-dressed Chinese tourists enjoying their slice of old Beijing.

We found Downtown Backpackers right in the middle of the *hutong*, and felt quite jealous of their location. Alas, 'proper' youth hostels, with their international clientele and multi-lingual staff, all seemed to cost twice the price of low-end hotels like the Beijing Dreams – and that was for single beds in dorms.

The trip they offered was a 6km (3.7miles) hike, crossing through 22 towers, 'on rugged, up and down mountain inclines' – and they reckoned it would take on average three and a half hours to do it. I was sold the instant I saw the phrase, 'Recommended you have a good level of fitness for this challenging trek!'

We booked in for an 8am departure the following morning, then went outside and splurged on donuts, ice cream, and kebabs as long as swords.

*   *   *

We were up early the next morning, brimming with

anticipation. We were first on the tour bus, and sat for what seemed like an ice age waiting for it to fill; evidently not everyone was as enthusiastic as us. It took over an hour to get out of Beijing, and a further two to reach *Jinshanling*. I guess that's the main reason why this section of Wall remained comparatively unvisited. The guide's spiel was quite informative. Like most people I'd assumed the Great Wall was one continuous edifice, built in one titanic effort, whereas in actual fact it is made up of hundreds of different walls, all of which have been built, destroyed, rebuilt, re-destroyed, repaired, upgraded, combined and then neglected again in a continuous cycle for over two thousand years.

The famous bits, that feature on all the post cards and the covers of National Geographic magazine, date from the 'Ming' dynasty (yes, like the vases), or around the 15th Century CE.

He carried on:

"The Wall came under attack during the *Manchu* invasion in the 1600s, and wasn't rebuilt until the 19th Century…"

"Heavily damaged by fighting with the Japanese, a plan to rebuild parts of the wall was undertaken in 1956…"

"Partially destroyed with explosives by the Red Guard during the Cultural Revolution, the wall was extensively repaired in 1985…"

I started to wonder if there was anything of the real Great Wall left.

"This next section was entirely rebuilt by my Uncle Steve last Thursday," I quipped.

"Steve works hard," Roo replied.

"Nah. Steve works with Styrofoam and spray paint."

The bus dropped us off on a short approach road, and suddenly there it was – the silhouette of a tower, looming high above us on the crest of a steep hill. A shiver of excitement ran down my spine. All joking aside, this was a major bucket list item, not just for me but for half the people on the planet. I'd always wanted to see the Great Wall, but had never envisaged a scenario which would take me to China. And now… here I was.

Practically wetting myself.

There was nothing else out here, and the meagre influx of tourists merited only a couple of stalls selling cold drinks. This I took as a good sign. The climb up to the Wall was tough, steps upon hundreds of carved stone steps, twisting back and forth through the forest as we snaked our way up the hill. Panting, dripping with sweat, we arrived at the base of the tower – and at the start of our day's trek.

I'm not quite sure what I expected, but something was not quite right.

At first I couldn't put my finger on it, climbing the steps to the top of the tower and gazing out over the parapets. Then I realised.

This tower was pristine.

The bricks were all clean and crisp and uniform, which meant... yup! Sure enough, they were thin veneers, glued onto whatever this section had been rebuilt from. Concrete blocks, presumably. There was a row of shiny black cannons, fresh from the set of *Pirates of the Caribbean*.

The view, however, could not be faked.

It was incredible.

Lush green hills rolled over each other to the horizon, where they met the shadowy, insubstantial mountains. From this vantage point I could see ridge upon ridge, fading into the distance – each one capped by a diminishing ribbon of stonework. Aside from the car park immediately below us, the only man-made structure in sight was the Wall itself – and it stretched on to infinity.

After a couple of photos we sped off on the hike, hoping to get ahead of the tour group. For now, we were the only ones on this section; if we put a bit of distance between us and the rest of the group, it was quite possible we would have a stretch of Wall entirely to ourselves.

It was easy going at first, the smooth, recently re-paved road deck offering no difficulty.

After the shocking Disneyfication of the first tower, I was relieved to find the Wall reverted to a much older version of restoration. Rough black bricks had been used, with carved stone lintels between the battlements. Although still heavily rebuilt, it felt significantly more authentic, as though it had been done in much the same way as it would have been a thousand years ago. Leaning out I could see that only the battlements had been restored in this way. Occasional openings, small doorways and windows that led to the north appeared far older, exposing red bricks and crumbling mortar that seemed to pre-date even this renovation. But the most ancient component of all was the scenery; unchanging, unspoilt and ancient, it accompanied us every step of the way.

We stopped often to gaze across enormous gulfs of space, at the line of the Wall as it vanished over some distant peak. It was hard to believe that in an hour or so we'd be standing over there, looking back at this spot with equal disbelief. The Wall provided endless photo opportunities as it rose and fell, vistas so spectacular they brought tears to my eyes. Always the green mountains surrounded us, a sumptuous backdrop, as the Wall looped and twisted impossibly. It reminded me of a cartoon road, a stripe bisecting every hill for miles around, with no clue as to how they might be connected.

Even now, looking back at my pictures, I can hardly comprehend the scale of it.

I've been racking my brains, trying to think of a way to describe it. I mean, I could quote numbers (culled from Wikipedia, as I didn't have a tape measure with me), but that won't mean anything to anyone. I find big numbers so arbitrary; I can't grasp the size of something without a common frame of reference. Let's try this: imagine the biggest-sized coach you've ever seen. I'm talking about those giant National Express buggers, with two axels at the back and drooping wing mirrors like butterfly antennae. Park two of them side by side. Then take another two, and stack them on top of the first two. Climb up to the top of the whole pile and, along with intense vertigo, you'll get a sense of how massive the Great Wall is.

Some sections are bigger still.

And that's not counting the towers.

Oh, and it stretches, in some form or other, roughly the same distance as from New York to Berlin.

It. Is. Freaking. *HUGE!*

The entire Jinshanling area is a series of mountain ranges. Rather than being content with these already formidable barriers, the Great Wall runs atop the mountains, right along the ridgeline from crest to crest. In places it climbs so steeply that it's built vertically rather than horizontally; hundreds of steps replace the paved walkway atop the Wall, and it climbs towards a watchtower on the pinnacle. This pattern repeats itself endlessly, the Wall plunging down the side of the previous mountain before rising to climb the next one. Stretches for some hundreds of metres may seem flat by comparison, but the Wall in those areas is constantly changing in height to compensate for the terrain. I don't think there is a single patch of genuinely flat ground in the entire length of the Jinshanling Wall. To have built it at all is mind-boggling. To have built it so spectacularly, is… well.
Must have been aliens.

A particularly steep section left us winded, gasping, on the roof of one of the larger towers. We found a patch of shade cast by the pagoda-like roof and sprawled in it to eat our cream cheese sandwiches. The air was roasting; one disadvantage of the gorgeous clear sky was the sun, which was doing its level best to cook us alive. A bit further along the roof, another couple had collapsed in the same strip of shade. He was tending her; she had literally collapsed, and was unconscious on the deck. Roo offered help and water, but he waved us away. "She does this a lot," he explained, so we decided to leave them to it.

Reaching the halfway point, we'd managed to outpace almost everyone else. A young English couple were our only companions, and it was here that we achieved the Holy Grail of Great Wall tourism: beautiful, atmospheric photos of the Wall snaking off into the distance, *and not a single other person on it.*

We took photos of the English couple, and posed for them to take some of us. Back on the bus we would eagerly exchange email addresses, promise faithfully to send each other our photos – and then forget completely, only to wonder, years later, why we have so many pictures of grinning strangers mixed in with our shots of China.

The condition of the Wall deteriorated dramatically once past the halfway point, with missing sections of battlements, and loose and missing pavers offering us a window into the layered heart of the Wall.

And then, climbing into yet another tower, we discovered a disappointing letter from the management. Literally, a letter, printed on a stained and tattered sheet of A4 paper, taped to the wall, which said:

Hello visitors
We are very sorry Houchuan pass temporarily closed, please go back to Little Jinshan Tower take cable car or to Shaling Pass.
Jinshanling Great Wall management.

To which we replied; "No."

Bollocks to that!

Our tour bus would be meeting us at a specified location. As far as I was concerned, that gave us carte blanche to get there, by whatever means necessary. If this meant ignoring official notices and clambering around on sections of the Wall deemed unfit for tourists, well then – so much the better!

So we hiked on, leaving the piece of paper where it was and hoping it wouldn't deter the rest of the tour group.

But there was a reason for that warning.

Beyond it, the Wall was a ruin.

Utterly unrestored, the brickwork looked every minute of fifteen-hundred years old. The top surface was reduced to rubble. Piles of stone lay here and there, most of the battlements were gone, and there was a sense that the rest of it could collapse into dust at any moment. The core of the Wall was exposed underfoot; sometimes underlying courses of bricks, sometimes just sand. It was slippery and treacherous, particularly on the steeper sections. At some points we had to scramble upwards, climbing ruins that had once been stairs. Here was the history I'd been looking for, that elusive authentic experience! This was the Great Wall as I had dreamed of seeing her, the original, unspoiled, barely surviving legacy of so many centuries past.

It was magnificent.

The last section we climbed was properly closed. We'd reached the finishing point of our tour, but our earlier burst of speed meant we had plenty of time in hand. So ignoring a more substantial sign that read 'This Section Is Closed', we climbed on, discovering a stretch of Wall in even worse repair than the previous bit. It's a sad fact that much of the Wall has been lost, and that even more will be lost as time goes on. The Chinese government simply doesn't care, beyond beautifying short stretches to maximise the tourist dollar, and even if it did, sufficient resources would be near impossible to find. The size of the structure belies its fragility, particularly the Western sections, many of which are constructed from rammed earth rather than brick and stone. This last section was the worst we'd seen, and we were defeated by the first steep incline.

The bus ride back to Beijing was a quiet one.

Sheer exhaustion claimed some of the group; for me, it was awe. I looked out of the windows at the pristine lushness of the foothills, and marvelled anew at the idea of carrying tens of millions of bricks up those forested slopes. No matter how hard the Chinese government worked to turn their most treasured national monument into a caricature of itself, it was simply too big for them to destroy. Centuries of peasant farmers pilfering the stone hadn't killed the wall either, and wild sections of it were still out there, begging to be explored.

We could come back here, I thought, one day…

Then we plunged back into the gloom of Beijing, and I started to change my mind.

No matter.

We'd come to see the Wall, and boy had we seen her. In all her current guises, from brand-new tourist imitation to ongoing restoration project to wreckage, she had one thing in common – she had majesty. I don't have the poetry in my soul to do her justice, so I'll end by saying this: go and see for yourselves. Go now, while there's still so much to enjoy; before the Government turns it into a theme park, and the rest crumbles into dust. It is really, honestly, every bit as incredible as you could possibly imagine.

And, at the risk of outraging conservationists the world over, if you get the urge – bring a piece home.

I did.

No-one will ever know!

And at least I'll look after my bit.

Templed Out

The only problem with seeing the Great Wall first, was that everything else paled by comparison.

Feeling braver, the following day we took the underground to visit the Summer Palace, and found ourselves slightly underwhelmed by the place. It was impressive, of course; the ancient Chinese dynasties did nothing by halves, and when they decided to build a palace... man. They *really* built a palace. They started off by excavating a 540-acre lake – all by hand, of course – and the spoil had been piled up to create the sixty-metre high Longevity Hill.

We picked up a map brochure, and paid the extra fee for an audio guide, as neither of us had any idea about what to expect. Our (highly illegal) copy of *Lonely Planet: China* mentioned a Marble Boat, which Roo was keen to see, and a tower, which I wanted to climb. Beyond that, the Summer Palace was most famous for being repaired in the 1890s by the Empress-Dowager Cixi. Presumably pissed off that she had such a crap title, she went on a power-spree, restoring the Palace as a birthday present to herself, and stealing the money for it from the Navy. The three-million *taels* of silver she took had been earmarked for upgrading the cream of China's naval forces, the *Beiyang Fleet* – which was subsequently annihilated by the Japanese.

Perhaps understandably, Cixi was not widely loved.

The first thing we came to in the Summer Palace was a sort of mock-village on the edge of a canal. Little shops lined the stone-paced banks, where people in traditional dress were doing traditional tasks, like Chinese calligraphy and selling ice creams. It was a bit 'Ye Olde Chinaland', with over-the-top costumes and plenty of twee fakery, but the ancient stone bridges made for wonderfully atmospheric photography. We just had to time it right, to avoid scores of Chinese tourists in baseball caps eating candyfloss. Bizarrely, we were the subject of dozens of photos ourselves, as we sat on the edge of the canal eating our cheese and ham sandwiches. I think some of the tourists found us more interesting than the Palace; then again, we didn't see a single other Westerner the entire day, so perhaps we were a rarity.

Once we got over the 'mother of God, this is huge!' reaction, a lot of the palace began to look the same; courtyards upon courtyards, terrace after perfectly-paved terrace. The distance between locations was substantial, but the scale of the buildings made it seem like the whole place was normal-sized, and we just weren't getting anywhere fast.

We piled on the speed, stretching muscles that were still complaining from the previous day's hike, and checked out the brochure to see where we were headed.

Several of the locations were simply described with, 'This Area Contains Some Halls and Pavilions'. Which could be construed as rather lazy guide writing, but I had to sympathise. I could just imagine the poor bloke writing it; "Jade-Dragon-King-Emperor-Fire-Pavilion... sits next to the Cloud-Wind-Jade-Emperor-Phoenix-Dragon-Pavilion... Oh sod it! You know what? No-one really gives a shit. Let's just call it 'Some Pavilions'."

We navigated our way towards the 'Tower of the Fragrance of Buddha'. Buddha being a cheerful but rather portly fellow, who was fond of extended travel in abject poverty through some of the hottest countries of earth... well, I'm sure his fragrance was lovely. But just to be on the safe side, they should probably have called it 'Tower of the Fragrance of Buddha after a Bath'.

This was the tower I was looking forward to climbing; a giant wooden pagoda eight stories tall, the upper levels glimmering with promise. The view of Kunming Lake and the famous gardens of Longevity Hill would be awesome from up there. And it probably was, but we'll never know; the stairs were fenced off, the upper stories closed, leaving us to marvel at yet another example of a beautifully painted and carved wooden pagoda.

Next we explored the Long Corridor, and found that it was in fact quite long. At the far end, it led to the sight Roo had been looking forward to seeing all day; the Marble Boat.

Which was closed.

A wall of scaffolding surrounded it, draped in a giant sheet showing a picture of what it would look like when it wasn't surrounded by a wall of scaffolding. The audio guide had long since lost us; it was still singing the praises of the Phoenix-Dragon-Emperor's-Jade-Silk-Pavilion or some such.

We moved on.

"I don't know what else I want to look at," Roo moaned, "now that the Marble Boat is shut."

"I didn't even want to see the Marble Boat," I admitted.

Instead, we watched a worker trying to corral the pedal boats on Kunming Lake. It was an exercise in futility, like trying to put frogs in a basket. Every time he thought he'd got them all, one at the far end would start to drift away and he'd start frantically tugging on ropes again. It was hands down the most entertaining thing we'd seen all day.

The trip home on the subway was a riot.

Or, put another way, on the trip home there was a riot on the subway.

For some reason, Line 6 had been closed completely. The transfer station was filled with angry commuters, facing off against station officials and a pair of machine gun armed soldiers.

"Should I try and ask what's going on?" I asked Roo.

"Please, please, don't," she replied.

So we took the scenic route home.

We suffered the same mental malaise the following day, when we returned to Tiananmen Square to visit the insanely-huge Forbidden City that fronts onto it. I think my awe-chip had been overloaded; after a while, one immense monument began to look like another, and the otherwise stupendous began to seem mundane and repetitive. It's how I imagine working in a chocolate factory would work out; for a week or so I'd eat everything in sight, and then lose all interest.

Still, the sheer scale of the Forbidden City was staggering. The walls were eight metres high and eight metres thick. Built without the aid of modern machinery, the Chinese had a unique advantage in terms of manpower. "Build it, or else," the Emperor had presumably said – and it took *one million* labourers fourteen years to accomplish his wishes.

At that time, (circa 1400 CE), the entire population of England and Wales totalled just three million.

We entered via one of five tunnels through the bright red Meridian Gate. It cost us $10 to get in; that didn't include admission to the world famous Palace Museum, housed inside, but we didn't need to wrestle with our conscience about visiting it. Much as we'd have loved paying again to stare at their unnecessarily vast collection of blue porcelain vases, we couldn't; only 80,000 tickets are available each day, and it was booked up.

Released into a courtyard big enough to play model railways with real trains, we trudged across towards an enormous pavilion which housed another gate. Beyond that... why, an even larger courtyard, with the mother of all pavilions dominating it from the far end.

Three hours later, our legs were getting tired.

It felt like we'd been walking forever, and we were stuck inside some colossal Chinese version of Groundhog Day. The northern half of the Forbidden City was a warren of smaller halls, each in its own walled enclosure. We saw a map on a signpost, which for some reason we found hilarious – it featured a large square filled with dozens of smaller squares, each containing a series of Chinese glyphs.

For us, it was the equivalent of a blank sign with a 'You Are Here' arrow pointing to the middle of it.

Still, prize for my favourite sign of the day went to a brass plaque affixed to some railings. 'HELP PROTECT THE CULTURAL RELICS,' it implored, translating the row of symbols above it. Below that came a second row of Mandarin, again translated underneath; 'HELP PROTECT THE RAILINGS.'

We'd explored huge areas of the Forbidden City, but there was something oddly boring about it, which I couldn't quite figure out. I mean, I love old buildings. I'm obsessed with castles, and quirky little construction details usually excite me. (This is the part where you all start feeling incredibly sorry for Roo, and subtly withdraw all those dinner party invites you've sent me).

But there was something spectacularly uninteresting about the buildings here.

Then Roo solved the mystery by asking, "Where do you want to go next? The 'Hall of Benevolence and Longevity', or the 'Hall of Happiness and Longevity'?"

That's when it hit me.

They were all the same.

Every hall we'd been through, from the most massive to the most humble; they were just big empty wooden boxes; no upper floors, balconies, internal staircases, room dividers, basements, plumbing, furniture... just four walls in a rectangular shape, covered by the same ornate, yellow-tiled roof. Occasionally one would contain a statue, or a culturally significant footstool, but by and large there was very little to distinguish one place from another. My ambivalence spilled out in my answer; "I don't really care, to be honest."

"Good," said Roo, "neither do I. Let's go."

And we went.

Or, we would have gone, except that leaving the Forbidden Palace was every bit as difficult as the name suggests.

Because there aren't any other exits. We had to navigate our way back through the warren of corridors and courtyards to the nearest colossal square. Then cross it, climb the stairs and pass through the giant pavilion above, then back down the stairs and spend fifteen minutes crossing the next enormous square.

At some point during this process it occurred to me to feel sorry for the Emperor, back in the day. I mean, if he wanted to nip out and get the paper, or someone rocked up at the front door with a delivery he had to sign for, well, that was his whole morning gone.

I'm all for a bit of decorative driveway, but getting in and out of that place must have been a real bastard.

Slave: Your highness, there's someone at the door!
Emperor: Who is it?
Slave: Sorry sir, I don't know.
Emperor: Find out!
Slave: Yes sir, see you in an hour!
One hour later:
Slave: Your highness! It's Fred.
Emperor: What does he want?
Slave: Um… I'll just go check…

I later did a spot of research, and discovered that the Forbidden Palace covers an area of *a hundred and eighty acres.*

No wonder we were knackered!

It contains nine-hundred and eighty separate buildings. That means, if you could make it in, around, and out of each building, and over to the next one in five minutes – and if you did that without pause for eight hours a day – it would take just over ten days to see them all.

I was kind of glad we stopped when we did, to be honest.

Commercial Success

We did a lot of walking in Beijing.

The underground stations, though numerous, were still spread out over an enormous area. The nearest one to the Beijing Dreams, for example, was a good twenty-minute walk away. Whilst exploring the streets, we frequently saw two girlfriends holding hands, and quite often two men – but not couples. The opposite sex's do not touch each other in public, in China – and for the most part, they don't touch in private, either. Instead, couples commonly displayed their affection by wearing head-to-toe matching outfits. This horrified Roo, which inevitably led to me suggesting we do the same, to try and fit in. Luckily for her, she'd packed mostly leggings, so was able to call my bluff with impunity. Embarrassing Roo is my favourite hobby, but even I won't go *that* far.

Our walks also revealed slightly more disturbing habits. Spitting was one; apparently it's considered lucky in China (though presumably not for whoever stands in it). Men, women and children hocked up thick mouthfuls of phlegm at will, peppering the pavement with piles of mucus.

It made me regret wearing sandals, that's for sure.

But this wasn't the worst abuse the streets were subject to.

Everywhere we went, we saw women carrying babies,

usually in homemade slings. Nothing unusual about that, you say? Indeed not. The unusual part is that, most of these infants had no clothing on their bottom half. The ones that did, mostly older babies and toddlers, wore outfits with no bum in them.

The reason for this was depressingly obvious, but we didn't dare admit it to ourselves until the first time we witnessed a woman grab her baby and hold it out over the pavement to do its business.

A stream of runny shit splattered the ground – and no-one batted an eyelid.

The woman replaced the child in its sling, and carried on about her day, caring not one whit about the mess she left behind her. Nor did anyone else – because, as we were to discover, this was considered perfectly normal behaviour. Several times a day we were treated to the sight of kids up to maybe four years old, being encouraged to piss in the gutter.

And that *really* made me regret wearing sandals.

We'd been exploring the city for nearly a week when we decided to find the legendary Silk Market. This is a place that has gone down in traveller lore as the home of cheap fakery; counterfeit brand names are pretty much the only things available, with appropriately rock-bottom prices. Having worn out quite a few of our clothes – the downside of alternating the same handful of garments for months on end – we were quite keen on finding some budget-friendly replacements.

The Silk Market I was hoping to find was a claustrophobic alleyway crammed with bartering foreigners and over four-hundred stalls; a slice of atmosphere and the chance of a few bargains all rolled into one.

I should have known that was too good to be true.

The original Silk Market, which had been trading, albeit dodgily, for twenty years, had been abruptly demolished in 2005. Citing 'fire risks' amongst a flotilla of other reasons, the Chinese government had struck again – eradicating the alley and surrounding buildings, and replacing them with a brand new mega-mall.

Which they still called the Silk Market, to con tourists into visiting it.

Apparently the real reason for the redevelopment was to eradicate the trade in knock-offs – thereby eliminating the one thing that had made it famous in the first place. Then Subway and Lavazza moved in and, well, you can guess the rest.

Of course, I didn't know this at the time – otherwise I wouldn't have spent two hours on foot looking for the damn place.

We were a bit surprised to arrive outside the titanic, seven-storey warehouse of a building. But we'd walked all the way there, dodging pools of assorted bodily fluids, so it seemed a shame not to go in.

First though, I spotted a phone shop on the outside of the building, and led Roo inside. We'd been buying pay-as-you-go SIM cards in each country, allowing us to use our phone as more than just a back-up camera. I chose the imaginatively-named China Mobile to run our mobile in China; there wasn't a whole lot of options.

Next came the tricky part.

You probably don't remember this, but the last time you bought a new mobile phone, you had to set up the internet on it. Or more realistically, you had to take it back into the phone shop and get them to do it. What they did is enter a series of codes and server addresses, known collectively as the Access Point Name.

And that's what I needed these guys to do.

I mean, I could do it myself – had done, in Borneo and Vietnam.

All I needed was a few little details, like the name of their server, the Proxy Setting, and the Port Number.

Yeah… good luck with *that*.

After playing 'let's push buttons then shrug and hand the phone to someone else' with all four staff members for half an hour, they finally came up with the idea of calling Customer Service. There I was transferred to a semi-English-speaking operator, and on his third attempt he managed to send me a text message with all the details.

Whew!

The Silk Market was not far off closing by the time we got in there.

But we didn't mind, as it turned out to be a major disappointment – and the most invasive shopping experience of my life.

About as far from what I'd imagined as possible, it was a market in name only. Inside the aircraft hanger sized building were hundreds of glass-fronted booths, each run like a stall by its owner. The 'market' was divided up into districts, based on the merchandise available; there was a pants area, a luggage area, and so on. Within each zone, every glass booth was stuffed to the gills with an identical selection of gear to the one next door. Wandering the luggage area, for example, showed us booth after booth crammed floor to ceiling with handbags, always the same styles and colours as every other booth we passed.

Perhaps because it was late, we were almost the only people there. Unfortunately, this made us that much more obvious a target to the booth-keepers. They bawled at us, thrusting their goods in our direction as we walked past, not daring to look, staring only at the floor in front of us. If any of them would have shut up for a few minutes, I'd have quite liked to browse their stock; if any of them had been less aggressive, I might have been tempted to try haggling for something. Instead, their repellent sales tactics resulted in zero sales. Would they ever learn? Would the day come when a light bulb went off in some trader's head, and he realised that he might gain more customers if he didn't verbally assault them all? It's such a no-brainer that I can't understand how none of them have figured it out. I just wanted to grab one of them and shake him, shouting, "leave me the fuck alone, and I might buy something!"

Suffice to say, we did a decent loop of both upper and lower storeys, looked in no shops and bought precisely nothing.

We were debating the virtues of a second loop when we passed through the Fake North Face Jackets section. Again, almost every booth featured identical stock, and each booth owner was stood in his doorway, shaking a jacket at me and shouting, "100 *Yuan*, 100 *Yuan!*"

I'd got all the way around and back out of the section before it occurred to me that 100 *yuan* was only about $20. Not bad for a decent fake; certainly cheaper than the conmerchants in Vietnam had demanded.

Roo bravely agreed to a second loop, despite the added danger that now the stall holders recognised us. They knew that something had convinced us to make a return visit, and they redoubled their efforts to sell us something.

When one guy stepped in front of me with his jacket, bellowing "100 YUAN!", I mock-surrendered, and let him lead me into his booth.

"Whayouwan?" he demanded.

"This," I said, touching the jacket. He immediately began rummaging amongst piles of merchandise stacked against the back wall of his booth.

"No, no, just this one," I pointed. I was perfectly happy with the exact jacket he'd thrust at me, although he continued to produce ever more garish versions from his supply. Eventually, he seemed convinced that I wanted his demo model.

"So," he said, "howmuchyoupay?"

"Ah... 100 yuan?"

"NO! NO NO NO NO! 100 *dollars!*"

Ah, Jeez. I should have known it wouldn't be that easy.

"Right, I'm off," I said, making to leave.

Only, I couldn't leave. He was stood in front of me, blocking the exit from his booth. "Howmuchyoupay?"

"Look, I don't want the jacket. I only wanted it for 100 *yuan*." I tried to step around him, but he turned, thrusting an arm to pin me in place.

"NO!" he roared. "100 DOLLARS!"

"Okay, but if that's the price, I don't want it."

The next twenty minutes were spent with me desperately trying to squeeze out of the booth, and the man and his wife refusing to let me go. He swore, she pleaded, they offered lower prices, and still I tried to escape. Finally, after his wife finished begging me not to make her husband lose face, his livelihood and his family by selling it for less than he paid, they allowed me to leave.

With the jacket.

For 100 *yuan*.

By this point I really didn't want the thing, but it was the only way I was getting out of there. The husband stomped around the booth, throwing things, kicking boxes and swearing violently, while I paid his wife and slipped away.

"Holy shit!" said Roo, as we regained the safety of the stairwell, "I thought he was going to punch you!"

"Yeah, me too! I wasn't even haggling, I just wanted to get out. Talk about a captive audience."

"Nice jacket though."

"Yeah... So, do you want to buy anything?"

With the Silk Markets a bust, we set off back to the hotel. It was at least an hour's walk, as none of the subway stations here connected with the line we needed. We'd only gone a few steps when it started to rain, rapidly building into a full-blown storm. The wind picked up, blasting us; crowds of locals were huddled in the subway entrances, looking terrified at the sudden downpour.

Roo took out the miniature umbrella she'd carried since Borneo, without ever using it. She opened it, held it up to the sky, and watched in dismay as it was instantly destroyed by the wind.

"Made in Vietnam," I commiserated. "Should have got one that was Made in China!"

Chinese superiority was then proven unequivocally by my new jacket, which, in spite of being fake, kept her dry the entire way home.

In fact, it looked so damn good on her that I decided to get one for my sister, Gill.

We returned to the Silk Markets on our last night in the city, and whilst I wasn't able to pull off the same near-miracle of extreme haggling – I was too scared to try, to be honest – I did manage to get a halfway decent deal on a snow-white ladies' version. Serendipity kicked in when, on the way out, I spotted an ideal present for Gill's husband, Chris.

It was a t-shirt that made perfect sense as a souvenir of

Beijing, but taken out of context – or anywhere else on the planet – took on a completely different meaning.

And of all the people I knew, only Chris would really appreciate it.

It was nothing fancy; just a plain white t-shirt with a slogan.

'I ♥ BJ!' it said.

I don't think he ever dared wear it in public.

Mortal Instruments

One of the biggest difficulties we had in China, was finding things.

Any things.

For example, when it came time to leave Beijing, we had to buy train tickets to *Zhengzhou,* our next destination.

In order to avoid the seething cauldron of chaos in the station, *Lonely Planet* listed several agencies where train tickets could be purchased.

We couldn't find any of them.

In most other countries we'd visited there were signs, either with some English, or with words we could train ourselves to recognise. Not so in China. Even the Underground only used bi-lingual signage since the Olympics were held here in 2008.

Likewise, we usually relied on being able to ask around until we found a token English speaker who could help us – but here, the chances of that happening were practically non-existent. China is ranked 47th on the English Proficiency Index; countries with a better average understanding of the language include Peru, Uruguay and Guatemala.

This made for a frustrating afternoon wandering disconsolately up and down the same handful of streets, looking for something we had no way of recognising.

In the end, salvation came in the form of a young Chinese bloke in a leather jacket. He came up to us wanting to practise his English, and I explained the trouble we were having.

"We need to buy tickets to Zeng-Zoo," I pleaded.

His brow furrowed. "Where you go?"

I dug out my journal and showed him the word.

"Oh, you go *shing-shoe!* No problem, I have friend!"

And he led us back along the street, to an unassuming, single-story building.

There was nothing at all to suggest it was a ticket office – because it wasn't.

Our helper led us down the side of that building, and around the back to an unadorned hut the size of a garden shed. It's usually at this point that I start to worry, but our new friend was as good as his word. He took us inside, to a bare room with a counter and a few plastic chairs. He chatted to a lone woman who seemed to work there, translating our request – and she pulled out a pad of receipts, and booked us tickets on the phone. At least, I hoped that was what was happening. She wanted paying, at any rate, and a few minutes later we were back on the street, clutching squares of paper covered in Chinese symbols that might or might not have been tickets to Zhengzhou. It was all so unlikely that I was half convinced we'd been scammed, right up until we surrendered the tickets at the station.

On our last morning in the Beijing Dreams, we found we were quite looking forward to leaving.

We'd had an interesting time, but between the constant grey skies, the incessant traffic, the massive, featureless buildings and the general difficulty of getting anywhere, we'd found the place a bit oppressive.

Moving on would hopefully show us a different side to China; a bit of the countryside perhaps, and a bit less smog.

I normally try to avoid overtly touristy places, but we both felt the urge to find something familiar; a touchstone if you like, something recognisable. I'd settle for a single person who could tell me what the hell was going on around me. The last time I'd had any kind of clue was in Mongolia.

A fistful of the hotel reception staff in collaboration managed to translate what I wanted, and wrote some vital phrases of Chinese in my journal. I considered this a success. Less successful was my attempt to get the same people to check the post for me. Final verdict: no bank cards. I still felt sure they'd been delivered and misplaced, as more than enough time had passed since they'd been posted in England. But nothing I could suggest would elicit more than a shoulder-shrug from the reception staff. It looked like another set of my bank cards would be floating around Asia ad infinitum. Which was a little worrying.

We packed carefully, keeping easily accessible bags of snacks for our journey. It was a muscle-cramping seventeen hours by train to Zhengzhou – the duration of which we would spend on the enticingly-named 'hard seats'.

My buttocks might never forgive me.

The walk to the subway station seemed to take forever. We were laden with far more weight than previously, as having the supermarket so close to our hotel was too good to ignore. Who knew when we'd next get the chance to buy Laughing Cow and Fanta? It was hot, as always, and we sweated copiously, the straps of our rucksacks starting to chafe as our t-shirts became ever more moist.

Eventually, breathing heavily, we hauled our bags down the stairs to the subway, along the corridor, and came to the scanners.

I may not have mentioned this before, but for some incredibly paranoid reason, every subway station in Beijing has airport-style x-ray machines that you have to put your bags through before you can go any further. Bizarre, yes. And a pain in the arse, But nothing more than that – until...

As my bag was going through the machine, there was a sudden debate amongst the operators. As it came out, a security guard took it, and beckoned me to follow him into an interview room. I shit bricks, obviously, and poor Roo tagged along behind me, not wanting to be abandoned on her own in the Beijing subway.

Inside the room, the guard's superior had a chat with him. They pulled my rucksack up onto a desk and started opening pockets. I watched, wondering what they hoped to find.

Then, with a shout of triumph, one of the guys pulled out my can of deodorant. Now, I should probably admit here that I still use Lynx; the B.O. basher of choice for sixteen-year-old boys everywhere! I've never graduated to a more grown-up brand because, well, I've never grown up. And I used to work for Lynx. In my underwear. But that's a different story.

So anyway, these two guards started jabbering at me, brandishing the spray can, as though I'd been caught red-handed committing a capital crime.

Which perhaps I had? As I mentioned earlier, sometimes in China it's hard to tell.

The boss guard had a few words of English – enough to say, "No, no!" at least – and he seemed to be telling me I couldn't take my deodorant on the subway.

I turned to Roo. She was visibly starting to panic, as we had a train to catch, and a station to get to. We'd allowed plenty of time, but the walk with bags had taken much longer than expected. These guys were now in danger of causing trouble for us.

"Look, you can keep the damn can," I said, making flicking-away gestures with my hands. I pointed at the Lynx, shook my head vigorously, and said, "No, no!"

This seemed to do the trick.

Until the first guy dug his hand into my bag again, and came out with the knife.

My 'ancient souvenir' knife, from Mongolia.

And the temperature in the room dropped a few degrees.

Oh, I thought. *Oh shit.*

The man held the knife out to me, a questioning look on his face.

Oh, crap. Here goes.

"It's from Mongolia," I explained, "very old, bought from the nomads. It's a... gift? From my holiday."

"No! NO!" said the boss guard.

It suddenly occurred to me that I had very limited choices.

Shave My Spider!

These guys were security guards, but not police, as far as I could tell.

It was clear their experience of dealing with foreigners was minimal.

I had to take control of the situation fast, before they decided what to do with me.

But one thing was for sure; we weren't about to ride the subway.

"Right!" I said. "That's enough! Give it to me. I'll go. I'll take a taxi to the station instead, I don't need to endanger your subway." I said all this rapid-fire, as I crossed the room, took the knife off the security guard, and stuffed it back into my bag. Grabbing the Lynx, I stuffed that in as well, along with other possessions that had spilled out. All this time I kept talking, explaining my plans in a slightly annoyed tone. I was hoping they were trying to figure out what I was waffling on about, and it would distract them from what I was doing.

Which was leaving.

I flung the bag onto my shoulder and strode from the room, following Roo back out into the scanning area. Without looking back, we turned towards the exit and marched down the corridor.

"They're following us," Roo hissed, as we made the bottom of the stairs.

"Keep going," I told her – and we did. Out onto the street, out into the smog-shine – and freedom.

The guards, presumably out of their jurisdiction on the surface, had paused at the bottom of the stairs.

So we legged it.

A block away, I flagged a taxi by sticking my arm out. An old woman scolded me, ranting unintelligibly and trying to wave me away, but I had no idea what had offended her. Maybe you're not allowed to flag down taxis in Beijing? Well, it worked for me – thank the Goddess! We were both getting seriously stressed as time ticked down. Our only Chinese taxi prior to this had taken substantial queuing to get, and I had no confidence we'd even find a taxi, much less convince one to pick us up. But Fate's cosmic elastic band did its twanging thing, and this driver not only knew the words 'Train Station' – he even put the meter on!

He was our salvation.

I was so grateful I tipped him $16 on a $4 ride. Also, I didn't have any change.

And just like that, we'd made it.

Our fears of getting lost in the subway system, of getting lost between the subway and the station and, latterly, of being arrested for possession of a deadly weapon, were all laid to rest.

At least until we entered the station, and found ourselves in a queue for the x-ray machines...

I was sweating bullets as I placed my bag onto the scanner belt.

Guessing that the machine was designed to look from the top down, and that most bags passed through it flat on their backs, I tried a little trickery. Using my daysack I wedged the much larger rucksack so it stood up on its base. This meant that the knife, which was stored vertically inside, would be presented point-on to the scanners – hopefully masking its tell-tale shape.

It was a tense couple of minutes, as I prayed the bag would remain upright on its journey through the scanner. I totally forgot to empty my pockets, or take my belt off, so the metal detectors went wild when I stepped through, and both Roo and I had a thorough wanding-down by a very serious-looking midget.

After that I collected my rucksack, which had managed to avoid drawing attention, and we put as much distance as possible between ourselves and anyone wearing a uniform.

"What are we going to do about that knife?" Roo asked me.

"Bloody hell, I've no idea."

"This is going to keep happening, everywhere we go! You'll have to post it home as soon as we find a post office."

"Yeah..."

She caught my hand and gave it a squeeze. "I bet now you're glad you didn't buy that samurai sword!"

Training Day

Trains in China have a hierarchy.

The carriage class system is necessary to keep those who can afford comfort (as defined by their 'soft-sleeper' cabins) safe from the riff-raff, who were travelling with us on the 'hard seats'.

This was only the second-worst class of ticket.

There's a Class system in the UK, too, but in practice the vaunted First Class carriages are little different from the rest of the train – the only major exceptions being that they have little lamps on the tables, and power sockets – and that they are almost entirely empty. You'd have to be mad to fork out twice the price for such an insignificant gain in comfort. After all, it's not like you're going to be there forever; most train journeys in the UK average around 40 minutes, and the longest possible single trip takes 6 hours.

Not so, in China.

This train, taking us south from Beijing to Zhengzhou, was a seventeen-hour ride.

That didn't even take us halfway down the country; there were at least three more similar-length trips in our immediate future. When we exited into Laos, from one of the southern-most border crossings, we'd have covered well over 3,500 kilometres – that's like going the full length of the UK, from Land's End to John o' Groats – and back. And back again. And back *again*.

(For my friends from over the pond, it's from LA to New York, and then about a quarter of the way back again.)

It's quite a long way.

And, in hindsight, rather ambitious on a thirty-day visa.

Getting onto a train in China should be made into a game show.

Thanks to our helpful taxi driver we'd arrived half an hour early for the train, but it was clear from the scene in the station that most people had been there much longer. Blankets were spread out, sleeping bags being put to use; it goes without saying that every chair in the hall was taken, but by the time we arrived most of the floor-space was as well. Many people had tiny plastic stools, like short folks use to reach things in their kitchen cupboards; I'd wondered about the popularity of these things, as they seemed to be on sale everywhere.

Now I knew.

With less than fifteen minutes to go, there was a palpable air of excitement. The makeshift camps were being packed away, crowds were starting to form around the barriers, and station officials had to be deployed to hold them back. People from the back of the hall surged forwards, building the pressure, and all eyes were on the mouth of the tunnel.

Minutes ticked down, until barriers were removed by the station staff (at considerable personal risk) – and then the whistle blew.

We'd experienced the notorious Mongolian Scramble, but China's population is four-hundred-and-sixty-five times that of Mongolia; it's like comparing a garage sale full of old women with handbags to a World Cup football riot.

Fervently wishing we'd been able to afford a GoPro, we inserted ourselves into the seething mass of people and were carried along by the current.

It was only afterwards that we realised this was a mistake.

What we should have been doing was using our superior size and weight to our advantage, forcing our way through the throng to reach our seats first.

Because there were roughly two-thousand seats on that train, and approximately triple that number of people aiming to get on it.

And luggage space for around two-hundred.

By the time we found our carriage, it was already rammed.

To add to the fun, some genius had decided to place coat hooks directly above the numbers that labelled the seats. With personal space at a premium, every hook bristled with hats, scarves, handbags, jackets and shopping bags full of peanuts, through which we had to root to find out where we were.

The next challenge, once our seats had been identified, was to negotiate with the people already sitting in them.

They, along with a couple-thousand others, had purchased 'standing only' tickets, and were fervently hoping they'd manage to occupy an empty seat for at least part of the seventeen-hour journey. I can't figure out why they'd try this, as I've never seen a single free seat on a Chinese train, and typically every inch of space down the aisle, every patch of floor, the gaps between the carriages – even the toilets – is taken.

So, we presented our tickets, and the offenders struggled out of their seats against the flow of people getting on, ending up propped against our seats anyway. I had to strategically employ elbows to remind one of them that my ticket price included the right to put my head on the headrest, instead of his arse.

We paid for our reticence in the boarding-crush by spending the journey with our rucksacks between our knees and our carry-on bags on top of them. My bag in particular is rather large, so straddling it felt like riding a hippo; it also caused my leg to occupy the aisle, rather than the miniscule space in front of my seat, which made it a serious impediment to the hordes of people straggling up and down the carriage in a never-ending stream.

"What the hell is with these people?" I growled, as for the hundredth time I pulled my knee up to my chest to let someone past. "Why can't they just be content with wherever they're standing?"

I put my bag in the aisle to give my leg a rest, just as a stewardess arrived with her food trolley.

"Oh, you have got to be kidding me," I moaned, before hauling the bag up onto my knee. As she pushed the trolley past I noticed it contained almost entirely Pot Noodles. "Who the hell is she selling those to?" I asked Roo. "Anyone dumb enough to forget their lunch, but foresighted enough to pack a flask of hot water?"

The two oddities dovetailed neatly when I battled my way down the aisle in search of the toilet. In the cubicle where I expected to find it, instead there was a counter with a massive steel urn, and a gaggle of passengers filling their instant noodle cups with steaming hot water! I was amazed. And a bit embarrassed that I'd already unzipped my flies. I had to refasten my trousers and fight my way through two more carriages to find a crapper, but there was a giant urn in every one of them.

I got back to find my bag occupying my seat, as yet another stewardess forced yet another trolley down the aisle. Figuring if you can't beat 'em, join 'em, I forked out for two Pot Noodles with what looked like Paddington Bear on the lids. I couldn't read the labels of course, but I imagine it said something like "Real Bear Flavour!"

"What are you going to do with those?" Roo asked, once our airspace was free again.

"Just watch," I told her, heading back the way I'd come.

"Wait!" she called, "you're not going to *pee on them,* are you?"

A few minutes later, slurping our urine-free noodles, we felt quite civilized. It even occurred to me that I could have made coffee in the empty cup, had I but known. Although that would inevitably result in another battle towards the toilet. Certainly, it altered our snack-packing habits. Instead of subsisting on bags full of chocolate and squashed sandwiches, we knew that in the future we need only bring a pocket full of change and some napkins. I now consider freely available hot water to be the first miracle of Chinese trains.

The second miracle is that no-one is severely burned by scores of people struggling up and down the aisles, clambering over luggage, feet and prostrate passengers, whilst carrying a Pot Noodle brim-full of boiling hot water in each hand. I became quite skilled at this myself eventually, though I never dared try it with more than one at a time.

Our bellies full, we settled down with Roo's tablet to watch an entire series of something I'd downloaded (by way of finding some use for an internet devoid of Facebook, YouTube, Twitter and all blogging platforms). This time we picked 'Game of Thrones' – we'd missed the latest series, as we hadn't seen English language TV in months. Ahhh, TV! It makes a seventeen-hour journey feel more like twelve.

However, any action which adds enjoyment on a train trip has an equal and opposite reaction. In this case it was the weirdest one yet.

A woman in a conductor's uniform made her way down the carriage, stopping beside my chair. I reluctantly pulled my rucksack onto my knee again, and she carefully placed the baskets she was carrying in the resulting space.

Then she took a deep breath and began screaming.

I nearly soiled myself.

She waved her arms for attention, still screeching.

Every eyeball in the carriage swivelled to fix on her, as she reached down into the basket by her feet.

From the volume and the shock-value, I half expected her to pull out a machine gun and start shooting – but she didn't. Instead she produced a small white towel, brandishing it above her head as the noise continued.

Was she surrendering?

I realised she was speaking, only at such high pitch and volume that it barely differed from a scream.

What was going on? Was some kind of disaster about to befall the train? Was this our emergency safety briefing?

Then, not bothering to pause for breath, the woman produced a bottle of water and poured it onto the carriage floor. Bending, she swiftly mopped the mess up with the cloth, before presenting it to the train again. She wrung the cloth out with no effect, then held it out for inspection to the nearest person. He took the cloth, staring at it in awe, and suddenly everything fell into place.

"She's... she's *selling* those cloth things!" Roo breathed in disbelief.

"What the...?" I noticed the basket by her feet was stuffed with cellophane-wrapped packages. "Oh my God! You're right!"

The amazing wonder-cloth did a circuit of the entire carriage, passing through every pair of hands at least once. The woman did not shut up for a single second of this time, having somehow mastered the art of breathing through her nose whilst shouting continuously. I honestly couldn't have talked for that long about my whole life to date, so God knows how she found so much to say about a frigging sponge.

I don't think she sold any, but it was not for want of trying.

An hour later she was back – this time assaulting our eardrums with a deafening presentation on universal phone chargers. It was like living in the Shopping Channel, with the volume stuck on a hundred.

Over the next several hours we were forced to sit through 120-decibel sales pitches for mops, a light-and-sound toy train (woo-woo!), a screwdriver with interchangeable heads, magic-trick puzzles, wooden bead necklaces... and of course, the unbelievable, incredible, amazing wonder-cloth. Again. Because of course, not everybody was going all the way to Zhengzhou. Some people were getting off halfway, and for every one that got off, at least three more people tried to get on.

And none of them had seen the cloth yet.

A student-looking lad sat opposite us for a couple of stops.

"Where from?" he asked me.

"Australia," I told him.

"Ahhh! Australia! Where you go?"

"Shing-show," I replied, confidently. I'd been practising.

"Ahhh?" He looked at me like I'd just said we were going to *Teletubbyland*.

"Um… zeng-zoo?" I tried. Then I gave up and handed him my ticket.

"Ah! You go *Chong-Chow!*"

Well, shit.

If even the locals couldn't agree on pronunciation, of one of the biggest cities in the country, what the hell chance did we have?

Lost In Transit

Everything is massive in China.

Well, apart from the people.

Zhengzhou train station was a monster.

Its ticketing office, where we now found ourselves, was frikkin' *huge.*

Seriously – a 747 could have parked in there with room to spare.

And, in common with the trains it served, it was absolutely rammed.

There were forty serving windows, each with a queue that stretched back to fill the hall behind it. I've seen shorter queues at a U2 concert.

This vast open space was roiling with chaos, as people struggled through the melee with kids, pets and luggage; the ubiquitous stack of cardboard boxes fastened with copious amounts of string, that seem to be the suitcase of choice throughout most of Asia.

It was terrifying.

It was, however, surprisingly efficient.

Unable to read any signs other than the numbers, I chose the window with the shortest queue, leaving Roo guarding a pile of bags near the entrance. I felt bad about splitting up, but these queues had expanded to fill all the space in between them; wearing rucksacks would cause too much collateral damage.

I waited less than half an hour in the first queue, although when it came to my turn at the window, I was already wishing I was still at the back. I smiled at the lady sitting in her little booth, and pushed forward my ratty journal, with the lines of simplified *Han* characters. Theoretically, this single scrawled sentence contained all the information she needed to book our onward travel: the destination, number, time, and date of the train, all of which was the result of several hours' painstaking internet research – plus a request for two seats.

The woman read the sentence a few times through, while I crossed my fingers, toes and ankles in hope. My worst fear was that she would simply dismiss the note as nonsense, leaving us effectively stranded here. She looked confused, and I swear she turned my journal upside down at least once to see if it made any more sense that way. Then she started to flick through the pages, and I had to stop her – there was nothing else of use in the book. I had pinned all our hopes on that sentence, penned by the reception staff at the Beijing Dreams. It had seemed such a simple request at the time... had something got horribly lost in translation?

The woman shook her head slowly, sadly, whilst looking at me. I was on the verge of leaving, to break the news to Roo that we needed to find an internet café stat, when my tapping finger drew her attention to one of the glyphs on the page.

"*Xi'an?*" she asked, pronouncing it 'She-Anne,' and I knew the word in spite of her different accent. I'd been calling it 'Shan,' but either way it was the place I was trying to buy tickets to.

"Yes! I mean, *shì!*"

(It should be noted that '*shì*' does not actually mean 'yes' in Chinese, because there is no word for 'yes' in Chinese. Just to make things a bit more complicated.)

The woman, delighted that she had solved my puzzle, gave me a new one; she spoke to me. In Mandarin. Telling me something very important, no doubt, and at great length – but something that was about as much use to me as a sandal full of spit.

So I fell back on the universal gesture of confused tourists everywhere: I shrugged.

She shrugged.

Then her face lit up with the afterglow of an idea. She opened a clean page on my journal, jotted a few Chinese characters down for good measure, and then drew a large Roman numeral 22.

Still a bit confused (because I'm an idiot), I pulled out my wallet, and started looking for any note larger than 22. She waved me off, tapping the glass, then pointed upwards with her pen. Right towards the number atop her booth…

And it all fell into place.

Booth 22!

Xiè xiè!

(It should be noted that, although *xiè xiè* is the right way of saying thank-you, it is only one of three possible ways, depending on the situation. In Mandarin. There are two more in Cantonese, and dozens of others depending on the local dialect. Unsurprisingly, we used *xiè xiè* pretty much exclusively.)

I left the head of the queue at booth 37, and joined the back of the queue at booth 22. Somehow, this still felt like progress.

The lady at booth 22 was far more receptive to my offer of the journal, presumably because she was responsible for selling the tickets I was after. I'd been another half-hour in her queue, but the transaction was completed in moments. I paid the fare I'd expected, and was handed tickets which I prayed were for the right train, on the right date, at the right time, as I couldn't read a word of the buggers.

And then I re-joined Roo, who was starting to think I'd been abducted by aliens. Or the secret police. I couldn't decide which was more likely in China.

And so, with tickets bought, we crossed the road to the bus station to begin the process all over again. Because we weren't actually going to *Xi'an* – not yet, at any rate. First we had planned a little side trip, with the boundless enthusiasm that comes at the beginning of an adventure like this. Part of me was starting to wish we were jumping on that train to *Xi'an* right away – but only part of me.

The other part could hardly contain its excitement, because this was not just any side trip. We were off to a remote mountaintop temple, a simple, unassuming place whose influence has spread throughout the known world. It is a place synonymous with action and adventure, a place that has spawned more popular culture than almost anything on the planet, *Star Wars* excepted.

Hell, even bits of *Star Wars* were based on the teachings that came from this place.

We were going to *Shaolin*.

*   *   *

The bus to *Dengfeng*, the nearest town to Shaolin, took about three hours.

I didn't care that my seat was broken, causing me to slowly recline backwards into the lap of the dude behind me; that stuff was small fry, compared to the challenges we'd overcome just by getting this far.

I was starting to feel pretty good again, regaining confidence in my ability to achieve things. Sure, China was hard, but isn't that what travel is all about? Otherwise, we may as well just spend six months on the beach…

Damn! Wish I hadn't had that thought.

It was too late now, anyway. We were in the middle of China, and it was time to put up or shut up. Whatever that means.

It was dark by the time we arrived on the outskirts of Dengfeng. This didn't bother me either. What did bother me was that we weren't supposed to be arriving on the outskirts of Dengfeng. I'd plotted our route very carefully, using three different travel blogs, the official bus timetable, an online map of the area and Google Translate; all this told me that we should be arriving in the centre of Dengfeng, a mere two streets away from the hostel I'd booked.

Not so.

We made a valiant effort to stay on the bus, refusing to

move until we saw our bags being dragged off and dumped on the pavement. Then we had no choice, and became the last passengers to vacate the bus. We were followed out by the driver, who turned the lights off and locked it, giving me very little indication that he planned on completing our journey.

A crowd of taxi drivers buzzed around us, as we collected our bags. It reminded me so strongly of Vietnam that I didn't dare trust them, so we shoved our way clear and ignored every shout that came our way. A short way up the street, we paused to adjust our bag straps and collect our thoughts. Mine went like this:

Shit! We're screwed.

From the look on her face, Roo's thoughts were the same, so there didn't seem much point in comparing them.

It's fair to say my new-found confidence was already taking a nosedive.

All around us, large, featureless office buildings stretched into the night.

The bus had pulled up on the side of a main road, but nothing on it looked open. Traffic was sporadic, especially once the last of the taxis sped away.

Maybe we should have let them scam us, I thought. Anything would be preferable to this.

It was the nightmare; we were lost, in some random outlying business district of a major city. It was dark. Everything was closed. There was no-one around to help us, and even if there were, the chances they would be able to help were slim to none.

Come to think of it, screwed was a fairly accurate description.

Then Roo came to our rescue.

"What about the phone?" she asked.

"What about it?"

"Can you get Google Maps up on it?"

"I dunno. Probably, yeah. But how the hell do we find out where we are?"

"Duh! The phone's got GPS on it. *It knows* where we are!

And Google Maps will show us the way to the hostel."

It sounded a bit too much like science fiction to me, but I booted up the Maps App, and lo and behold! She was right.

"Now all we have to do is figure out which direction we're walking…"

We followed that green dot for hours.

At first, it seemed like a great idea. Hell, it *was* a great idea, it just didn't take into account a couple of factors; one was that it took the better part of an hour to figure out which direction we were moving in – GPS not being quite as accurate in mainland China as it is in, say, central London. The second factor was the heat; it was stinking hot, we each had over twenty kilos on our backs, plus daysacks on the front. We sweated copiously, the straps chafed, the weight bore down, and the hike rapidly approached intolerable. The third factor was the distance; it's not easy to get a sense of scale from a map that's only three inches by two inches, but much like Beijing, we found that blocks that looked small seemed to take forever to cross; it was much, much further than we thought at first.

And the fourth issue was one of veracity; because Google Maps is also not quite as accurate in mainland China as it is in Central London.

Consequently, the hostel was in the wrong place.

We'd been walking for a long time – and staggering for even longer – when we saw the cops.

By this point I was reasonably sure we were on the right street. We should only be a block or two away. In desperation we went up to the cops, three of them, hanging out on a street corner, smoking. I dug in my daysack for the address of the hostel, printed on the Booking.com reservation page. I showed it to them, passing my phone over too, as proof that we were trying our best to find our way.

The cops looked at each other and shrugged. Looked at my phone and shrugged. Then one of them pointed in the direction we were going. That seemed to settle it, so we trudged on.

Several blocks later, opposite a brightly-painted day care

centre, we were forced to admit we'd gone wrong. But where? We weren't in the happiest of moods as we turned and headed back the way we'd come.

"Try calling the hostel?" Roo suggested. "Surely there'll be someone there who can direct us."

"If there's anyone manning the phones at this time…"

I dialled the number from our paperwork, and was relieved to find the bloke that answered spoke English. "Where are you?" he asked.

"I'm pretty sure we're on the right street… *Chong Gao Street?*"

"Yes, Chong Gao. Where are you?"

"Well…" I peered around me into the darkness. I was surrounded by unidentifiable buildings. "I think we passed a nursery…"

"A nursery?"

"Never mind."

"Okay, go along Chong Gao, you find us for sure."

"Which direction?"

"Uh, I dunno. Where are you?"

Half an hour later we plodded past the cops again. They hadn't moved, were still smoking, and watched our progress with the same bemusement as before.

I'd have sworn at them, if I'd had the energy.

We kept going for another couple of blocks, but were close to despair. We couldn't just give up – there was no alternative, unless we wanted to sleep on the street. But then, a whine in the distance announced the cops' return to the stage. They had acquired a small electric vehicle, like a police milk-float, and they beckoned us on board. Too grateful to care, we piled in, and kept a watch on the buildings as the vehicle crawled by. Suddenly, Roo gave a cry – her eagle eyes had picked out the hostel's sign, unlit and obscured almost completely behind a tree.

The cops let us go, shaking their heads for the peculiarities of foreigners, and sped off at around six miles an hour.

We hauled our bags over to the hostel, and were

delighted to find the front door unlocked.

It was about a mile away, and on the opposite side of the road from where Google had pinned it, but this was the place alright – and John, the receptionist, had been dozing in his chair, waiting for us to check in.

We had arrived!

"Thank God that's over," Roo said, collapsing into a chair.

"Sorry love, I had no idea it would end up like that…"

"No, me neither. But you know what?"

"What?'

"Next time, we're taking a frigging taxi!"

Hostel Negotiation

John, the receptionist at the Shaolin Traveller Hostel, spoke pretty good English.

He used this straight away, to apologise to us.

Our room had been double-booked; the other parties had arrived before us, and were currently in it.

But not to worry, as their sister-hostel had a room free – and he was going to call the manager from there to come and pick us up. This was actually a major blessing in disguise. This hostel had been a reluctant second choice, after deciding we couldn't afford the other one; we were basically getting a free upgrade, to the 'Kung Fu Hostel'. This was a brand-new place, and the only piece of accommodation that was actually *on* Shaolin mountain – mere minutes away from the temple itself! I could barely contain my excitement.

"Oh crap!" A thought had just occurred to me. "I've got to draw some cash out before I can pay. They don't take Mastercard up there?"

John shook his head.

"So, is there a bank here, with a cash machine? I know it's late…"

John directed me to a bank two blocks away, and I took off at a jog. Roo, still collapsed in a chair by the front desk, refused to move until the car came to collect us.

The bank was closed, obviously, but had one of those enclosed lobby service-thingumies. The glass doors slid open for me, and I approached the row of ATMs. Roo had bequeathed me the sacred bank card for this venture, so I stepped up to my chosen machine and inserted it.

As soon as I pushed the card into the slot I realised my mistake. My stomach lurched with the potential for disaster, and I looked down at the keypad.

It was all in Chinese.

No numbers.

No red buttons. No green buttons. Nothing.

I looked back up at the screen. How could I punch in the PIN code without numbers? And why wasn't I being asked for a PIN? I scanned the icons, each lined up with a button on the edge of the screen. One had a picture of coins. One had a book. A couple looked like diagrams of the stock market crash...

I couldn't recognise any of it.

But I had to do something, so I pushed the one with the picture of coins on it.

And was greeted with a chilling message:

PLEASE INSERT CARD.

Oh crap, I thought.

Panic.

Roo! Roo could help. Inwardly I cringed at having to admit my stupidity, but in fairness she knew I was an idiot when she married me. She should be expecting this kind of thing. I tried to calm my breathing as I dug out my phone and hit redial. John answered again, and I begged him to put Roo on.

"Is everything okay?"

"No love, it's not! We're screwed. The card got swallowed. Again! I'm full-on shitting myself here. What do we do?"

"Hang on," she said, and she muffled the phone while she spoke to John.

"John's coming over," she told me when she came back on the line. "Don't worry, he'll sort it out."

Thank the Goddess for Roo! There'd been times on this trip when I'd had to stop her panicking, and now she'd repaid them in full by keeping a cool head. I was a mess, close to the end of my tether after a long and difficult evening, but Roo was there to ground me and comfort me. Without her, I'd have cried.

Well, I might have cried a bit anyway.

John arrived, and spent a fruitless few minutes playing around with the machine.

"I think this one is only for bank books," he said, pointing out a hatch I'd assumed was the cash dispenser. He opened it to show a small scanner bed inside – I'd used the wrong machine completely, and probably would have at least managed to retrieve my card from one of the other machines.

"You might want to warn people about that in future," I suggested.

John nodded, and pulled out his phone to call the bank. Having a Chinese speaker here made everything seem so normal, so *possible* – and at that exact moment I had a revelation.

This is why you have to book a tour to come to China, I realised. Even the government knows it's too difficult to do it on your own!

By circumventing the rules and getting our visas on the sly, we'd blundered into unforgiving territory; China, even in the touristy places, simply wasn't set up for international visitors. It was *too foreign* – delightfully so on the surface, when there was someone nearby to hold your hand. But once things started to go wrong? That's when the idiots stupid enough to sneak into the country on their own found themselves up shit creek and sinking fast...

Without John, we'd have no chance of getting our card back.

Having said that, without John directing me to the bank, we'd probably still have the damn thing.

When the manager of the Kung Fu Hostel arrived to pick us up, we were in a sorry state. We had no money, no possibility of getting any money, and after forty hours awake since the subway debacle, we must have looked like the penniless bums we were. We climbed into the back of his Mercedes, feeling rather out of place when our sweat-drenched clothing stuck to the leather seats.

It was a quiet journey. As far as I knew, the manager spoke English... just, not to us.

By the time we reached The Kung Fu Hostel, I was back in a positive frame of mind. I felt relaxed enough to laugh at the little weirdnesses, which every place we stay in has. It was pretty obvious in this case; the en-suite bathroom consisted of a large glass box taking up about a third of the room. It was completely transparent, with frameless glass doors like you get on upmarket shower enclosures. I imagine the idea had been copied from some high-end hotel – where presumably they had that special glass that turns opaque at the flick of a button. Whereas here they'd just used regular glass, which was very stylish, if a bit lacking in privacy.

"I'm busting for a poo," Roo said, her tone and wrinkled brow conveying apology.

"That's alright," I told her, "I don't mind watching you poo."

"Can you... not watch me?"

"Ah. Well I can try!"

So I sat on the other side of the bed, and listened to the sound effects instead. It turns out that glass is not substantially better at blocking noise than it is at blocking light.

"I'm sorry," she said, when the toilet had finished flushing, "is the romance dead?"

"That depends. Do I get to watch you take a shower now?"

The trip back to Dengfeng in the morning was quite complicated. A hike down to the Shaolin Monastery, where we hopped aboard (and paid for) an electric golf cart for a ride to the entrance. From there we took a regular bus down the mountain, meeting up with John outside the local bus station.

He arrived on his bike, and led us several blocks up to the bank from the night before. Inside, a lengthy negotiation with a variety of clerks led us to a cashier's window, where our precious card was returned to us. John listened to the warning that was delivered along with the card, then translated it to us, looking sheepish. "They don't take international cards here," he admitted.

The nearest bank that did was in the opposite direction, and John had to get back to the hostel, so I thanked him – somewhat wryly – and asked one last favour of him.

"Where do we catch the bus back to Zhengzhou tomorrow?" I asked.

"Oh, same place," he said.

"The local bus station? Where we just arrived?"

"Yes! That place."

"And is there a Post Office in town?"

"A what?"

"A… place where you… post things?"

"Ah… no, not here."

And he was off on his bike, waving us towards the bank.

"Okay then," I traded nervous looks with Roo, "here we go again. Take Two."

The familiar logo of the ICBC, a bank we'd used in Beijing, comforted me greatly. I still made Roo chose the machine and insert the card, though. "In fact, you should just do that every time from now on," I told her, "it's much safer."

She agreed.

With money in our pockets we felt much more secure. Next I was hoping to solve another tricky, potentially re-occurring problem; if I didn't find a way of sending my Mongolian knife back home, sooner or later it was going to be taken off me.

A free night in a Chinese police cell was quite likely to accompany such an event.

Google Maps having been so helpful the night before, I turned to it again to find a Post Office. The closest it could come was the Central Office of the China post Service. This seemed like a good start, as it was only a few streets away, so once again we followed the green dot.

When we arrived, it didn't look much like a post office. But nothing in China had looked as we'd expected it to – it was part of the trouble we were having, being unable to identify restaurants, for example – and the only solution I could think of was to expect the unexpected, and go with the flow.

So in we went.

There was a car barrier and an empty booth next to it, but we walked around those and found ourselves in a yard, with buildings on all sides. The China Post logo was on one of them, and an open roller door beckoned, so in we went again.

Inside was some kind of distribution centre or sorting office; packages and parcels were stacked here and there, and a few blokes in overalls were trying to fix a conveyor belt.

"Excuse me," I shouted to get their attention, "can you help us?"

"I don't think we're meant to be in here," Roo whispered.

The guys were approaching, so I started to mime posting a parcel.

"Are you doing the Macarena?" Roo asked, incredulous.

"No, I'm.. never mind. Can I post something to Australia?" I asked the workers.

They looked at each other in confusion.

"I want to send this," I said, pulling the knife out of my bag," to Australia…"

For some reason, all three guys started backing away, eyes wide.

"Oh, crap. No, I want to *post* this…" I pointed to the knife and waved it, trying to find a gesture that looked more like posting a parcel and less like 'I will stab you now.'

"I think we should go," said Roo. "Quickly."

So we left.

Monkin' About

Following our escape from the post office, we decided to lay low for a while – in case the cops were out in their milk float, looking for two knife-wielding Westerners.

Roo was close to fainting with hunger, so we approached a noodle house that John had pointed out to us the previous night. I'd asked him where locals went for lunch, and apparently this was it – so to make up for missing out on a morning at Shaolin, we ventured inside in search of an authentic meal.

It goes without saying that we didn't recognise anything, but we were feeling much more relaxed now that we could pay our way. We queued up at a window, and when it was our turn I simply pointed at a young couple who were sharing a tasty looking plate. A few questioning finger-jabs later I'd conveyed my message, and we collected a steaming plate of noodles and a porcelain bowl each of tea. Then we picked a table, sat, and copied everyone else – shovelling fresh noodles into ourselves as though we hadn't eaten since this time yesterday. Which, apart from sharing a packet of crisps, was true.

Locals came and went, as noisy and chaotic as ever, and the noodle house seemed like a happy place – sort of like the coffee shop in *Friends*, where everyone meets to joke about the crazy things that are going on in their lives. And about the two gangly white people hiding in the corner, struggling to use their chopsticks and splattering themselves with soy sauce in the process.

Back at the Shaolin Monastery we bought tickets for the kung fu show I'd dreamt of seeing for years. Real Shaolin masters doing real Shaolin kung fu – for me this was more central to an experience of China than the trip to the Great Wall. Kung fu is one of two things that pretty much define the Western impression of China; the other being cheap crappy products from electronics to clothing to housewares. Out of everything that's 'Made in China', martial arts is the only export I have faith in.

Waiting for the show to start (because the manager of the Kung Fu Hostel had told us the wrong times), we snuck into one of the neighbouring schools and watched the students practise with their weapons. Tiny lads as young as five, shaved bald like the monks and wearing only their pyjama pants, leapt and flipped and flailed around themselves with swords and spears; it was a bit surreal, like wandering into a land of half-dressed fighting gnomes. Their tricks were very impressive though, and Roo must have taken a hundred pictures trying to capture that perfect moment.

"I'll delete some of them later," she lied.

The show itself skirted as close to disappointment as is possible, whilst still kicking arse – quite literally, on more than one occasion. The monks giving the show were spectacular, leaping around the circular stage like their legs were made of springs. Weapons flashed, the monks' concentration so intense that their blades and whips blurred too fast for the eye to follow. They gave individual demonstrations and perfectly synchronised ones, culminating in that greatest of crowd-pleasers: iron shirt kung fu.

One disciple channelled *chi* into his abdomen, reaching around him for the life-energy and gathering it in his diaphragm. Then he climbed up onto the point of a spear, impaling himself at the belly-button, and hung there, transfixed, as the others rotated the spear with him atop it.

He was unmarked afterwards, as were the monks who bent spears against their throats and had iron bars smashed across their arms, legs and backs.

From start to finish, the monks' abilities were breathtaking. Their flexibility, agility and precision were incredible. From lying on their front, they could bend their legs up backwards until they were standing on the stage in front of their own heads! I couldn't think of a practical combat application for that particular skill, but it was certainly wince-inducing. The ability to throw a sewing needle through a pane of glass, miraculously puncturing a balloon held on the other side of it, was similarly crowd-pleasing. Again, not a skill I could seeing being of much use when accosted in a dark alley – unless they were being accosted by balloon animals – but I understood the level of mastery behind this almost impossible feat.

The show was only marred by being just half an hour long, and by spending over half that time in unintelligible audience participation. When it became obvious they were asking for volunteers, I had an odd reticence. I couldn't follow even the simplest of instructions in Chinese, so I let my fear of looking like an idiot for the wrong reasons stop me from doing what I wanted – which was to look like an idiot for the right reasons. Instead, a handful of Chinese tourists were called up to the stage, and invited to copy a sequence from Shaolin's famous animal forms. One at a time, each monk performed a blindingly-fast series of moves. Then his tourist partner gave a half-hearted flailing of his arms, tried to do a cartwheel and fell over. The crowd went wild.

I guess with political satire off the menu, along with anything which could be construed as morally offensive, complaining about one's station in life, or one's superiors, or anything controlled by the government (like jobs, public transport, taxes) or anything distasteful (sex and toilet humour) – the local comedy scene was kind of stagnant. It was understandable, but a bit frustrating. I could think of much better ways to spend $30 than to watch five-hundred Chinese tourists piss themselves laughing as a fat man stood on stage trying to do the splits.

"Does the kung fu make you want to stay?" Roo asked,

as we wandered along the pedestrianized boulevard linking the various schools and temples.

I thought about that for a minute. "Yes."

"We could come back, and you could study?"

"But it would take months to get any good. And you'd be bored."

"I'd find something to do..."

"And they live in cells and only eat rice and vegetables."

"Oh."

"Yeah, it's not the most glamorous of lives."

We watched the kids training again, because it was impossible to avoid them; every field or stand of trees had groups of students under them, all in formation, repeating the same pattern of movements with their weapons over and over again. Finally we came across a gigantic courtyard, ten football pitches wide at least, that was absolutely thronged with them. Thousands of unnaturally-muscular boys shrieked and groaned, all frighteningly identical in their matching trousers.

"Makes you think, if China did want to take over the world..."

"Yeah." Roo lowered her camera briefly – presumably to stop it exploding from over-use. "How many kids are down there, d'you think? Five thousand?"

"At least."

"I bet they could conquer Australia on their own."

"And that's just one school. On the bus to Dengfeng I saw dozens of them – pretty much everything between here and there is a kung fu school."

There was one last stop to make. We'd missed the chance to explore the monastery proper, as by the time we got back from town we only had time to do one thing. But the gates, although closed, were still there; characterful old wood, bound with iron, atop a stone staircase. It was the perfect place to strike a pose or two – or would have been, were it not for two rather large Chinese chicks who were doing the same thing. For an hour.

Eventually we gave up waiting, and took it in turns to

pose for photos in front of a lesser gate fifty metres away. I'd pulled off my t-shirt (purely for authenticity, of course), and ascended the stone steps. I'd picked up a stick, and was using it to do half-remembered staff moves, ending with a mighty high-kick – when there was a tearing sound from behind me.

Nooooo...!

Roo could tell straight away that something was amiss. "Tony? What's wrong? Are you okay?"

"Oh crap. Um... I'm afraid I've got a bit of a problem."

"What? Did you hurt yourself?"

"Ah... no, not exactly."

"Then what's happened?"

"I think I've, um, split my shorts..."

"Oh?"

I turned around for proof.

"Oh my God! Tony! Shit!"

"What?"

"Half your arse is hanging out!"

"Oh-oh."

"You didn't think to wear underwear?"

"I didn't know I was going to split my pants."

"Bloody hell! You've split them right up to the waistband at the back."

"I thought I could feel a breeze..."

She burst out laughing. "This could only happen to you!"

"Serves me right for showing off, you mean?"

"No, I mean, most people wear underwear as a general rule. Just in case."

I stuffed my t-shirt into my waistband, letting it hang down to cover my modesty, and we began the walk back to the hostel.

As we laboured up a steep bit of hillside, a police car crawled up behind us, hanging back as though checking us out.

"Can they see my arse?" I hissed at Roo.

"I don't know! I'm not stopping to look!"

"I'm going to get arrested for indecent exposure! And then they'll search my stuff and take that damn knife anyway!"

"If they decide you're a psychotic pervert, what are they

going to say about me? I've got about a thousand photos of half-naked children on my camera…"

*   *   *

The trip back down the mountain to *Dengfeng* was the same on the day we left, only with the added impediment of a time limit. Our train tickets were booked, and we had to accomplish the relay of hike to golf-cart to bus-down-the-mountain to long-distance-bus in sufficient time for us to somehow defeat the x-ray scanners and join the throng back at *Zhengzhou* station.

It went well.

And not at all to plan, which for once was a good thing.

We'd made it as far as the local bus station, and tried to get off when I was physically restrained by the conductor. The driver was also waving at us, very determined that we not get off. So we didn't – we sat back in our seats, and watched the time tick down as the bus criss-crossed the city, making pick-ups and drop-offs, with no further clue as to what we were waiting for. I assumed the bus would swing back into the station and meet the bus to Zhengzhou. Surely that's what they were trying to do? Save us from a long wait in the heat?

But no. Pretty soon it became clear that this bus was heading out of the city. I got up to demand an explanation, when it pulled up in a layby.

A suspiciously familiar lay-by.

The conductor shooed us off, and we looked around. There was the street of looming office blocks, vanishing into the distance. There was our bus, parked in the lay-by. And behind it…

This was where we had been dropped off, when we showed up in Dengfeng.

This was the middle of nowhere.

Or not. Because in the daylight we could see that, behind the row of trees that screened the layby, was a great big sodding bus station.

A *long distance* bus station, in fact.

If we'd got off where John had told us, at the local bus

station in town, we'd still have been stood there. Whereas the bus to Zhengzhou was here.

And missing it would inevitably have meant missing our hard-won train to Xi'an.

Climbing aboard, we shook our heads in disbelief.

I was suddenly reminded of a thing I'd read, the origin of which had long since escaped me. In some places, it is common to tell a person what they want to hear, even if you don't know the answer to their question.

China was obviously one of those places.

Despite running an international hostel, John didn't have a clue what banks could be used, or what bus routes were commonly frequented by foreigners. But of course, he wasn't going to let that stop him advising us.

Circumnavigaxi'an

The train journey from Zhengzhou (Chong-Chow) to Xi'an (She-Anne) followed a familiar theme.

One thing we couldn't help noticing, as the suburbs of Zhengzhou slid past our windows, was the epic scale of construction happening on the outskirts. I think we'd noticed it on the way out of Beijing, too, but had been too traumatised by the incessant infomercials to take note.

Now we stared, mouths agape, as we processed past tower block after tower block. These were brand-new high-rise apartment buildings, at least twenty floors high. And they were being built with mechanical precision, in identical groups of a hundred. My brain shies away from multiplying big numbers, but as we continued past mile upon mile of these developments, bristling with tower cranes, one thing was clear; they would house *a lot* of people.

Arriving in Xi'an was considerably easier than getting out of it.

We'd been a little concerned when a phone call to the YHA ended with them explaining that the free station pick-up was only for people arriving in the morning. As our seven-hour journey from Zhengzhou wouldn't be over until 6pm, this meant we would have to find our way to the hostel ourselves. "But is easy," the receptionist informed me, "take bus 603 and get off when you see the walls."

Oh no.

I hate directions like this.

Possibly because I struggle to follow arrows the right way, let alone process clues that involve an element of guesswork. When someone says, "keep going till you see the big shop, then next left at the crossroads," I go into panic mode. Every shop seems huge, and what exactly constitutes a 'crossroads' in their parlance? Do I take the 'next left' even if it's an alleyway? Or were they referring to the much bigger junction up ahead, which has a shop, but it's slightly smaller than the last one we passed…

So I was pleasantly surprised to find a sign with bus numbers on it outside the train station, directing us to a substantial queue. A few minutes later, the entire queue seemed determined to cram themselves onto one bus, so we followed suit. The driver saw us lumbering up, heavily laden, and waived the fare. The press of people kept us upright as the bus wound through clean, well-manicured streets, until I saw an immense, medieval structure looming above us.

"That'll be the walls," I said, as we struggled from the bus.

They were titanic – an order of magnitude bigger than the Great Wall itself, which was an eye-opener for sure.

"And there's a sign!" said Roo. The YHA generally does things right, and their signs directed us around the corner and down the street to a pair of iron-bound double doors, which led into a building dating back to the construction of those monumental walls.

We checked into a snug underground room, created in what used to be catacombs, and spent a while admiring the traditional wooden interior of the building above.

Then we went to bed, and when we woke up the next day, we decided to stay there.

If modern China is best typified by slightly terrifying megacities like Beijing and Zhengzhou, then Xi'an embodies the country's ancient majesty. Continually inhabited since the Neolithic Period, there'd been a city on this spot a thousand years before Jesus handed the Romans some nails and asked if they'd put him up for the night.

At the founding of 'modern' Xi'an, around 200BCE, Emperor *Liu Bang* built the largest palace the world has ever known – 1,200 acres, or roughly 11 times the size of Vatican City. We'd thought the Forbidden City was big; unfortunately (or perhaps fortunately, for our legs), the mighty *Weiyang Palace* is now an empty field.

Those towering walls, though, were very much in evidence. Six-hundred years old and perfectly preserved (or perhaps, perfectly rebuilt), they were impossible to ignore, always visible, brooding over the city like a jealous lover.

It rained all morning, giving us a chance to catch up on our journals and plan our next few trips. But when the rain cleared up mid-afternoon, we set out to explore. As usual, the lack of signage made things more difficult. We ventured outside the walls, following a footpath that led straight into a construction site, and with nowhere else to go we retraced our steps. Then we saw a way into what looked like another construction site, but turned out to be the main entrance to the wall-walking experience.

And an admission gate, which charged us $20 each for the privilege.

Having said that, the walls were impossibly vast, utterly beautiful, and worth every penny.

As wide at the top as a four-lane highway, the walls sloped twelve metres down to a base half as wide again. The core was rammed earth and rubble, but they were thickly-lined with layers of tan-coloured bricks, creating a fortification so massive it would take a nuclear blast to breach it.

It's possible to walk the whole way around the top without needing to climb back down; the four hour, twelve-kilometre trip gave us a great perspective on the city, seeing all sides of it in one circular stroll.

Immediately obvious was the contrast between the inner city and the outer.

Beyond the walls, skyscrapers clustered thickly, bearing

the emblems of banks, financial corporations, hotels and other indecipherable logos. Strict preservation rules and a two-storey height restriction had created an island-city inside the walls, where traditional clay-tiled roofs and venerable wooden buildings could survive; in the world outside, they would have been swallowed up in a heartbeat. It was old China versus new, and nowhere was this more apparent than in the thick grey fog which clung to the top of the high-rises, blotting out the sky. It was grey inside the walls too, with buses and cars clogging the main roads, but the smaller alleys were devoid of traffic, presumably also due to some heritage legislation. It meant that, despite the glitzy main shopping street lined with glass-fronted Gucci and Chanel stores, the character of the ancient city could still be appreciated from on high.

Over the walls, the modern world gazed with hungry eyes.

As we approached one of the many-tiered corner towers, we spotted a pattern of bricks bearing stamps of the workers who had laid them. A series of Han characters were followed by a date in Roman numerals, revealing that this part of the wall had last been repaved in 1984.

So, not *quite* as ancient as we thought.

When darkness fell, hundreds of red lanterns hung from iron posts all along the walls lit up. Actually they lit up quite a while after darkness had fallen, leaving us blundering about barely able to see for quite some time. But when they lit, they were lovely. The towers and gatehouses, however, had undergone a more excessive transformation. Dripping with multicoloured neon lights, they blazed like fairground rides. Even looking at them made it hard to see anything else afterwards.

We completed our circuit in the dark, and couldn't help but stop when we heard music coming from below us. Leaning through the battlements, we watched as a seniors' dance class took place beside the base of the wall. Accompanied by a trumpet, cymbals and a guy on bongos, a group of pensioners in floral-print pyjamas performed the hokey-cokey with parasols on their shoulders. It was so surreal we could hardly tear ourselves away. Doing it out in the open made it look to us like they were putting on a performance, whereas they had probably done it to save hiring a hall. It made me aware of a vast gulf between our cultures, based entirely on self-consciousness; the only person I know who will dance in public without at least three beers and a shot of vodka inside them is me. As for exercising in public... forget it!

But that's exactly what was happening in a square on the other side of the wall; a mixed-age class stood in lines, wearing their regular clothes, following the dubious aerobic advice of four instructors in jeans and jackets. They looked absurd; beyond absurd, actually. There's a reason we work out in the gym, safe from the critical eyes of others – two reasons, in fact. One is that, no matter how good you are at them, doing squats and star jumps always looks stupid. The other is that, in the gym, you actually *get* a work-out. If these guys and girls though they were transforming themselves by marching on the spot and occasionally issuing a group, "Huuuuuuuuuaaaaooo!" – then they were very much mistaken.

Dinner that night was hard to come by. Finding food was bizarrely difficult, even in a tourist-friendly city like Xi'an. One issue was that restaurants and cafés simply didn't *look* like restaurants and cafés – all the visual cues we used to identify the nature of a business were absent. We ventured into offices, shops and an estate agent, before happening on a bright red and yellow façade that screamed *fast food*. Inside, we found a delightfully convenient picture menu over the counter, so we used point-and-choose to order some noodles.

When they came, they were stone cold, but we were too hungry to care. They tasted okay, if a tad on the slimy side. We narrowly avoided adding the sauce that came with them when I dipped a finger in, licked it, and nearly burned a hole right through my tongue. All in all, a strange but interesting experience.

Later that week, still struggling with meal options, we tried again – this time, giving in to our urge to order burgers and fries.

They also came stone cold.
Apparently, it's a thing.

The day after our wall-walking expedition, based on advice I'd read online, we decided to buy our tickets out of Xi'an.
We were only partially successful.
We bought the tickets from a tiny window in a location that would have proved impossible to find without precise instructions from the staff at our hostel. It was a booth the size of a phone box, built into the side of a department store as far as I could tell, and manned by one woman – I had no idea if this was the sole agency for ticket purchase in the whole of Xi'an, or if the city was littered with such windows.
Anyway, the news was less than great.
The day we wanted to leave was already fully booked.
That's beds, seats – even the dreaded standing-room-only tickets were gone.
As were the three days afterwards.
When we finally found a ticket out of Xi'an, it meant we would be stranded here for a week.

With no-one else to complain to, I aired my grievances to the hostel receptionist.
"Oh, the rules, they change," I was told. "Before, can only book train tickets for one week ahead. Now, you can book one month!" He seemed ecstatic about the change, which would dramatically alter his ability to travel around the country. For us, it was a solid kick in the testicles. It meant that most of the tickets we would need to travel China – and more importantly, to get the hell out of China – would have been snapped up already. I knew that every train in the country was booked solid within a few days of tickets being issued. We'd just learned that, as of now, every ticket we needed to buy had been made available over a fortnight ago.
I felt like we'd only just entered China, but now it was a race – *get out, before it's too late!*
Before our visa, which had a little over two weeks to run at this point, expired.
And like it or not, we'd be spending a week of that in Xi'an.

If we wanted to leave China without getting into serious trouble for overstaying, we were going to be cutting it mighty fine.

Buried In The Ground

One of the main reasons we were in Xi'an was to see the Terracotta Warriors.
Probably the most famous attraction in China after the Great Wall, and the most visited, the Warriors are actually part of a much larger complex of underground palaces and tombs. The crazy thing is that the vast majority of it is completely unexcavated. According to our guidebook, at current speeds it would take another 200 years to unearth the entire complex! I've said it before, and I'll say it again – nobody does BIG like the ancient Chinese.

With so many travel websites blocked, I was doing all my research via a couple of blogs and reviews left on Trip Advisor. From these slightly imperfect sources I put together a plan of attack; the same bus we'd taken from the station, only in reverse, followed by another bus we hoped to discover in a parking area to the station's left. The official bus left at 7am, leaving unofficial buses to take those lazy bastards who liked to sleep through the dawn. We fell firmly into this category.
There were no further instructions I could glean, beyond a warning that all the restaurants in the area ripped off Western tourists mercilessly. For this reason, we built a

McDonald's stop into our schedule (although there was no accounting for the ladies bathroom queue, which Roo spent forty-five minutes in).

The bus journey only took an hour; a welcome surprise, as I'd been expecting three. There was an American couple sitting slightly further back, and they seemed equally unsure of themselves. "Is this the right bus?" the girl had asked me, when they got on. "Your guess is as good as mine," I admitted – though the full-colour mural of the Terracotta Warriors running the length of the bus gave some indication. We didn't get chance to speak to them again – and they were the only other Westerners we saw all day.

We arrived in a gravel car park lined on one side with stalls selling racks and racks of mink hides – a few turned into hats and stoles, but most with their teeth and claws still attached. Closer inspection revealed that, amongst the more expensive furs, it was also possible to buy dog and cat pelts – Alsatian being a popular choice, from the look of things. It was an unusual way to showcase one of the world's most treasured archaeological finds, and I struggled to think what logic had prompted the stallholders to set up there. It must have been a premium location, requiring a decent chunk of change to rent and/or bribe the appropriate officials. But how many people want to go and visit the Terracotta Warriors, and bring home a skinned weasel as a souvenir? The two don't really go together. And call me crazy, but a dog-skin rug is hardly an impulse buy.

Ah well. The mysteries of China!

Beset by touts, we were pushed into a queue, and spent a good fifteen minutes there before getting to the front and realising it was a queue to hire electric golf carts. There were no 'This Way!' type signs, so we blundered around between restaurants and market stalls, and found the entrance to the Warriors Centre about a kilometre away. It was up a long series of steps and through several small squares full of kiosks selling drinks, crisps, postcards... and bladed weapons. Now, as far as I'm concerned, a broadsword *is* an impulse buy. I'm sure not everyone agrees with me here –

maybe it's a guy thing? Or maybe it's just a me thing. But I was itching to walk up to one of the counters and say, "I'll take two cans of Coke and a six-foot battle-axe, please!"

Sadly, as Roo pointed out, anyone buying these lethal objects would have a hell of a job getting them home. They certainly wouldn't be taking them on the train...

Once inside, we headed first for the museum.

One blog had suggested seeing this first, and it was the right thing to do. A large part of the collection was photographs of the warriors in various stages of excavation – this probably wouldn't have seemed nearly as interesting after nipping next door and seeing the actual excavation. There were reconstructions showing what the warriors would have looked like when first created, with brightly-coloured paint jobs, glossy black hair and ruddy cheeks. It made them look a bit cartoony compared to the impassive, stony features they have today, but someone had put a lot of effort into painting them – each statue is life-sized, and current estimates suggest there are more than 8,000 soldiers, 130 chariots and 670 horses buried in the ground.

A series of boards told the tale of their discovery; two peasant farmers digging a well in 1974 came across shards of the statues, and reported the find. Since then three giant pits have been uncovered, thousands of statues have been painstakingly reassembled from the fragments, and groups of Terracotta Warriors have travelled as far afield as London, Sydney, Washington DC and Mumbai.

The display didn't mention whether or not the farmers got a finder's fee.

The rest of the museum was fairly lacklustre. Most of the pieces had little to do with the warriors, and fully a third of the glass cases were empty, bearing little signs that said 'This item is on loan.'

It didn't matter. The museum was just an appetiser; following our 'save the best till last' philosophy, the next item on the agenda was Terracotta Warriors: The Movie, as projected inside a standing-room-only dome theatre.

This was also crap.

The first five minutes of the twenty-minute film consisted of an aerial view following the roads leading to the site. I could only guess this was meant to simulate the experience of driving here, in which case it was fairly redundant, as everyone in the room had done that quite recently. Inexplicably, the last five minutes of the film were simply the first five minutes played in reverse. In between these two life-affirming experiences, we were treated to an out-of-focus reconstruction of the warriors being made, narrated in English by a voice from the 1960s BBC World Service. "Here you can see, clay being made, and placed into a mould…"

And, well, that was about it.

I still never got to find out what happened to those farmers.

But at last we were going to visit the site of their well, which is clearly marked in Pit One. As we stepped inside the first of three colossal aircraft hangers, there they were! Rank upon rank of warriors, grimly facing the gateway that had been buried with them. After two-thousand years underground, their wooden-roofed corridors crushed under five metres of soil, they were still things of beauty. Every single soldier was unique; after separate firing of the hollow pieces – arms, legs, bodies and heads – individual facial features had been sculpted on, with moustaches, eyebrows and hairstyles adding distinction. Seen all ranked up, the six-thousand repaired soldiers made an awe-inspiring sight – but I had to stifle a giggle at the thought of pushing the first one over, and seeing how far along the domino effect would go. A terribly disrespectful thought, of course, given the countless hours it had taken to piece these guys back together. At the time of discovery, every one of them was shattered. It must have been the biggest jigsaw puzzle in the world, and efforts were still ongoing; towards the back of Pit One we watched archaeologists with paint brushes acting out the pictures we'd seen in the museum. Hundreds of fragments were labelled, and dozens of half-built warriors lay around in various stages of completion.

It had reportedly taken an army of over 700,000 labourers and craftsmen to complete this horde. It was to be a thankless task; the mass grave containing their bodies was only a short distance away.

We spent several hours going from pit to pit, starting with the unexcavated areas full of broken bits and working our way up to Pit One. We were guided largely by chance, and by very occasional signs; my favourite featured a slanting directional arrow bearing the legend, 'Warm Prompt'.

Roo took hundreds of photos, including some lovely ones of the 'no photos' signs. Everyone else was ignoring them; there must have been several thousand Chinese tourists there that day, and every one of them was carrying a camera *and* a smartphone. Stopping them taking photographs would be like standing in front of a tsunami armed with a dustbin lid. Personally, I'd have given anything to stop them *talking*. We'd noticed that, when in public, the Chinese tend to speak in what we would deem a shout. Combined in large tour groups, this became a wall of sound that drove us to seek refuge anywhere they weren't. It had been a thorn in the side on every excursion so far – along with surfing on the incessant tide of spit – and there was only so much of it we could take.

The bus we caught back was a bit of a scam. It took an hour longer to make the trip because it took the longest, most circuitous route possible, stopping to pick up people even when it seemed doubtful another human could possibly squeeze in. We didn't much mind, as our only plan for the evening was to find the Muslim Quarter, a warren of backstreets inside the northern stretch of Xi'an's walls, and eat as much street food as possible. This we achieved, standing in doorways to munch whatever looked most appetizing as the alleyways bustled with activity.

It was there that Roo spotted her dream vehicle – we came to call it the Bubble Bike, a motor-scooter inside a spherical Perspex cockpit.

She practically squealed when she saw it.

"Oh Tony, I want one!" she said. "Imagine it – we could put a solar panel on the roof and travel all over Australia in one!"

Shave My Spider!

I've sometimes been accused of leaving cliff-hanger endings in my adventures, so I'll put this one to rest right now: it never happened.

Of course, two years later Roo still hasn't shut up about it, so I guess anything is possible...

That night I read as much as I could find about the Terracotta Warriors. They'd impressed me even more than I expected, and I couldn't stop thinking about the kind of civilization that could create something like that. It had been the doing of Emperor Qin, beginning in the year 246 BC. Not only had he been buried with an army, he'd been buried with palaces full of officials, all kinds of rare animals and precious objects and his entire bevvy of concubines – all of which lay undiscovered, somewhere beneath the 76m high mound of earth at the foot of *Mount Li*. Radar scans and other archaeological techniques have revealed that, thirty to forty metres beneath the surface lies the tomb itself – a hermetically-sealed chamber the size of a football pitch.

That grabbed my attention. Just imagine – what could be in there?

Chinese historian *Sima Qian,* writing in 109BC, said the underground tomb complex had included artificial rivers made of mercury, which had been designed to flow automatically. What other marvels of ancient technology could be lying in wait down there?

It was enough to give me chills.

The Chinese government doesn't believe the techniques currently available are sufficient to adequately protect the tomb, if opened.

And so the tomb remains closed.

Undisturbed for over two-thousand years... it must be one of the last remaining mysteries on this planet.

I'm kind of glad it's stayed that way.

Getting High

Sometimes, people send me things.

Since publishing my first book, I seem to have acquired a reputation on the internet for being a daredevil. I've no idea how, as I still faint at the sight of blood and jump three feet in shock every time a car door slams.

Personally, I think people are confusing bravery with stupidity.

For example, I regularly walk out in front of traffic – not because I have no fear of cars, but because I'm usually thinking about something else and don't even notice I'm in the middle of the road.

Back in my university days, my friend James was the first person to notice this trait. We used to walk back to his house after class, and he would save my life on average three times per journey. It used to amaze him how, once I started talking, all my other senses were completely tuned out. I hung out with him for three years, and I still don't have a clue where he lived.

But anyway. That doesn't stop people from sending me things, pictures and videos of the world's craziest bastards tackling the world's craziest challenges – usually accompanied by a note saying something like, "You should totally do this!"

And without fail, I *always* want to do them.

Hua Shan is one of China's five sacred mountains. I first came to know about it when someone forwarded me a blog post entitled 'The Most Dangerous Hiking Path In The World!'. Now, I defy anyone to read that and not think, 'Dangerous? Pah! I'll show them!'

Well, that's how my mind works.

Roo has recently started deleting this kind of email.

At least a decade ago, a random bloke who had never been to China, started collecting accounts of people who had climbed Hua Shan. He turned these stories into a hobby blog, which was filled with alarmist statements and third-hand reports of alleged deaths. The blog became quite a fixture on the internet, doing rounds of Facebook largely because of one incredible photo: a pair of staircases, both vertical, carved into the rock about halfway up the mountain. With dangling chains to help pull yourself up, these impossible stairs had become synonymous with insane adventure, and the legend of the World's Deadliest Hike was born.

Back when we'd decided to travel Asia, China hadn't been on the cards. But Roo had desperately wanted to see the Great Wall, and when I'd added China to our itinerary, Hua Shan had been my condition.

Lying in hostel beds in Vietnam and Mongolia, she'd voiced her concerns time and again. Always I'd replied by telling her that we'd wait and see – if Hua Shan was doable, we'd try and do it. If it became too difficult, we'd stop doing it. And if it became dangerous, well, that's what travel insurance was for.

Not that I'd bought any travel insurance.

I'd thought about climbing Hua Shan, and about those crazy stairs, for months. I'd lusted after them like a drug. Because they were *there*, and other people had climbed them, and more than anything, I hate feeling left out.

After today, I wouldn't have to worry about that any more.

Because today, at long last, we were going to climb Hua

Shan; 'The Most Precipitous Mountain Under Heaven'.

Which I took to mean it rains a lot there.

First though, we had a chore to take care of.

We'd visited Xi'an's central post office twice already, on the advice of our hostel staff. Both times it had been closed, showing once again that if they didn't know the answer to one of our questions, they merely told us what they thought we wanted to hear.

This time it was mid-morning, mid-week, and the place was bustling. I'd done everything I could to get my Mongolian knife safely back to Australia; I'd wrapped it up like a birthday present, and packaged it with a few bits of clothing we no longer needed. I placed a note in the box addressed to Australian customs, explaining that the knife was wrapped to fool Chinese customs, and paid $20 for it to be sent by the cheapest method possible. 'SURSACE' was stamped on the parcel, proving that even government officials getting rubber stamps made up don't bother to have their text proof-read first.

We caught the bus to Hua Shan from outside the Xi'an train station as planned, but just before we arrived at our destination the conductor gave a long and angry-sounding lecture in Chinese. Roo and I looked at each other and hoped it wasn't important.

Then we pulled up outside a café, and the rest of the passengers bolted inside and started chowing down on noodles.

We dawdled on the pavement, not sure what to do. The conductor barked at us a few times, made emphatic 'you're in or you're out' gestures, then gave up and pulled a sliding door closed across the entrance.

"What just happened?" Roo asked.

"I'm not sure, but I think he's co-opted the entire tour, and turned it into a trip to his brother's restaurant."

"Shit."

"Yes, quite."

This was a bit of a bugger, as we were on a tight schedule to climb the mountain. We had a long way to go to, and the place we were staying in for the night – the only place we could afford – was on top of it. So, with absolutely no advice forthcoming, and zero English spoken in the immediate vicinity, we did what we usually do; wandered vaguely around looking confused.

Luckily, the seven-thousand foot mountain looming over the town was hard to miss. We were on what appeared to be the main street, and it had a distinctly uphill direction, so we went that way. We passed shops and businesses, and a car park with a huge brown tourist sign written entirely in Chinese.

I pointed it out to Roo. "You see, for all we know that sign could say, 'This way to climb Hua Shan, tickets available right here! And free ice cream for foreigners'."

"Yes, but it leads to a car park."

"Well, true enough."

The road terminated in wide stone steps, which we climbed hoping to find a clue. It was like a treasure hunt, only with the added incentive that if we didn't succeed, we'd be sleeping rough on a park bench. Assuming we could find a park.

What we did find was a small square in front of an ornately-carved wooden gateway.

"This looks like the entrance to a temple," Roo said.

And she was right!

It was naff all to do with Hua Shan though, which was a bit frustrating.

Finally, Roo spotted a sign about the size of a car number-plate on the side of one of the temple buildings, which said, 'Climb Hua Shan'. It had an arrow on it, so we followed that down a lane at the side of the temple. It didn't look particularly promising, but after a while it turned a corner and we came to a row of ticket booths.

"This is it!" I declared. "We made it!"

Roo was also exultant, and we did a little dance to celebrate.

Then we bought tickets and followed the path towards the mountain.

We walked for half an hour before we realised we were still in the wrong place.

You see, there are three ways up Hua Shan. The vast majority of people take the cable cars – even though a round-trip costs $32 per person, in addition to the $20 Scenic Area entrance fee we'd just paid.

The second most popular route, which we figured we were on, is the 'long' path – a steep, 6km hike, ascending the mountain via paved walkways. I'd been referring to this as 'the boring way up'.

The third is the damn hard path, which is climbed only by the very dedicated and the very stupid, because it's damn hard. It starts right under the cable cars, and pretty much follows their route – except that in place of giant winches hauling six-man gondolas up the mountain in six minutes, there are just stairs. Lots, and lots, of stairs. This path is compellingly titled 'The Route Intelligent Take-Over Of Hua Shan' – which is probably why everyone calls it 'The Soldiers Path'.

And that was the way I wanted to go.

Bollocks.

We retraced our steps to the raised area outside the temple.

We were quite literally back to square one.

It's fair to say we were a bit pissed off at this point.

Faced with no obvious alternatives, we wandered past the brown sign into the car park. A couple of guys were manning a barrier, and out of desperation I approached them.

"Hua Shan, Hua Shan," I said, waving my hands over my head to mime cable cars.

The two men exchanged a look that transcends language barriers; *Why do we always get the crazies?*

Much frantic questioning and repeated pantomiming of cable cars finally conveyed the right impression, and they waved us in, pointing us towards a minibus parked in the corner.

Which had a picture of a mountain on it.

"Oh, bloody hell! Roo, you know what this car park is?"

"What?"

"It's the shuttle bus station for the Hua Shan Visitors Centre."

"Ah."

"Why did it take them so long to figure us out? Every Westerner who ever visits this place is going up the mountain. Those guys have *one job,* which is to put people like us on *that frigging bus!*"

Roo nodded her agreement. "I think they just liked watching you wave your arms around and go *Woooosh!*"

The ferry bus to the visitors centre was empty, because by this time no-one in their right minds was *starting* the climb. The rather expensive (but compulsory) shuttle bus from the visitors centre to the cable car terminal was similarly empty. Our timing was perfect. Despite everything that had happened that day (or perhaps because of it), circumstances had conspired to send us up this mountain at 4.30pm – entirely alone. The whole climb, we only saw three people – and they were right at the beginning, on their way down. I'd read that taking the more popular route could be like queuing up the mountain, especially at the weekends. Instead, Roo and I had the place to ourselves. It was glorious.

They weren't kidding about the 'damn hard' bit though. We'd been going for less than ten minutes when we had to stop, panting and wheezing.

"Thought we were fitter than this," gasped Roo.

"Me too," I admitted, "but don't worry, we're nearly at the top…"

"Are we?"

"No."

"Bastard."

I won't bore you with the next section. Suffice to say, there were steps.

Lots of steps.

Thousands of them.

Tens of thousands.

It was quite tiring, actually.

But the view was spectacular.

We stopped to catch our breath at every landing, and took the chance to look across the hazy gulf of nothingness to the mountainside opposite. At times we had unobstructed, 180-degree views of the surrounding landscape; I could really see why the cable cars were so popular. To be able to sit and stare at all that, effortlessly drinking in the forests, the lakes, the smudge of cities on the horizon…

Pah! Where's the adventure in that?

"You know what we should do?" I asked Roo.

"No. What?"

"Climb some more steps!"

My mind wanders when my body is busy.

Which is probably not ideal when I'm on a narrow staircase halfway up a mountain, but there you go. As the stairs stretched endlessly ahead of us, I began to marvel at the effort involved in creating this path. It had to be one of the most inaccessible patches of mountainside in China, so ridiculously steep that only a staircase of stupendous proportions could get people up there. But then, how do you make that staircase? Why, with stone, of course. Massive great blocks of granite that must have weighed as much as a small car. I had the same feeling I'd experienced standing in front of the Pyramids at Giza; that sense that, without modern technology, what I was seeing was simply not possible. In the absence of tower cranes, how do you haul stone up a mountainside? With a donkey? What if the stone is heavier than the donkey…?

Next I found myself dwelling on the mountain's history. Originally I'd assumed the 'Soldier's Path' was called this because it was so physically demanding, but now I knew different. The name 'Route Intelligent Take Over Hua Shan' referred to a group of seven People's Liberation Army soldiers who climbed Hua Shan by this ancient, forgotten route. At the top they surprised a garrison of a hundred enemy soldiers, capturing them all. This must have made them rock stars with the army brass, though quite why it was necessary is a mystery. I mean, what harm were they doing up there? It's not like they could get down quickly. Whatever they were up to, it would make sod all difference to the rest of the country. It's like being at war in England, and realising there's a hundred enemy soldiers stationed in a swamp in Belgium. And you're like, "Damn! We must devise a cunning plan to capture those troops…"

Or, you know, *leave them there?* They're in Belgium. What are they going to do, send an aggressively-worded note by carrier pigeon?

Finally, I worried about the depressing amount of Disneyfication in evidence.

At some point in the distant past, the same poor buggers who hauled stone steps all the way up here had also hauled stone balustrades for the more exposed sections. Now, those ancient chunks of granite were getting a make-over. They had been encased in cement, which was rounded off and had rough grooves scraped into it. Several sections were still wrapped in plastic film, waiting for the cement to dry, but others had been painted brown – turning the raw stone handrails into poorly-sculpted concrete logs. It was heartbreaking. Some complete douche-canoe in the Communist Party's high command had obviously visited Frontierland in Morecombe, spent half an hour in the queue for the Rusty Mine Cart Ride, and decided to restyle China's ancient monuments after it.

Epic. Fail.

The most frightening thing was, no-one was trying to stop him.

About halfway up, we finally came across the thing I'd been waiting for.

The stairs!

Yes, I appreciate we'd climbed a lot of stairs already. My thighs would be reminding me of that for days to come. But this was *it*; the scene of that infamous internet picture, the ridiculous vertical stairs that scared Roo so much it had taken me three months to convince her to come here.

And now here we were.

And they were closed.

Like ladders, the slender staircases were carved directly into the cliff face. Fifteen, maybe twenty metres of sheer rock, they could only be climbed by putting your toes onto the shallow step-ledges whilst clinging for dear life to a pair of dangling chains. They did look a *little* dangerous…

But then, that was the point.

It was a bit annoying that some health-and-safety minded bureaucrat had decided to close the most famous staircase in the whole country, but luckily all they'd done is fasten the handhold-chains across the steps at the bottom.

It was no effort to climb past them.

And I figured I wasn't really breaking any rules; 'No Striding' said the English language warning sign.

As if striding was ever an option.

I have to admit, I went a little crazy.

I'd been fantasising about these steps for months, which in any other relationship would be grounds for divorce. I'm very fortunate to have Roo; not only did she stand at the bottom and film me as I climbed up, and down, and back up the steps, time and time again – she also let me try climbing them *with* the camera. This resulted in the most boring video ever made: ten minutes of me panting like a sex-pest over shaky footage of my feet.

Running on adrenaline, I explored every inch of those stairs. Climbing them was much easier than it looked. Each step was a tiny shelf cut into the rock; enough space for my toes to rest, but that was all I needed. As the steps were so small, each one only raised me a handful of inches, and the chains on either side could easily hold my weight. A couple of metres up, the steps were caked in dust, suggesting it was a long time since anyone had bothered to climb that far. Perhaps everyone else took the 'CLOSED' signs seriously? Ha! More fool them. I made several ascents to the top of the biggest stairs, but could only get halfway up the other one, as the top section had been obliterated by a landing for a new concrete staircase. Complete with faux-log handrails…

Oh, China. For shame!

Finally, Roo advised me to stop.

Otherwise I'd probably still be there.

Or, bits of me would.

But she made a good point; the light was starting to fade, and it wouldn't be *ideal* if nightfall caught us on the side of the mountain.

"Was that enough adventure for you?" she asked.

"Yes," I panted, "for now."

"Right then! What's next?"

"Well, I figure we're about halfway up the mountain. So…"

"We climb some more stairs?"

"Pretty much."

Roo sighed.

"See, that's the spirit," I said, "aren't you glad I talked you into this!"

What Goes Up...

We arrived atop the North Peak of Hua Shan, absolutely knackered, a little over three hours after setting off. It had been a relentless, leg-busting, lung-bursting, fatigue-inducing, Oreo-fuelled odyssey.

We felt a powerful urge to sit down for a bit.

To be perfectly honest, I think we'd both have been happy if we never saw another carved stone step in our lives.

But that was not going to happen. Because as we admired the view from the top, we came to realise something.

This wasn't the top.

Even though it had a cable car station and a swanky hotel.

And a photogenic stone archway for taking 'I'm at the top!' style photos.

There was also a sign – the first one we'd seen in English, unless you count 'No Striding'. It listed the relative heights of Hua Shan's five peaks, and we couldn't help but notice that the North Peak, whilst it sounded impressive, was also the lowest. By some 600 meters...

"Good news!" I informed Roo.

"Is there?" she asked.

"Well, it depends on your definition of good."

She just looked at me.

"A glass-is-half-full person would say we're nearly there."

"So, we're not nearly there."

"No, we're a little over halfway."

She lifted her eyes to the ridge which soared above us, where tiny ant-people toiled endlessly upwards. "And we're climbing *that* next?"

"Apparently so…"

But first I had a quiet chuckle at the uniformed Tourist Information Officer, sitting stony-faced at his open-air desk by the cable cars.

'Safety Propaganda' was the title emblazed on the desk.

He obviously didn't appreciate the irony, and I wasn't about to tell him as he was armed to the teeth. Like all good Tourist Information officers.

I didn't fancy his job though;

Distraught woman: "Help me officer, my son has just fallen to his death!"

Officer: "No he hasn't."

Woman: "Yes he has! That's his body down there…"

Officer: "NO. IT. ISN'T."

Anyway.

We had to get a move on.

Our next obstacle, called Dragonback Ridge, was only the beginning of an immense, circuitous route which visited each of the five peaks of the sacred mountain. It led from the North Peak, where we were standing, over the much-higher Central Peak, to the West Peak, where our hostel was located, and on to the notorious East Peak, where we planned on going tomorrow. I forget what the other peak was called.

Owing to the slight delay in our starting time it was now 7:30pm, and daylight was failing rapidly. It made for some gorgeous sunset pictures of the valley below, where the distant lights of Xi'an city were very nearly visible through the smog.

And then, breath caught, it was time to turn our eyes upwards once more.

The scene in front of us was like something from Lord of the Rings.

Through the Posing Pillars of False Hope, the path narrowed as it climbed, rapidly becoming the stuff nightmares are made of.

Dragonback Ridge followed the barest knife-edge of the rock, a stone staircase at times less than a metre wide, with sheer cliffs plunging down hundreds of feet on either side.

Not a great place to be drunk, I thought.

Or to meet anyone coming the other way…

At first I thought we were lucky with this; later I discovered the Dragonback is a strictly enforced one-way system, as it is simply too dangerous to allow people to try to pass each other.

Climbing that ridge was an experience I'll never forget. The steps stretched on in front of me, but to either side there was nothing; a skinny metal handrail, and an empty expanse of sky. The clouds were below us, the far peaks were opposite, and the setting sun made them glow with otherworldly promise. I've seldom seen a view as beautiful; that was the most dangerous part of the hike so far, as the temptation to stare in awe was great. And staring in awe is not really compatible with negotiating steep, uneven steps barely as wide as you are.

Few others were daft enough to attempt the Dragonback ridge in the evening, so we had it almost to ourselves. We could even stop for photos, and to admire that incredible view, whereas all the pictures I'd seen online showed the Dragonback in the daytime as the world's steepest queue.

Beyond the ridge, we came to an unexpected guesthouse. It wasn't listed on any of our maps (although by 'maps' I'm referring to a 2-inch line drawing on the back of our ticket, labelled in Chinese).

The official hiking route appeared to continue right through the centre of the building, taking advantage of their internal stairs – it's possible that the signs suggesting this were put there by the owner, but no-one seemed to be telling him to stop it. Constructing anything up here most have cost a fortune, but I could only imagine the bribes he must have paid to secure such a prime location.

The manager was stood out front, and his eyes lit up when we trudged up the steps to his courtyard.

"Stay here, stay here!" he cried, rattling off prices in English.

"No, we book a room at the West Peak," I told the man.

"West peak very far!" he said, and immediately offered us a discount which brought the price close to what we'd expected to pay at the West Peak. Roo and I had been in China long enough by this point to expect a scam of some kind, so we pressed on, hauling ourselves up the ragged stone steps until a gap in the foliage allowed us a glimpse of our destination.

"Oh bloody hell," said Roo.

The West Peak gleamed in the distance, the last rays of sun picking out a tiny building clinging to the slope facing us across the gulf.

It was friggin' *miles* away.

Very far was a serious understatement.

"Bollocks to that," I said.

Roo agreed.

So we retraced our steps and took up the hostel manager's offer, booking into his cheapest dormitory.

Roo was proud of me for making such a grown-up decision.

Or as she put it, "Hiking in the dark, whilst knackered, on an unfamiliar mountain known for being lethal to hikers, would probably be a mistake. Even by our standards."

I guess I could see the truth in that.

We scored some free hot water from the manager to make our instant noodles; in China boiling water is always freely available, in hotels, on trains, in supermarkets… if you stop any person in the street and ask them, there's a better-than-average chance they'll have a flask of the stuff in their bag. Cold water, though, is a different story. No matter how hard I tried, I couldn't convince the manager that it was safe to give me any. I had a bag full of water purification pills and a state-of-the-art UV steriliser, but instead I spent two hours pouring boiling water from cup to cup until it was cool enough to refill our plastic drink bottles.

Then, utterly exhausted, we settled in for some sleep.

We didn't get any of course, but what were we expecting?

It was a small room with eighteen other people in it, packed so tight I could feel tremors in my bunk whenever the guy in the far corner scratched his arse. It was hot, it was sticky, and the pungent stench of unwashed hiker was strong enough to bottle. It was nearly bad enough deter the mosquitos... but not quite.

And then, there was the human factor.

One of the eternal mysteries of the universe is this: how do people who snore like a drunken sumo wrestler always get to sleep before everyone else? Within minutes of the lights going out, a fat bloke two beds over started moaning like a water buffalo with its balls caught in a barbwire fence. His vocal range was impressive; from squeaks to ecstatic sighs, he covered every noise the human body is capable of making – all with the volume knob set to 11. None of it sounded healthy. Every so often he would lapse into silence for up to a minute and I would have the happy thought, "Thank God, he's died!"

But no. After an hour, I got up and shook him awake. He jabbered at me in Chinese, and I gave him my best pissed-off look and went back to bed. He sat up, hacked and coughed for a few seconds, then spat a massive gob-full of phlegm onto the floor.

And went straight back to sleep.

I don't think anyone else in that dorm slept. Three other people got up and woke him throughout the night, and each time he was snoring again before they climbed back into their bunks. One girl on the opposite side kept throwing her pillow at him. I spent at least an hour contemplating tipping him out of bed, and making some kind of scene so that the whole dorm could tell him what he was doing to them – but then the faintest stirrings of light in the room made me realise that dawn was on the way. My phone alarm was set for 5:00am anyway, so it hardly seemed worth bothering.

At 4:00am the room came alive. Watching the sunrise was a vital part of the Hua Shan experience, but that was still an hour away; I think everyone just wanted to get the hell out of that room. More than a few stern words were directed at the snorer as the room emptied, a torrent of angry Chinese invective that seemed to surprise him. This ended abruptly, however, when he stood up, hocked a lungful of snot onto the floor… and began pulling on a police uniform.

Suddenly you could hear a pin drop, as the last occupants of the room packed their gear in shocked silence.

It made me quite glad I hadn't physically assaulted him in the night.

We ate our last pots of instant noodles on the darkened deck, and slowly, feeling every step in leg muscles still burning from the previous day's climb, we headed upwards.

As we went, we passed hundreds of people waiting to see the dawn; they thronged the path, making it more of a shoving match than a hike. Many of them had followed the 'boring route' up overnight, in a throwback to times where climbing in the dark was considered safer because the danger was invisible. There was no sign of the sun as we moved past them, nor would there be; a dense curtain of vegetation shadowed most of the route. But hell, they were the ones who'd invested all this effort in seeing the sunrise. Let them stand wherever the hell they wanted.

I was more concerned with something else that Hua Shan had to offer – something every bit as infamous as yesterday's crazy vertical staircases.

As it happened, we did see the dawn. By not waiting for it, we'd already climbed higher than most by the time it arrived, and emerged onto the crest of a bare ridge. It wasn't as impressive as the crowds suggested; even this high up a sacred mountain, we were still only an hour from the city. As a result, it was more of a smog-rise than anything else.

But there were other benefits to being up early.

By the time we reached the East Peak, we were alone.

Which was perfect, as we were about to walk the plank.

Possibly more famous even than the photo of the vertical stairs, internet footage of the Hua Shan Plank Walk has gone truly viral, with millions of views cementing its status as the World's Most Dangerous Hiking Trail.

Now though, a system of safety wires had been rigged up, and a simple shoulder harness was required to be worn by anyone attempting the plank walk. The thrill-seeker in me would rather have done it without, but Roo never would have, so the harnesses at least meant she could join me on this adventure.

Amazingly we were the first customers to arrive, and the staff were still setting up as I handed them the equivalent of $15.

Together, clipped onto the safety wire, we descended a series of metal rungs fastened into the rock. From the top they simply vanished into the abyss, but following them down several metres brought us to a tiny ledge chiselled from the cliff. From here a pair of gnarled wooden planks hung suspended in fresh air; bolted to the rock face, they looked as old as the mountain itself, and utterly unsuited to the task of bearing the weight of a person.

Onto the planks we ventured, shuffling along them with our safety clips clacking. Beside and below the planks was nothing at all; a sheer drop thousands of feet down the mountainside, with no handrail, no lip – nothing but the narrow, weather-beaten boards, which between them were less than two feet wide.

It was awesome.

With no-one else there, we stopped for photos, daring each other to lean out into the void, trusting our harnesses to prevent a long fall and a violent death. Even knowing I was safe, I couldn't quite force my body to let go; my hands clutched the strap that connected me to the safety line, which had an alarming degree of elasticity to it. People viewing the photos later on were disgusted, pointing out just how little protection such a simple harness really gave us. But it allowed us to overcome the heart-stopping sensation of being so exposed, so impossibly high up, and so utterly far from the comfort and security of solid ground.

It also allowed me to make the world's worst attempt at *Gangnam Style*, which Roo filmed with trembling hands. I'd promised myself I'd do this, hoping I would finally create a video worth sharing with the world. As of this moment, it's had almost thirty-five views on YouTube, proving once and for all that I should stick to what I'm good at.

I just need to figure out what that is, first, and then there'll be no stopping me…

After twenty minutes on the plank walk, other people were starting to arrive. We'd been incredibly lucky to have the place to ourselves, as the trip back across the face of the cliff was now littered with Chinese tourists. Passing them meant unclipping from the safety lines whilst they squeezed between us and the rock – definitely one of the more brown-trouser-inducing experiences of the trip. Climbing the metal rungs meant literally climbing over the newcomers, as it obviously hadn't occurred to the staff to develop any kind of turn-taking system, or to limit the number of people on the planks at any one time.

We emerged from the top of the rungs shaking with adrenaline, wide-eyed and exultant, and struggled out of our safety gear. The staff were glad to get their hands on it; the queue for harnesses stretched out of sight back around the mountain.

With that excitement over, we set off to hike the circuit between the peaks – another 8km trek that took us over four hours. I couldn't help but notice more examples of the ongoing Disneyfication process. It beggared belief. We watched a gang of workmen with hammers *chipping the ancient stone steps into gravel* – while another gang built the formwork to pour concrete replacements! Whoever came up with that plan needs shooting, but I bet the government think he's doing a great job.

I also bet he owns a cement factory.

On the other hand, the labour they were using to facilitate these 'repairs' was amazing. We passed several porters, almost all scrawny-looking old men, carrying everything from huge granite blocks, to five-metre-long bundles of steel reinforcing bars on their shoulders! Some of the guys had special back-baskets, and carried walking sticks that they could prop underneath the baskets when they stopped for a breather. I didn't want to think how many times these guys must have climbed this mountain. Today. With thirty kilos of stone on their backs...

Incredible.

The circuit of the peaks was, unsurprisingly, full of stairs. They branched off the main trail, winding away up random rock faces for no apparent reason. Some were crazy-steep, some utterly-ridiculously steep – and then, joy of joys, we found more of those fantastic vertical stairs!

I'm a big believer in stepping outside my comfort zone, and because I love Roo so much, I'm a big believer in making her step outside her comfort zone as well.

She doesn't always thank me for it.

But on this occasion she took very little convincing to try the climb – and once she'd had a taste of it, she was eager to try it again. We spent over an hour mucking around on various staircases, taking endless photos and videos which will doubtless never see the light of day.

It was exhilarating, physically demanding, and at times genuinely scary. But we did it – over and over and over, because this expedition had already cost us more than $200, and it was highly unlikely we'd get to come back.

Especially after this book is released.

I doubt they'll even let me into China again.

Eventually, close to dropping from two days of extreme effort, with no sleep and only pot noodles and a handful of Oreos to eat, we decided to call it a day.

After all, we still had to get back down...

Anyone who has climbed a lot of stairs knows, it's toughest on the way down.

Going up burns your thigh muscles, but that's what they're designed for. On the way down, knees and ankles bear the brunt of the punishment; gravity, rather than helping you, makes each impact more powerful, hammering the cartilage in your joints and sending shockwaves up your spine.

All in all, it wasn't something we were looking forward to.

Shave My Spider!

Plus, we were now perilously low on water.

And it was scorching hot – we were sweating like whores on payday.

As we stood at the top of the Soldier's Path, I glanced at Roo.

She looked like I felt. We were trying to brace ourselves for another stair-climbing odyssey, another vertical marathon, and neither of us were particularly enthusiastic.

"Bugger it. Shall we take the cable car?" I asked.

"Oh hell yes," she replied.

So we did.

Please don't tell anyone.

Water Features

The following day, we caught our train to *Chengdu*.
For once, the journey went off without a hitch, which was just as well – the hitchless version consisted of sixteen hours on hard seats, swamped by our luggage, beset by noodle-sellers, constantly jostled by the infinite queue for hot water and deafened by live infomercials every half an hour.
If there had been a hitch, I don't think we'd have survived it.
Not with our sanity intact, at any rate.
Amazingly, the station had a taxi rank – an incredibly rare phenomenon we'd encountered only once, outside Beijing train station, and something we would never see again after Chengdu. We waited in line for taxis next to a fence, the other side of which was thronged with hideously disfigured beggars. This was a tragic side of China we hadn't encountered so far, and what I saw now turned my stomach. One man lay sprawled on a blanket, his ruined leg exposed – and I mean, exposed to the bone. It looked like a prop from a zombie movie, the flesh completely eaten away leaving the grey-ish bone to protrude from his angry, putrid flesh. I'd never seen a wound like it, and could hardly believe the man was even alive, let alone camped out in front of the station. I pushed a few notes through the fence, but that was a mistake

as every beggar in the place suddenly pressed towards us, thrusting pox-ridden hands, gigantic tumours, shrivelled claws and stumps of limbs through the fence at us. I threw up in my mouth on the way to the taxi, and couldn't get the image of that poor bloke's leg out of my head for days. I remembered a friend telling me, after his visit to Hong Kong, that he'd been mobbed by beggars in a subway, and had been advised by his Chinese contacts never to walk through the underpasses beneath the freeways. He'd been told that a depressingly common practice amongst peasants, who found themselves with mouths they couldn't afford to feed, was to cut the legs off their children so that they could 'work' as beggars in the city.

The phrase 'life is cheap' was never more appropriate than in China.

I guess that's what happens when there's over a billon of you.

The taxi driver found our hostel, which was another stroke of luck as we never would have; the only sign of its presence was a scrolling LED sign above a single darkened doorway. 'COMFORT INN' the sign read, if you watched it for long enough.

Except the name of the place, at least as far as Booking.com was concerned, was 'Dexin Coatin Hotel'. Clearly, they were in disguise – a popular ruse for attracting customers, or so I'm told.

From the check-in desk, stairs led up to a lobby on the first floor, which was decked out with chairs and tables made from beautifully-polished solid tree stumps. The area, which doubled as a restaurant, was dominated by a huge homemade pond – complete with its own breeding population of mosquitos.

Our room, however, was simple and relatively clean-ish.

And the bed was so comfortable that we fell into it, and didn't surface for the better part of two days.

By the time we emerged, we had established that our mission here in Chengdu was twofold; firstly, we were here to visit the world-famous Panda Research and Breeding Centre, where we'd be able to see more of the cuddly black and white chappies in one morning than most people do in their entire lives.

Secondly, and more pressingly, we had to accomplish the first phase in what had become known as Operation: GetTheHellOutOfChina! The difficulty we'd encountered so far in booking train tickets paled in comparison to the task we now had to accomplish; with only nine days left on our visa, we somehow had to navigate from Chengdu, via overnight bus to the ancient town of Lijiang, where we could again pick up the train as far as Kunming – which, rumour had it, was the only place where the twenty-six hour cross-border bus into Laos could be caught. When I say rumour, I'm not even joking – the only clues I'd been able to find to this bus's existence were in the comments on a travel forum, and the blog of a bloke who'd done it two years ago in the opposite direction. Booking websites featuring price guides and illustrated timetables may well have existed in Chinese, but the only references I'd been able to discover in several hours of patchy internet trawling were incomplete and inconclusive.

But they had to be right.

Because as far as I could tell, there was no other way out of China. Not without going back to Beijing and getting on a plane, and we were already a bit late for that.

Back when we'd met Tim and Charlotte in Vietnam, they'd bequeathed us a document that became our Chinese Bible. It was half a piece of A4 paper with a list of destinations scribbled in biro. Beneath each city, Charlotte had added the name of a hostel or hotel they'd stayed at, and a piece of advice about something to do there. Because Tim and Charlotte were already vastly more experienced travellers than me and Roo – and because I am, at heart, a very lazy person – I'd based our trip around China entirely on the contents of that piece of paper.

And so it was that we'd come to Chengdu, hoping to stay in a hostel called the Traffic Inn, where the English-speaking staff would be able to help us with our ticket booking dilemma.

Except the Traffic Inn was full.

Which was why we were staying in the hotel that was pretending to be a Comfort Inn. Pretending badly, I might add; the advertised free breakfast, which I'd stupidly allowed myself to get excited about, turned out to be a bowl of hot water with rice in it, a soggy steamed bun which tasted like polystyrene, and a cold boiled egg. The Egg Marketing Board in the UK use the slogan, 'Eggs make a meal out of anything!'. I wanted to send them a photo of what was in front of me and say, "Prove it!"

We still needed help to book our escape from the country, so we resolved to visit the Traffic Inn anyway, navigating our way there on Chengdu's excellent underground railway.

It was belting it down with rain when we arrived, and the river running past the hostel was in full spate. There was an arched stone bridge a short distance downstream, and the water level had risen so high you could barely float a canoe beneath the centre arch.

The Traffic Inn was the kind of place I wished we'd stayed in throughout China. It would have made everything so much easier! In one visit we were able to fill our bellies with delicious western food, book seats on their trip to the Panda Sanctuary, and check into a room that had become available at short notice.

Ahhh!

We'd planned on exploring more of central Chengdu, but the deluge proved too fierce. We made it back to our hotel soaked to the skin, showered, and immediately packed our stuff for the return journey. We couldn't wait to be surrounded by fellow travellers – people we could chat to, compare notes with, take advice from or just reminisce about our adventures. We'd missed out on this throughout China, because these places were priced to take advantage of the typically cashed-up Western backpacker; in a bizarre reversal, the cost of a private en-suite room in the hotels we'd stayed at would barely buy a single bunk in a youth hostel dorm.

But sometimes, you just have to take one for the team.

The Traffic Inn wasn't cheap, but it would make all our dreams come true.

We woke up in plenty of time for our panda excursion, feeling well-rested and positive. Our bags were ready to go; the only things we hadn't packed were the various bits of technology, all of which I'd left charging overnight.

All of which were now sitting in a puddle.

The rain had returned overnight, battering the Traffic Inn with its fury.

Our room had only one window, which some stroke of design genius had placed directly above the only power socket. The window didn't open, but it didn't need to, as the rain had come straight in anyway, running down the walls to flood the area where every piece of gadgetry we possessed was sitting, plugged into the four-way adaptor. Which was plugged into the mains electricity.

Shit!

Scrambling for our laundry bag, I emptied its contents into the puddle and began mopping. One by one I removed the devices; the phone, which made a squelching sound when I picked it up; Roo's tablet, with water dripping from its plug adaptor; and the battery charger for our waterproof camera, which, ironically, was the only bit of it that wasn't waterproof.

Miraculously, most of it survived – even the four-way, which I actually had to pour the water out of! The phone was never the same again, having become stuck in 'car mode', which was a bit of a pain as it was the only camera I was allowed to touch. Between that, and the deteriorating condition of Roo's lens (since landing on it in Vietnam), we were running out of options for photos.

"I know I say this a lot," I admitted, "but this time it's *really* not my fault!"

Before we left for the Panda Sanctuary, I mentioned the flooding incident to the young lad on duty in reception. I brought my phone up to his desk, opened the back, and tipped the water out onto the surface. It wasn't a vast amount of liquid, but it was rather more than you're meant to have inside your phone.

"Oh!" said the lad, "Sorry!"

And that was the extent of his interest.

"You might have a problem with the window," I explained, trying to make it seem important, "you might need to get it fixed."

"Oh yes – window, very bad," he agreed.

I gave up.

I borrowed a piece of paper from his desk and used our permanent marker to make a sign for the power socket:

'WARNING – DO NOT USE WHEN RAINING!'

I was probably wasting my time. No maintenance report had been filed. Only the receptionist had any idea what had happened, and he didn't seem terribly concerned. The cleaners wouldn't be able to read the sign, and would almost certainly throw it away as soon as we vacated the room.

Frowning, I tapped the socket, causing water to spill out of the housing. It seemed likely that rain penetrating the wall was travelling down it using the same channel as the electrical conduits. Assuming the wires were even *in* conduits...

I crossed out **'WHEN RAINING'** and replaced it with **'EVER!!!'**

For all the good it would do.

Pandamonium

Let me get this out first: Pandas are utterly adorable. They lumber. They waddle. They fall over. They peer around themselves myopically, have a permanently-smiling mouth and a friendly expression that seems to say, "Come here! I won't slice you with my claws! I only want a hug…"

They may be rather flatulent, and a bugger to keep clean, but they are gorgeous beyond belief.

And the only creature in the entire animal kingdom where the cuddly-toy version actually looks more realistic.

We were lucky right off the bat, overhearing a German tour guide telling his group it was baby-feeding time. We followed them and came to an enclosure with half a dozen chubby panda cubs, about the size (and fluffiness!) of Old English Sheepdogs. They didn't look much like babies, but we watched them flop around on the wooden feeding platforms, whilst their keepers delivered a spiel in Chinese. The enclosure wasn't amazing, given how much importance both China and the world in general places on these animals. The whole centre felt more set up for the tourists than the pandas, but that could be my personal prejudice talking. I'm well aware of how breeding programs like this draw attention away from the plight of the wild panda. Every time a new baby is born, the media of the world crowd round for the best footage, beaming it triumphantly to every corner of the globe. But the truth is, no panda cub born in captivity has ever survived in the wild – largely because the Chinese government seems to have no interest in protecting that wild, or the handful of pandas it still contains. They've created dozens of reserves which serve only to make it appear like they're doing something; most have no pandas in them, some are only a mile wide, and all are open to wealthy Chinese tour groups who pay a mint to glimpse pandas in their natural habitat.

I should point out that all of this relates to the Giant Panda, the familiar black-and-white furball on the WWF logo. As opposed to Red Pandas, an equally gorgeous, though unrelated species, that is also found in China, and is also highly endangered.

When rich Chinese tourists go in search of Giant Pandas, Red Pandas are also included in the trip – only, they are on the menu.

Apparently they've become a delicacy.

Speaking of Red Pandas, there were several at the Research Centre – thankfully not being served up in the restaurant. They had an enclosure of their very own, which Roo and I headed for as soon as we could tear ourselves away from the 'babies'.

We did a circuit of the Red Panda pad, Roo's sharp eyes spotting two of the animals hiding amidst a decent habitat of living trees and dense undergrowth. I could just make out their cat-sized silhouettes, but it was enough to get me excited.

Red Pandas are one of my favourite animals ever. They're like the lovechild of a bear and a raccoon, only infinitely more adorable – go to Google, if you don't believe me, I guarantee you'll be instantly smitten.

Roo was desperate to get a good photo, but there was a problem; Chinese tourists can generally be heard long before they are seen, and the groups here were amongst the worst. Picture the loudest, most raucous drunk in a Saturday night bar brawl; every Chinese tourist we saw acted like that, shrieking, squabbling, spitting and shoving their way around every attraction we visited. Amusingly enough, shortly after we returned from Asia (spoiler – we survived!), the Chinese Tourist Ministry issued an official directive to its holidaymakers worldwide, demanding they be less rude, less noisy, and show more respect to the nations they visit! You know it's bad when the government has to step in, and being China they didn't stop there – the new rules were written into law, threatening fines as high as $10,000 for tourists who make China look bad on the international scene.

Red Pandas being notoriously shy animals, and nocturnal at any rate, we knew the odds were against us getting a good look at them under these conditions. But we settled in to wait, hopeful they would patrol their territory once the crowds thinned out.

It was a long, frustrating vigil, as tour groups followed family groups, each as loud as the last. After about an hour it began to rain, and finally we had the place to ourselves long enough for the pandas to emerge. Quietly, respectfully, we crept closer, and Roo got her prize photo – though the animal in question was dripping, soaking wet.

It was not alone in that.

After staring at the pandas, there wasn't much else to do.

In fairness, it was a panda sanctuary – the clue is right there in the name. I'm just used to places in the UK, where they've long since had to diversify their activities in the face of dwindling public interest. This place, arguably China's most popular animal-based attraction, had no need of such shenanigans – on a good day as many as 3,000 Chinese sightseers descended on it, and annually it receives over a million visitors.

Compared to, say, Edinburgh Zoo, which gets 600,000.

We bypassed the shiny new information centre, as we'd have left puddles right through their displays. I had a feeling most of the information on display there would be fairly biased; I seriously doubted the true depth of the Giant Panda's plight, or the lack of a decent government response to it, would be showcased.

And neither would this little fact:
China still owns *all* the world's pandas.
True story!

Back in the 1970s, several breeding pairs were given away to other countries as diplomatic gifts. None of them ever bred successfully though, leading to the common belief that all pandas are gay. Sadly, all the 'gifted' pandas have since passed on, and in 1984 China adopted a new strategy. Its pandas, still highly coveted by the outside world, would now only be available to rent – with a price tag of *one million* US dollars, per panda, *per year!* And get this – under the terms of the standard ten-year loan agreements, all cubs born to rented pandas immediately belong to China, and must be transported back there as soon as they are able to be separated from their parents! Every panda, in every zoo in the entire world, is currently subject to these conditions.

I know, right? Hard to believe. And no wonder the Chinese are more interested in breeding captive pandas than protecting wild ones. But it just goes to show the kind of terms you can achieve, when you're negotiating from a position of total market dominance.

To be honest, if I had a million dollars lying around somewhere, I think I'd be sorely tempted.

They are pretty cute…

Back at the Traffic Inn, I managed to make some headway in the ticket booking process. I very carefully counted the days forward, gave all the details to the receptionist, then sat back and watched as he made the ten-minute phone call that I never could have. He arranged to have our train tickets from *Lijiang* to *Kunming* delivered later that afternoon, and explained that the bus to Lijiang departed from a terminal less than a block from the hostel. He then made a flurry of calls to sources in Kunming and established that there was indeed a long-distance bus leaving daily from there to Laos.

It should always be like this, I thought; China made easy!
And I guess, for most people it probably is.
I just make bad decisions.
Lots of bad decisions.

After a picnic lunch in our room, we went for a walk along the river. The rain had stopped, and the water level had receded dramatically, now passing a good metre below the bridge's arch.

"The river's still raging," Roo said.

"Oh! I was just about to say how much slower it seemed."

"Yes," she agreed, "it's quietly raging."

It's moments like this that inspired me to keep a folder on my laptop called 'Hilarious Things Roo Says'. That way I can look through it every so often, and remind her of my favourites.

It also means I get to use them in my writing.

Like this:

Roo: (reading a book) "This book is going in one ear and other the other."

Me: "That sounds quite painful."

And:

Roo: (spotting a classic car) "What's the little statue on the front of that Jaguar? Is it a horse? Or a dog?"

Me: "Um… it's a jaguar."

I think the lesson to be learned here is, never marry a writer, because we are all bastards.

Later that afternoon we strolled around the centre of Chengdu, snacking on cheap street food. On the advice of Tim and Charlotte, we wandered over to the 'People's Park', the largest green space in the city. It was quite a trip – and by that I mean, the kind of trip people get after taking hard drugs.

For starters, the People's Park was full of people.

Nothing too surprising in that, I hear you say. And you'd be right. Except, the people in People's Park weren't behaving like people normally do.

The Chinese have a wonderful attitude to outdoor activities. They seem to embrace any opportunity to stand outside, doing things most Westerners prefer to keep behind closed doors. They obviously don't care what other people think of them – or perhaps they've grown up in a society where people are less judgemental of each other, and are less insecure as a result?

Either way, it's a positive and refreshing trait, to be able to partake of their favourite hobbies in full view of the world.

And more importantly, it gave us the chance to point and laugh.

Everyone was engaged in an activity of some kind, each group completely ignoring the next. No-one seemed the slightest bit self-conscious, which was amazing considering the ridiculous things many of them were doing.

Dancing, for example, was well represented. Not well organised; there were small groups and individuals scattered all over the place, some practising their moves in rows as though in class, some pin-wheeling around the park on their own. Not all of them had music.

Lots of people were doing exercises. None of them were actually getting much exercise though – walking backwards, marching slowly on the spot, or turning in circles, they were the kind of exercises one could do without risk of breaking a sweat. Which was probably for the best, as most of the participants were dressed in business suits and shiny shoes, posh dresses or jeans.

Following the path, we came across a large group of octogenarians armed with broadswords. Carefully, precisely, they flowed through the motions of Tai Chi, slicing the air around them with their blades. We watched, spellbound, as the old ladies completed their pattern, and swapped their broadswords for spears.

I bet their grandsons never got bullied.

In yet another area, people were painting intricate Chinese characters onto the flagstones with water, creating beautiful calligraphy even as it evaporated seconds later. They had specially-shaped sponges on sticks, allowing them to write standing up – it occurred to me that someone, somewhere had identified this niche market and set about designing and selling these things. Sponges on sticks. For people that wanted to write in water on the pavement.

Seriously.

There was even an inter-park dating site, where despairing mothers hung hand-written personal ads for their sons from low-hanging tree branches! Oh, how badly do I wish I'd been able to read them?

But my favourite had to be a small group of middle-aged women who, with laser-beam focus and deadly seriousness, were practicing their fiercest catwalk moves. Honestly, I couldn't make this up. Wearing what appeared to be their ordinary, day-to-day clothes, they strode down a strip of red fabric laid out as a runway, pouting left and right to give the imaginary paparazzi their best angle. At the end of their walk they posed, smouldering, then turned and pranced back the way they'd come, making way for the next lady in line. All this, in an unmarked area in the middle of a paved square in the park.

Surreal is the only word that describes it.

Right beside China's next top models, an old bloke in a vest and trousers was camping it up like crazy, dancing freestyle to music only he could hear. He twirled, he lunged, he cha-cha-cha'd. At first I thought he was trying to hit on the catwalk-walkers, but then he seemed to be taking the piss out of them. Or something in between? They didn't even seem to notice him, being far too focused on perfecting their poses. I pride myself on being impossible to embarrass, but this was too much; inwardly I wanted to cringe on their behalf, only I couldn't decide who I felt more awkward for.

Before I could decide, I was accosted by a trumpet player. He was part of a loose group of men standing a few metres away, playing an assortment of instruments. Not together, you understand – just playing their own tunes, in their own time. Whilst together.

"English?" asked the trumpet player.

"Australian!" Roo replied.

"Oh! Australia!" said the man, and proceeded to play a chorus of *Waltzing Matilda* on his trumpet.

"Thank-you!" we shouted, as he shimmied off, still playing.

By this point my grip on reality was becoming tenuous.

We dodged past people playing twelve-a-side

badminton, side-stepped a group who seemed to be just *bouncing,* and found ourselves back on the edge of the park. Beyond a last fringe of leaves, traffic and commerce and concrete pressed in again.

Roo turned to me. "Did that really happen?" she asked.

I shook my head, doubtfully. "I honestly didn't think China could get any weirder."

"That's it," said Roo, "Next time we eat street food, I'm picking off the mushrooms."

Slumber Party

Having been on several sleeper buses in Vietnam, we were pretty sure we knew what to expect from our twenty-two hour, overnight trip to *Lijiang*.

We were wrong.

Vietnam may not be famed as a centre for advanced technology, but compared to China they had freakin' moon rockets. The Chinese bus, far from being a sleek, purpose-built modern conveyance, was a shitty old coach retrofitted with welded steel frames and plywood planks for beds. It didn't have pillows. It didn't have mattresses! It also didn't have a toilet, which was of some concern. Despite the best efforts of the doctors in the UK, I was back to peeing every two hours – into a bottle, if I couldn't find a toilet. So far, in nearly four months of travel, I'd managed to avoid this unique humiliation – but if it was going to happen, it was going to happen in China. I'd never seen a long-distance bus without a toilet.

Before we boarded it, I bought a spare water bottle. Just in case.

The journey began quite promisingly.

The driver sent us right to the back, into what were either the best seats on the bus, or the worst. Time would tell. I took the top bunk, as Roo was afraid of falling out of it – a very real issue given the lack of seatbelts, or any other form of protection. Roo caught a couple of cockroaches trying to snuggle up with her, but apart from that the bus was practically empty.

At least until we crawled across Chengdu to a different bus station, where we sat for another two hours. By the time we left, the bus was so full there were people lying in the aisles.

Getting out of the city took another two hours. It was endless; a forest of skyscrapers, the traffic gridlocked in between them, the sky a relentless battleship-grey.

In the bed in front of me, a shrivelled old woman coughed and hacked, sounding like she was mere minutes away from dying of TB. Each sickening session concluded with her spitting a great wad of what had to be lung tissue into a small plastic bin the bus company had thoughtfully provided for just such occurrences.

Well, she didn't always use the bin.

She had a young boy with her, maybe five or six years old, and the two of them fitted quite well into their bunk. Unlike me and Roo, who lay there with our knees up to make room for our heads.

The first part of the journey was made on the freeway, and wasn't too bad.

The bus stopped for dinner at around 9pm; we bought and ate pot noodles, and congratulated ourselves for coping so well with the journey.

Then we set off again, into the night.

And began the journey from hell.

Leaving the freeway without slowing down, the bus climbed high into the mountains, on roads not substantially wider than the bus itself. The terrain switched from relatively smooth asphalt to the surface of Mars, throwing vehicle and passengers all over the place. Before long torrential rain engulfed the bus, but that didn't give the driver pause – he kept the pedal relentlessly to the metal, swinging around corners so tight I could feel the back end skid out. Never a good thing when there are precipices with a thousand-foot drop on one side, and a solid cliff face on the other. Lightning blasted the mountainside all around us, the accompanying thunder so loud it shook the bus.

"Rubber tyres means we can't be struck, right?" Roo called up from below.

I've never been entirely convinced about the physics of this.

"Yeah, that's right," I called back down to her. Hoping it was true.

We stopped in the middle of nowhere to take on more passengers, the driver caring not one whit that the bus was already chock-a-block. The newcomers obviously didn't have tickets and were simply bribing the driver, which probably why he was keen to squeeze every last one of them on.

We ended up with a bloke reeking of booze lying in the aisle right next to Roo, which given the uncomfortably narrow nature of the cots we'd been allocated meant they were basically sleeping in full body contact. She was more than a little freaked out by this, so I offered to switch with her – just as the bus lurched off, and began ascending once more.

How big was this bloody mountain? We'd been going uphill forever. The road was so knackered the bus was shaking itself apart. I braced myself with all four limbs against the metal bed frame and the roof, but it was impossible to sustain – every time I shifted position a sudden jolt would throw me against the window, or, on at least two occasions, right out of the top bunk and into the aisle.

Which wasn't much fun for the bloke lying there.

But that's what you get for not buying a ticket.

Gratefully, Roo hauled herself up into the top bunk, but getting any kind of rest was impossible.

Apart from the insane angle of the bus up the mountain, the terrifying speed it was making, and the sheer violence of its passing, she discovered something else when the rain got harder – her window leaked. She quickly decided that sleeping in a puddle was the lesser of two evils though, and learned to cope with it, whilst I continued to enjoy the company of the stinking Chinese stranger – who had miraculously fallen fast asleep, and was snoring like the village drunk.

It remains one of the worst nights of my travelling life, but dawn found us stopping at a filthy concrete shack which contained a long trough for us to piss into. It was the toilet! After seven hellish hours without one, I didn't give a toss that twenty Chinese men of assorted ages stood and stared at me as I peed.

It did make me wonder about the quality of the female facilities, though.

One look at Roo's face as she climbed back on the bus told me not to ask.

Now, I'm generally quite a positive bloke, and when things get bad I tend to say, "it could always be worse."

This bus journey was the exception to that rule.

I didn't think it could possibly get any worse.

Until the old woman who'd been spitting into the bin all night shuffled back on. The young lad she was traveling with hadn't got off the bus to use the toilet. Instead, as we looked on in horror, she encouraged him to drop his pants and piss into the same bin.

He was less than three feet from my head when he did it, and that was where the bin full of piss stayed for the rest of the journey. The old woman congratulated him afterwards, as though he'd been a good little boy.

Suddenly I needed the toilet again – and not to pee into. It's remarkably hard to vomit into a plastic water bottle.

I spent the next stage of our journey contemplating the stench, as the driver pulled the bus up by the side of the road, in the middle of nowhere – and went to sleep in the aisle.

For four hours.

Amazingly, against all the odds, exhaustion won out and I dozed off.

I woke up when the wet patch from Roo's bunk started dripping on my face.

I was still three feet from a bucket of fresh piss, my bunk was vibrating in time to the old ladies' death rattles, and I was being spooned by the alcoholic tramp in the aisle.

Yup – I've had better nights.

It's fair to say, we weren't in the best of moods when we arrived in Lijiang.

When none of the taxi drivers hanging around the station would take us, a local woman waved us into her funky red Postman Pat van and gave us a lift. She was very friendly, chatting away, not at all concerned that we couldn't answer her back. She unwrapped her lunch as she drove, and must have noticed my eyes tracking her sandwich – so she gave me half of it.

The kindness of strangers can go a long way towards righting what's wrong in your world. Such a shame there wasn't enough sandwich for Roo.

Lijiang is a tiny place, with little over a million inhabitants.

Sorry, I meant that it's a tiny place *for China.*

The Old Town was the bit we wanted to see – a UNESCO-designated World Heritage Site, and one that has miraculously doubled in size since being awarded this status. Planning regulations have been put in place to ensure that all new buildings resemble the old, historical buildings – meaning there's nothing stopping you from demolishing a piece of 800-year-old architecture, so long as what you build in its place looks similar.

It was happening all around us, with several rows of 'authentic' ten-storey apartment blocks nearing completion opposite the Old Town entrance.

But I promise, that's the very last time I'll moan about China's approach to preserving their heritage.

Bloody idiots.

However, the preserved part of Lijiang is beautiful.

It was based around three rivers, the buildings following them as they twisted and turned, resulting in a labyrinthine network of tiny streets with no discernable order. Getting lost is pretty much the number one activity in Lijiang, so after checking into our guest house – a delightfully restored, two-storey courtyard house – we set out to do just that.

The narrow alleyways bustled with local tourists, but here and there we spotted the occasional Westerner. Cafés and souvenir shops lined the wider streets, swathed in ivy and bedecked with flowers.

We ate all kinds of snacks from a wide variety of vendors, filling ourselves with noodles, fried potato twists, curry and steamed dumplings, for considerably less than the price of a meal in one of the posh cafés. After this we simply roamed, finding picturesque bridges, small squares that opened unexpectedly, and as we worked our way further from the touristy areas, more twisting, narrower alleyways, where ramshackle brick buildings struggled to hold each other upright, old women scrubbed their doorsteps and washing hung from upper-story balconies.

Roo took so many photos she got cramp in her trigger finger.

Sadly, Lijiang was only a stepping stone for us. We passed one very pleasurable night in the Garden Inn hotel, though we couldn't help but nip out to roam the streets again after dark, and probably spent more time outside the hotel than in it.

The next morning a taxi arrived to take us to the train station, squeezing through alleyways so tight we couldn't have opened the doors. Cars were banned in the Old Quarter after 6:00am, for obvious reasons, so we were actually glad of our early start.

"Such a pity we have to leave," Roo said, staring out the windows as the old buildings crawled past at point-blank range.

"I know. I really like it here."

The taxi crept around a bend and in front of us was the main road, already congested, heralding our return to contemporary China.

"If we'd been here a bit longer we could have gone right to the top of Jade Dragon Snow Mountain." Roo pointed to a single peak rising beyond the haze of modern Lijiang.

"Cool! That sounds like it would have been a challenge!"

"Not really," she said. "It's got a chairlift."

The Difference A Day Makes

Our brief stay in Lijiang left us feeling restored.

Sure, we'd had some rough times, but from here on in it should be plain sailing.

We had our tickets, supplied by the Chengdu Traffic Inn, that would take us as far as Kunming, and from there we had only one task to accomplish: booking the bus out of China.

The timing would be tight. I'd allowed two days from arriving in Kunming to departing on a bus we had yet to buy tickets for. This left us with a single spare day on our visas, before we became criminals in the eyes of Chinese Immigration.

I was saving this day for emergencies.

Standing outside the sweeping, modern façade of Lijiang train station, I felt free. Uplifted. Not only because we were on our way out of China but because, for that brief moment, I felt quite content to be *in* China. Roo was by my side, happy and talkative, full of the plans she had for her photographs of the Old Town.

We joined the queue of people entering the station and heaved our bags onto the now-familiar conveyor belts for the x-ray machines.

I wondered if they'd ever actually stopped a genuine

threat.

Probably not.

But they stopped me.

Roo was struggling back into her rucksack when a rather severe-looking lady pulled mine off the conveyor belt onto an inspection table. Her colleagues called out to her as she peeked into the various pockets. Then she opened the velcro pouch attached to my rucksack's waist strap, and pulled out my *other* knife.

Oh nooo…

It was my penknife. A small folding one with a locking blade, it was what we used to cut cheese and salami for our picnics. It had travelled with me for as long as I can remember, always there on my waist strap through country after country. I'd carried it through at least twenty different airports, and as part of my checked-in luggage it had been around the world twice. It had been fastened to my bag throughout the length of China, and no-one had commented on it once.

And it was the first Valentine's Day present Roo had ever bought me.

I was *not* losing it to some damn Chinese bureaucracy.

"No, no," the scanner lady was telling me. She opened the blade and pointed at it, shaking her head.

I sighed. "Look…"

I argued with her for some time, getting nowhere because she had about as much English as I had Mandarin. Roo was getting nervous, so I sent her to join the crowd shuffling through the ticket barriers.

"Get on the train and save our seats," I told her, "I'll have one last try at sorting this out and then I'll come to you."

"You promise?" she asked.

"Of course."

"Okay. But don't do anything stupid…"

"I won't."

Turning back to the woman, I tried a different tack. "What's your name? Write it down for me." I pulled a pen and paper from my daysack.

"Eh? Name? Eh?"

"I want to complain to your supervisor. I need your name."

"Oh! No, cannot…"

"You can write your name, here. Now. I need it to complain."

"No, cannot," she said, covering her name badge with one hand.

"Then get your supervisor."

She left with the knife, and I stood there, eyeballing the rest of the x-ray staff for what seemed like an age. If the supervisor didn't show soon, I was going to have to abandon my attempt and make a dash for the train.

Then a slightly older, immaculately-groomed lady emerged from an office and came towards me.

"I'm sorry," she said, her English sounding far more confident, "you cannot take this knife on the train."

"But I've taken this knife from Beijing to Zhengzhou to Xi'an, to Chegdu. On many trains. Every time my bag was scanned. No-one else had a problem with it."

"Yes, maybe different there. But here, you cannot take."

"But why?"

"Because, can be used… as weapon. Is dangerous."

"Are you kidding me? It's a penknife! And I'm on holiday, here. Do you really think I'm going to stab someone? And spend the rest of my life in a Chinese prison?"

"Yes, not you, but someone on the train can take."

"I promise that no-one on that train is going anywhere near my bags. I keep them very close and safe."

"You don't know, maybe you sleeping… is too dangerous."

"Look – I'll wrap it. Or you wrap it. Use tape, so it can't be used."

"No, sorry, cannot take."

"I'm not leaving here without it."

"Cannot take…"

I was getting nowhere. Waiting for the supervisor had cost me valuable time; Roo had disappeared, along with all the people waiting for our train. The tunnel leading to the platforms contained only a solitary ticket-checker, cooling her heels.

I had a sudden moment of revelation. This knife, sentimental as it may be, was just a thing. A possession. In the grand scheme of things, it didn't matter at all. Whereas Roo was up there somewhere, alone on a train bound for Kunming, almost certainly starting to panic. Announcements had come and gone over the PA system. I had no idea what they were about, but it was a good guess at least one of them was a warning of imminent departure.

Roo would be as upset as me by the loss of that knife, but not nearly as upset as she'd be if I missed the train over it.

Time to go.

"Okay, okay," I told the woman, "keep the knife. It cost one hundred US dollars – maybe you can sell it."

I grabbed my rucksack, swung it onto my back, and pulled my laptop bag on in front of me. The dreaded backpacker turtle – my least-favourite mode of travel, slow, ungainly, and an obvious target for thieves and pickpockets. I waddled across the empty station concourse and flashed my ticket at the lady by the barrier. She snatched the thing off me and studied it intently, which I thought was a bit unnecessary. Then she thrust it back at me and yelled in my face.

I ignored her. Now was not the time to fight the language barrier. Whatever her problem was, she would have to deal with it on her own.

I made to move past her, but she blocked my way, still jabbering at me. I glanced around; she was making a scene in the otherwise empty station, and the few people still around were staring at us.

No matter.

I strode on, shrugging the woman off as she grabbed my arm. She was definitely agitated about something, but I couldn't deal with it right now; *just get to Roo*, I thought, *that's all that matters.*

The woman was screaming into her walkie-talkie as I set off down the tunnel. I could feel the ground sliding out from under me, a sense of vertigo I get when things suddenly go horribly wrong.

What the hell is happening?

I glanced back to see her gesticulating frantically towards the staff at the x-ray machines. Another announcement drowned out any sound she was making, and I recognised the word *'Kunming.'*

Oh-oh.

Roo was about to be transported halfway across China on her own.

I *had* to get to that platform.

I was speed-walking down the tunnel as fast as possible, and as I turned onto the ramp up to the platform I noticed a group of people in uniform doing the same about twenty metres behind me.

Only they were armed with automatic weapons.

Shit!

I had no idea what was going on, but someone must be pissed off about something. It was a race now – as long as I could get to Roo before they confronted me, we could straighten this all out. If they managed to collar me before then – well, shit was going to get complicated real fast. I had all the details of our hostel in Kunming. Roo would have no idea where to go, and no way to contact me since I had our only phone. And the bastard thing still didn't work.

She had all the money – every single *yuan*, and our only bank card, tucked away in her purse. She also had every scrap of food, every mouthful of water... and I had her passport.

Words can't even begin to describe how utterly buggered we would be if she was on that train when it left, and I wasn't.

Halfway up the concrete ramp I broke into a jog. I swung around the bannister at the top and surged onto the platform, adrenaline pumping. The row of carriages beside me stretched off into infinity, but they weren't moving; doors were standing open here and there, so I still had a chance. I took a break from scanning the carriage numbers to check behind me, and immediately wished I hadn't. A pair of what looked like SWAT troopers were giving chase, charging down the platform towards me. I passed a window with a '13' in it; our carriage was only three cars ahead. With little choice, I accelerated, running like a drunkard with the weight of my rucksack swaying me from side to side.

Just... Don't... Fall...

I was close now; I'd passed the mid-point of the previous carriage, and there had been no whistles or obvious signs of imminent departure. I was going to make it!

An angry cry sounded behind me as I came abreast of the right door and hauled myself up through it. By some miracle the carriage wasn't crowded, and I pushed my way down the aisle with minimum commotion. Roo wasn't hard to spot – her brightly-coloured hair, her pale face, and the terror writ large across it – all these were visible from the other end of the carriage. I bustled up to her, dripping sweat, panting from my exertions, and grabbed the back of the chair opposite her to keep myself upright.

"I'm here love!" I gasped.

"Thank God for that!" she sobbed.

"But I've got a bit of bad news..."

Her eyes went wide – and then focussed on the uniformed officers storming down the aisle towards me.

"Tony, what...?"

And that was when they grabbed me.

Later, Roo told me it was possibly the most scared she'd been in her entire life. Sitting there in what was already approaching blind panic, she'd been treated to the sight of me leaping aboard and sprinting the length of the carriage, closely pursued by two Chinese policemen armed with machine guns.

Quite how she maintained bladder control is beyond me.

I was collared from behind and hauled round to face the officers, and by then the lady from the security barriers had caught up. Her high-speed jabbering produced one recognisable word – ticket – so I held it up, somewhat crinkled and slightly soggy from being in my hand during my 100-metre sprint.

The ticket was snatched away, carefully scrutinised, and then thrust back in my face.

"NO! NO!" was all I could make out, shouted by the security woman in time with her finger stabbing the ticket. "NO!"

I shrugged. I was past caring. I was back together with Roo, and whatever happened we were going to stay that way. This woman could shriek and yammer all she wanted, but unless she found a better way of convincing me what her problem was, I was determined to stand there making puzzled faces at her. Then another pair of uniforms joined the party – including the supervisor from the x-ray machines. I could hear Roo's sharp intake of breath when she recognised the woman.

"Oh God Tony, what did you do?"

"Love, I have no fucking idea."

And then a much calmer voice entered the conversation. The x-ray lady was a higher level of authority, and she clearly had more practice at this sort of thing. "Your ticket," she told me, "it is no good."

"What? I bought it yesterday! From my hostel in Chengdu."

"But is no good. Is already gone!"

"What? I don't understand?"

"This ticket. Is for train already gone! Go, ah, day before."

I blinked. Then studied the ticket more carefully. Amongst boxes and boxes containing microscopic Chinese characters, it had the date on it.

It had yesterday's date on it.

We'd been screwed.

"I only buy yesterday," I told the lady. "Can you change it?"

"Is no good."

"I know. I understand. Can you change ticket? For today?"

"Change ticket? No. Train is full."

I looked down at Roo. She was still sitting in her allocated seat, looking horrified at this turn of events. Poor girl, she was reaching her limit. And about to be stranded here for another night, or longer, with no accommodation booked, nowhere to go, and every possibility that if we missed this train, we'd be too late at the border and would end up illegally overstaying our visa.

Fuck it.

"I'm staying on this train," I told the woman. "I don't care about the ticket. I paid for it, so I'm staying on the train. You can sort this out however you want, but if you want me off this train, you'll have to drag me."

I knew she didn't understand most of what I was saying, but I hoped the tone would convey my message; I was pissed off. And I wasn't going anywhere.

The train gave a lurch, nearly knocking me off my feet, and Roo put her arms out to steady me. The uniformed types exchanged glances and a high-speed debate ensued. The train lurched again, and I could hear the heavy doors being slammed up and down the platform. Again the woman tried to demand something of me – one last attempt, at which I just shook my head – then, as the cops turned and made their way back down the train, she followed. The sight of that heavily armed posse retreating was my happiest for some time. I don't think I'd taken a proper breath since they grabbed me. Now they turned and scowled at me from the far end of the carriage, each waiting their turn to climb down the steps to the platform.

Somehow, I had made it. We had made it.

Roo marvelled at the sight of the officers, clustered around the woman in heated discussion, as the train pulled away. I unfastened my rucksack and collapsed into the seat next to her, a sweaty, trembling mess.

"They kept the knife then?" she asked.

"They did." I was suddenly too weary to imbue the words with emotion.

"Thank God for that," she said.

"Eh?"

"When I saw them chasing you with guns, I thought you'd grabbed the knife and made a run for it."

"What? As if I'd do that!"

"I never know, with you. And they were chasing you! With frigging *machine guns!*"

"I know! Because my ticket had expired. Talk about overreacting."

"I thought you were going to prison for sure."

"Me too, for a minute."

"Please don't leave me again. Not ever."

"I won't, my love. I promise."

She was silent for a few seconds, breathing deeply to calm down.

When she spoke again, there was a quaver to her voice. "Tony, why does this keep happening to us?"

Coming to Kunming

Against the odds, we made it to Kunming.

A guard had forced us to buy another pair of tickets at twice the price. They were valid for standing room only, but our carriage stayed miraculously uncrowded – perhaps because we were approaching the remote fringes of the country – and by switching seats we'd managed to stay sat down for most of the nine-hour journey.

We joined the hordes leaving the station, following signs for 'Taxi'.

They led down a tunnel and onto an access ramp – but not to any taxis.

The rest of the hopefuls shuffled off up the empty ramp, so we followed – out onto the main road outside the station.

Where it looked like a football game was letting out.

Or ten football games.

Thousands of people crammed the pavements, thronging a row of bus stands opposite. It goes without saying there was no taxi rank.

So we walked around for a bit, pushing our way nervously through the crowds.

We both hate being encumbered this way, the size of our bags restricting our view and limiting our manoeuvrability. Crowds are the worst place to be in this situation, so we stood for a while in the middle of the road and tried unsuccessfully to flag down every taxi that passed.

The next half hour was spent dodging a filthy old tramp who kept jumping in front of us and jabbering at us. I showed him the address we were headed to on several occasions, but he hardly glanced at it – just said something that sounded like 'bathroom', and tried to grab my hands.

We did our best to ignore him, but he trailed us, still shouting, as we headed back into the station. I had a new plan, which involved finding the Customer Information booth and asking *them* where to get a taxi. The booth was easy enough to find, labelled as it was in English, but neither of the staff knew a word of the stuff. "Taxi?" I pleaded.

Blank looks.

I wrote 'Taxi' on a piece of paper and showed it to them. Roo pantomimed driving, though to me it looked more like she was milking a cow. After another flurry of discussion, one of the ladies took us outside and pointed us to the row of cash machines.

Hm.

Perhaps it was time to have a word with Roo about her miming skills.

Back on the main road, we looked on in disgust as an elderly bloke squatted in the middle of the pavement, his pants round his ankles, and took a shit.

No-one around him seemed to care.

Was this a common occurrence? I didn't want to know.

"We came out of there at exactly the wrong time," Roo observed.

"Or the right time," I added. "Five minutes later and we might have walked right through that."

We shuddered collectively.

"I really, *really* want to get out of here," Roo moaned.

"Me too," I agreed, glumly. "But how?"

Within minutes we were accosted by our stalker again.

Shouting at us in Chinese and waving three fingers, he followed us down the road. He was irate now, practically screaming at us, but making no other gestures, no attempt to explain what he wanted or was offering. Finally, Roo swung around and bawled at him; "If you don't FUCK OFF, I'm going to punch you!" She was actually trembling with rage – and fear, and borderline panic – and at last the guy took the hint. He skulked off into the crowd, leaving us exactly where we started. Literally; we were stood outside the access ramp, where the 'Taxi' signs had led us.

"Please get us out of here," Roo begged me.

Then, from behind us, I heard the four sweetest words known to man: "Can I help you?"

"YES! Please!" I turned to find a young Chinese girl standing with her friends. "It is very hard to get a taxi here," she said (at which I nodded so fast my vision blurred) – "so, maybe we can share?"

I showed her the address.

"Oh! No, it's the wrong way. Sorry!"

And she was gone.

But an older woman was also craned over our paperwork, and Roo tentatively asked her, "you drive?" She did her best udder-squeezing mime again, and this time the woman nodded. "Forty!" she said.

"Uh... twenty?" I tried.

"Thirty," the woman replied.

"Okay!"

So she beckoned us, and we set off – walking down alleyways, past building sites, mostly down the middle of the road. Buses beeped at us and thundered past with inches to spare, but the woman forged on ahead, heedless. She led us through gridlocked intersections, threading her way between honking cars and scooters, and I joked to Roo that she was leading us to the hotel on foot. It was only 3.5kms away, according to Booking.com...

After a fifteen-minute hike we came to a strip of shops with cars parked outside. She led us to a tiny minivan, and left us squeezing into it while she walked back up the road, shouting into the distance.

"She's gone to look for the driver," Roo said.

"Ha! I just hope it isn't *that* guy!"

But you know what though?

It was.

He snorted when he saw us crammed into the back of his

van.

Roo and I exchanged looks of horror.

Hopefully he wasn't *too* offended that I'd repeatedly told him to bugger off. As we were now kind of at his mercy...

The old bloke ranted at his wife for the entire trip, while she hacked up phlegm-wads and spat them out of the window. I needed no language skills at all to understand their conversation:

"What the eff-ing hell did you say to these arseholes?" he was asking. "I tried to catch them for an hour and a half, and all they did is run away! I chased them all over the bloody station!"

To which I'd have replied (had I been able), "learn the word 'Taxi' you frigging idiot. It is, after all, written on the top of your car!"

I should probably mention at this point that I had made a strenuous effort to learn the Mandarin for 'taxi'. It was difficult without access to Western search engines, but what I found was a five-word phrase: *chéng chū zū qì chē*. It is every bit as difficult to pronounce as it looks, and no-one understood what the hell I was saying anyway. Like we'd discovered with *Zhengzhou*, every stress and accent changed the word completely – and every dialect uses a different accent. No wonder people ignored me – I was probably stood there shouting, "Armpit-octopus-bedspread?"

They'd have thought I was less weird if I'd taken a shit in the street.

It seemed our worst fears were about to be confirmed when the van pulled up in a neighbourhood so unsavoury it made my stomach clench. It looked like the kind of place murderers came to kill time. Ruined apartment blocks and filthy façades hemmed in an alleyway that stank of poo. A canal bordered the road, its water black as pitch and full of floating unmentionables. I scanned the area as we got out of the van, wondering which of the hideously grotty buildings facing us was our destination. None of them appealed. I turned to Roo, and stoped. There behind us, on the other side of that fetid canal, rose a gleaming pink and gold palace. Massive and

gaudy, it looked like a great gay Taj Mahal.
"That can't be it," I breathed.
But it was.

I'd picked the Royal Garden Hotel because it was an amazing deal; a 4-star place at cheaper-than-backpacker prices. It was bound to have something wrong with it, but so had every backpacker's we'd stayed at. At least with 4 stars, there was a long way to fall before it became intolerable.

At this point I'd be happy if it was waterproof.

And to be honest, it looked fantastic.

We crossed the black canal by a footbridge and entered a lobby the size of a nightclub. Marble gleamed everywhere, a vast chandelier hung above us; it was like stepping into the grand ballroom on the Titanic.

The staff seemed a little surprised to see us. I got the impression they thought the place was closed for renovation. The receptionist held the print-out of my booking confirmation as though he'd never seen such a thing in his life. But a Chinese equivalent of Google Translate helped smooth the check-in process, and minutes later we found our room on the second floor. It was clean, comfortable and welcoming, and as far as I could tell, we had the whole place to ourselves.

Well, a group of Buddhist monks were living in the opposite wing, and (we later discovered) greeted the dawn with a cacophony of chanting, bells and gong-bashing – but hell, I could live with that.

Safe at last, we ditched our bags and collapsed on the bed.

That evening, Roo had a panic attack.

We'd been reeling from accident to disaster ever since entering China, and the stress had finally caught up with her. When I offered to go in search of food she begged me not to leave, convinced I'd be killed if I set foot outside the hotel.

I wasn't quite as concerned, but decided to heed her intuition. After all, my rusty kung fu skills probably wouldn't cut much ice with muggers in China.

Instead I held her as she cried, promising never to leave

her alone again. Then we shared the only food we had left – an apple I'd kept because it had the word 'SOD' stencilled on it, and a muesli bar that had been in the bottom of my bag since leaving Perth – and went to bed early.

You see, travel is not always glamour and excitement.

Sometimes, it can be downright difficult.

Sometimes, while everyone else you know is hard at work, dreaming from their desks about the adventures you're having, they don't realise – that you're stressed out and hungry, crying into your duvet, wishing fervently that you were back home.

There And Back Again

The staff at the Royal Garden's front desk were very enthusiastic, but convincing them to let me use their phone took about twenty minutes. I've done my fair share of miming over the years, due largely to being crap at learning languages. I figured 'phone call' would be a fairly universal gesture. But these guys were like something out of a Monty Python sketch. They hadn't a clue – they just kept guessing at random, offering me things, pushing different objects in front of me while I stood pointing at their telephone with a questioning look on my face.

Finally, I walked around the desk and picked up the receiver. There was a chorus of "Oooh!" and "Ahhh!" as the collective penny dropped. Of course, I had no idea how to use the phone – and neither did the receptionists, who tried valiantly for some time to get through to the number I was showing them. I'd pulled it from the internet; it was the number for Kunming's only Western-style backpackers hostel. I'd assumed that, presented with a phone number located in their home town, these guys would immediately recognise which bits to dial and in what order. Like when dialling locally, you know instinctively that you can drop the area code, right?

Nope. It was like trying to crack a safe – I encouraged

them as they tried every possible combination of every number on that page.

When I heard a voice on the other end of the line, I nearly wept with joy. I took the phone off the receptionist and launched into phase two of my dilemma.

"Hi there! Do you speak English?"

"Yes, of course."

"Is this Cloudland youth hostel?"

"Yes, of course."

"Great! I need to book some bus tickets to Laos, for my wife and me. Can you help me do that?"

"Yes, of course! But you have to come here, to the hostel. It can only be done in person."

"That's okay, I thought so. I'll come straight away, but I'm afraid the staff at my hotel don't speak any English. Can you please tell my receptionist to put me in a taxi to your place?"

"Yes, of course," came the reply.

I was ecstatic.

The phone debate that followed seemed unnecessarily long. There was much scribbling of Chinese characters, followed by much crossing out of same. By the time the call was over, I was back to being nervous. But now we were out of options, so I collected Roo, and we followed the female receptionist out onto the street.

I'd been hoping she'd phone for a taxi – like they would anywhere else in the world. Apparently this isn't something they do in China, even at four-star hotels, so instead she led us past the disturbing black water of the canal, and onto a side street.

Where we waited.

And waited.

This didn't look like the kind of place taxis passed through very often.

When a battered yellow cab did pull up beside us, the driver had a few quick words with our receptionist and buggered off at top speed.

Two more taxis pulled the same trick – I don't know what she was saying to them, but it clearly wasn't helping.

So when a shady-looking bloke wandered over and took

an interest, we were only too pleased to be waved towards his minivan.

He took the paper with the hostel's address and examined it minutely, as though the mysteries of the universe were written on there somewhere in invisible ink.

Much debate then ensued between this bloke and our receptionist, including a lengthy phone call they both partook in. Then she asked me for the phone number of the hostel – by tapping the number written on the paper, which *was* the number for the hostel. Then they both stood around for a while, glancing up and down the street, as though divine inspiration might streak past on a scooter. Eventually the bloke shrugged, the woman wrote '40' on the paper and showed it to me, and I thought, *sod it, triple the price, but I'm past caring.*

I climbed in, and we were off.

Of course, this didn't entirely quell The Fear. Because as we drove along, the driver frequently picked up the piece of paper and frowned at what was written there. Then – always a bad sign – he turned it upside-down, to see if it made more sense that way.

"I don't want to worry you," I said to Roo, "but..."

"I know," she replied. "I saw. Oh God, not again..."

Twenty minutes later we sat facing a dead end in a residential ghetto of delightful cold-war era apartment blocks. The driver gestured at us to get out, as though he'd given up trying to find our destination.

Both Roo and I refused to move.

"How hard can it be to find one hostel?" I moaned. "When we have its name, address and phone number right there? Is it mythical? Has it been destroyed by the Empire?"

Then a traffic warden shoved his head into the car – presumably to tell the driver to get lost. Or more lost. But this was the lucky break we needed; a few terse questions later we were back on our way, and after crossing a series of junctions the driver spun us round into an identical alleyway several blocks further up. And there it was; the Cloudland Hostel, home of everything a traveller could want in Kunming.

We were saved.

Once in the hostel, the bus (which apparently went to *Luang Prabang* in Laos), proved simple enough to book. Although we'd have to wait an extra day for it. Tomorrow night was full, which meant we'd be crossing the border with mere hours left on our visa.

Providing the bus was on time. And didn't break down.

I didn't fancy explaining to Chinese border officials that we'd become illegal over-stayers due to mechanical failure. But you do what you've got to do in these situations, and for us that was pay for the ticket, triple check it was for the right day, and then get the hostel staff to write down in Chinese every conceivable thing we might need to say to anyone for the next two days.

Like, "Take me back to my shitty hotel in the middle of nowhere, please!" and, "Which one is the bus to Laos?" and, "You are fucking kidding if you think I'm sharing my bunk with an old Chinese bloke who couldn't afford his own ticket!".

All of which were to come in handy over the next 24 hours…

With business taken care of, we threw caution to the wind and tucked into a delicious, homemade beef burger with all the trimmings, courtesy of the Cloudland bar.

Other than an apple and half a crushed, four-month-old muesli bar, it was all we'd eaten since getting off the train from Lijiang. It was so good, and so rapidly devoured, that we decided to sit there while it went down – and then buy another.

Unfortunately the Cloudland staff also wouldn't call us a taxi, instead suggesting that we wait for one on the main road. I was in a food-coma by that point, blissfully ignoring the fear in my heart. We followed their instructions, and after waving at every taxi that passed for close to an hour, we crossed six lanes of traffic to the other side of the road where there was a queue for the lights.

We found an empty taxi sitting in the queue and simply got in without asking.

The young man driving it didn't seem too keen when I showed him the Royal Garden's business card, but he flipped on the meter and took us back at cost price: twenty *yuan*.

I was so grateful I gave him thirty.

The Royal Garden staff were surprised to see us again. It seems they thought we were checking out, which made me a little concerned as everything we owned was still up in our room. At least, I hoped it was. It also proved that, when checking us in, they hadn't managed to find our two-night booking despite holding the printed evidence in their hands.

It took a few minutes to straighten things out, again employing their PC's translation program. But I couldn't fault their customer service – it was smiles all the way, regardless of the confusion we were causing them.

The icing on the cake was when one of the younger girls approached Roo shyly, holding out her iPhone. She had the same translation software on it, and she giggled as she tilted the screen for Roo to read.

'You are very beautiful," it said.

"Oh!" said Roo. "*Shay-shay!*" (Thank-you!)

The girl blushed and everyone laughed.

I liked those guys.

That evening I couldn't resist exploring a little, though Roo was feeling nervous about us being the only ones there and decided to stay in our room. The Royal Garden was a massive place; hundreds of rooms arranged in a square around a central courtyard big enough to train dragons in. Construction was underway in several areas, and everything was a little faded or broken – but old fashioned, in a way that suggested it had once cost *a lot* of money to stay here.

An Olympic-sized swimming pool took pride of place in the courtyard, but was full of brackish, brown water.

I bent down for a closer look, and jumped about three feet into the air when a big fish surfaced just in front of me. I couldn't decide if this heralded the pool's conversion into a giant Koi pond, or if the builders were simply keeping their lunch in there.

Roo was watching me anxiously from the window, and

when I got back she asked me why I'd been walking so weirdly.

"I was trying to be quiet. You know, not draw attention."
"So that was your 'surreptitious' walk, was it?"
"Yes. Why?"
"You were shuffling along one foot at a time, staring at the ground with your hands behind your back."
"Maybe that's what it looked like from up here, but I assure you it looks very discrete at ground level."
"You looked like a penguin that's shit itself."
"Oh. Okay. Thanks for your feedback."

And that was the end of a fairly arduous day. All we'd achieved was a pair of taxi rides to and from a hostel across town, and the purchase of some bus tickets.

The stress of those accomplishments had taken years off my life.

Roo had developed a mantra, which she was reciting like a shield to keep her sanity safe from the madness surrounding us; "Only one more day in China. Only one more day in China…"

Cloud Nine

The next day we paid our bill and left.

To be on the safe side, we'd decided to spend our last night at Cloudland.

Even though it sounded like a retirement home for Care Bears. Even though it would be more appropriately named Smogland.

It was more than twice the price of the Royal Garden Hotel, for a room with no en-suite, no air conditioning, no breakfast, no TV and no WiFi. But the staff spoke English, and the 'luxury car' we'd been forced to book to the long-distance bus station was leaving from there. Roo had found a website that hinted Kunming had an underground railway, and that it had a stop at the bus station, but none of the hostel staff had any idea about it. It was like that in China; no-one seemed to know anything, least of all the people whose job it was to know stuff. Opening times, bus numbers – even the existence of an entire underground train network – all seemed to hang in the air with big grey question marks over them.

But no matter.

All we had to do today was check in to the hostel – after getting there by taxi.

Even the prospect of that brought tears to my eyes.

It was like Groundhog Day. I watched in disbelief as the third bloke that stopped to pick us up scrutinised the card I had given him. 'Please take me to Cloudland Hostel,' was printed on it, complete with the address, in two different sets of Chinese characters as well as English.

He stared at it for so long I thought he'd fallen asleep on his feet.

Clearly, whatever was written there made no sense to him, just like the last two drivers. Just like our driver from yesterday...

And that's when it dawned on me.

He was illiterate!

It was like the pinging on of a light bulb, shining new insight onto all the confusion we'd experienced in China. There's a proportion of people who can't read or write in every country, but in China? There was a good chance that half the population was illiterate.

And given the complexity of their alphabet, I can't say I blame them.

It might make it difficult for them to become, say, a teacher, but it wouldn't stop them from working as a taxi driver. Suddenly all the pieces fit. No wonder none of the other drivers wanted our business! Kunming was hardly a tourist hotspot. Unless they got saddled with the only pair of backpackers dumb enough to get lost here, when in the rest of their careers would they ever need to read?

But interesting though this revelation was, it didn't help us one bit. Apart from reaffirming my decision to never again visit China without some kind of tour guide. I mean, it's hard enough to get by when you can't understand the language, but when the locals can't either? That's when you know you're screwed.

After a further bout of perusal, the driver handed the card back to me and shrugged. I shrugged back, and watched him walk off.

Take Four: a young woman stopped her taxi about ten minutes later. We passed the card back and forth, and she grudgingly waved us into her cab.

Success!

I think...?

What was disconcerting, is that the woman kept glancing back at us as she approached every intersection, and pointing her arms in different directions, asking us to choose which way to go. Roo and I exchanged worried looks. This was not an encouraging sign. Several times she pulled up and tried to convince us to get out. We couldn't risk being lost again – not now – so each time we stayed where we were until, shaking her head, she set off again.

Then, coming onto a long, wide road, Roo decided she recognised a hospital in the distance. Trusting her instincts (which are much better than mine), we let the woman drop us off, and watched as she sped away in relief.

"I really hope you know where we are," I said to Roo.

"Me too," she agreed.

"Okay. So... which way do we go?"

"I'm pretty sure it's this way."

After a few minutes, even I recognised the road. We were a little way up from where we'd caught the taxi back to the hotel yesterday.

Up ahead was a door.

Just a door, brand new, in its frame, leaning against a tree.

"I think it's for sale," I said, pointing to a scrap of paper taped to it. "It's for that moment when you're walking down the street and you realise that you're fresh out of doors."

"I get that all the time," Roo added.

Sweating into the straps of our backpacks, we walked on, coming to a shop that sold safes.

Proper steel safes, with those spin-y dials you turn whilst listening to them through a stethoscope. Dozens of them sat outside the shop, ranging in size from bar fridge to chest-freezer. They were lined up as though to encourage browsing by the casual passer-by. Of all the myriad items on sale in the shops of the world, I was hard-pressed to think of anything less likely to be an impulse-buy.

"I wonder if they sell many," Roo mused.

"Yeah. Bet there's no job security…"

Further down the road we passed the entrance to some sort of army base or depot. Heavy barriers were in place, and a single armed guard stood outside a glass sentry booth.

Next to him was a huge sign, which nearly made me wet myself.

'GUARD IS INVIOLABLE,' it said, in a no-nonsense military typeface.

"Oh Roo, you've got to get a photo of that one," I said.

"But what does it mean?" she asked.

"Well, it means no-one is allowed to violate that guard. Even if he wants them to."

Roo's camera bag was strapped across her front, so she pulled out her DSLR and took aim.

Just then a shout went up from inside the gateway.

That's when I remembered the rules about taking photographs of military installations in China.

Or rather, not taking them.

"Shit! Roo, let's go!"

She thrust the camera back into her bag and marched off down the street.

I caught sight of a uniformed soldier running towards us as I turned to go.

"They're after us!" I told Roo, "Quick! Run!"

"No," she hissed, "don't run! They'll chase us. Walk!"

So we made our escape at full-saunter. Being a foot taller than anyone else on the street made it close to jogging speed for the average Chinese soldier, whilst still maintaining an air of casual innocence.

There was a brief shout from behind us – probably the Chinese equivalent of, "Hey! Stop right there!" – but we ignored it and strolled on.

Our backpacks were our armour, hopefully convincing our pursuer that we were clueless tourists rather than a credible threat to national security.

And my backpack was stuffed so solid it was bound to be bulletproof.

It was a tense few minutes.

At some point the guard must have decided it wasn't

worth chasing us.

Luckily. Otherwise this adventure would have ended very differently.

I didn't dare look behind us until it was time to cross the road, but when I did the soldier was gone.

"Next time you have an idea like that..." Roo started.

"I know, think of the consequences. But it would have been such a great photo."

"Worth going to prison for? You know what happens in prison, right? You wouldn't be 'inviolable', that's for sure."

"True enough! But imagine if we'd been arrested, and we had to explain what we were doing to a Chinglish-speaking officer. 'Well sir, we liked the sign because what it means, in colloquial English, is: *It is not allowed for another man to make love to this guard's bottom.*' Surely they wouldn't hold that against us?"

We killed time that evening on the hostel's groaning old desktop PC, sifting through the accommodation options in Luang Prabang. Even the name of the place sounded exotic; I could picture half-forgotten temples peeking out of the jungle, sunrise over the mighty Mekong River and the kind of culinary delights we'd been bereft of since Vietnam.

Laos (unfortunately pronounced like 'woodlouse') is a nation of contrasts. It's French and Asian, Communist and Buddhist, and has a newly-booming tourist industry despite – or perhaps because of – its extreme poverty. This meant there were plenty of places to stay in the cities, although getting off the beaten track could prove tricky.

"I'm sick of 'off the beaten track' anyway," Roo exclaimed. "We've been there already. Off the beaten track *sucks.*"

She had a point.

So we booked into Liberty, Luang Prabang's top-rated youth hostel, delighted by the prices – we could spend a week there with all mod cons for the price of two nights at Cloudland.

"I've got a good feeling about this," I told her. "I think Laos could be *it* for us. It's set up for backpackers, and cheap enough to do whatever activities we want. We can live a bit more extravagantly, and find great local food whilst still staying where there are people that speak English… We might even make some friends!"

"You know what I want, more than anything?" Roo asked.

"A bath? A shopping spree? Another cheeseburger?"

She ignored me. "I want, just for a little while, to *not* be lost."

"Ha! Yeah…" I shuddered involuntarily.

I'd lost count of the number of times we'd been stranded in China – booted out of a bus or taxi to stand surrounded by unrecognisable city blocks, soaring skyscrapers and screeching traffic, scooters whipping past us on the pavement as we turned in circles, gazing all around us, desperately searching for any sign of what to do next.

Getting lost for fun, from a position of relative security, is one thing. Being lost and scared is something entirely different. I hated it. And I hated putting my wife in the position where she was lost and scared.

It felt like failure.

More than anything, China had been a monumental tribute to my failure; a catalogue of errors for which I was mostly responsible. I was, after all, *meant to be good at this shit.*

Perhaps mistake number one had been believing in my own press.

Because in reality, I was crap at it.

Poor Roo.

"I'll try not to get us lost in Laos," I said to her, softly.

But I couldn't make any promises.

Escape

The border between China and Laos was one of the most welcome sights I've ever seen.

It had been another traumatic bus journey.

I now knew exactly which bunk was the worst, because I'd been in it; the front-top, on the middle row. With no walls either side to brace against, there were two metal guardrails designed to keep me from falling out. I'd been flung back and forth between them so violently I was bruised on every part that bruises. Two drivers had alternated, meaning the bus hardly ever stopped; they even smoked as they drove rather than taking fag breaks. I was lying right behind them, and smoke billowed around my bunk like fog; I figure I smoked at least half a pack myself.

We arrived early, and had a couple of hours to kill before the border opened.

We got off the bus to stretch our legs, and Roo hugged me, resting her head on my shoulder. "When we get to Laos, let's spend a whole day in bed."

"Yeah? Bollocks to it, let's spend a whole *week* in bed."

"Oh really! Can we? Wow, that's like heaven!"

"Yeah, we can veg out, watch movies, eat junk food... and do lots of naughty things."

"Oooh! We'll have to ask the hostel if they have a room

that's nice and far away from the others, so we don't disturb anyone..."

She giggled in a manner I find quite appealing, and suddenly things didn't seem so bad. We were safe; more importantly, we were together, and that made us able to cope with almost anything. China had been a rough ride – with highlights, certainly, but the challenges and difficulties we'd encountered had soured our overall impression. Neither of us could wait to get out of there. Especially now we were on a promise...

That first week in Laos was looking pretty good.

Leaving China was much easier than I'd anticipated.

When the immigration hall opened, we stood in line and presented our passports for inspection. I resisted the urge to say anything that could be misconstrued, and endured the icy gaze of the Immigration Officer in silence. He made no attempt to question me about my choice of exit; technically I'd needed a flight out of the country to qualify for my visa, but either he didn't know that or he didn't care. He stamped me out, and moments later Roo joined me. At long, long last, we were free of China!

I could have kissed the bloke.

But better not.

We strolled down the road towards Laos, which was represented by the gaudiest golden monstrosity of a building you could imagine. It looked like a scaled-up version of the plastic shrines they sell on market stalls in Buddhist countries. It was huge, covered in gold leaf and ridiculously ornate, and seemed very out of place amidst the scrubby countryside surrounding it.

Inside were long lines of people waiting for their passports to be stamped, which most of our fellow passengers immediately joined. I remembered something about a visa window, and spotted it on the far side of the building. All visa-on-arrivals had to be processed through here, which meant the rest of the passengers were in for a frustrating experience when they got to the head of the queue.

The $2 bribe I'd read about was impossible to avoid,

because they simply tacked it onto the cost of the visa, declaring, "Price go up!" when questioned.

This was bullshit of course, but not something we could easily call them on.

Not without being refused entry to the country...

And being sent back to China.

So we smiled sweetly and paid the extra.

Outside again, I spied the toilet; a squalid shack set well back from the other buildings. It wasn't until I'd finished relieving myself that it hit me; this toilet was equally accessible from both sides of the border. There were no gates, no guards, and a swirling melee of travellers coming and going, queuing and queue-jumping, all shouting, swearing and laughing at each other.

All those uniforms and stamps and official paperwork, yet there was absolutely nothing to stop people going to the toilet from China and leaving it via Laos, or vice-versa.

"We could have just gone around by the loo," I explained to Roo, "then it wouldn't have cost us a penny!"

Roo eyed the toilet shack warily. "Yes, but then we'd be in Laos illegally. That kind of thing never ends well."

"Makes it nice and easy for smugglers though," I commented.

Roo gave me a black look. "Don't even think about it," she said.

We spent the next two hours sitting on plastic chairs outside a food stall fifty metres up the road. No-one told us what we were waiting for, or why, or how long it would be, but we figured it out when a group of Laos customs officials wandered over to our bus and gave it an inspection so half-hearted it barely qualified as lip-service. A couple of them climbed onto the bus and strolled up and down the aisles, before getting off again. Given that no-one had been stupid enough to leave their belongings on the bus, I struggled to think what they expected to find. Then they ordered the luggage hold to be opened, and stood staring at the staggering amount of crap wedged in there. Boxes and bags of every description threatened to spill out and bury the men;

if they had to look through every one of them, we'd be here until Judgement Day.

But no – such attention to detail was clearly not necessary.

We were all good people, right? I could tell the men trusted us implicitly. As a token effort, they hauled one large cardboard box out of the hold and opened it up with Stanley knives.

Oddly enough, there was a safe inside it.

I guess they sold a few of those bad boys after all.

At some point on the journey we'd taken on a young Buddhist monk, resplendent in his pristine orange robes. He was just what we needed to lighten our mood as we hung around watching the customs inspectors falsify their paperwork.

He can't have been older than fifteen. His head was freshly shaved, revealing a pale pink bonce, and his otherwise tanned form was so slender his robes went round him about half a dozen times. He was engulfed in them, with just one skinny brown arm sticking out – and from it dangled a large, diamante-encrusted handbag by Dolce & Gabbana.

As far as I can remember, monks are only allowed to own what they can carry in one bag; either this lad didn't have a bag, and had to borrow his mum's, or else he'd been attracted by the sparkles and bought it for himself. He seemed quite keen to show it off as he minced back and forth, one hand on his hip, striking poses with it tucked under his arm. Perhaps he kept his lipstick in it.

I'd seen fighting monks, and praying monks, and begging monks; in the Forbidden City Roo had taken a great photo of a monk taking a photo of her! I even helped a monk dangle his pet water buffalo from a tree once. But this was the first time I saw a monk that looked *fabulous.*

We got back on the bus to find the driver's mate had already sold our beds. We chased a pair of old women out of them, feeling thoroughly righteous about it, and ignored them while they argued with the driver. Then one of the women looked down at the bundle in her arms – a squirming infant –

and realised something was about to happen. She hefted the kid, checked that the butt-flap in its babygro was open, and held it out over the aisle. The child was quite clearly straining to take a shit.

"WOAH! No fucking way, lady!" I yelled.

She ignored me completely, but the bus driver, alerted by my yell, looked around and saw what was about to happen. He bawled at the woman too, and she reluctantly raised the toddler over her head and carried it off the bus.

Outside she repeated the gesture, and a stream of runny brown filth gushed forth onto the side of the road. Satisfied, the woman shook the kid the way you'd shake a wet umbrella, and tucked him away again. It was a lucky escape; a few seconds later and I'd have been staring at that mess all the way to Luang Prabang.

Which was still twelve hours away.

The carpet would have smelled pretty bad by then.

* * *

Laos, from China, was as different as George Orwell and Robinson Crusoe.

Vast swathes of skyscrapers wreathed in smog were replaced by stick huts and overgrowth.

The jungle ruled this land, and was bent on reclaiming as much as possible; here and there people had kept it at bay, but tendrils curled around every structure, just waiting for a chance to engulf them once more.

The villages we passed through looked positively medieval, disorganised straggles of homemade shacks that clustered around the road as though it might save them from being swallowed by the forest.

Quite frankly, it was paradise.

Well, I thought it was. There's a lot to be said for 'the eye of the beholder'. I mean, anyone else could have looked out of that bus window and seen a landscape of despair; torrential rain lashing down from a sky the colour of lead; battered hovels held together with rusty nails and shattered dreams, and all of it drowning in sucking, squelching, splattering mud.

Because that's exactly what it looked like.

But to me, there was something else out there. Fresh air, for starters, which was a novelty by itself. Untamed natural beauty, in the kind of quantity you couldn't tame even if you really wanted to. And for us, at least, there was freedom.

Poverty, depressing as it was, had not been absent in China – it was just out of sight behind a forest of skyscrapers. Here, the rural people scratched a living much as the peasants did over the border, only it was more obvious because there wasn't any urban sprawl to confuse the issue. Acres of semi-submerged rice paddies gleamed like emeralds whenever the sunlight caught them – which admittedly wasn't much, on a day like today – but somehow, it all seemed a lot more wholesome.

I liked Laos immediately.

And not only because it wasn't China.

The condition of the road, however, was awful. Especially considering this was the main – and only – road to the border. We swerved past pot holes big enough to swallow the bus, and hugged the cliff for long sections where the edge of the road had crumbled into the abyss. It compared to Chinese freeways like the villages we passed through compared to the centre of Beijing. Which is to say, *delightfully rustic.*

Night had fallen by the time we reached Luang Prabang.

The outskirts resembled a shanty-town, unlit and dilapidated, but we quickly found a *tuk-tuk* driver to take us from the bus station to our hostel.

Liberty turned out to be a cheerful two-storey building, with wooden shutters on the windows and a little roof over the gate.

We trudged in, dripping, and straight away the brother-and-sister tag team that ran the place introduced themselves in flawless English.

In the few minutes it took us to check in we heard their life story, shared a couple of jokes, and soaked up a measure of their happiness and positivity.

Of Vietnamese nationality, the pair had sunk every

penny they'd saved throughout their lives into this guesthouse, and were determined to build its reputation.

The only downside was the room they'd allocated us; it opened directly off reception, the door only a few feet from the desk that was, they assured us, manned round the clock by one or the other of them. They even took turns in sleeping on a mat beside the desk, in case they had a late arrival.

"Well, bugger," I said, as we leaned our backpacks in opposite corners.

"Bit close for comfort, you mean?" Roo had noticed, too.

"Yeah! Was sort of hoping... well, you know. Naughtiness."

"It'll be fine," she said. "Maybe tomorrow we'll ask if they've got something a little more private. Honestly, tonight, I don't think I'm capable. I need food, and then I need to collapse."

She was right, of course. Neither of us had slept in over forty hours; I could feel the weariness threatening to overwhelm me at any moment. Even opening my rucksack was a chore.

"We'll be okay to go out in these clothes?" I asked.

Roo sniffed herself, and made a face like she was going to be sick. "Okay," she said, "but we eat at the first place we see, and we sit as far away from anyone else as we can."

"Deal."

It wasn't perhaps the most auspicious start to a new country, but I felt very good indeed about it. For the last couple of weeks, getting out of China had become such a huge obstacle that it had dominated my thoughts. All my fantasies were focused on nothing more than reaching Laos; it had become the promised land for both of us. Firmly ensconced on the backpacker trail, for better or worse, food here would be recognisable and edible, accommodation would be well-reviewed and affordable, and more than anything we'd be back amongst people we could communicate with.

Hell, we might even get a spot of internet access now and then.

Oh yes – Laos would make all our dreams come true.

And Luang Prabang, with all its exotic promise, was ripe

for exploration.
>We would do well here…
>Or so I thought.

LAOS

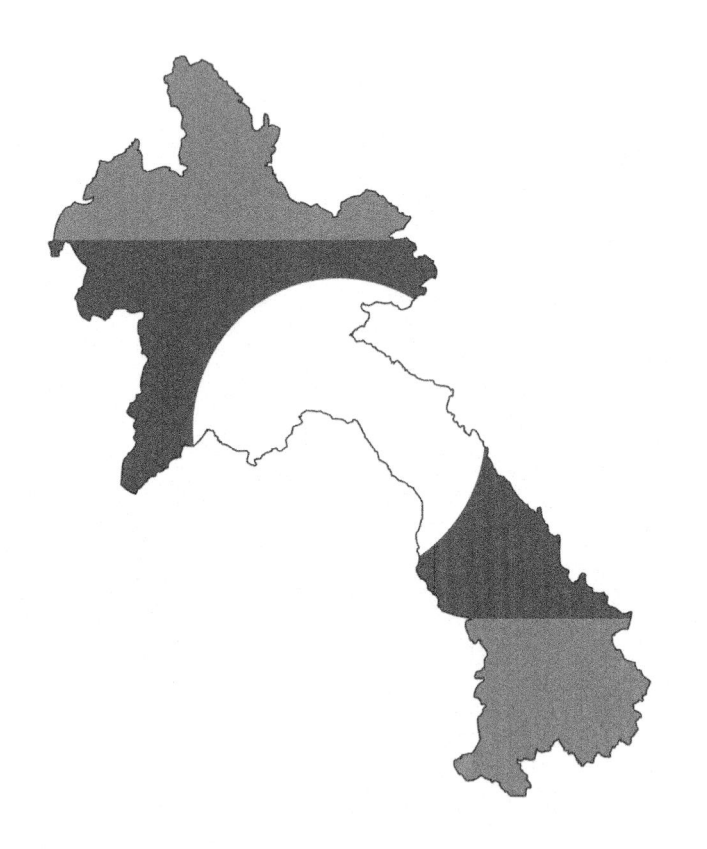

Poison Café

As Roo and I dragged our weary bodies out of Liberty Guesthouse and into the surrounding darkness, we had one overriding goal: find food, as quickly as possible.

We were aided in our quest by the fact that Luang Prabang only has one main road, and within minutes we were on it. We headed towards the centre of town, and came across a perfectly adequate café straight away.

'Delilah's', it was called. I took this to be an excellent sign; for starters, I could read it, and that bode well for the menus. Sure enough, Delilah's was exactly the kind of place I'd been hoping to find – ever since leaving Vietnam, actually.

The menus were in English, and promised such mouth-watering fare as spaghetti, lasagne and all-day breakfasts!

"Something easy," Roo pleaded, "so it won't take an hour for them to cook."

We settled on *pad thai*, my personal favourite noodle dish – a meal that can be cooked in less than three minutes on a motorbike stall at the side of the road.

The kitchen staff knocked it out in fairly short order, and it was delicious. They even served us a free glass of water each, while we waited – now this was service!

"Just what the doctor ordered," I said to Roo.

She had her head propped on one arm, while she shovelled food in with the other. She didn't bother answering.

We lingered for a few minutes after the meal, letting the feeling of contentment suffuse us before our return trip. It was raining, inevitably, and though we didn't have far to go, we'd be well and truly soaked by the time we got back.

But all we had to do was crawl into bed. No alarms, no schedules; nothing that had to be accomplished the following day, nowhere we had to be besides right where we woke up.

Now *that* is paradise.

At the last minute I thought about supplies for the night.

"Do you have any bottled water we could buy?" I asked the waitress.

"No, sorry, no bottled water left," she replied.

"Okay. No worries!"

At the time, I thought nothing of it. After all, our hostel sold water, and it was probably more polite to buy it from them than to walk in with it.

So we paid our bill and left, rejoicing in how easy it was to find food here, and how easy everything was going to be from now on.

"I already love it here," I told Roo. "Surviving China was a test, and Laos is going to be our reward."

Liberty's owners, Minh (named for Ho Chi Minh) and his sister, Nang, gave us such an enthusiastic welcome-back that we felt like old friends.

"Tomorrow, you want to go to the waterfall?" Minh asked.

"Ah... maybe," I told him. It sounded more respectful than the truth, which was, 'Bollocks to the waterfall, I'm not getting out of bed tomorrow!'.

I bought two big bottles of cold water from a fridge right outside our door, and we bid our hosts goodnight.

As we snuggled into our blankets, utterly exhausted but happy with it, I shared my positive vibes with Roo.

"Good things are going to happen to us now – I can feel it."

Not long after midnight, I woke up. I could feel something now, alright, and it was anything but good. I leapt out of bed and bolted to the bathroom, making it just in time; a torrent of poo blasted out of me with such violence it must have woken everyone in the building.

Woah... Those night buses really did a number on me. Something about disrupted sleep cycles combined with junk food, weird food, and not enough of either – my guts often punished me for treating them so carelessly.

I thought no more of it until Roo bolted for the bathroom an hour later, with equally explosive results.

"Well, that's the last bit of China out of our systems," I joked, "literally!"

And we fell into the deep sleep of those who really, *really* need it.

By morning, we had to admit that we had a problem.

It was called 'Tony shit the bed.'

Actually, we had two problems; the second was called 'Tony shit the floor'.

I won't go into the state of the bathroom, but let's just say it was in need of a damn good hosing down.

Unfortunately, neither of us felt strong enough to even contemplate such a task. It was all we could do to drag ourselves out of bed each time we felt a new wave coming. It was the same for both of us; a sudden clenching of the stomach. Ominous sounds of the kind no healthy digestive tract should be making, immediately followed by the certain knowledge that another eruption was imminent.

"Oh God, Tony, it's happening again! I've got to go..."

She crawled back to bed afterwards, and we lay there comparing notes.

"I can hardly move," I admitted. "I feel so weak..."

"I'm the same," Roo said. "I can hardly lift my head up! I'm so tired..."

"Oh no! I gotta go..."

And it was my turn to make the two-metre dash.

On the one hand, I was grateful for the compact size of the room; having so little floor space between the bed and the toilet meant a lot less chance of me voiding my bowels all over it. Again. But being so small, the room filled fairly rapidly with a variety of pungent aromas; our wet, stinking clothes, the sweat of our now feverish bodies, and the all-pervading odour of the toilet.

"How are we so ill?" I couldn't understand it.

"It must have been the food last night," Roo said, "we didn't eat anything dodgy on the bus. We didn't get the chance."

"But the food was so good! And all we had to drink was…"

Realisation hit us both at the same time.

"…water," I finished.

"No bottled water left," Roo repeated.

So what had they been serving us…?

Sewage water, with a side order of plague, if how we felt was anything to go by.

Lunchtime came and went; we felt no better, dozing in between bathroom visits and persuading each other to drink as much water as we could.

It kind of goes without saying that all forms of naughtiness were off the cards.

"I'm sorry," Roo said, "hopefully we'll feel better by tomorrow!"

I hoped so too.

Tomorrow was my birthday.

And, coincidentally, our second wedding anniversary.

"At least we'll get to spend the whole day in bed," she joked.

I had to chuckle. Ironically, my first thought when we'd been shown into the room directly adjacent to reception was that it would be awkward for sex – not being the most soundproof of buildings at the best of times, we'd have to make an effort to keep the noise down. Now, sex was about as likely as being mugged by a unicorn, and all I could think of instead was that Minh and Nang had been sitting there all morning listening to us violently abusing their toilet every ten minutes since 6am.

So it was with more than a hint of reluctance that I crept out of our room and over to the reception desk – a journey of about three metres.

I had one burning question on my mind.

"Ah, excuse me... I don't suppose you have any more toilet paper?"

On our second night in the country, neither of us was capable of going out for dinner. Facing further weakening, having involuntarily rid ourselves of every scrap of nutrition we'd been able to consume, I pulled my shit together (not literally this time) and ventured out. I could only face going as far as the restaurant we'd eaten in the night before – it was the only place I knew, and the closest. Roo was less than thrilled when I announced I would try to reach the Poison Café, but we didn't have a lot of options. I made my way there as fast as I could, horribly aware that I was on a time limit.

I half expected the café to be deserted, having been identified as ground zero for a viral apocalypse, but for everyone there it was business as normal. I asked for two servings of plain chicken and rice, and managed to muster a snigger when I saw it on the menu.

'Survival Rice,' they called it.

Obviously they'd encountered this situation before.

Which was hardly surprising, given they were the cause of it.

I sprawled on a bean bag while they cooked my order, and eyed the waitress bringing round glasses of water on a tray. When she approached me I waved her off – but then couldn't help asking, "is that tap water?"

"Yes!" she said brightly, like I'd just won a prize.

"I'll pass, thanks."

She placed a glass each in front of a couple sitting at a table in front of me.

"Don't drink that," I warned them.

"Really?" the bloke asked, in a strong Scottish accent.

"See what I look like?"

He narrowed his eyes, and then nodded.

"This is what you'll look like tomorrow night if you drink that water."

"Oh. Shit." And they both pushed their glasses away.

Shit is right, I thought.

I barely made it back to the guesthouse before my next episode.

I was shaking when I emerged from the bathroom. "This is ridiculous," I said to no-one in particular.

Roo was forcing the rice down, barely able to sit up for it.

I ate mine half-heartedly, then made yet another foray back out to reception.

Minh was on duty, and gave me a sympathetic smile. "You okay?" he asked.

"Getting better," I lied, pulling two big bottles of water from the fridge. "Can you put these on my bill?"

"Of course!" He scribbled a note on his desk-diary. "So, you want to go to the waterfall tomorrow? It's very beautiful..."

"Erm... not really. Sorry!"

Nang had thoughtfully provided a stack of fresh towels, which she'd left outside our door. I couldn't blame her for not disturbing us – I was quite relieved I hadn't had to let her into the room. She'd also left some other essential supplies, which I tossed straight over to Roo.

"More toilet roll! Thank God for that. I was afraid it was my turn to ask..."

"Think of it as an anniversary gift," I told her. "At least I know you'll use it!"

Drugged

That single glass of water was responsible for more discomfort than anything I have consumed before or since. Whatever it was we caught from it, we were absolutely buggered.

It lasted for an entire week.

The day of my birthday, and mine and Roo's wedding anniversary, was spent tag-teaming with my beloved wife on the toilet.

And they say romance is dead!

Once again I struggled out as far as the Poison Café, bringing back simple food that we felt would have the best chance of staying inside us for more than ten minutes.

It was not to be.

Having drunk six litres of water each the previous day, and still feeling weak and dehydrated, we switched to Coke; Roo's theory was that we had to replace the nutrients we were losing somehow, and in the absence of something more specialised, a big hit of sugar and caffeine might at least give us some energy to fight the bug. It's kind of hard to talk about this delicately, but suffice to say, it was a losing battle; no matter how much liquid went in, there was considerably more coming out.

That night, as we lay sweating into sheets already

saturated, I broached a topic we had studiously ignored until now.

"If we're not better tomorrow," I told Roo, "we'll have to go to hospital."

She nodded her agreement, too tired to bother with anything more vigorous.

The next day we were still sick, but a Skype chat with my parents in England had made me feel less miserable about the situation.

"At least it happened here," Roo reminded me, "and not in China. Or worse – on the twenty-two hour night bus out of China!"

She had a point.

And looking on the positive side helped me to find a bit more strength, so I outlined an alternative to the hospital plan. This was well-established backpacker territory, so surely there'd be a pharmacy around?

I crawled out of our room, closing the door quickly so the miasma of pestilence couldn't escape into the lobby. Ming was on duty, sitting attentively at his desk.

He gave me directions to a medicine stall in the market, which didn't sound terribly promising, but the good news was he didn't need to transcribe my symptoms into Laotian. "They all speak English," he explained, which went a good way towards reassuring me.

The stall turned out to be as well-stocked as any modern pharmacy, with thousands of boxes piled high. Every medication I could ever wish for was here, including plenty that you'd need a doctor's visit and a prescription for back home.

I bought a shopping bag full.

That afternoon Roo and I started on a course of strong antibiotics, dosed ourselves with Imodium, and took painkillers to ease the aching in our joints.

Sadly, there was little we could do about the most painful side-effect of our condition; all that excessive wiping had left us with a nasty case of ring-sting.

The oral rehydration sachets proved to be the least-popular of the mix.

Mixed with warm water to help the powder dissolve, the resulting concoction was tepid, viscous and salty.

Pretty much what I imagine a mouthful of sperm tastes like.

It made Roo gag, anyway.

"Let's get this straight," she said, spreading the cards of pills out on the bed. "We take three of *these* per day, four of *those* per day, these big white ones whenever the headaches come back, and two green ones after each arse explosion?"

"That's right," I told her, "and try to take them with the semen-water if possible."

With little to do but trawl the internet, I'd managed to identify our mystery guest; *E-coli,* the little bugger, was touring our guts the same way we were touring Asia, only with even messier consequences. Now, having declared war armed with the very best weapons a Laotian medicine stall could offer, I felt the worst of our battles had passed.

"Are we still going to hospital, if we don't get better?" Roo asked.

"We'll have to," I admitted. "But let's give these antibiotics a chance. And I'm a lot less worried now about the cost of medical care in this country!"

The bag full of drugs had come to $20.

The following day, neither of us could have pooed, even if we'd wanted to.

On reflection, it's possible that we may have overdosed somewhat on the anti-diarrhoea meds. The desperate urge to shit was replaced by gassy bloating, and I made another trip to the medicine stall for something to ease the discomfort.

A day later, we had the balance right. Our short course of antibiotics came to an end, and we decided to try venturing out together in search of food.

We didn't get very far, but at least we made it past the Poison Café.

Luang Prabang has only one main road, with a handful of smaller streets and alleyways bisecting it. In the late afternoon the stalls lining the road blossom, tripling in

Shave My Spider!

number, until around 5pm they spill into the main road and cover it completely. This night market occurs every day, blocking the only road through town all evening. Imagine doing that anywhere else!

The market was a delight though, full of spicy smells and splashes of colour and low-hanging awnings that constantly threatened to take my eyes out.

We struggled through, marvelling at how much effort it was requiring just to stay upright. Normally at ease in crowds, instead we walked hunched over, holding on to the poles supporting the tarpaulin roof, still feverish and shivering.

We ate in the first place we found beyond the market, and struggled home as best we could.

The illness had dominated another day of our adventure, and looked set to claim a few more before it was done.

"Oh, you look so much better!" Minh commented, as we staggered past him.

"Yes, much better now, thanks," I wheezed.

"So! You want to go to the waterfall tomorrow?"

Yet another day passed, with us venturing no farther than a sandwich stall on the edge of the market. This day, we told ourselves, was about regaining our strength for the rest of the trip – so we spent it in bed, watching movies on the laptop. I battled the patchy internet to post a blog about our Hua Shan experience, and we caught up with our diaries and our diarrhoea. I sincerely hoped that this would be the last of it.

The following morning, we dragged ourselves out of bed before dawn, and made our way through the shadowy streets to one of Luang Prabang's many temples. There was a famous alms-giving ceremony Roo wanted to witness, and it was about time for us to start testing our strength again.

We held up well, watching from a doorway as a procession of monks arrived with the first grey hints of light. It was still too dark for photography when they began their daily ritual. Local people lined the main street, interspersed here and there with keen tourists. Some stood, some knelt, but almost all held insulated containers of cooked rice. The monks, wrapped in orange robes that can't have provided much warmth, filed past carrying empty rice bowls.

Every person the monks passed placed a spoonful of rice into their bowls, so that each monk received dozens of individual donations towards his breakfast. The alms giving was conducted in respectful silence, and it took about an hour for the monks to complete their procession along the main road and back to their monastery. It was slightly anticlimactic, with the onlookers shuffling away as soon as the monks had passed them. We bought our breakfast at 6am from our favourite sandwich stall – I don't think the woman that ran it ever slept! When she saw us approaching she fired up her griddle, cooking fresh bacon and eggs for us, adding cheese and creamy guacamole, and serving it up in a home-baked roll. My stomach wasn't big enough to give this woman the amount of business she deserved, but I did my bit for the local economy by eating one of her delicious sandwiches every time I walked by. Which was pretty often, as her stall sat on the corner of the main road, directly between town and our hostel.

We spent that day visiting several of Luang Prabang's identikit temples. There were dozens of the things, littering the town, clustering on the outskirts and scattered across the surrounding hills. All followed the pattern of one large, mostly empty main building, with three or more layers of curving roofs. Roo took plenty of photos to get back in practice, but the temples were quite ordinary compared to others we'd seen.

We ate well, using the rebuilding of our strength as an excuse to splurge. The restaurants along the main street were all equally enticing, and it seemed that every one we ate in managed to outdo the last. Of all the places we'd visited, Luang Prabang had the most interesting, most diverse, and most downright delicious culinary experiences.

We also explored the night market properly, admiring the quality (and most importantly the price) of the goods on offer. Roo bought colourful trousers and silver trinkets as presents for her sisters, because we were starting to realize that our grand adventure was heading towards its natural conclusion. We'd been away for over well over four months now, and like it or not, we had to spare a thought for what the real world would hold when we returned to it.

We also had to make plans for the last few weeks of our trip, which inevitably began with booking a bus to our next destination; the infamous backpacker party town of *Vang Vieng*.

Liberty's owners had been friendly, helpful and understanding to a fault. After everything we put them through during our stay, I now feel like I owe them a massive apology – and an even bigger thank-you.

Unfortunately, I'm too embarrassed to go back there.

But if any of you happen to be in Laos, and you decide to visit Luang Prabang, please pop into Liberty and tell Minh and Nang that Tony and Roo from Australia say thank-you.

Seriously – it's only been two years. No chance they've forgotten *that* yet.

We'd now been in Luang Prabang for twice as long as we'd intended. It was a gorgeous town though, and I doubt we could have found a better place to convalesce. Bedecked in greenery and bracketed by rivers, it had a tranquil and relaxing ambience – the kind of peace I could have easily spent six months absorbing.

But we didn't have six months left; hell, at this point we barely had six weeks.

And that meant our time in Luang Prabang was coming to an end.

We never did see that damn waterfall.

Alternative Therapy

On our last evening in Luang Prabang, I got to have my first go at acupuncture.

Receiving, not giving, just for the record.

My left shoulder had been causing me a lot of pain ever since Vietnam – much as I hated to admit it, that *liddew owd lady* had broken me. For months I'd been complaining about it, every time I put on or took off a t-shirt; raising my left arm above my head made me howl, and it's surprising how often you need to do this on a day-to-day basis.

So, having already recovered from one ailment in Luang Prabang, I decided to try my luck with the other. I'd been interested in acupuncture ever since meeting Milos back in Borneo. Somehow I'd managed to go right through China without finding any; although, given the difficulties we'd encountered just trying to find something to eat, it was perhaps for the best that I hadn't asked someone to stick needles in me.

Over the past week I'd had plenty of time to study *Lonely Planet: Laos*, and had found an acupuncture practitioner listed on the far side of town, right by the river.

We found the place easily enough, and the wizened Laotian lady who ran it.

At first she resisted my request, offering me a hot stone

massage in preference. This was a new experience for me, in Asia – someone who actually *didn't* want to sell me something! But she explained that acupuncture takes several sessions to achieve results, and since we'd mentioned we were leaving tomorrow, she didn't want me to be dissatisfied with her efforts. It took some doing, but I convinced her – I said I'd find another acupuncturist in the Laos capital *Vientiane,* when we passed through. This placated her, and she suggested the city's main hospital as the best place to get a follow-up dose of treatment.

And then she led me into her inner sanctum, lay me down on a massage table, and went to work.

I'd heard that acupuncture needles are so fine that you can't even feel them go in.

This is a lie.

I felt every one of the buggers, as she pierced the muscle of my shoulder and slid them deep inside my flesh. I felt them go all the way down, and gritted my teeth expecting them to hit bone. She placed over a dozen needles, all down the affected arm from shoulder to wrist, and though initially uncomfortable, it wasn't too bad.

Then she did something I wasn't expecting.

She wired the needles to a bank of electrodes and flipped the power on.

And that *was* bad.

Jolts of electricity shot through me without warning. My arm thrashed around like a landed fish, the muscles spasming with each surge of power. "OOoww!" I yelped.

"Too much?" the lady asked.

The liddew owd lady.

"No, I can take it," I told her.

Because some mistakes are worth repeating.

She left me there, laid out on the table with my arm leaping around like a possessed thing. I had no idea how long she'd be gone, but my muscles were already starting to complain about their treatment. The pain ratcheted up another notch with each burst of electricity. My arm was tensing harder than I'd thought possible, as though at any moment my biceps would turn green and tear through the shirt I wasn't wearing.

I clenched my jaw to keep quiet, and tried to think happy thoughts.

I could eat a nice juicy— Argh! Bastard!

Maybe after this we'll go buy— ARRRGH! BASTARD!

Ten agonising minutes passed. Twenty.

It felt like the woman had been gone for a century. I was counting to a hundred in as many languages as I could, which wasn't taking very long.

What the hell? How long was she leaving me here for? Had she abandoned me completely? Was I being punished for arguing with her?

But then, right when I was on the verge of crying out in pain, of screaming for her to come back and save me – she did.

She flicked off the power switch and calmly withdrew her needles.

"Was okay?" she asked, passing me a towel to mop my forehead.

"Yes, fine thanks," I told her.

Because, after all, I *am* British.

I paid the lady at her front desk – surrounded by healing crystals, with chakra posters on the wall and incense curling through the air. I couldn't help but notice the contrast between the relaxing vibes this room implied, and the torture I'd just undergone in the chamber beyond.

Tricky little... I bet she was laughing all the way to the bank.

"How was it?" Roo asked, when I collected her from the waiting room.

She'd been enjoying a milkshake.

"It wasn't the most relaxing thing I've experienced," I said. Then I described the electro-shock therapy I'd just received.

Roo listened with eyes wide. "Are you okay, though?" she asked, when I was finished.

"Well, yeah, I guess so. I mean, my shoulder doesn't hurt any more, but that could be because my entire nervous system has been fried."

"Was it really that bad?"

"Well, put it this way – I wish I'd agreed to the hot stone massage."

*   *   *

The bus to Vang Vieng only took seven hours. It was refreshing to be back in a country where distance was measured in sensible increments. The journey took in some of the most beautiful scenery Laos had to offer; vibrant green fields and hillsides, sheer-sided mountains with exposed granite faces, and rivers winding back and forth between them. The villages we passed through were ramshackle things, tin-roofed huts made of badly-fitting planks, where scrawny dogs roamed and half naked children played in the mud. We absorbed it all, the beauty and the poverty intertwined, and wondered what the future held in store for Laos. Tourism is the fastest-growing industry in the country, contributing over a billion dollars to the economy. If developed sensitively and sustainably, the sky is the limit – some of the money might even filter down to improve the lives of the subsistence-farmers, who make up eighty percent of the population.

The town we were heading for, on the other hand, could be viewed as the downside of tourism. Vang Vieng is on the international map for one reason: it's become a Mecca for insane drunkenness, with a party scene said to rival the best in Asia. Cheap booze, readily available drugs and a river running through it brought backpackers to the town in droves; some never left. A guilty part of me was looking forward to a few drinks and a bit of a boogie, but I was painfully aware of how damaging this kind of development can be. Any culture Vang Vieng once displayed has been annihilated by bikini-clad babes and shirtless dudes, smoking spliffs as they stagger down the streets towards techno music thumping from a dozen different bars. It's the kind of place you'd love to visit, but hate to live – only, there *are* people who live there. And we've basically turned their home into one giant, seedy, all-night disco.

The stunning journey was only slightly marred by the rain,

which beat down on the bus with unrivalled savagery. When putting together our six-month itinerary, there hadn't been enough wiggle room to avoid everything – hence, we were here smack bang in the middle of the rainy season, and would be for our entire stay.

I didn't mind too much. Growing up in the north of England, it rained pretty much continuously for the first ten years of my life. Still, the monsoon-intensity made it hard to imagine exploring the sights. Unless they included shopping centres, which, in Laos, I seriously doubted.

By a supreme stroke of luck, the bus stop in Vang Vieng was right outside the hotel we'd booked into.

As we fled inside, hunched over to protect the electronics in our daysacks, the entire busload of passengers followed us. They milled around in the lobby for a while, staring sullenly out at the rain – then someone asked if there were any rooms available, and within minutes every single one of them had checked in. I had a feeling that happened a lot.

Apart from the most convenient location in town, the hotel didn't have much to recommend it. A fairly soulless, two-storey concrete box of a place, both floors consisted of one long central corridor with rooms opening off either side. The room did have air-con – not that we needed it at the moment – and a TV that, according to their website, got Cable. And maybe it did, when it wasn't raining.

We never got to find out.

After ditching my rucksack in a corner, I raised my left arm experimentally, and when I encountered no pain I did some slow circles with it. It felt much looser. My neck did, too, and I realised I'd been holding it stiff to avoid making my shoulder hurt.

"Bloody hell," I said to Roo, "that Guantanamo Bay shit really worked! I think my shoulder's fixed."

"Yay! Do you want to try and find an acupuncture place here to do you another session?"

"Ah... maybe not just yet. I'll wait till we get to Vientiane. I might not even need a second treatment."

Roo's eyes narrowed suspiciously. "Are you just saying

that because she electrocuted you?"

"Maybe."

"Okay, you want my advice? What I think you should do, at least for the next few weeks, is..."

"Yeah?"

"Stay the hell away from little old ladies."

Later that night, we had something else to celebrate – or rather, Roo did.

I was writing on the laptop when she emerged from the bathroom like a match-winning goal scorer, yelling in triumph, and danced a victory jig around the bed.

"Guess what?" she said, "I just did a solid poo!"

"Well, that's great," I told her. "Do you want me to post it on Facebook?"

"No, thank-you very much. I don't think strangers want to read about my bowel movements."

"I dunno. You'd be surprised... I've got Facebook open right here."

"NO! Look, I don't mind you writing about your own bodily functions, but I'd prefer it if you left mine alone. Alright?"

"So, just to be clear, *not* on Facebook?"

"No. And you're not blogging about it, either!"

"Fair enough."

But she didn't say anything about the Asia book.

Probably because, at that point, I wasn't thinking of writing one.

It has to be said, there are downsides to marrying a travel writer.

Circles of Life

The rain continued unabated for our first two days in Vang Vieng. Perhaps because of the weather, the crazy carnival atmosphere of the place had fizzled a bit. Instead we dashed from bar to bar, reclining on long cushions while looped episodes of *Friends* played endlessly on TV. It was great – whenever an episode came on that we'd seen, we just nipped next door and watched a different one. Of maybe fifteen different establishments we frequented during our time there, almost all of them showed back to back *Friends*.

The only two that didn't were showing back to back *Seinfeld*.

We stayed well clear of those places.

The number one attraction in Vang Vieng – well, apart from drinking – is tubing. This involves floating sedately down the *Nam Song* River on the giant inner-tube from a tractor tyre... whilst drinking.

I was very keen to have a go, obviously, but Roo was a little more apprehensive. She was concerned about the slightly shonky safety record the activity had; official statistics show that at least twenty backpackers die every year whilst tubing in Vang Vieng.

"And literally hundreds more are seriously injured," she

explained, "and they have to go all the way to Vientiane for treatment."

"Yes, but most of those people get hurt because they get paralytically drunk, and then think it's a good idea to dive headfirst into the river."

"And we won't be doing that?"

"Ah... no, of course not."

I crossed my fingers behind my back while I said this, because life can be pretty weird sometimes; you never know what it's going to throw at you.

And also because, getting drunk and jumping into rivers is, like, one of my favourite things *ever*.

(At this point I'd like to add, for anyone who remains unconvinced, that I'm not known for being particularly sensible.)

My timing was perfect.

I'd convinced Roo to go tubing on the only day it was actually possible.

The intense rain of the last few days had swollen the river, supercharging it to a speed and violence which even the people renting out tubes had deemed too dangerous. And they didn't seem like overly-cautious types.

Today, however, the rain had stopped. The sky was blue... well, blue-ish grey, but the forecast was good – at least until tonight. We had a narrow window of opportunity here, and Roo bravely agreed to take it.

Although my suggestion of a few drinks for Dutch Courage didn't go down too well.

We showed up mid-morning, in shorts and flip-flops, and took possession of our tubes. It was a low-tech set up; the tubes were still actual tractor inner-tubes, rather than purpose-made versions, and the start of a day's tubing involved flinging the tubes on the roof of a minibus, piling in, and being driven to a rickety wooden jetty about ten miles upstream. We slid our tubes into the sluggish water, wrestled ourselves into the things, and drifted into the current.

The river was still bloated, still chocolate brown with churned up mud and silt, and still flowing along at a fair old clip. We relaxed into it, bumbling along next to each other, spinning in circles to admire the scenery.

The first bar-stop was indicated by a hand-painted sign nailed to a tree. As we came around a bend we spotted the flimsy wooden bar, with dozens of tubes piled up at the water's edge. We weren't sure exactly what to expect, but we knew the bar had staff on hand to assist with getting there.

Two blokes stood on the riverbank, and they sprang into action as soon as they saw us.

Each was armed with a grotty rope, attached at one end to a plastic milk carton; they were meant to throw these at us, allowing us to catch them and be pulled in to shore.

Only, I made the mistake of waving at one of the men, and that was just enough distraction to screw things up. They both waved back at me – and then they threw their ropes. Both towards me.

"Help!" Roo cried, as she drifted past the rope that should have been hers. I had mine in hand, but she'd had no chance of catching one.

"Don't worry!" I shouted, then flung myself off the tube and into the water. Catching Roo was easy, because the river swept me right into her. Holding onto her, and the rope, and my tube, was not quite so easy. Both men on the bank were now hauling on the other end of the rope, straining to pull us back against the current. It was a hell of a struggle, and when we swung close to a beached canoe I grabbed that instead. Roo clambered off over the top of me, and I pulled myself back to the beach hand over hand.

"That wasn't too bad," I gasped, as Roo came to relieve me of my tube.

I had a feeling she didn't agree with me.

The only reason to stop at the bar was for drinks, so I ordered us a couple of rum-and-Cokes. The bar was busy, but not packed, mostly with tweenagers. They were all drunk; dancing in a muddy mosh-pit, crowding the bar, and playing slip n' slide with a hosepipe on the riverbank. We sat surveying the scene, sipping our drinks, feeling a bit old.

"We can still party, right?" I asked Roo.

"Of course we can party."

"Now?"

"Um... I was thinking, if we finish these drinks we could get back to the hotel. I'm in the middle of this great book..."

"Yeah." I necked the last of my drink and slumped on my stool.

"But we could have *one* more drink," Roo said.

"Sweet! I'll get 'em!"

The drinks, it has to be said, were rather strong. I was being given a free shot every time I turned up at the bar, as well as one for Roo. She's not really into shots, or the consuming of alcohol for no other reason than 'it's there' – so I figured she wouldn't mind me drinking hers.

When I got back she was chatting to a pair of Dutch girls, and a little while later we were all dancing in the mud. Then it occurred to me to try the slip n' slide; I raced up and threw myself along the bank, tumbling and bouncing down the rocky slope to a torrent of yells and jeers from the crowd. I'd just picked myself up when another party-goer gave into his urges, and threw himself into the mountain of tubes. There were shouts of dismay this time, as his impact collapsed the pile, sending half the tubes into the river where they quickly vanished around the bend.

"I should have jumped in and saved some of them," I slurred.

Roo cast a critical eye over me. "I think it's time to go," she said.

"Are we stopping at the next bar?" I asked.

"Ah, we'll see," she replied, evasively.

The rest of the trip passed without incident.

We 'accidentally' missed the next bar, somehow ending up on the opposite side of the river from the bar's rope-throwers. A leisurely drift later we passed under a footbridge made of wood scraps and wire, and realised we were nearing the end. The river split in two, and we washed into the quieter stream, fetching up against some concrete steps. We recovered our tubes and hiked through town to return them.

"See," I said to Roo, "I told you we wouldn't die!"

"Yes, we seem to have narrowly avoided disaster this

time."

"Well, you know those Dutch girls were planning on doing another circuit... What do you think? Wanna try again?"

Having decided to quit while we were ahead, we went for an early dinner at an Irish bar in the centre of town. I mean this literally; Vang Vieng is five streets wide by three streets deep, and Gary's Irish Bar was in the middle from both directions. They did great comfort food, and I risked ordering a full (Irish) breakfast; it was hands down the best cooked breakfast I ate in all of Asia.

As we lingered over our drinks, I noticed the Dutch girls we'd met at the tubing bar. I wandered over to see if they'd followed through on their plan for a re-run, discovering that they'd arrived back too late to make a second trip.

"I think we looked too drunk," one of the girls, admitted.

I nodded diplomatically and made no comment.

"Hey, are you guys going to the Jungle Party?" she asked me.

"I dunno! What is it?"

"It's... a party. In the jungle."

"Okay. I guess I deserved that. So how do we get there?"

"Just show up here, at eight. All the tuk-tuks leave from out front.

"Great! We'll be there!"

So, that night, Roo and I went to the Jungle Party.

I think.

I must have got pretty drunk, because I have absolutely no memory of it.

I tried asking Roo what happened; she just rolled her eyes, muttered something about me being an idiot, and then refused to talk about it.

So I'm afraid my report on the Jungle Party will have to wait until next time... well, assuming I'm allowed to go again.

I wouldn't hold your breath.

The next day was spent in recovery mode.

Fortunately, Vang Vieng is ideally suited to this – I can't imagine why! Whether your preferred hangover cure is vegging out in front of the telly with a full cooked breakfast, or starting to drink again as soon as you wake up, both methods are adequately catered for. There's even the option of a brisk walk through unspoiled nature, though I don't think that's a popular choice.

Especially not in the rain – unspoiled nature, pretty though it might be, tends to get a little soggy in the wet season.

We did manage to achieve one thing that day. Having identified the various companies that offered rock climbing trips, I chatted with the staff at each place and ended up saving $50 by going with one of the smaller, less flashy outfits. Roo wanted to do one full day, whereas I was keen on pushing the envelope; I booked in for a three-day course, covering complex-sounding techniques like 'lead climbing' and 'multi-pitch'.

Whatever they were.

Later that evening, back in our room, I packed a bag for the following day's course.

Roo was checking herself out in the mirror. "I can't believe how much weight I've lost," she said, turning sideways. "That E-coli was a great diet!"

I pulled off my shirt to have a look, and was delighted to see my abs rippling with new-found definition. "All that clenching probably helped, too," I mused.

But Roo, stood behind me, was staring at my back in horror. "Tony... holy shit!"

I swung around to check the mirror.

My back was covered in scratches – dozens of them, criss-crossing every inch of skin. It looked like I'd been having an affair with Catwoman.

"How...?" I began.

"Sliding down that muddy riverbank!" Roo realised. "It must have been full of sharp rocks. Didn't you notice?"

"Uh... Maybe? No, not really."

"How?"

"I was just... excited, I guess."

She shook her head. "Thank God they closed the 'death slide'."

We'd been reading up on tubing, wondering why the experience didn't quite match the insane party we'd seen footage of. A ropey video playing in the tube-rental shop had shown people plunging into the river from giant ropes swings, shooting off the end of lethal-looking slides and strutting their stuff in several different theme-bars. It turned out that the death toll had gotten too high; six months ago the government, under the auspice of making Vang Vieng safer for tourists, had bulldozed the lot of it. The two bars currently on the route were recent additions, highly illegal, and not likely to stay there for long. Tubing was being cleaned up, and the focus of Vang Vieng was being forcibly shifted away from drunken revelry and onto more wholesome pursuits, like climbing and hiking.

Part of me applauded the change, whilst at the same time, part of me wished I'd been here at the height of it, to sample the ultimate craziness that had spawned a thousand urban legends.

Roo, I think, was rather glad I wasn't.

Vertical Limits

At the risk of repeating myself, it rained that night.

Boy did it rain.

We stared in disbelief at the fury of the storm, as the street outside our hotel became a lake. All night we listened to it, a dull roar like a distant waterfall.

In the morning, the roads were still submerged. We slogged through giant puddles to reach the climbing shop, half expecting the day's activities to be cancelled.

"No, the climbing place is dry," our guide reassured us.

The route there, however, was a different story.

At first we rode in a pick-up truck, surrounded by piles of gear. There are plenty of foot bridges over the Nam Song River, most of which look like props from an Indiana Jones movie, but there is only one drivable bridge. We headed for that, and joined the queue to cross – noticing as we did that something was amiss. As we edged closer to the bridge it became obvious; the river had burst its banks, flooding the properties on both sides. We looked down into the grounds of a nice hotel; one of the staff was standing waist-deep in the brown water, presumably wondering what he could possibly do about it. The answer, of course, was nothing – the river had effectively annexed everything between it and the nearest parallel street. The clean-up bill would be enormous.

Our driver paid the toll and started onto the bridge. Roo and I had walked across this bridge a few days earlier. The river had already been in spate at that point, but since then its level had risen by *over a metre!* It demonstrated the power that even this relatively minor river had over the surrounding communities.

At the other end of the bridge we were in for another surprise.

The reason for the queue was now revealed; the far end of the bridge was impassable for cars. That hadn't stopped the toll booth dude charging us for the crossing, though.

A bunch of enterprising locals had brought their canoes, and were ferrying people back and forth across a pool where the road had been; as we watched, they floated a scooter across, its rider poised nervously astride it. When it came to our turn we hauled as much gear as we could carry into a pair of canoes, and sat there feeling foolish while our guide paddled us across with his flip-flops.

Luckily, a few taxis had been trapped on the far side of the river, so we were able to catch a lift for the next stage of our journey.

When the taxi dropped us off, our view was dominated by a titanic limestone karst formation. Its craggy outline rose abruptly from the landscape, massive and majestic. And, for those of us about to try climbing the thing, not a little intimidating.

And we weren't even there yet.

We trekked across the field, through a stand of trees and reached a gate. Our guide unfastened a twist of wire and led us through – into a swamp.

My feet sank into the mire up to my ankles; pulling each foot out took a fair amount of effort, and was rewarded with a delightful slurping sound.

On we went, holding on to each other for support. I couldn't stop laughing, as every step of our progress was punctuated with a *'schhhhlop!'*

"This is more adventurous than climbing," I said to Roo.

And then we came to the river.

Not the Nam Song, but a minor tributary; still, it seemed

like a fairly formidable obstacle. My heart sank a little, as I expected our guide to pull the plug. Unless he knew another way around, our trip was over before it had begun.

As it turned out, our guide didn't need another way around – he was perfectly happy taking the usual route.

"Careful!" he warned – as he stepped off the bank and into the river.

Being a typically tiny Laotian bloke, the water came up to his arse. It was churning, roiling, barrelling along, and he was struggling to stay upright. But he forged his way forwards, one step at a time, and gestured for us to follow.

Awesome!

I stepped in, the water thigh-deep and so powerful I staggered a few steps before I could brace myself. Roo took my hand and stepped daintily in, shrieking as the force of the water pushed her into me. "Shit! It's deep!"

I took a step forwards and plunged into a hole of some kind; suddenly the water was over my waist and I was in danger of being swept away. Roo hauled me back, and pointed to the guide.

He was waving at me. "Don't go that way!" he warned.

Following in the guide's footsteps as closely as possible, we navigated the river for several minutes. I'd assumed we had to cross it; in fact, we had to follow it, as this *was* the path. "Normally, not so deep," our guide explained.

"How deep?" I asked him.

"Uh, maybe, here?" he held up one foot and drew a line across his ankle.

Once out of the river, we followed a track through small, scrubby trees until we hit rock. This outcrop was the base of a cliff that soared over two-hundred metres straight up; a short, slippery scramble over sharp rocks in muddy shoes brought us to our destination. Above us, the rock face towered.

And we were about to climb it.

If I could pick one thing to suddenly acquire ultimate skill at, *Matrix* style, climbing would be it. Nothing else comes close; it challenges me, it adrenalizes me, and it scares the crap out of me. Probably because I'm rubbish at it. Climbing requires a high strength-to-weight ratio, which is my first barrier to greatness; I've been told (by qualified healthcare professionals) that my bones are made of lead. Possibly that's why I've never broken one – well, unless you count my nose, which is just too big to avoid.

Starting on easy routes and progressing to harder ones, we spent the whole day crawling up and down that rock face. By the time we were done, I couldn't feel my arms, but that didn't matter in the slightest.

It *did* make it slightly harder to get back through the river and across the swamp, but I managed without serious incident.

Hell, I was walking on air.

The second day of climbing followed a similar pattern, but with an added bonus; only three of us, all young(ish) blokes, had stayed on for the full course. The focus of this day was lead climbing, which was an altogether more frightening experience. Lead climbing involves being the first person up the rock; rather than being tied to a safety rope which goes up through a steel ring at the top and back down to a partner on the ground, you get to take the safety rope up with you. Your mate still has hold of the other end of it, but for the first few minutes of climbing, that's all he's doing: standing around, holding your end.

I set off nervously, taking much longer to scale the same bit of rock I'd climbed yesterday. There's just something about doing it without any form of protection – kind of like sex, really. If something goes wrong, well, you're screwed.

There were bolts driven into the rock at regular intervals, and each time I reached one I had to take one hand off the rock, reach around to the gear dangling from my belt, pull off a 'quick draw' karabiner, clip it into the bolt's eyelet, and then clip my safety rope through it. Done with trembling fingers, braced in a precarious position by heavily fatigued limbs, it was quite a struggle. But there was no choice; until my rope was connected to that bolt, the only protection against a fall was the last bolt I'd clipped into. So if I fell – and a few times I thought I was going to – I'd tumble back down to that point, praying the whole time that the bolt down there would hold me.

Reaching the top, and clipping the rope into the anchor ring, felt like Christmas morning. And then I could relax, abseiling down the cliff or simply dangling, admiring the view over miles of submerged rice paddies whilst my partner lowered me to the ground.

On the third day, we practised multi-pitch climbing. This involved all of us lead-climbing up to the anchor point, then hanging there while we pulled up the safety ropes – and then taking it in turns to start lead climbing again, from that point upwards.

Now that was serious brown-trouser territory, I can tell you.

By the end of the three days, I was knackered. Scratched and scraped and bruised, I sat in a rickety bar overlooking the river. Roo and I were celebrating our last night in the party town with a drink and a schnitzel. Our bus to Vientiane was booked for the following morning; I planned on sleeping the whole way.

I'd been high on adrenaline for three days straight, and my body was starting to crash. I was trying not to use alcohol as a replacement, but I was failing.

It was kind of hard not to get drunk when a bucket – literally, a child's sandcastle bucket, full of whisky and Coke – came free with every meal.

"So, you're all adventured-out for a bit?" Roo asked me.

For an answer, I groaned, wearily.

I took a sip of my drink and stretched out full-length on my cushion, staring up at *Friends* on the TV.

The life of an adventurer is a tough one, I thought.

During our time in Vang Vieng, Roo had received a crash-education in my favourite American sitcom. One of the few disadvantages of a cradle-snatching relationship is differing appreciations of pop culture; when *Friends* first hit the big time, Roo was only nine years old.

That was pretty terrifying.

What made it worse was that, despite her being so much younger than me, she was somehow still more responsible.

She'd even refused the free bucket. *Madness!*

Interestingly though, rock climbing, rather than drinking, had been the highlight of Vang Vieng for me. Maybe I was actually growing up? I guess it had to happen sooner or later. The climbing had really pushed me, physically and psychologically, and I'd found new strength and confidence. I don't know where they'd come from – some poor bugger must have left them lying around unattended – but they were mine now.

I was starting to like this climbing-with-ropes malarky. It had one major advantage over my usual climbing style; two actually, if you count the significantly reduced risk of dying. When I used ropes, Roo could climb with me – which was a vast improvement on her standing at the bottom, shouting, "Get down you bloody idiot!"

Vientiane

Someone once said that Vientiane, the capital of Laos, wasn't really worth writing about.
　　They were right.

Temple of Manhood

In fairness to the Laotian capital, it wasn't horrible or anything. Merely, unremarkable. We checked into an ultra-modern hotel called 'iHouse' – now there's a lawsuit waiting to happen! The room was only two feet wider than the bed; if I'd been six inches taller, I could have touched all four walls at once. We dodged intermittent rain long enough for a walk along the river, which at that point was so wide it felt more like a walk along the sea front. And we went in search of the night markets, which are a popular sight – sorry, *the* popular sight – outside the wet season.

Alas, we were well and truly inside the wet season, and the handful of sodden stalls that braved the downpour didn't really make the walk worthwhile. Especially as Roo had insisted we wear the waterproof ponchos we'd been given on the Kinabatangan River. The bright yellow plastic billowed around us, rustling and crackling with every move we made. If there's a way to draw more attention, whilst looking and feeling like a total dickhead, I have yet to discover it.

We ate delicious *laap* (minced pork and herbs, especially mint, on rice), sitting on plastic chairs in an abandoned warehouse. We'd stumbled on the place by accident; only locals seemed to know there was a restaurant in there. Or else, only locals dared to go in and find out. There was a distinctly temporary feel to the place, as though the police could arrive at any time to close it down. Our meal was therefore competitively priced, at less than two dollars each.

We had another windfall the following day, when Roo discovered $30 worth of Chinese Yuan in a jacket pocket. If there's one thing better than free food, it's free food you can't normally afford – so we went a bit crazy, eating breakfast burritos at JoMa bakery, waffles and ice cream for lunch, and pizzas at a posh-looking Italian restaurant for dinner.

Ahhhhh!

By the end of the day we were back to being broke again.

It was worth every penny.

It was a short (five hour) bus ride to *Pakse,* aka 'the Gateway to Southern Laos.'

The *Lonely Planet* team normally pull out all the stops when describing a place, making the humblest of destinations sound so enticing you'd sell your grandmother for a one-way ticket. This is what they had to say of Pakse:

'Most travellers don't linger long, because there's not much to do.'

And they were dead right.

I would even go so far as to add, 'get the hell out of Pakse, because it's a shithole'.

Maybe they'll add that to the next edition.

Then again, my dislike of the town was perhaps a tiny bit my fault.

You see, by this point in the trip I was starting to get nervous. We'd had an amazing adventure, but if I didn't rein in our spending a little, we'd be arriving back in Perth without a pot to piss in. With job prospects not terribly high due to our habit of buggering off around the world on a moment's notice, it could be a long time before we had a decent income again. And as one of the most expensive cities on the planet, Perth is a pretty rotten place to be poor.

Originally I'd planned on visiting the cheapest countries in Asia, the better to eke out the eight-grand we'd nearly spent on a car. Since then, the trip had morphed into a bucket list style adventure, ticking off a whole bunch of stuff that, even individually would be considered by most people to be trips of a lifetime.

Which was all well and good, except it ignored the defining principle of a bucket list adventure: you're supposed to die at the end of it.

Unfortunately, neither of us were dying.

We still had to eat when we got home – and the way things were going, just *getting home* was looking dubious.

We still hadn't looked at flights back to Perth, for instance.

I had a feeling they might be expensive.

So, crazy as it may seem, I decided that, from now on, we would try and stick to a budget.

Starting with Pakse.

Where I had booked us the cheapest hotel room I could find, at $5 per night.

The tuk-tuk driver who brought us from the bus station struggled to find the place at first, heading instead to the various hotels and hostels commonly frequented by Westerners. When he finally got his head around the address we'd given him, he said, "Ahhh! Yes! Only Laos people stay there."

I decided to take that as a good sign. Cultural immersion, you know.

It was not, in fact, a good sign.

The room looked like something from a 1970s Butlins holiday camp – one that hadn't been cleaned since 1970. There was no window, but given the squalid state of the surrounding junkyard, I considered that a mercy.

Besides the bed – which was broken – there were only four other items in the room; a broken shelf, a broken mirror, a broken chest of drawers and an air-conditioner that looked like it had been on fire recently. It was broken.

We also had an en-suite bathroom, which Roo refused to enter without being vaccinated. The scent of mildew and misery hung in the air. *This is where dreams go to die,* I thought.

I tried to look on the bright side, but all I could find was a slightly less mouldy side. "No-one would ever come here looking to steal things," I pointed out.

Which was probably for the best, as the door didn't lock.

"And we're here for *two* whole days...?" Roo didn't sound keen.

I can't say I blamed her.

The room was so demoralising that we had to get out of there.

The staff spoke no English, a rarity for Laos, so we walked into town, hoping to find a company that ran tours. *Wat Phu Champasak*, a thousand-year-old Khmer temple complex, was the main reason we'd come to Pakse; the only other being that the bus stopped here. Our eventual destination was an archipelago in the Mekong River called the Four Thousand Islands; Pakse's biggest claim to fame was as a ferry port.

After a long and fruitless wander through a town that seemed almost entirely closed, we found a shitty café, had an awful breakfast, and tracked down 'Discover Asia' – Pakse's travel agent. Which was also closed. The only other option I could think of was the youth hostel, where most of the other passengers from the Vientiane bus had been staying. They were easy to find, and they did run tours – only, their tour bus had already departed.

We could still visit the temple of course, by hiring a taxi to take us – only, this would cost twice as much.

Bollocks!

It was like the universe was trying to tell me something.

Some of the poorest people in the world are happy, and plenty of the richest are miserable; the worst part of not having any money is worrying about it.

We were never likely to starve to death. At some point in the future we'd be solvent again, and our only regrets would be things we'd missed out on because I was being miserly.

"Bollocks to it," I said, "let's take a taxi."

It was the right decision.

Roo brightened visibly, and the matching lift in my spirits gave me another revelation: when she was happy, I was happy. It was the ultimate two-for-one – I could devote the rest of my life to making her smile, utilising every ounce of selfish determination I possessed. At the end of the day, so long as she won, so did I.

My new-found sense of maturity lasted until Roo walked up to the taxi driver sitting outside the hostel, and asked him, "Wat Phu?"

To which the only acceptable answer is, of course, 'That poo!'

Off we set.

The taxi, inevitably, was a tuk-tuk; a three-wheeled motorbike taxi with two bench seats in the back. It bounced and jounced down a road which barely qualified for the name, so bad was its condition. The journey took over an hour, driving at speeds that made my teeth rattle.

After miles of rice paddies, we passed several rows of neat little bungalows, like mass-produced versions of the typical Laotian shack. Concrete stilts protected them from floods, raising each house above a small parcel of arable land.

"They army," our driver informed us, "you join army, get house."

It seemed like a fairly sensible policy.

The driver deposited us outside the temple grounds, parked up, and went to sleep in the back of his tuk-tuk. I doubt he was rich, but he seemed content with his lot.

Wat Phu Champasak temple exists for one rather odd reason.

About fifteen-hundred years ago, someone was poking around on *Phu Kao* mountain, and they found a stone at the top that they thought looked like a penis.

And that's it! A big stone willy.

The official word for a stone phallus, in case you ever need to know, is 'linga'.

Once, in Thailand I found a stone that looked like a penis. Boy did I laugh! I kept it in my bungalow for a week, and must have showed that thing to three, maybe four different people.

Whereas the ancient Khmer rulers had overreacted slightly and decided to build their capital city beneath it. Almost nothing remains of *Shrestapura,* which lay at the foot of Wat Phu, on the banks of the Mekong, but fortunately the temple complex itself was maintained and upgraded by each successive empire, and is still a place of worship today.

Proving once and for all that the penis is mightier than the sword.

The paved path through the centre of the complex was lined with 'linga' statues – they were roughly the same shape and height as fence posts, so I didn't even think about putting my hand on them, until Roo asked me if I was going to fondle every bell-end in the place.

The first two temples were closed off, undergoing one of those interminable restorations that you never actually see anyone working on.

What we *could* see was a group of children playing inside the forbidden ruins. Presumably they lived in a nearby village, in which case they had the best playground the world has ever known. The largely unprotected monuments were ripe for exploration, and with no-one around to chase them away, these kids were playing a truly epic game of hide-and-seek.

I felt a bit jealous, actually.

So I waited until I saw them leave, then Roo and I snuck in the same way they'd come out. Inside wasn't all that different, to be honest; the same intricately-carved stone walls, braced here and there with heavy wooden frames. Over half the temple was missing, most likely carried away for house building by generations of farmers.

"I'm not sure you should stand there," Roo said, as I leant in to study a doorframe. "That wall looks like it could come down at any minute. I don't think it's very safe in here."

"Well, it *is* closed," I pointed out. "Maybe that's why."

We beat a hasty retreat back to Penis Avenue, and followed it further up the hill. We stopped for photos on a set of steps that had buckled spectacularly, and were now curved up at the edges like a half-pipe. Here we found an old lady selling bottles of fizzy drink, and felt it was our duty to unburden her of a couple. The day was hot and humid, and we'd been walking uphill since getting out of the tuk-tuk; ice cold Coke, from the cooler the lady was sitting on, was the perfect antidote.

From there it was a quick, sweaty hike up to the

Sanctuary, wherein lay the focal point of the ancient Hindu religion. The focal *shaft,* I should say.

Not that we got to see it.

Some king or other had carted the thing off, presumably to help fertilise his new empire. The temples were still there though – and they were magnificent.

Most of the Sanctuary was standing, the carving on the lintels and friezes worn with age, but still telling their stories of battling Hindu deities. As always, the size and weight of the stone blocks, so far up a mountainside, put me in awe of the builders. This modest temple, now largely forgotten to the outside world, had been lavished with exquisite detail; hundreds of artisans devoting years of their lives to craft such delicate sculptures. Who were they? Had this work been their passion, a proud labour of love? Or a thankless task imposed by a heartless ruler? I pondered these mysteries whilst exploring the ruins of several smaller temples. It was impossible not to feel like Indiana Jones as we scrambled over mossy blocks of stone, climbing thousand-year-old steps which lead nowhere, and brushing vines back to study carvings that had been reclaimed by the jungle.

I'd been secretly afraid that Wat Phu would be an anti-climax; having visited so many citadels and ancient monuments on this trip, there was a very real possibility that it would all blend in, becoming just another pile of artistically arranged rubble to gape at.

But this was our first jungle temple – our first real experience of the kind of thing we'd been wanting to see all along. Forbidden Cities were all well and good, but decades of restoration and crowds of tourists lent them a sanitised, theme-park-esque vibe. This was the real deal; a fantastic ruined temple, its origins obscured by the volatility of the ancient Khmer. From vantage points atop millennia-old stonework, we could look out over the vast expanse of surrounding forest. We could look, and we could wonder; *what else could lie there, half buried in the jungle, undisturbed for centuries? Were there still, even now, tiny fragments of these ancient empires still waiting to be discovered?*

Probably not.

And unexploded landmines from the Vietnam War were far more likely discoveries for anyone wandering randomly into the jungle.

But still...

It was exciting.

And that was good news. Because if Wat Phu aroused the wannabe explorer in me, then just wait until we got across the border into Cambodia.

To Angkor Wat.

Hammock Time

We only stayed one night in that God-awful hotel.

I'd managed to book our trip south to the 4,000 Islands a day earlier than expected, so we paid the princely sum of $5 for our night's accommodation, and fled.

It started to rain as we left, so we huddled in a doorway to wait for our ride. I was a little dismayed by what arrived. The minivan was in decent condition, but it was full; room for the pair of us to squeeze in (with Roo sitting on my knee), but nothing more. This meant our rucksacks would join the rest of the luggage on the roof, tied on with a mess of string and getting wetter by the second. It took some doing, but I convinced the driver to throw an old tarp over the luggage; it hadn't occurred to anyone else in the van to mention it.

The van drove us out of Pakse to a small shanty town which seemed to exist solely because of the docks at the far end.

The driver let us out, then sat there while I climbed onto the roof and handed down everyone's luggage. He pointed us towards the docks and then strolled off in the opposite direction, leaving me with that sinking feeling again.

"Seriously, that guy has *one job*," I moaned.

We found the 'ferry terminal' - a poorly-built wooden hut - at the furthest end of the docks. A handful of other

Westerners were sitting on benches, waiting for seats on a pair of long-tail motor-canoes.

When a smartly-dressed man came over to sell us tickets, I tried to explain that we'd paid already. He wasn't convinced.

"Damn that driver," I said to Roo, "he's pocketed the boat money and buggered off!"

Leaving her to guard our bags, I sprinted back down the docks and up the road, spotting the minivan we'd been traveling in. The driver was nowhere to be seen, but I spied a pile of tickets on his dashboard. I tried the door and it was unlocked, so feeling thoroughly vindicated, I grabbed a handful of the tickets and ran back to the docks.

Where Roo was waving frantically at me. Our driver had materialised, and was handing tickets to the boat guys; Roo had already dragged our rucksacks down the jetty. I jogged up, cursing the half-assed way people did things here. If the driver had given us our boat tickets, or told us we needed boat tickets, or even said, 'I'll be back' – well, it would have saved me a 500-metre dash and about twice that many swear words.

And it would have saved him six boat tickets, which I'm guessing he'd already paid for. They made the trip to the islands screwed up in my pocket.

The Mekong River was enormous by this point, its turbulent waters slapping the boat as we motored across. The rain had all but stopped, mercifully, as everything we owned was now lying exposed in the front of the canoe. Roo, sitting next to me, tensed up every time a wave set the boat rocking. I knew what she was thinking; the narrow canoe wasn't the most stable of vessels in these conditions. She wasn't afraid for herself, of course, or for me – she was afraid for her camera.

Four Thousand Islands is, somewhat predictably, a misnomer. Even the most ambitious tally would reveal only a few hundred – and that's counting every mound and molehill that protruded from the river in the middle of the dry season. In every way that matters, there are actually *three* islands; the backpacker's paradise of *Don Det*, the slightly more upmarket *Don Khon,* or twenty-five kilometres to the north, the seldom-visited *Don Khong.*

Don Det was to be our base for the next few days.

After recovering our bags from the canoe, we lugged them all the way up the narrow strip of bars and resorts to the northernmost point of the island. Then, having seen nothing better, we retraced our steps to the bungalows directly opposite the jetty where our boat had docked, and rented one of those.

I'd learned my lesson; these were certainly not the cheapest places to stay on Don Det. However, having walked past the cheapest, I was confident I'd made the right choice.

There's a first time for everything, right?

Our wooden bungalow was quite cute; one room inside, with a bathroom at the back and a raised veranda at the front. It wasn't overhanging the river, as most of the competition was, but it looked like it had been built by someone who actually built things for a living; the others, not so much.

Don Det is known as a place where not much happens.

At all.

The most popular pastime is relaxing; chilling out comes a close second, with resting and/or napping bringing up the rear. So having established ourselves in a comparatively comfortable resort, and with nothing better to do, we set about soaking up the local vibe.

For dinner that evening, we traipsed back along the muddy path known locally as 'Sunset Boulevard'. One of only two 'roads' on the island, the recent rains had turned much of it into a bog. Boards and planks had been thrown down to help people negotiate the worst stretches, and we quickly learned to walk with care.

Adam's Bar was the nicest wooden shack in a string of them, so we ventured in.

'Been There, Don Det,' said the t-shirts dangling from the eaves, which made me chuckle. As well as Western food, the bar sold 'Space Cookies', 'Happy Shakes', pirated music and movies by the hard drive full – and weed, at $8 a bag.

"I guess that explains the famous 'laid back' vibe," I said to Roo.

"No kidding," she whispered, "look around!"

From the path, it had seemed like the bar was full of people; it was only from inside that we could tell most of them were asleep.

*   *   *

I lay in the hammock outside our bungalow, looking out at the miserable weather. The sky was iron-grey; the drizzle we'd woken up to a few hours ago was in no danger of quitting. The narrow strip of path running past the resort had become caked in thick, slippery mud, and this was one of the few paved parts; a minute's walk in either direction would plunge the walker into an ankle-deep quagmire from which few flip-flops ever escaped.

Roo was considering hiring a bike. She'd been considering hiring a bike for the last two days, but her passion for the idea was starting to wane. Hiking through thick mud is a given, but cycling through it? That sounded like a good way to end up eating it.

What she really wanted was to get out and about, to venture beyond the ribbon of shanty-shacks that stretched up the coast of our tiny island. She wanted to explore – but most of all, she wanted to find something to photograph. And if there's one thing less compatible with expensive cameras than rain, it's throwing them forcefully into a swamp and then dropping a bike on them.

So instead, Roo was reading. It was my turn in the hammock, and I was rocking it gently, with one foot on the deck. All was at peace.

And then I became aware of a sound.

It was a buzzing, such as would be made by a bee, only it seemed to have an undercurrent of urgency. *Wow, that must be one mean-assed bee*, I thought.

The sound grew louder.

And louder.

A sixth-sense I never knew I possessed was doing some weird triangulation-type thing, and the data popped up in my head with a red flag attached to it.

Ha! Sounds like it's coming right for me!

I decided to make a joke about my imminent doom to Roo, and opened my mouth to say something.

And then it hit me.

Now, I've been known to use that as a figure of speech, but no – I mean *it really hit me*.

In the face.

Like a cricket ball.

"AAARRRRRRGGGHHHHHH!"

Roo leapt out of her chair in shock. "Tony? What—"

In reflex I swiped my hand across my face, far too late to protect it from any impact – but as it swung through the empty air in front of my eyes it *connected with something*. Whatever had hit me was still there, sitting on my left eye, and my hand clipped the back end of it and knocked it away.

"What the fu—?"

And then the pain began.

Searing, white hot, it radiated out from my eyeball, burning through my veins until half my face felt like it was on fire.

At that point I said some not-nice things, which I won't relate word for word as I get enough complaints about the swearing in my books as it is.

Suffice to say, I was not a happy bunny.

Roo was trying to help me, but she didn't have a clue what I was raving about. I'd gone from reclining peacefully in a hammock to a screaming, cursing mess almost instantly, and poor Roo didn't know what to do.

She hadn't seen anything.

But then, neither had I.

And the agony lancing through my eye socket told me it could be a while before I'd be seeing anything again.

Vespa Mandarinia

An hour or so later, the pain had died down to manageable levels. My whole head was throbbing, and opening either eye was still out of the question. The left eye, where The Thing had hit me, felt raw and hot, like it was boiling in its own juices. That whole side of my face was so sensitive that the wind on my cheek felt like it was filled with airborne needles.

Roo had finally gotten some sense out of me, and was starting to believe my wild tale that "it just *came for me!*" As far as she was concerned, it was a bee sting, but she'd never known me to overreact this badly.

Eventually, with gentle fingers and much repetition of the phase, "It's okay, let me look," - she prised my hand away from my left eye.

"Oh, fuck me," she said.

Which is generally not a good sign.

"What's wrong? Is it okay?"

"Ahhh…"

"Come on, what does it look like?"

"Umm… you've got one hell of a black eye," she began.

"Yeah?"

"And there's a mark, like a birthmark on your eyelid, and all the way into the corner of your eye. It…"

"What?"

"It looks like a *burn*."
"Shit. That's what it feels like, too."

I'd known pain like this before, I realised, though thankfully not in my eyeball.

When I was thirteen, I'd tried to fill a hot water bottle for my sister. Copying what I'd seen Mum do, I filled it directly from the kettle, holding the bottle against myself to check its temperature.

Never the most co-ordinated of kids, I squeezed too forcefully. Boiling water slopped from the rubber mouth of the bottle, scalding me through my t-shirt.

I screeched and leapt back, flinging the hot water bottle away from me. As part of that gesture, both hands ended up above my head – and one of them was still holding the kettle.

Which was upside-down.

The lid fell off, and the entire contents of the kettle poured straight down my front. That's when I screamed.

I remember dropping the kettle and grabbing my t-shirt, peeling it up over my head. Most of the skin on my stomach came with it.

The pain of that burn, now a dull memory, was suddenly rekindled in my mind. *That was just like this*, I thought, *but how the hell can I have burned my eyeball?*

My head was splitting for the rest of the day, and the area around my left eye never seemed to cool. I was seeing mad flashes of light and colour, but my eye was screwed up shut. I chewed through some painkillers from our first-aid kit, but even with double the maximum dose inside me I was only just keeping a lid on it.

"Maybe we should go to hospital," Roo said doubtfully.
"Yeah, right!"

We were on a scabby little island populated entirely by stoned backpackers.

The boat to the mainland left once a day, and had to be booked at least a day in advance. And even that only got us as far as the nameless shanty town around the docks – the chance of finding emergency medical care was slim at best.

Beyond that... well, we'd have to catch a minibus back to

Pakse.

And I *really* didn't want to do that.

"I'll be fine," I said to Roo, feeling not particularly confident about it.

"But I'm worried about you," she replied.

"Me too," I said, and meant it.

That evening, I munched the last of the painkillers from our kit. We'd been fairly unlucky so far in Laos, and our little first-aid kit was sadly depleted. The last few anti-nausea meds languished in there alongside the anti-diuretics, but between us we'd emptied the thing of Band-Aids, sterile wipes, Paracetamol and Ibuprofen.

So Roo did the only thing she could.

She pulled on her filthy trekking sandals and made her way through the muck to Adam's Bar, where she bought me a big fat bag of weed.

We'd been married for a little over two years at this point; I was surprised it had taken me so long to turn her into a criminal.

The next morning, I still couldn't open my eye. In fact it was stuck to the pillow with some kind of crust, and made a delightful tearing sensation when I prised it away.

"Ugh!" said Roo, on seeing the nastiness on my pillow.

Then she looked at my eye.

"Oh my God! It looks like you've got third-degree burns!"

The eyelid was swollen shut and bright, shiny purple. I didn't dare try and open it – I could just tell that would be a bad idea.

"I think we need to see a doctor," Roo said quietly.

She helped me wash the eye out with bottled water, and again I described the rising tone of the insect as it beat a path straight towards me at top speed. It was uncanny – like it had some kind of personal vendetta, and had flown halfway around the world just to line up that shot.

"But I've never seen a bee sting do anything like this," Roo said. "You're not allergic are you?"

"No. And it was *not* a bee!"

Roo conceded the hammock to me for the next couple of days, and I spent most of that time snoozing, struggling to read with one eye open, listening to music and watching passers-by slogging through the mud.

On the second day after 'the incident' I tried to open my left eye for the first time.

(I'd taken to calling it 'the incident' as a defence mechanism; Roo kept referring to it as 'the bee-sting', and I was concerned that anyone overhearing her might be inclined to believe I was being a bit pathetic.)

The first time I opened the eye I couldn't see out of it, but repeated attempts were rewarded with a bit of vision. It was surreal; I could see through that eye, but only in low-resolution black and white. That damn insect, whatever it was, had downgraded my visual technology by about thirty years.

That evening we sloshed through the mud to the nearest restaurant, and as I waited for my cheeseburger to come I did a bit of Googling.

I was determined to find out what had hit me, if only so I could prove to Roo it wasn't a just a bee.

This is what I found: The Giant Asian Hornet.

Also known as the 'yak-killer wasp' – presumably because it kills yaks – it is the largest and most dangerous stinging insect in the world. Found in Indochina (including Laos), and also in Japan, where it kills thirty to forty people every year. Its venom contains neurotoxins and flesh-dissolving agents; apparently a high enough dose can be fatal to humans, whether they are allergic or not. I figured I'd been lucky – knocking the thing off my eye had caused it to inject only part of its venom, splashing the rest across my eyelid like the climax scene in a bizarre insect-porn video.

Which was why my eyelid was starting to dissolve.

But there wasn't much we could do about it, so we ate our cheeseburgers and decided to Google happier things from now on.

Day Three found the eye looking slightly worse; Day Four found it looking worse still.

"It isn't healing," Roo pointed out, "and if it was going to, by now it would have started. It should be looking better. The bruise has faded, but the skin on your eye still looks scalded and..." she craned over me for a better look. "Shit, Tony, I think the bit around your eye is... I dunno, but it's not good. It looks like it's... decomposing."

"Necrosis." The writer in me couldn't help supplying the word.

"Yeah. Exactly. I really think we need to take you to a hospital."

And yet we didn't, for all the afore-mentioned reasons. I was feeling okay apart from the fire in my eye and a permanent, pounding headache, and neither our schedule nor our budget could easily stretch to a trip back to the mainland.

"I'll see what it's like when we get to Cambodia," I said, to ease her worries. "If it's not getting better by then, we'll look for a hospital in the first decent city we come to."

We booked our combined boat and bus tickets back to the mainland, but via a different route; when we left the Islands, we'd be heading further south, into Cambodia.

To the appropriately-named town of *Stung Treng*.

"If they can't help you, no-one can," Roo quipped.

With our chores accomplished, it was back to the hammock.

I was sitting there, pondering the future, when I saw something amazing.

"Roo! Come quick," I hissed, "and bring your camera!"

She joined me on the veranda and followed my gaze to where the resort-owner's daughter, a slender child of about three or four years old, had plonked herself down to play. She was sitting cross-legged on the path that ran along the front of the bungalows, intent on her game.

In one tiny hand she held a block of polystyrene packaging (what my American readers will know as Styrofoam). In the other hand she gripped a razor-sharp carving knife as long as her forearm, presumably borrowed from the kitchen. With the complete focus of the child at play, she delicately shaved strips off the polystyrene block, systematically reducing it to ribbons.

She was in full view of her mother, who must have chased her out of the kitchen while she prepared a meal; and learning by imitation, as kids will do, the little girl had decided to play chef.

I hardly dared to breathe, for fear I was about to witness the loss of a finger.

But the girl wasn't remotely concerned. When she was done, she carefully gathered up all the shards of foam she'd made, picked up the ten-inch blade, and toddled off back towards the kitchen.

Roo lowered the camera and shook her head in disbelief. "If someone saw that back home, they'd be calling child support about now."

I nodded. "They barely let kids use scissors back home…"

I was to regret using the word 'scissors', as it reminded Roo of an ambition she'd had for some time.

She wanted to cut my hair, and having nothing better to do, she quickly decided this was the perfect opportunity.

"But why?" I asked.

"Because you've needed it doing for ages, and you chickened out in Luang Prabang when you said the hairdresser's shop looked like Frankenstein's surgery."

"It did! I'm telling you, that chair had straps on it for holding people down."

"This hammock's not too scary for you, is it?"

I'd have rolled my eyes at her, if I'd been able. "I'm just… afraid you'll make a mess of it."

Now *that* cracked her up.

"Are you kidding?" she asked, when she'd stopped laughing. "Tony, you look like an extra in a zombie movie. Trust me – nothing I do to your hair could make you look any worse."

Ouch.

It's times like this I think that honesty in a marriage is totally overrated.

CAMBODIA

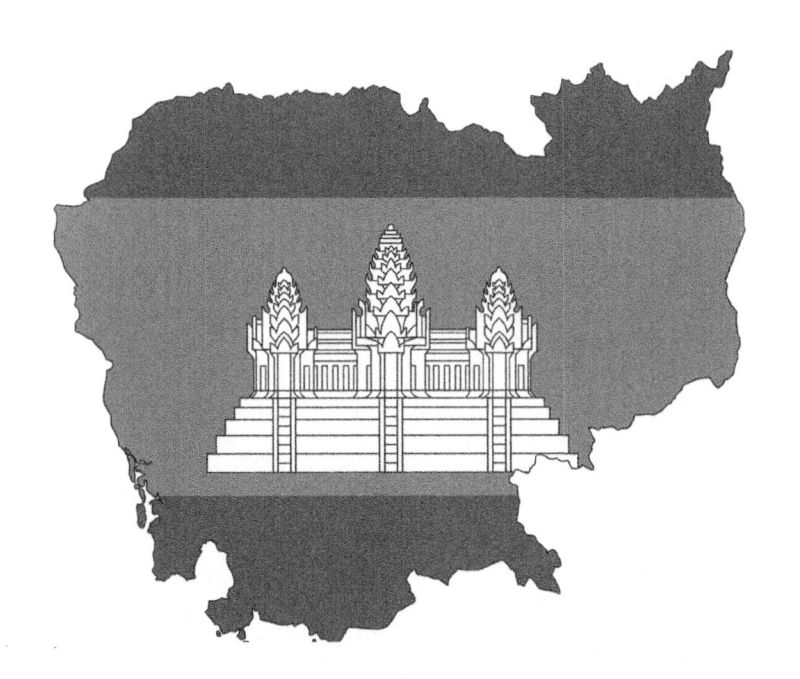

Rough Crossing

Despite the afore-mentioned incidents, our time in Laos had been thoroughly enjoyable. We'd spent a lot of time reading, relaxing and, in my case, getting in some precious writing time. I knew we hadn't really done justice to the place, hadn't tried nearly as hard to explore it as we had previous countries. We'd definitely shifted gears into a slower pace – maybe we were getting lazier as the trip wore on? Or maybe China had been such an assault on the senses that it took us the best part of a month to recover? Whatever the case, Laos was firmly established on my mental list of places to come back to.

Ideally when it wasn't raining.

The boat from the Islands and the bus to the Cambodian border were unremarkable, except for when the driver's mate tried to convince us all to give him our passports ahead of the border crossing. He wanted paying to handle the paperwork on our behalf, and was quite insistent; we chose to keep hold of our precious passports and face the bureaucratic music ourselves, as I'd done a bit of research and didn't entirely trust the guy.

Sandwiched between Vietnam in the east, and Thailand in

the west, Cambodia is widely regarded as one of the most corrupt nations on earth. It is also one of the poorest, which goes some way towards explaining this struggle. In the 1970s, after a decade of ensnarement in the Vietnam War, Cambodia was taken over by a communist faction called Khmer Rouge. Basing itself on the China of genocidal People's Hero Chairman Mao (remember him?), the Khmer Rouge, led by dictator Pol Pot, sent the country into its darkest years. The population was relocated from cities to the countryside, forced labour camps were created, and intellectuals – including anyone who wore glasses – were murdered as enemies of the dominant ideology. Including deaths from widespread starvation, as well as government-sponsored massacres, the Khmer Rouge regime succeeded in killing over a quarter of the country's population – that's over two *million* people.

Although the evil regime was deposed and mostly destroyed by the Vietnamese in 1978, Cambodia has been under totalitarian rule ever since, with the current prime minister – or, 'Lord Prime Minister Supreme Military Commander', to give him his full title – being a former captain in the Khmer Rouge.

None of that should discourage people from visiting the country, of course; you just have to be prepared to encounter a bit of corruption.

Approaching the narrow northern border with Laos, Roo and I braced ourselves to do battle with the scammers we knew would be lying in wait.

The bus dropped us in the shadow of a huge, temple-like structure – an acre of tiled roof supported by dozens of giant columns. It looked like the banqueting hall of an emperor, except that most of the sides were open to the elements. After some of the border structures we'd seen, this was a seriously impressive customs house.

It was also closed.

Whatever it was they did in there, it wasn't being done right now; customs business was being conducted from a garden shed about fifty metres further down the road. We walked past the enormous edifice, trying to image what on earth it was for, and arrived at the barrier separating the two countries – which we walked around.

This was the signal for the con to begin.

First we were offered to exchange money. We declined. There was a bank with an ATM in Stung Treng, our first stop – actually, the bank was pretty much the only thing in Stung Treng.

Next we were informed we had to have medical checks performed… at the side of the road. Quite what they were expecting to diagnose was never mentioned, but there was a suspicious absence of medical equipment on their folding wooden table.

Luckily, I'd read about this, and knew it could be safely ignored. That's one of the difficulties you face in a country where corruption is endemic – just because something is obviously a scam, doesn't necessarily mean it can be avoided. When the people in power are the ones perpetrating the hustle, sometimes you have no choice but to smile sweetly and reach for your wallet.

Not this time. "No thanks," I said, and we pushed past the 'doctor' – who, in stained jeans and an ancient Manchester United top, wasn't doing a terribly good job of appearing official.

Nonetheless, he pursued us down the road, demanding that we get checked out.

"No thanks, we're fine," I repeated.

"Then I will tell the guards!" he declared; his final ultimatum.

"Okay!" I said, cheerfully, and we strolled around a second barrier. The man didn't follow. He knew his turf, and he knew we'd beaten him – but there was a long line of passengers from our bus waiting by his stall, digging in their pockets for the $5 examination fee.

And so we came to the Immigration Hut, where the official business of stamping us into the country would take place. At least, we hoped it would.

Inside, a stern-faced fellow with an army uniform two sizes too small and the attitude to match, refused to believe me when I told him he was not allowed to charge us anything other than the recognised $25 visa fee.

"This is more price," he repeated, tapping a sign written in Magic Marker. "Stamp fee. Process fee. Four dollar each." I could tell he was getting pissed off with me.

"No. We're not paying it."

"Okay. You sit over there."

What he'd neglected to tell us was that we would sit over there *until we decided to pay*. We waited, expecting some higher-up official to come and talk to us – but no-one was coming.

We sat there for a long time.

When the bus driver found us, he was frantic.

The next two bus-loads of passengers had come through the hut, some clueless, some complaining – but they'd all paid the bribe in the end.

It was getting ridiculous. We had no guarantee at all that our bus wouldn't just drive off without us, so I went back to the customs officer and said, "How much."

"Four dollar," he said.

I paid it.

"Four dollar," he said, indicating Roo.

"No. That's all the money we have. No more."

He looked at me, and at Roo, and at the panic in the eyes of the bus driver – and stamped us both into the country. It wasn't a victory – not quite – but it was as good as we were going to get.

"So, we saved four dollars," Roo confirmed, as we were frog-marched back to the bus. "I know it's about the principle, but in hindsight, that particular stand might not have been worth taking."

As though to demonstrate his displeasure, the bus driver decided not to bother calling at Stung Treng. Instead, he simply pulled up on National Highway 7, roughly opposite the turn-off for Stung Treng, dumped out our bags, and left us by the side of the road. One other person followed us off the bus, and luckily for us he was Cambodian. Evidently used to such service, he whipped out his mobile phone and called for a tuk-tuk to come and get us. We hadn't bothered getting a SIM card for our phone in Laos, because the soaking in China had rendered it temperamental at best; now we were extremely grateful for our new friend, and more specifically his functioning phone. Had he not climbed off the bus behind us we'd have been left standing there in the rain, with no clue how far away town was, waiting there for a miracle as the sky darkened into evening.

The tuk-tuk whisked us 2km into the centre of town, depositing us right outside a hotel. We hadn't been faced with an abundance of choices when it came to booking accommodation – in fact we hadn't been faced with anything. Of all the places we'd visited, Stung Treng was the only one to have not a single hotel listed online. So we were kind of glad to be dropped outside one. At least, we were until we checked into the place. The shower, our first port of call after any long bus journey, wouldn't stay on the wall – not a serious problem though, and I quickly fixed it with gaffer tape. The power socket also didn't want to stay on the wall, and was dangling by its (presumably live) cable. I fixed this with a bit of gaffer tape too, which made me feel very much like MacGyver.

The room was pretty awful, but it *did* overlook the river – along with a petrol station, which provided my first source of amusement. A farm truck had just pulled up to the only petrol pump, its driver jumping out to commence filling. Only, he wasn't just filling the truck – the open back of the vehicle was crammed with battered ten-gallon jerry cans, at least fifty of them. He was still there, filling his sixth or seventh, when we gave up watching and headed downstairs in search of food. A handful of scooters had showed up by then, and were queuing up behind him. I imagined they'd have quite a wait.

We'd come to Stung Treng hoping to see the highly endangered Irrawaddy River Dolphins for which the town was famous. Well, *famous* might be a bit of a stretch; let's just say that, if it weren't for their dolphin watching tours, there probably wouldn't be any hotels. We stopped by the front desk to ask the manager if he could help us out.

"No," he replied, gruffly.

"No...?"
"No tour."
"Oh. Why?"
"No dolphins."
"Ah. Right."

We decided to have a scout around anyway, as it was dinner time; judging by the overall cleanliness of the place, we'd didn't fancy eating at our hotel. So we did a quick circuit of the block, and came to the conclusion that our hotel was the only place to eat. There were plenty of other buildings, but none of them were open; the entire town had that abandoned look, with deserted streets, signs creaking in the wind, and a slightly-thicker-than-normal layer of dust coating every locked steel shutter. I'm not saying there was tumbleweed blowing down the road, but it wouldn't have looked out of place.

The wet season had confounded our chances of seeing dolphins from the 4,000 Islands, and it had struck again in Stung Treng; there clearly weren't any tours in the offing.

Rain stops play.

It's my own fault, really, for getting my hopes up. I mean, what did I expect?

Everyone knows dolphins hate getting wet.

With our only reason for staying gone, we returned to the manager and booked ourselves on the first bus to *Ban Lung*. Roughly five hours away to the northeast, Ban Lung wasn't on the typical tourist trail, but it offered an unusual attraction; a circular lake inside the crater of an extinct volcano, which we were hoping to swim in. We'd managed to book into an eco-lodge with the alluring name of 'Treetops' – whether this was an appropriate description or not we would soon find out, but it would have to work very hard indeed to be worse than where we were staying now.

One advantage of town being practically non-existent was that the minibus to Ban Lung departed from the only major landmark: the petrol station right opposite our hotel. Sorry, *the* hotel. You've heard the phrase, one-horse town, right? Well, it fitted Stung Treng perfectly. In fact, judging by the shape of our bed, that damn horse was the last thing that had slept in it. We couldn't get out of there fast enough.

Road Rage

The ancient minivan was stretched to capacity and beyond, with the inexplicably large pile of luggage that local people always seemed to travel with. It didn't matter what country in Asia we visited, one thing seemed to hold true; whenever a local person travelled cross-country, they invariably took with them at least three giant, disintegrating cardboard boxes full of dried fish. Or fruit? Hell, they could have been crammed with iPhones and knock-off Nike Airs for all I knew, but they were always right on the edge of bursting, restrained only by copious amounts of sticky tape and string.

The driver grudgingly found room for our backpacks, and we joined an American couple and a trio of Cambodians in the car. The journey was uneventful, right up until the driver decided to stop and pick up two more people standing by the side of the road. Unfortunately he decided last-minute, no doubt due to that eternal dilemma of having no more space in the car. Debating the pros and cons, he decided it was worth trying to squeeze them in – so he stomped on the brakes, performing what amounted to an emergency stop on the side of the freeway.

His brakes were pretty good, stopping us dead with six cases of whiplash for no extra cost. However, the young Cambodian girl on the scooter behind us wasn't so lucky.

Whether it was her doubtless shoddy brakes, or her inability to predict some maniac performing an emergency stop just to pick up extra passengers, she couldn't match the manoeuvre. Instead she swerved desperately, slammed into the back corner of the car, skimmed the side of it, wobbled a bit, then bounced off the front wing and went flying. Her bike pin-wheeled through the air – as did her body – and the two of them crashed to earth in a tangled heap about ten metres in front of us.

Oh shit, I thought, she's dead for sure.

The driver sat in shocked silence for a few moments, then he cautiously slid out of the cab. I leapt out, followed by Roo and the American couple, although the driver cursed us and waved us back into the car. Instead we all pushed past him, and ran to see if there was anything we could do.

The girl looked to be about seventeen, which meant she was probably closer to thirty. Still, she was skinny as a rail, bleeding from several lacerations, and lying bundled beneath her bike in a way that looked extremely uncomfortable. But she was moving – and whimpering – and that was all the proof we needed to set about lifting the damaged motorbike off her. The bike itself was in pretty bad shape. Two giant cardboard boxes had been strapped to the back of it, and their contents were now strewn across the verge. It was fruit, mostly. (*I KNEW IT!*)

The girl was in a lot of pain, but she managed to sit up. She yelped when she tried to put weight on her left arm, and it hung in a way that suggested her shoulder was dislocated. None of her cuts seemed life-threatening, but she seemed to have a badly sprained ankle, and was in shock – possibly concussed. We helped ease her into a less painful position, by which time the minivan's Cambodian passengers had wandered over. After a bit of a chat with her, one of them made a brief phone call, and then our driver started shouting at us to get back in the van.

I couldn't believe it – he was planning on leaving her like this? We ignored him, as his tone and gestures became more insistent. There was every danger that he would simply leave us there, stranded by the side of the road, but before long a young bloke showed up on another scooter. He knew the girl, and while he chatted to her we helped to gather up her scattered cargo and the broken pieces of her bike. By this point our driver was spitting curses, practically dragging us backwards towards the van. When the newcomer gave us a thumbs-up, we succumbed, allowing ourselves to be bullied back into our vehicle. The driver gunned the engine and sped off without a backward glance, leaving us feeling terrible.

Should we have stayed?

My heart said yes.

But what more could we have done?

For the honour of the thing, and for her sake, I felt we should have stayed.

But then we'd be lost, in the middle of nowhere, and quite likely would have been separated from our luggage when the driver's patience ran out.

I wracked my brain trying to think of some other way in which we could have helped. I came up with nothing; not without medical training, or Cambodian language skills, or any way of conveying her to the nearest hospital.

Sure as shit our driver wouldn't take her.

It was a sullen ride from then on. In whispered conversations, we told the Americans that we would report the accident, and the driver. They said the same, and we left it at that; but nothing could keep that image out of my mind, of the girl's bike spinning past us at terrible speed, and her limp body tumbling after it.

As first days in a country go, this hadn't been the most promising start for Cambodia.

Arriving at our accommodation in Ban Lung made us feel much better.

We were so relieved to be out of that minibus that any place would have seemed like paradise; that said, the bungalows at Treetops Eco Lodge were the nicest we stayed in during our entire time in Asia.

Raised amidst the trees on a forested hillside, they were individual and private. A path of logs snaked down the hill, with spur trails shooting off to each separate residence. By spacing them out and angling their orientation, the builder had managed to achieve that most rare and sacred quality of privacy. He'd also made each bungalow unique, crafting them to nestle into their particular patch of forest. Ours featured a wraparound deck, with hammocks at mid-foliage level, and a large picture window that made up most of the front wall. Inside, the single room was simply furnished; a generous bed, with towels laid out, a pair of chairs, and a small table with tea, coffee and a kettle on it. In keeping with this style of bungalow, the interior was entirely wood – in this case though, the bathroom had been clad in smooth river stones, and every detail was finished beautifully.

We stayed there for a week.

Not just because we loved the airy, yet secluded ambiance, and not because the food served on the main balcony overlooking the forest was great; it was though, and cheap with it.

We stayed mostly because, after everything we'd been through, we felt the need to *stop*. Between high-stress environments, illness and injury, and the constant rush to repack, rebook and move on, we were drained. A spot of R&R was just what the doctor ordered.

And speaking of doctors, every single day Roo recoiled in horror from the ruin of my eyelid and suggested we call one. But the pain was lessening. I was still a little scared, but my colour vision had returned, so I figured I was mostly off the hook. And ten days after the sting, my eyelid showed its first signs of healing.

To celebrate, Roo and I sat drinking mojitos on the extravagant main deck. It had tables, beanbags, fire-pits, and best of all, a view across the treetops of a fiery Cambodian sunset. *This* was how I'd dreamed of our Asian adventure.

As Roo gazed at the horizon, lost in reflection, I felt an upwelling of pride. She'd matched me step for step, every inch of the journey so far, and had pulled me through some truly difficult moments. Technically, I was doing this for a living, or at least trying to; she was just doing it for the love of it. And the love of me.

"You look beautiful," I told her, and meant it.

"Thanks!" she said, startled from her thoughts. She smiled back at me. "You look... hideous."

Healing was going to be a slow process.

*   *   *

Renting out bikes is big business in Ban Lung. Or so we'd assumed, after passing four separate rental shops on the main street. But the first two were entirely unoccupied – racks of chained up bikes outside, and no-one home. The third place clearly didn't want our custom, as the only bloke in there flat out refused to talk to me. He probably thought I had leprosy.

The fourth place was much larger, which is why we'd avoided it, thinking to spend our tourist dollars with the little guys. But this time we had more luck, and emerged with a pair of shabby, unbranded mountain bikes. The owner kept our passports, which had me a little concerned as they were probably worth ten times what the bikes were. We just had to hope he didn't try to make a quick buck by selling them while we were gone.

And we resolved to take damn good care of those bikes.

Crater Lake was only three miles away, so I figured it would be a leisurely jaunt. The rain had stopped, the sun was out, and we were quite looking forward to a swim.

We'd made it out of town, and got to the bottom of the first hill, when Roo's bike chain came off. I put it back on as best I could, but there seemed to be a problem – even wrapped around the biggest gear wheel, it was way too slack. It continued to fall off every five minutes for the rest of the day – whether she was on the bike, or not.

I was having a few problems of my own; my saddle slid further down its post with every bump I went over, until I was struggling to pedal uphill with my knees higher than my arse. I had to stop to adjust it; Roo had to stop because she was laughing too hard.

That ended the first time she bashed her boobs on the handlebars. The slipping chain had left her pedals spinning freely, just as she pushed down with hill-climbing force. The resulting injury left her with matching bruises above both nipples.

"I'll kiss them better," I promised.

That bastard hill lasted the entire first half of the journey. It was the kind of long, gruelling slope that hardcore bikers seem to relish – one reason why I've never trusted them. (The other reason, in case you're wondering, is the Lycra fetish. I mean, really? Does it make you go any faster? If you were in the Tour De France perhaps, but how much difference does it make to a chubby estate agent from Ramsbottom?)

At long last we reached the crest of the hill, and turned right onto a muddy gravel track. Sweaty, oil-stained and sore, we needed more than a swim – a stiff drink wouldn't have gone amiss. But joy of joys! Our long climb was over, and we only had a mile and a half to go.

"Don't worry love, looks like it's all downhill from here!" I called back.

Which is when we realised that none of our brakes worked.

Crater Lake, when we finally got there, was gorgeous.

It was, however, just a lake. All the pictures we'd seen illustrated its perfectly circular shape, puncturing the dense forest like a blast from a laser cannon.

That's because all these photos were taken from the air. When you stand in front of it, all you can see is a flat, clear expanse of water, with the jungle closing in on all sides. That was good enough for me, though, and I spent a pleasant hour jumping in off the railings of a wooden swimming platform.

Roo, being wary of the pack of children running around, decided to stay and watch the bikes.

And then it was time to face the ride back.

A mile and a half uphill, through mud, on bikes that didn't do well uphill. To put it mildly.

And then a mile and a half downhill, on one long, straight stretch of smooth tarmac – on bikes with no brakes.

By the time we made it back to the shop I was seriously considering throwing the damn things through the window.

"Now I know why they kept our passports," I said to Roo, as we limped back towards Treetops. "It's not to stop us stealing the damn bikes – it's to stop me shoving them up his arse when we got back!"

Delicate Matters

I could have stayed in Ban Lung forever.

There was sod all else to do there, but it's amazing how little that matters when you're staying in a comfortable place with good food, gorgeous views, and someone you love.

It was a fleeting insight into how people survived without travel. *Maybe I could too, one day?* I thought.

Ha! Not a chance.

We'd been saving *Siam Reap,* the top destination in Cambodia, because we wanted to end our trip with a blast. Most tourists don't even bother going anywhere else in Cambodia; but then, most tourists are on a strict time limit. Staying in Ban Lung had been cheap and relaxing, and was the perfect advertisement for travelling slow. We hadn't exactly immersed ourselves in local culture, but we'd explored the town and made a couple of forays into the surrounding countryside. We'd also spent a lot of time listening to the rain rattling on the roof of our bungalow, appreciating the tranquillity of the natural environment – and snuggling. Now I'd caught up on my journaling, my eye had mostly healed... and Roo still hadn't started sorting her orangutan pictures.

I had a feeling they'd be with us for the long haul.

We were squelching through the mud on our way back from the market when Roo's eagle eyes picked out something on the ground. "Tony! Quick!"

I looked down, and couldn't believe it – right between her feet, torn and filthy and half-disintegrated – was a US $100 bill!

Crouching down, I very gingerly extricated the note. It was in terrible shape, possibly beyond saving – but if there was any chance at all, we had to try. Surely Fate had planted this in our path, as a reward for all our struggles?

Or perhaps as an apology.

Back at the bungalow, Roo went to work. She blotted the mud and water off the fragile paper, and used a Q-tip to gently unfold all the jagged edges. There were several holes ripped in the bill, and most of one edge was missing. It was stained and crumpled... but still. I did a bit of Googling and found all sorts of urban myths, that such notes could be returned to the US mint for replacement, or that it was still legal tender if more than half of it remained intact. There was nothing we could do about it in Cambodia – people entering the country are advised to bring pristine notes, for fear imperfect currency will be rejected – but once we got home, I'd figure out what to do.

And then we'd have a party!

Roo sandwiched our windfall between several sheets of toilet paper, and pressed it in my journal.

We pulled the note out periodically over the next few weeks, re-examining the damage, trying different methods of cleaning it, and debating whether or not it would pass muster. I spent a few more hours researching the legalities, and made a list of our options. Then Roo suggested checking for security features, so I looked up those, too. The note had its watermark alright, and there may or may not have been a special thread embedded in it. I was carefully turning the note back and forth in the light, trying to see if any part of it was glowing – when I spotted something a little more obvious.

"Oh SHIT! Roo! It's fake!"

"Nooooo!" She leapt up and came to look. "What's wrong with it? How can you tell?"

"Well, you can see the watermark here, which is fine," I explained.

"Yes?"

"But then when you turn it over..."

"Yes? What is it?"

I pointed.

"Oh, bloody hell!"

On the back, where it should have said 'UNITED STATES OF AMERICA' across the top, in the exact same typeface it actually said, 'ABODE OF THE DEAD BANK'.

"I'm no expert," I admitted, "but that *might* give the game away..."

*   *   *

The bus to Siam Reap was actually two buses. No-one had told us this when we booked it, but few things surprised us anymore. What was a tad concerning was the second bus, which we'd been told we'd be getting onto when it was ready to leave, listed its destination as Hanoi, in Vietnam.

"We really don't want to end up in Hanoi," I said to the lady in the ticket-shack.

"No, is okay, go, Siam Reap," she replied.

"Siam Reap? Really?"

"Yes!"

We had no choice but to trust her, so we looked around for something to occupy us for the next hour or two.

"Hey, you know where we are?" asked Roo.

"Middle of nowhere?"

"No, look! That lady on the food stall, see what she's cooking? She's frying tarantulas. This is..." she swiped through the pages of *Lonely Planet: Cambodia* on her tablet. "This is *Skuon*."

"Ahhh!" It all made perfect sense, now.

Spider eating had supposedly started as an act of desperation. The villages near Skuon had suffered badly during the rule of Khmer Rouge, and widespread food shortages forced them to look for other options. It's probably a mark of how extreme their hunger was that they even considered eating tarantulas – for starters, they had to catch the bloody things, and then de-fang them without dying. Cambodian tarantulas are roughly the size of an adult human's palm, and to see one in the wild, well, you'd be forgiven for thinking *it* was going to eat *you*. As spiders go, they are the stuff of nightmares – and that's coming from a guy who's lived in Australia for the last two years.

But after the years of famine ended, the villagers of Skuon had discovered quite an appetite for the spiders. As had people in other parts of the country, who now made regular visits to this tiny outpost to stock up.

Even I had to admit, the spiders didn't look all that threatening when deep-fried and piled on a serving platter the size of a dustbin lid. There must have been hundreds of them, all slightly shrivelled but otherwise intact. The old lady who ran the stall was doing a roaring trade, selling them by the bag to locals on scooters.

And no wonder. She was offering an outrageous bargain – *three* spiders for fifty cents! At that price, it was hard to turn her down. Specifically, it was hard to turn down the challenge, as I'd proudly boasted to Roo that I would eat anything – spiders included. Hell, after Mongolian five-organ soup, how bad could it really be?

Still, I decided not to go too crazy. Since Roo wasn't keen on partaking, I eschewed the special offer, and just bought the one for now.

Roo started filming me as I took my prize to a plastic picnic table. She was hoping to capture squeals of disgust and possible retching, whereas I was determined to take this thing like a man. In my mouth…

Now, if you've seen a spider's legs lately, you might have noticed that there's not a lot of meat on them. I pulled one off and studied it, wondering what the next step was. I mean, I was struggling to find anything edible at all in the 'meal' I had in front of me.

"Maybe you suck out the meat, like you do with crabs?" I mused.

I tried.

I failed.

"So, you don't suck out the meat like you do on crabs," I confirmed.

In the end I just stuffed the legs in whole, crunching them up as best I could.

"What does it taste like?" Roo asked, from behind her camera lens.

I thought about my response for a second, rolling the mixture around in my mouth. "Fingernails and soy sauce," I admitted.

Rolling it around in my mouth hadn't been the wisest of moves.

I cracked the chest cavity open, but found it hollow; whatever substance had been in there must have oozed out during the cooking process. I took a nibble anyway, and was rewarded with crispy shards of toughened carapace. They tasted about as good as they sound, which is to say, not great. The soy sauce was overpowering any natural spider-y flavour, which is a shame, as I can't stand soy sauce. I'd almost rather have eaten it raw.

Not that I'd actually found much to eat so far.

"No wonder locals buy them by the bagful," I commented.

Now I was faced with a dilemma. In my fingers I held the spider's abdomen – which is a polite way of saying, the arse-end of the beast. I dimly recalled reading something about this, but couldn't quite remember if the recommendation was to eat the abdomen, or not.

Might as well give it a go, I thought, after all, I paid twenty cents for this…

I held the spider's bum up to my mouth, steeling myself for the inevitable explosion of nastiness within. But just as I made ready to stuff it in my gob, I gave it a gentle squeeze. A bubble of brown goo welled up from within the thing, dribbling out onto the table. It was a substance so unspeakably foul that my mind was made up instantly.

"Yeah, I'm guessing you don't eat this part…"

It was a narrow escape. Later research revealed this rather poetic description: 'the abdomen contains a brown paste consisting of organs, possibly eggs, and excrement.'

Apparently, some people call it a delicacy.

As for what other people call those people, I probably shouldn't say.

So, all in all, not the most satisfying of snacks. Not inedible, and had I been dying of starvation in a remote jungle village, well, I'd have munched those little buggers like they were M&M's. But as a delicacy… let's just say, I'm glad I didn't blow the whole fifty cents. A phrase I use a lot is, 'When in Rome,' – and I'm delighted to say I have finally found the exception that proves this rule. When in Skuon, *do not* do as the locals do. Instead, point and laugh at the poor fools who *are* doing as the locals do – it really is far more entertaining to watch people trying to eat tarantulas than it is to eat one yourself.

Trust me.

"The worst part," I said to Roo afterwards, "is the leg hair. It's all stuck in my teeth."

"What? Eww! You're telling me they didn't take the fur off it before they cooked it?"

"Of course not! How could they? And that was a hairy little son of a bitch."

"No wonder you didn't enjoy it! No-one likes eating hair. Even if it is deep fried. You should go back and demand one that's been de-haired."

"Well, I could try, but she doesn't speak much English. And oddly enough, I don't know the Cambodian for 'please shave my spider'."

City of Stone

On our first morning in Siam Reap, I woke up already grinning.

This was a day that could well change my life forever.

I was going to do something I'd been wanting to do since I was ten.

Roo was so excited she was bouncing around the room.

"Yay!" she said, wrapping me in a bear hug, "We're going to feed the squirrels!"

"Ah... yes, love. Although, I feel you might be missing the point a little..."

This was the day around which the entire trip had been built – at least for me.

Today, we would be exploring the most impressive section of the nine-hundred-year-old temple complex of Angkor Wat.

Where apparently, there lived a large population of mischievous squirrels, who had become expert picnic thieves. Roo had become obsessed with feeding them ever since she read about it in *Lonely Planet*.

That guidebook had a lot to answer for.

We rented bicycles from a shop in town, preferring to be our own bosses for the day instead of being shepherded around by a tuk-tuk driver. It was an appropriate start to our adventure; just riding out of the city felt daring. As swarms of scooters and tuk-tuks zipped by on both sides, it was exhilarating to be a part of the flow. And a bit scary, too – there obviously hadn't been a 'watch out for cyclists' campaign here recently.

One long, straight road led directly through the forest from Siam Reap to Angkor, passing a ticket booth the size of a bus station. It pretty much would be a bus station in peak season, if the vast coach waiting area was anything to judge by. Two million people came through here every year, as it was the only legal place to buy entrance tickets for the temples. Queuing up behind a dozen international tour groups would have been a nightmare – yet again, we were glad of our timing. Cambodia has a 'hot-wet' season, and we were smack bang in the middle of it. The lack of crowds was the most obvious benefit, but the major drawback was equally obvious – in every photo we took, our clothes were soaking with sweat.

Having paid for three-day passes to the Angkor Archaeological Park, we cycled on. Twenty minutes later we emerged from the tunnel of trees, to be rewarded with our first sight of Angkor Wat. It was majestic; the temple's towers rose spectacularly above the surrounding forest, beyond a moat so vast it was hard to believe it was artificial.

We followed the outline of the perfectly rectangular island, turning a corner towards the main gate. Here lay a chaos of motorbikes and tourists, a fraction of what it would have been a few months ago but still an unplanned, swirling melee. A wide stone causeway crossed the moat, leading to possibly the most-photographed gatehouse on the planet; a shiver ran down my spine as I recognised the entrance to Angkor Wat.

But we didn't stop.

We rode on, because we had bigger fish to fry.

You see, the Archaeological Park contains over a thousand temples.

Many of them are nameless piles of rubble, but over fifty are full-size structures with names like Angkor Thom, Angkor Bob and Angkor Freddie.

Okay, I may have made the last two up, but the point is, the most famous one is not necessarily the most impressive. We'd decided to spend our first day exploring Angkor Thom, a walled city almost two miles square, which contained most of the best-preserved temples in the area. My theory was that nothing could overshadow Angkor Wat itself, but if we saw it first, everything else in the region might seem kind of naff by comparison.

So! On we pedalled, around that enormous moat. We were gaining a real appreciation of its scale – if only because our arses were going numb from being in the saddle.

"How much... money did... we save... with bikes?" Roo panted behind me.

"About five dollars!" I called back. "But bikes are environmentally friendly!"

I didn't hear what she said next, but I don't think it was very complimentary.

Eventually we crossed a bridge flanked by statues of Hindu gods, passed through a gateway held up by chunky timber braces, and left our bikes chained to a railing inside. From here we scrambled up a grassy slope to the top of Angkor Thom's eight-metre high walls, and stood in another world. Trees grew atop the wall, forming a secluded walkway far from the main tourist areas. Bordered by a moat of its own, this temple complex was more than five times the size of its world-famous cousin.

Inevitably, we'd decided to do things a bit differently. Walking around the walls wasn't a common activity for tourists, as most of the amazing ruins were in the middle of the compound. Within a few minute's walk of the gate we found ourselves alone, surrounded by clouds of butterflies, and we settled down to eat our picnic. "Save some for the squirrels!" Roo reminded me.

We played around in the ruins of a corner tower, before continuing around the wall to a seldom-used gate at the next cardinal point. There we climbed back down, succumbing at last to the lure of the temples.

They did not disappoint.

From this direction, the first thing we came to was the

Baphuon. Reached by a raised causeway of its own, the Baphuon is a colossal three-tiered stone pedestal a hundred-metres square. To stand in front of it is to be utterly humbled; were it not missing its central tower, it would be taller than the Statue of Liberty. Restoration had only been completed two years ago, having taken fifty-one years in total. It must have been the ultimate face-palm moment; after spending eight years completely dismantling the temple, the records of where each stone came from were lost during the war with the Khmer Rouge, turning it into the world's biggest jigsaw puzzle.

Temples were everywhere. No matter which direction we walked in, we found gateways, walls, steps, shrines; all were beautifully carved, or would have been a few centuries ago, and all were ruined, to a greater or lesser degree. Trees were everywhere too, not caring one whit if they grew through an ornate stone window frame, split apart a lintel or collapsed a roof onto themselves. It gave the whole place a mysterious, undiscovered feeling – amazing really, considering it's one of the most-visited tourist attractions in the world. It had size in its favour, of course. I'd made fun of Beijing's Forbidden City, suggesting the Ming Emperors had some kind of compensation issues that caused them to build palaces the size of small towns. Angkor Thom was on another level again; there was room in here to fit twelve Forbidden Cities, and still have sixty acres left over for a vegetable garden. In this vast gulf of space, thousands of tourists were easily swallowed up. There were times when we had not just a temple to ourselves, but the surrounding landscape as far as we could see. Even in peak season, when visitors thronged the most important monuments, there would be pockets of quiet and seclusion for anyone seeking them. And it goes without saying, there'd be a temple in them.

We roamed the ruins until our feet ached, crossing a wide paved terrace edged with dozens of identical elephant sculptures, climbing down to examine an elaborately-carved wall recently discovered hidden behind another elaborately-carved wall, and posing for photos with all of it. In the near-distance we could see many more towers, but decided against heading over to them.

"They're *massive*," Roo pointed out, "so they look closer than they are. It'll take us half an hour to walk over there!"

Instead, we worked our way to the centre of the complex, towards a colossal edifice that had been looming over us all day. This was the *Bayon* – the largest structure at Angkor Thom, a titanic three-level ziggurat towering forty-seven metres above the surrounding landscape.

From a distance it looked gnarled and knobbly, owing to the stupendous amount of raised detailing on the stonework. Most famous of all are the giant faces, two-hundred and sixteen of them, that graced roughly half the postcards in the country. We climbed the ridiculously steep steps from level to level, eyeing great piles of stones still waiting to be sorted and catalogued. There was no set end-date for this restoration; it would quite simply never be fully complete. The constant presence of tourists is both too dangerous, and yet too financially beneficial, to allow much work to be done.

Standing at the top, beneath the benevolent stone smiles of the corner towers, I was moved almost to tears by the beauty of the place. Such a powerful, awe-inspiring monument, from a civilization long lost; I felt a sudden upwelling of respect for its builders, and a sense of fascination with their mysterious culture.

Also worth noting; the view was incredible.

We must have been suffering from heatstroke when we decided to ride the long way home. There were plenty of other temples to see in the surrounding countryside, and unfortunately most of them were marked on our map. This resulted in an extended excursion, cycling past more piles of eleventh-century religious rubble than was strictly necessary. We stopped for a breather at one of the grandest; *Ta Prohm*, which was used as a set in the movie Tomb Raider. It was an eerie place; completely reclaimed by the jungle, the ancient stone buildings were being strangled by roots as thick as my waist. Huge trees grew from rooftops, vines and creepers tangled the fallen blocks, and every surface was coated in fuzzy green moss. It was like a fairy castle, or perhaps an elven stronghold – but one that had long since been destroyed, leaving only ghosts and jungle plants to fight over the ruins.

We stayed for as long as we could, but got chased out by a security guard just before sunset. We'd already given him the slip a couple of times, and when he cornered us again we decided he'd earned his keep. This was a place so magical, so creepy and ethereal, that we knew we'd be coming back.

Night fell on the ride home, which made us wish we had lights on our bikes. In keeping with most forests, there weren't a lot of streetlights – none, to be precise, and we were seriously relieved when we broke free of the trees and sighted Angkor Wat. From there, we followed the stream of traffic around the moat and turned back towards Siam Reap.

Tuk-tuks buffeted us as they shot past, carrying tourists who'd lingered to watch the sunset at *Phnom Bakheng*. We gripped our handlebars tightly and pedaled on. Just ahead of us we noticed an eastern European couple of similar age, also on bikes. He was cycling for all he was worth – and cycling one-handed, because his other hand was on her bike, pushing her along. From the periodic shrieks she emitted, we could only assume that she couldn't ride a bike, and that without his support she'd be under the wheels of the next tuk-tuk.

"Look!" I called back to Roo, "I bet they're glad they saved five dollars!"

We rode straight back to the hotel, because knowing we'd be buying a three day Angkor pass, we'd paid to keep the bikes for three days as well.

Bugger.

We'd cycled nearly fourteen miles, and walked another six. Added to the many hundreds of steps we'd climbed, the sheer volume of sweat we'd pumped out, and the number of calories burnt by our brains going, "WHAAAAT?" – we'd had a pretty heavy day.

We collapsed into bed, rising only to answer the door when the hotel manager brought us our dinner. Room service in Cambodia, it turns out, is dangerously affordable.

So affordable, in fact, that the next day we did nothing

else.

As we lay there, sated and exhausted, my mind spun with images of everything we'd seen. I knew these pictures would stay with me forever. I rolled over to look at Roo.

"My only regret," I told her, "is that I didn't bring my Mum to see it. She'd have gone absolutely mental."

"We'll have to come back then, and bring her with us," Roo said.

"Now that is a great idea!"

We were silent for a while, both picturing that future. Then Roo rolled to face me.

"You know what my only regret is?" she asked.

"What?"

"NO SQUIRRELS!"

Best 'Til Last

Angkor Wat was every bit as incredible as I'd hoped.

After a day in bed resting our sore feet, and letting our arses re-inflate to their normal size, we set off for the temple – by tuk-tuk, this time.

We'd learnt our lesson; bikes are from the devil.

I'd been concerned that the driver, being on a flat day rate, would hurry us along, hoping to get finished early – but nothing could be further from the truth. He dropped us off at the entrance, stretched out a hammock in the back of his tuk-tuk, and went to sleep.

We looked up – and there it was! A colonnaded gallery, surmounted by distinctive beehive tower-tops, rising beyond the six-hundred-foot wide moat.

I'd been dreaming of this all my life.

Walking across that causeway gave me chills.

In case you haven't figured this out by now, I'm a bit of a geek when it comes to this sort of stuff. But not everyone is – if you're sick of temples, please feel free to skip ahead to the next chapter! I won't hold it against you, I promise.

Once we passed through the entrance building, we could see the central temple itself – the single largest religious structure on the planet. Made almost entirely of sandstone, around ten *million* 1.5 tonne blocks were quarried and shipped to the site by barge. We followed a paved avenue lined with lion statues, which I couldn't help but notice had extremely well-defined buttocks.

The path ran between two flanking temples, known as libraries, though their real use is unknown. And then we arrived, climbing steps to the raised terrace on which the temple was built. Even that most subtle of elements was staggering when I thought about it. Roughly two-hundred metres (700 feet) a side, the central section of the temple was built on a square stone plinth maybe two metres high. Imagine the volume of space that had to be filled, just to create that level deck to build on! Millions of tonnes of sand and rubble must have been carted here, all to disappear into the structure's most unremarkable aspect – its foundations.

The lowest level of the temple is a square of open galleries, featuring hundreds of metres of incredibly detailed bas-relief carvings in near-perfect condition. A black-ish stripe around shoulder-height attested to countless hands that have reached up and touched them over the years, in places turning the sandstone as smooth as glass. We moved on, finding an entrance to the inner courtyard, from where the next level of the temple rose steeply. The stairs up the side of the next gigantic plinth were purposefully built at a seventy-degree angle; ascending towards heaven was never meant to be easy.

Reaching the next level, we were already at tree-top height. Whereas the lower courtyard had been grass, this one was paved; again, my mind reeled at the sheer quantity of materiel underfoot. Although Angkor Wat is the best preserved of the surrounding temples, owing to it being in continuous use since its construction, even here we saw a huge number of loose stones awaiting relocation. In this case they were laid out in orderly rows rather than heaped in jumbled piles, but it looked like an impossible puzzle – a giant jigsaw whose picture has been missing for nearly a thousand years.

Still another level loomed above us. This time the steps had been deemed too precipitous, so a wooden replacement had been laid over the top. We filed up, craning our necks back to take in the view of the lower levels, the acres of grass surrounding them, and the gleaming moat surrounding that. Then we were into the Sanctuary, at the highest point in the temple. Again, it was a square of galleries open to the inside, with two central corridors forming a cross. This divided the interior into four courtyards, each of which we explored. At the centre of it all was the highest tower, the 43-metre pinnacle of Angkor Wat – which has been sealed since the temple's conversion to Buddhism in the late 12th century. The four corner towers were still open though, so I went into one and looked up. The stone, so exquisitely sculpted on the outside, was left as rough blocks inside; I could see right up to the top. Those world-famous towers – which apparently are meant to resemble lotus buds – are hollow.

Standing beneath that tower, staring out at the complex below, I felt a sense of accomplishment like no other. Getting there hadn't been impossibly difficult, but it represented something more intangible. I'd always wanted to come here, much as I've always wanted to visit Machu Picchu in Peru and Petra in Jordan. Slowly, I was working my way through those goals, but for the first time, this was not a holiday. No-one else had paid for this adventure, and we hadn't saved up wages and taken two weeks off work. We were here because I'd written a book, and that project had funded this one. Roo had asked me several times if I'd be writing a book about our Asian experiences, and I'd always replied, "Probably not." I didn't think we'd done anything interesting enough, and it felt too contrived to seek out situations that would be worth writing about. And yet…

There was something to be said for this travel writing lark.

Especially now that I'd actually done some travelling.

*   *   *

Two days later, having explored the major sites to the point of exhaustion, we hired a tuk-tuk to take us fifty miles east to *Beng Mealea.* This was the last temple we would visit in the vicinity of Siam Reap – more than likely the last we'd visit in Cambodia. Which meant...

That element of our Asian Adventure would be over.

It had worked out well; as Roo pointed out, if we'd seen the temples of Angkor at the start of our journey, nothing else would have held a candle to them. Done this way, it was a fitting end to our trip; all we had to do now was wind down, kick back, and hit the beach.

There was just enough time for one last temple...

And oh man, was it a good one.

Forget everything I've said about Angkor Thom and Angkor Wat; Beng Mealea was the best by miles. But why? I mean, sure, it was photogenic as hell, with trees growing through collapsed corridors, and great piles of stone blocks lying where they'd tumbled. Plus, the layout was interesting, made more so by the extensive wooden walkways built to let tourists get around the place. And the ruined structures themselves differed from the lofty spires of the bigger temples, being on a more human scale – narrower, more enclosed and secretive.

But none of this compared to the single, overriding factor in Beng Mealea's favour: *you could climb on it!*

At least so long as no-one caught you.

The central tower was a huge mountain of rubble, but many of the surrounding galleries were largely intact. It was thrilling to stand atop the curved stone roofs, to scale the gatehouse pediments and cross from one area to another hand-over-hand along vines as thick as my wrists.

Local children were all over the place, leaping around the ruins with a grace and sure-footedness I could only envy. They must have spent most of their lives climbing the walls and trees of the ancient temple; it was an education I was majorly jealous of.

A slightly less romantic aspect of their education came to light when Roo tipped one young lad with a few small-denomination notes. He'd shown her the way down to a ledge we were crossing, and seemed such a bright and happy soul that she'd felt compelled to reward him.

But the other children switched instantly from play to beg, presumably having learned from their parents that all tourists were rich marks. Barefoot and skinny, they clustered around us. As far as I could tell, they'd learned precisely one word of English; a word much-beloved of tour guides and touts the world over.

"Cheap!" the first lad said, holding out his hand. He wasn't offering anything for sale, and there was no pretence of him playing tour guide – he just knew it was a word that adults used to encourage foreigners to give them money.

"Cheap!" said a tiny girl of about six.

"Cheap!" the first boy said again, not to be outdone.

"Cheap!" A third child thrust his hand between the others.

I shook my head, both saddened and amused, and moved away along the ledge.

"Cheap! Cheap!" The kids followed, five of them now, their high-pitched voices repeating the same word over and over.

"Cheap! Cheap! Cheap!"

It was like being followed by a flock of birds.

They persisted for a good ten minutes, before I cracked up laughing. Roo took the opportunity to film a few seconds of it; a surreal encounter, and one that still makes me chuckle when I think about it.

After spending the entire day climbing ruins, we had to help each other walk back to the tuk-tuk. Returning to Siam Reap, we got dropped off near the heart of the bustling tourist district. We knew we were on Pub Street because huge neon signs saying 'Pub Street' hung above every junction. The touting was more fierce here than anywhere else we'd been in either Laos or Cambodia – the worst I'd come across since Beijing's Silk Market. Wanting neither a massage, nor a tuk-tuk, we were accosted every few steps by locals trying forcibly to sell us both. We battled through, determined not to let this sour our day, and ducked into a Mexican restaurant called 'Viva', hoping to hide.

It was a good choice; the food there was so delicious, and so cheap, that as soon as we'd finished eating we ordered another meal between us.

And that was our last real experience of the city; we

staggered home in a shared food coma, slept the deep sleep of the truly knackered, and rose the next day to catch our bus out of Siam Reap. We'd loved the place; not the city itself, which had little to recommend it beyond low prices, but that wasn't what we'd come for. Angkor Wat, and all archaeological gems that shared its umbrella, had been even more amazing than I'd imagined. I was sad to go, but I knew I'd be back – much like the food at Viva, Angkor really was too good to resist a second helping.

"Last time," Roo said, as we boarded a night bus bound for the beach resort of *Sihanoukville*. I detected a trace of sadness in her voice, and understood completely. Sleeper buses (or, more appropriately, sleepless buses), had been a regular fixture on our itinerary, and one we approached with a mixture of hope and dread. There was always the chance, I firmly believed, that we'd get a comfy berth, a smooth road, a cheap night's sleep, and wake up somewhere new and exciting. The reality was usually the opposite; treacherous roads, treacherous drivers, cramped conditions and way too many bodily fluids on display.

Still, there was a definite melancholy to knowing this was our final overnight voyage; from here on, everything we did would be a 'last' – at least as far as this adventure was concerned.

I sincerely hoped it was the last time we'd have to wait three hours for a bus.

"Bus late," said the man in the booking office, shrugging. Which was obviously bollocks. With only a handful of passengers for the 8pm departure, they'd decided to cancel our bus and bump us to the 11pm. Which made perfect sense, and I wouldn't have minded a bit, if they'd just told us that. Instead, we stood shivering on the street outside the booking office, our luggage in a pile, gazing longingly at the strip of bars and restaurants a few blocks away.

Unsurprisingly, our 'late' bus arrived bang on schedule for the 11pm slot. It was a weird one; the permanently-reclined seats were packed in so tightly that the person in front of you was sleeping with their head directly above your groin. As Roo settled in behind me, I could feel her breath tickling my hair.

"I'm kind of glad this is our last night bus," I said to Roo. "Reckon that's the last time we'll be blatantly lied to?"

"Ha! I wouldn't get your hopes up."

Beach, baby!

We arrived in Sihanoukville to discover a tragedy.

Sadly, on our last night bus, less than ten days from the end of our trip, we suffered our second major theft of the trip.

Roo had known that boy was up to no good; when the bus made a pit stop in the middle of the night, she'd noticed the young lad of about ten, walking up and down the aisle. I'd been half asleep at the time, but she'd convinced me to go and check on our bags. An odd feature of the bus was that the luggage storage area could be accessed from a set of stairs in the middle – where in most buses that size, there'd be a toilet. I'd dragged myself out of my bunk and gone for a look, but the boy was long gone.

And so was something else.

My towel.

I was… perplexed, to be honest.

I mean, don't get me wrong – I loved that towel, as much as any man can love a towel – but what I didn't understand was, why?

In the wide world of senseless crimes, this had to be a stand-out case.

In some ways, I guess it was Karma, finally catching up with me. I'd stolen that towel myself, you see, at a time when I was almost as desperate as that boy must have been. During my travels around Australia, I'd found myself staying at a YMCA hostel. It was a terrifying place; grown men with bushy beards wandering the corridors in their underwear, singing hymns about the glory of God. Perhaps it was ironic that the YMCA made a criminal out of me; I couldn't afford a new towel, and the cleaners *just kept bringing more of them.*

In the end I caved, fleeing the scene with my sister, Gill – *who also stole a towel!*

You see, Gill? That's what you get! There's no honour among thieves.

Anyway, I'd used that towel for years. It was covered in hair dye (not mine), blood (mostly mine), and was ripped from where it had got caught in a van door once. So, the poor lad probably got less than he'd bargained for.

I think the lesson we should all take home from this, is, Fate never smiles on a towel-thief.

The hotel we checked into was another great find. Called Aqua Resort, it was set back from town amidst a kind of no-man's land of overgrown fields and abandoned building projects.

But what a place! Two stories, with rooms on three sides wrapping around a rectangular swimming pool, it fitted our needs perfectly.

Because our needs had changed somewhat, over the last twenty-four hours.

The other major development we'd discovered on arrival was this; my baby sister, arch-towel-thief that she was, had sent me an email.

She was about to have a baby of her own.

Like, *now.*

I could hardly believe it. At the start of this trip, she'd only just discovered she was pregnant; now, as we made our plans for coming home, she was ready to give birth. Sometimes I'm guilty of thinking that real life stops for everyone else while we're away. Certainly, we tend to get back from a trip to find nothing much has changed, and real life is right where we left it.

Not so, this time.

Gill was about to be a mum!

She'd had a roller coaster ride of it.

Starting with the warning from doctors that there was a good chance her baby had Down's Syndrome. She'd been terrified, of course, but hardly dared say anything. Only our Mum knew the story at that point, and weeks of stress and sleepless nights had been resolved with a test that showed the baby was completely normal.

It was small though – tiny actually, to the point where this had caused concerns in itself. For anyone that doesn't know, a baby's growth is tracked in the womb, and measured against a set of statistics to give what's called the percentile.

An average baby falls somewhere between the 40th and 60th percentiles; Gill's unborn child was struggling to reach the 1st.

Gill was less worried about this situation, as she knew the reason. Having inherited our Mum's gnomic stature, Gill isn't huge herself, but her husband Chris is tiny. On the day of their wedding, he weighed less than she did – and was shorter, by about half an inch.

So. A midget baby, born to Hobbit parents.

In New Zealand, which was perfectly appropriate.

Or would be, if it would ever come out!

Gill emailed a few days later to say she'd been induced, and then a few more days later to say she'd been induced *again*. I hadn't thought this was possible, but what do I know? The one time I managed to get through to her on the phone, she was out *shopping*, for crying out loud!

"I thought you'd been induced!" I yelled.

"I was. But it didn't work, so they told me to go out for a bit."

"But... but... *give birth*, God damn you! We're all sitting here, waiting for it to happen. You have no idea how stressful that is!"

In all honesty, it wasn't that stressful. Having chosen to stay put until we heard the news, Roo and I were propping up the bar at the Aqua Resort. The quality of their cooked breakfasts and the presence of a swimming pool didn't influence that decision in the slightest. So we whiled away the days, me drinking ice cold Angkor beer and writing, Roo reading the backlog of books on the Kindle and studiously ignoring the ten thousand photos she was supposed to be sorting.

And at 2pm on Tuesday, the 3rd of September 2013, Gill gave birth to baby Hazel Rose Robinson, who weighed a very respectable 5lb 4oz.

I cried tears of happiness for my sister, and I cried again just now, writing about it. Of all the accomplishments most amazing, and all the wonders most sacred... Gill had really outdone me this time.

I was over the moon.

We managed a quick Skype chat with my parents, Roo and I from the poolside in Cambodia, Gill from hospital in New Zealand, and Mum and Dad from their living room in Somerset, England. Modern technology, eh!

The first ten minutes of the call were spent in weeping, ecstatic congratulations.

And then Mum looked at me, down the barrel of her webcam. "So," she said, "your turn next!"

*   *   *

Our final destination in Cambodia – and of the entire trip, come to think of it – was the country's capital of *Phnom Penn*.

We hadn't left ourselves much time for it, but by this point we didn't mind. Our week of semi-enforced relaxation had given us ample time to reflect on the experiences we'd had, and let our minds wind down from the expectation of imminent adventure.

Hard to believe, but I was actually looking forward to going home.

We spent a last day on the beach in Sihanoukville, defying the brooding black thunderclouds and, eventually the driving rain, just so we could say we had a dip in the sea.

Then we caught the bus to Phnom Penn, booking just a single night in the capital before catching our flight back to Perth.

On our itinerary for our last day in the country was a visit to Cambodia's infamous Killing Fields. The site of horrendous

Shave My Spider!

massacres perpetrated by the Khmer Rouge, the fields are one of the 'must-see' spots for tourists.

Or, not, in our case.

"I just can't face it," Roo explained, as we sat in the hotel restaurant perusing the bus schedule. "It's too… I dunno. But it's our last day in Cambodia. It's the last day of the entire trip. I don't think I want it all to end on such a depressing note."

She had a very good point. The end of an epic trip like this gives rise to a melancholy all of its own; there was no point adding misery. We'd ticked off enough 'must-see' items to last a lifetime on this journey, and if I knew anything about us, it was that we'd be travelling again before long. There'd be plenty more to come. And I was fairly sure that if we looked hard enough, there were plenty of 'must-see' destinations around Perth that we'd never got around to visiting.

Adventure never ends, I thought, unless you let it.

Our adventure would be sure to continue.

So we crossed off the Killing Fields, and immediately felt a weight lift. The prospect of confronting such horrors as the 'Baby Tree', where Pol Pot's soldiers killed hundreds of infants by smashing their skulls against the trunk, had been a grim one. I'm not too emotionally stable at the best of times, and with our flight home less than twelve hours away I was fluctuating all over the place. But it was more than that; now, with the decision made, I felt free.

Free, because that choice was effectively the last one we had to make. With it, we had finally closed the lid on our Asian odyssey. Free because all we had to do now was watch and wait, read, reflect and remember.

And free because I was, and always am.

Life is good.

Instead, we wandered through the markets, idly browsing for last minute souvenirs. We ate a last indulgent lunch in the hotel, triple checked that our airport taxi was booked for two hours' time, and went out for a final stroll through the city. I'd remembered something over lunch – something I'd been putting off, but which had suddenly become urgent.

I needed a hair cut.

My last trim had been performed by Roo, on our bungalow balcony in the 4,000 Islands. It wasn't that she'd done a bad job, just…

She'd done a bloody awful job.

And whilst I hardly cared when we were mucking about in the jungle, we were soon about to arrive in a place where well-dressed people would be judging me. It wasn't enough that my last pair of jeans was starting to fray around the nether regions – I had to look like Shaggy from Scooby Doo on top of it. With a hair cut in Perth running to at least twenty dollars, I was determined to cram one in before we left for the airport.

So when I spotted a barbers across the road, I made a beeline straight for it.

There was no-one else waiting, so I leapt enthusiastically into the chair. A bit of simple signing explained the style I was looking for – a short back and sides, which I felt was impossible to screw up.

And the barber, a younger man, set to with gusto.

It was a far more relaxing experience than my usual barber's appointments, as I didn't need to keep thinking of pithy conversation. I just sat back, and let the man work. He was doing a very thorough job – a little too thorough, to be honest, as thirty minutes passed, then forty. I kept thinking he was finished, but each time, as I half-rose from the chair, he returned to snip at something invisible, and then carried on.

Finally, he presented me with a plastic hand-mirror, and I did that thing guys do after a haircut where they pretend to look, but don't really know what they're supposed to be looking for. From that point on, all we are usually thinking about is getting out of there as fast as humanly possible, and then recovering with a pint in the pub down the road.

The bloke seemed justifiably proud of his work, and I pulled my 'very pleased' face. I returned the mirror, made ready to stand up – and froze in my seat.

The barber had just unfolded a cut-throat razor, the blade

fully six inches long, and was holding it just to the left of my Adam's apple. Fearing a hold-up, I made no sudden movies – no moves at all, in fact – as he pressed the razor against my neck and began to shave it.

I honestly don't know if I was more terrified that he'd *not* demanded money. At least then I could have given him money, and he'd have stopped.

Instead he worked the razor expertly over the back of my neck, all around my hairline, shaved both ears – inside and out – and brought the blade right between my eyes to fix my mono-brow.

Then, while I sat transfixed, he adjusted his grip to use the tip of the razor, and deftly shaved inside my nostrils.

I've never sat so still in my life.

The whole process took him maybe five minutes; I swear I didn't take a single breath the entire time.

He charged me three dollars for the shave.

I was so grateful I was still alive, I gave him ten.

"You got your money's worth there," Roo said, as we jogged back through the city. She obviously hadn't noticed what was going on.

"I may have to change my trousers before we get on that flight," I said.

"What? You enjoyed it *that* much?"

"Honestly, it was the scariest moment of the entire trip, right there."

The best thing is, she thought I was joking.

It wasn't far back to the hotel, and we slowed to a walk as we passed a public square. We'd noticed how busy it was earlier, with uniformed police keeping order on the far side. Now though, the square was packed, with people streaming in and out from all directions. I had to have a look, and led Roo into the back of the crowd. Ahead of us we could see a startling mass of people, some holding up banners and placards.

I suddenly remembered something I'd seen on the news in the hotel.

There had been an election a few days ago, and the existing Prime Minster (and self-styled Supreme Military

Commander), Mr Hun Sen, had got in again. This was his latest victory in a premiership that now stretched back unbroken for over twenty-five years. Understandably, there were some who thought the election just *might* have been rigged. Protests had been brewing all over the country, but none so fierce as right here, in the capital. It was probably not a bad time to be leaving, actually, as although the protests had been mostly peaceful so far, there was a very real chance that violence would erupt in the next few days.

I grabbed Roo's hand tight, and pointed her into the press.

"Wow, Roo, this could be a defining moment in history! We should check it out."

"No, come on, we've got to go."

The crowd seethed with unrest, and rippled with promise.

"But – *how much* do you want to get caught up in a real live riot?"

She gave me a look – the kind of look you give to your toddler, when you've just noticed they're playing with a Stanley knife. Then, very slowly, she said, "Tony. We have a plane to catch."

And she was right.

– Epilogue –
Repatriation

We arrived back in Perth at 7:30am on the 18th of September, 2013.

We'd been away for almost exactly six months.

Including airport stopovers, we'd visited eight countries and travelled a fraction under twenty thousand miles – for only five thousand more, we could have circumnavigated the globe. We'd seen nineteen UNESCO World Heritage Sites, and used nine different currencies – three of which I still had banknotes in, only to discover later that they're 'closed currencies', and can't be exchanged outside their respective countries!

Which was a bit of a bugger.

And we'd spent a little over $16,000.

Roo's dad picked us up from the airport, and drove us back to the family home.

The first thing we did was eat, emptying his cupboards of all the comfort food we'd missed so much. The second thing we did was sleep, and we did a lot of it.

The third thing we did was unpack. Two great piles formed rapidly on the floor of the games room – one of clothes in desperate need of washing, and one of clothes so far beyond washing that they were destined for the bin.

Oh, there was a third, much smaller pile; this was the sewing pile, or as Roo put it, "stick anything your balls hang out of in here."

Next, Roo pulled out all the presents she'd bought for her sisters. They were almost entirely scarves.

I carefully removed and unwrapped the more illicit souvenirs I'd collected; a tiny piece each of the Great Wall of China, Hua Shan's interminable steps, and the majestic Bayon of Angkor Wat.

I know! I'm very naughty. But other than books, I don't collect much. If I ever own a house one day, I shall display these ancient treasures proudly. Alongside my piece of Hadrian's Wall, my piece of the Berlin Wall, a Roman mosaic tile from Jerash in Jordan, and a carved fragment of rock from Petra. Oh, and a piece of limestone casing from the great Pyramid at Giza, which (I was told afterwards) you could be shot for taking. Who knew?

Out came all our technology, most of which had survived remarkably unscathed. Man of the Match award went to the Steripen, which I'd used almost every night of the trip; I'd replaced the batteries twice, and it had saved us from contributing somewhere between two and three *hundred* plastic water bottles to landfill sites around Asia.

Next I removed the mosquito net, which had been used only once, at Mulu National Park in Borneo. It looked like it had been used considerably more often, and for something considerably more heinous than keeping out insects.

It went straight in the bin.

Last but not least, I felt around in the bottom of my bag, quite puzzled as to why it still weighed so much. Then, with a gasp of revelation, I withdrew around two kilos of scrunched up plastic; Vince the inflatable Velociraptor, who hadn't seen the light of day since we'd squashed him into my rucksack over six months ago.

"You took the Velociraptor?" Roo said, sounding surprised.

"Well, it was your idea! We were going to take photos of

him everywhere. You said it'd be hilarious."

She gave an exaggerated sigh. "Yes, but I wasn't *serious*."

*   *   *

The following morning, Roo's dad gave us a stack of post to open, as we'd had everything diverted to his house. Predictably, there was enough junk mail to fill a bath tub, and very little of consequence.

Except.

At the bottom of the stack, I discovered a more official-looking letter. I opened it, recognising the seal of the Department of Immigration and Citizenship – and as I read the text, my blood ran cold.

Readers of my previous books might remember that, shortly after Roo and I got married, I applied for a Permanent Residency Visa in Australia. Emigrating to Australia is getting harder and harder, and I'd been lucky; pretty much the only way a penniless, unskilled backpacker like me has a chance these days is by getting hitched to a native.

The application process had been complicated and horrendously expensive. Despite having been together for over five years, Roo and I had really struggled when it came to proving our relationship. Our vagabondish ways left little in the way of a paper trail, and we had no mortgage, no car loans, no life insurance and no way to prove our love for each other beyond sending them a graphic video. The result was a probationary period; for two years I would have the right to live and work in Australia, and if Roo and I were still together after that, the visa would become permanent.

That was the subject of the letter; my probationary status was now up for review. Or rather, it had been. This letter was inviting me to submit proof that my relationship to Roo was still ongoing. The decision about whether or not to allow me permanent residence in Australia would be based solely on the documents I supplied to them.

And the deadline for them to receive these documents had expired.

Two months ago.

I dropped the letter on the kitchen bench, and stared at it

in horror. My stomach was clenching in a way I hadn't felt since Luang Prabang; I was either going to cry, pass out, or shit myself.

Roo caught the look on my face and read the letter.

"Oh," she said. "That's... not good."

"No." It was all I could manage to say. "Not good at all."

I don't react well to stress.

That's why I picked the stress-free life of a happy-go-lucky traveller.

It hadn't turned out *quite* like that, but I figured that was mostly my fault.

Now, however, we were back in the Real World – and already it was going tits up.

All I could think was that at any moment another letter would arrive, informing me that I had twenty-four hours to leave the country. If my partner visa was refused, with no tourist visa and no other way of legally remaining in Australia, deportation was the inevitable conclusion. I was starting to panic.

Roo rescued me, as she so often does.

She got me sitting down, glass of wine in hand, while we calmly talked through our options.

A flurry of phone calls to different government departments followed, eventually resulting in a conversation with someone who actually worked for Immigration.

"The trouble is," he explained, "there *is* a way to get an extension on the deadline. But even if you had applied for, and been granted the extension, you'd *still* have missed it."

"So, what do I do?"

"It's up to the case officers, I'm afraid. The only thing you can do is gather all the forms and documents supporting your application, plus anything which explains why you missed the deadline, and overnight courier it to Brisbane."

"And there's absolutely nothing else?"

"That depends. Are you a religious man?"

It took most of the day to gather and annotate the evidence, which I'd been collecting since moving to Australia two years ago. I wrote a lengthy apology to include with the parcel, and sent it off just minutes before the post office closed. Now, like the man suggested, there was nothing else to do but pray.

I did think of one possibility though, and fired off a carefully-worded email to the Migration Officer who'd vetted my initial visa application. The ominously-named Mr Stern was anything but, and had guided me through several complications in the early stages. His office was in London, but he was the closest thing I had to an ally in the field.

A day later, his response came back. He couldn't promise anything, but he'd see what he could do. It was the first glimmer of hope, a single ray of light at the end of the tunnel; I could only hope it wasn't the headlamp of an oncoming train.

That one slight issue aside, our homecoming had been very welcome. I always suffer a burst of depression after the end of a big trip, but I've long since figured out how to manage it: start planning the next trip, asap! As we reacclimatised to life in Australia, Roo and I tossed around ideas for travelling South America, Europe – even the USA, which we'd both visited, but never really had the chance to explore. But America, like most of Europe, is a staggeringly expensive proposition when compared to Asia. It would be a while before our finances were back to a level where we could even consider something like that.

Actually, our finances were a bit of a problem.

I'd been using the money from my book sales to prop up our dwindling travel fund, with the result being we'd arrived back with almost nothing.

After the splendid freedom of our adventures, Roo couldn't face going back to her last job – cleaning toilets for the mentally disabled.

I can't say I blamed her.

So I promised to work extra-hard on my next book, and convinced her that it would turn us into millionaires. In the meantime, all we had to do was live cheap and keep our fingers crossed.

One way of achieving this, which had been suggested to me several times over the years, was house-sitting. I'd always wanted to try it, but the time had never been right. Now it was, so I signed up to a website called 'Trusted House-Sitters', which had several adverts requesting volunteers in Perth.

Figuring that the vast majority of advertisers wanted house-sitters to look after their pets, I put Roo's profession down as 'animal carer'. That's what she'd been, before I came along and completely derailed her career. And with only a slight hesitation, I listed myself as a travel writer.

"Are you sure that's wise?" Roo asked.

"Well, it's our only source of income at the moment. I might as well start owning up to it."

The hardest part of filling out the application form was finding a photo of the two of us that could be described as 'sensible'. I considered using one of our wedding photos, until Roo pointed out the unsightly bulge caused by me wearing trousers two sizes too small. In my defence, it *was* a medieval theme – and the tight-tights had been entirely Roo's idea. Eventually, I trawled through the pictures on Roo's big camera, finding one of us both draped around a stone head in Angkor Wat.

I wrote a cheerful introduction to us, mentioning that we loved to travel, but leaving out the fact that disaster seems to follow in our wake.

To top it all off, we even had a suitable reference.

We'd scored an unofficial house-sit once before, whilst visiting Gill in New Zealand. An elderly couple she knew were going on holiday; they had an equally elderly cat that they were very attached to, and asked if we would stay in their house to keep him company while they were gone.

It was a win-win situation; we got a free stay in the kind of comfy, well-equipped house we would never be able to rent, and they could enjoy their holiday, safe in the knowledge that a pair of devoted animal-lovers were taking good care of their precious baby.

It hadn't been the most successful of gigs.

The cat had died, for starters.

Fortunately for us, the beloved moggy had expired the day *before* we were due to move in. It had been taking more pills, potions and remedies than most octogenarians, and we'd been given extensive notes on the dosage and timing of every medication.

Not all of it was to be taken orally.

The couple went on their holiday anyway, having already paid for it, but it was a tearful goodbye as they left the house.

Roo and I stared at each other in shocked silence, as the sound of their car faded into the distance. I looked out of the window to make sure they were gone, then gave Roo a hug. "I never thought I'd say this, but thank God that cat is dead!"

A smile of relief flickered across Roo's face. "Yeah! Imagine if he'd struggled on for one more day…"

I shuddered at the thought of disaster so narrowly avoided. "And, on the upside, I don't have to spend the next week chasing the cat around the house with one finger inside a rubber glove…"

Dead pets aside, house-sitting was the perfect job for us. We both had plenty of experience owning and working with animals, we're both very tidy and respectful people, and we both have very trustworthy faces. Seriously – we practiced them in the mirror. As most of the contact was by email, I had the opportunity to write sensitive and thoughtful messages aimed at convincing pet owners we were the ones they needed – and before I sent them, Roo went through and cut out any swearing and/or references to my testicles.

Good job she doesn't do that to my books, eh!

Sitting Dogs

Our first house-sit was for a gorgeous golden retriever called Brittany. Well, more specifically it was for her owners, who had a luxurious family home in Perth's southern suburbs. We couldn't believe we got to stay in such an amazing place for free; not only did they have a heated swimming pool in the back garden, they had not one, but *two* different robots to clean it! There was a large home office; I set up my tiny, rather battered laptop with its taped-up power supply in between two wall-mounted iMacs that looked so mind-bendingly expensive I didn't dare touch them. The office had a daybed, which was perfect for resting my eyes while I wrestled with a story, and was round the corner from the fridge, which the owners had thoughtfully left well-stocked with wine.

    I locked myself in (to the office, not the fridge), only emerging for food and dog-walking duties, and wrote all day and late into every night.

    It's my own fault – you'd think I'd have learned to type with more than two fingers by now.

    Perhaps because of my night-owl tendencies, the early morning sales calls Roo started getting on her mobile were becoming a real pain. One morning when it rang at just after 6am, she sat up, cursing, and groped for it in the darkness.

"This number is on the Do Not Call Register," she mumbled into the phone, "and we don't want to buy *anything*, so fuck off!"

"Sales call?" I groaned.

"Bloody Indian call centre," she murmured, and was asleep again in seconds.

So when the phone rang again less than a minute later, she was ready to hit the roof.

"I'll get it," I said, "I might as well get up and take the dog out while I'm at it."

I put on my best disgruntled tone when I answered the phone. "Hello? What do you want?"

"Mr Slater?" came the voice, with a thick Indian accent.

"Yes."

"Please do not hang up, Mr. Slater."

"Why?"

"Mr Slater, this is Mr Singh, from the Department of Immigration."

"Oh."

"Yes, Mr Slater. I believe I was just speaking to your wife?"

"Oh! Yeah, ah, terribly sorry, we've, ah, been getting a lot of sales calls…"

"This is not a sales call, Mr Slater."

"No, sorry."

"This call is about Permanent Residency in Australia. Is that a product you would be interested in, Mr Slater?"

"Ah…"

That was my introduction to the Case Officer who would be handling my residency application from now on. He went on to inform me that, owing to intervention on my behalf from London, I was being given a second chance to have my claim assessed. He needed me to organise Police Records Checks for both of us, and to print, fill out, scan in and email back a form which explained why I'd changed my passport since the original application…

It wasn't great news, but it was hopeful. So long as they were prepared to review the evidence I'd sent them, it should be a foregone conclusion. The very fact that they were communicating with me, and asking for more paperwork, gave me reason to believe they were still considering my application. And that's all I could ask for.

When I got a second call a week later, this time from a lady, I was trembling in anticipation.

With good reason, as it turned out.

"There's been a problem with your application," she told me. "There have been allegations that your marriage is *not genuine,* and that you are attempting to gain residency in Australia through fraudulent means."

I felt like I'd been doused in a bucket of ice water.

"What? But... but... I... How? Who?"

"I am not at liberty to disclose that information, other than to say the allegation were made by an Australian citizen living in Vietnam. I'm afraid we have to take these claims very seriously, and have opened an investigation."

Suddenly, understanding flickered through my shock-shrouded brain.

Vietnam.

The only place in the world, as far as I knew, where I had an enemy.

"You have got to be kidding me..."

"I'm sorry? What was that, Mr Slater?"

So I explained to her, everything that had happened to us in Hanoi. I told her about our boat trip complaint, about the subsequent grilling which was now on YouTube, about the pornographic website created just to get back at me, and then listed the organisations I'd contacted to report the perpetrator.

She said she'd look into it.

A few days later, having read all the websites, watched the videos and reassessed my evidence, the decision was made in my favour. My palms dripped with sweat as I received the call, and I couldn't help asking what would happen to the person who told such blatant lies about me.

"I'm not at liberty to say," came the expected response, "but making a false statement to Immigration is considered a Federal offense here."

"Ah! Well. Thank-you very much."

"Have a nice day, Mr Slater."

"I will now."

A few days later I was sitting in the home office working on the book, when an email came through.

"Congratulations! Welcome to Australia!" It began.

Which I took to be a good sign.

My application had been successful. I was now allowed to work, rest and play indefinitely in Australia – and in New Zealand, too, should the mood take me.

After everything I'd gone through to get this far, it felt like a major victory.

So how did I celebrate? Why, with a glass of wine, of course. And a hug from Roo. And then I carried straight on with the chapter I'd been writing, feeling more than ever that Fate had something good in store for me.

Roo was my primary editor. She has eagle eyes when it comes to typos, and having spent rather a lot of time with me, she understands what I'm trying to say – even when the text I've written makes no sense at all.

She's also very handy when it comes to questions about Australia – specifically the weird-assed animals that inhabit this crazy country.

She could tell straight away, for example, which species of spider had chased me around the bathroom the previous night. "Those are the ones we kill," she explained, "because you really don't want to die on the toilet."

My next Aussie question was on marsupials. Roo had popped into the office to bring me a coffee – and, I suspect, to make sure I wasn't fast asleep on the daybed.

"Hey love, how do you spell *numbat?*" I asked.

Suddenly, Roo burst into song. "N says you're Nice, U are Unique, M says you're Marvelous, it's true! B, you are Beautiful, A you're Adorable, T, you're Terrific, and tiny too… You are a Numbat, and we love you!"

"Er… thanks for that," I said. "You know, N-U-M-B-A-T would have done."

It took two long months – with time off over Christmas for an extended pool party, of course – but a few days before we returned Brittany's house to its owners, I completed the first

draft of *'Kamikaze Kangaroos!'*
There was only one real problem.
It was rubbish.
Or so I thought.

It was another month before I dared release it.

Most of that time I spent changing every word in a sentence, only to re-read it fifteen minutes later and change them all back again. By this point our luck had changed, and we were living in a dilapidated old house with three huge rescue dogs that pretty much filled it. That's the downside of house-sitting; you have to take what you can get, if you don't want to end up on the street. Technically, it was illegal to own more than two dogs in that area. "Just walk them separately," the owner suggested. Which meant I had to go out four times a day; Roo simply wasn't strong enough to restrain any of the dogs (a Bull Mastiff, a huge German Shepherd, and the biggest Dalmatian I've ever seen). Almost as a passing thought, the owner mentioned to us that all three were rescue dogs, and all had different behavioural problems. The mastiff, for example, hated wheels, and would attack anything that had them – like children on bikes, or skateboards, for instance. "And feed them all separately, or they'll fight over the food," she told us.

That was a long month.

Eventually, Roo convinced me to stop farting around with my manuscript.

"Even if it doesn't take off," she explained, "you'll sell a few hundred copies to the die-hard fans. And we could *really* do with that money."

She was speaking from the heart. She'd just helped me pick up enough poo to fill two shopping bags from the back garden, and was understandably over the whole house-sitting lark.

So I put the book up on Amazon – hoping for the best, but expecting the worst. I've never had much confidence in my writing ability, and to be honest it still terrifies me when I think of people out there somewhere, actually *reading* my crap!

But this time, Roo's predictions came the closest. She's always had far more faith in me than I have; probably far more than I deserve.

Kamikaze Kangaroos, against all odds, was doing rather well.

When it became the top-selling travel book on both sides of the Atlantic – albeit briefly – I was so blown away that I nearly forgot to take a screenshot.

Luckily, Roo had my back on that one, too. "Look!" she stabbed a finger at the laptop screen. "Your book is no.1 in Travel. That officially makes you a best-seller!"

"Wow. Cool."

"You know what else that makes you?"

"No...?"

"A travel writer."

"Ah. Yes. Good point."

"So, does that mean you'll quit bitching about it?"

"Well... I guess I'll have to."

"Finally!"

I sat there for a bit, savouring the heady rush of endorphins. This is what success felt like, I realised. Well, kind of – I mean, I was still flat-broke, living in a house so disgusting that Roo stood outside to eat, and we'd be homeless again in a couple of weeks. I was about to be dragged around the neighbourhood by a pair of dogs so powerful it was more like water-skiing than walking, only to return and repeat the process with a beast so fearsome-looking that most people crossed the road to avoid me. And if they were on roller skates or a scooter, they really needed to.

But apart from that... things were looking up.

"So, what's next for my famous travel writer husband?" Roo asked.

I sighed.

"First I've got to sacrifice a few children to Cerberus, and then I've got a bajillion emails to answer."

"Oooh! From readers? What do they say?"

"Dunno. Let's see." I brushed the ever-present pile of dog hair from the laptop and clicked on an email.

'Dear Tony,

My husband dealt with cancer for over 2½ years, prior to October when he passed away. During this time, the only thing that made me laugh was reading about your escapades. So now I am dealing with the loss of a partner of 56 years. Finding your new book is just what I needed.'

I sat back, stunned.

"Wow…" Roo was lost for words, too. "Are they all like that?"

"No! Most of them are just, 'Hi there, I love your books, if you're ever passing by Palm Beach in Florida, come and stay with us, we'll show you some real southern hospitality.'"

"That sounds great! We could go to Palm Beach."

"Ah… I think the US is a bit out of our price range."

"How many of those emails have you got?"

"Oh, millions. Billions. Or thousands, at least."

"How many in reality?"

"Err… about 50."

"And are they all offering you a place to stay?"

"I dunno. Most of them say something like that."

"Oh my God! We should totally take them up on those offers!"

"What – go to America?"

"And visit the fans! Imagine it – all those people who want to meet you, and all they have to do is find us a bed, or a sofa to crash on, maybe buy us dinner… and in return, they get a visit from a real live author!"

"Ah… I can see where you're going. But you might be overselling me a bit. I'm not sure any of them *really* want to meet me. It's just something nice they put in an email, because they know I'll never *actually be in* Palm Beach."

"That's their bad luck then, isn't it!"

"Ha! It really would be, given what normally happens when we travel."

"Yes, but that was Asia. Surely that can't follow us to America."

"Whaddaya think? Should we find out?"

"Hell yeah!" Roo danced a little jig, before remembering

something important. "One thing though," she said, her voice taking on a serious tone, "if we're going to be staying in other people's houses, you *have got to* buy some underwear."

I thought long and hard about this.

It seemed like a sacrifice I'd be willing to make.

So! It turns out that the next adventure is this: I'm coming to see YOU!

Whether you want me to, or not.

And where I go, Roo goes too. And we all know what that means…

Be afraid. Be very afraid!

And put the kettle on.

I'll see you soon.

Tony
xoxo

THE END…
…FOR NOW!

A Message from Tony...

Hiya! Thanks so much for buying and reading my ridiculous book. If you enjoyed it, I'd REALLY appreciate a brief review on Amazon! It doesn't have to be epic, or poetic – a couple of honest words is all I need. Word of mouth is the best form of recommendation an author can get, and I love reading my reviews! Thanks in advance.

Now, if you'd like to check out the photos that accompany this book – and there are quite a few of them – just head to my website at:
www.TonyJamesSlater.com

In case you're wondering about my other books, here's a list:
It all stared with **'That Bear Ate My Pants!'**, which followed my stint as a volunteer in an exotic animal refuge in Ecuador. Spoiler alert! I got bitten by a crocodile.

This was followed by **'Don't Need The Whole Dog!'**, which chronicled myriad adventures in the UK and then me following my dreams to Thailand.

Next came **'Kamikaze Kangaroos!'** – all about the two years I spent travelling around Australia in a knackered old van. This was when I met Roo!

And last but not least was the story of my wedding to Roo, told in **'Can I Kiss Her Yet?'**

Weirdly, I then released another book, which is a kind of prequel – all about the years I spent trying (and failing) to become a world famous actor! It's called: **'Don't You Know Who I Am?'**

You can also catch up with me on Facebook, Twitter or Instagram by searching for Tony James Slater – or check out what's happening on my crazy blog:

www.AdventureWithoutEnd.com

About the Author

Tony James Slater is a very, very strange man. He believes himself to be indestructible, despite considerable evidence to the contrary. He is often to be found making strange faces whilst pretending to be attacked by inanimate objects. And sometimes – not always, but often enough to be of concern – his testicles hang out of the holes in his trousers.

It is for this reason (amongst others) that he chooses to spend his life far from mainstream civilization, tackling ridiculous challenges and subjecting himself to constant danger. He gets hurt quite a lot.

To see pictures from his adventures, read Tony's blog, or complain about his shameless self promotion, please visit:
www.TonyJamesSlater.com
But BE WARNED! Some of the writing is in red.

Printed in Great Britain
by Amazon